RENEWALS 458-4574

DATE DUE

GAYLORD			PRINTED IN U.S.A.

COUNTERCURRENTS

SUNY Series, The Margins of Literature

Mihai I. Spariosu, editor

We regret the passing of our colleague
Peter Salm, whose contributions to
German, Comparative Literature, and this
volume will always be gratefully appreciated.

COUNTERCURRENTS

On The Primacy of Texts in Literary Criticism

Io credo, per l'acume ch'io soffersi
del vivo raggio, ch'i' sarei smarrito,
se li occhi miei da lui fossero aversi.
Dante—*Paradiso* XXXIII. 76–78

edited and with an introduction by

RAYMOND ADOLPH PRIER

State University of New York Press

Library
University of Texas
at San Antonio

Published by
State University of New York Press, Albany

©1992 State University of New York

For information, address the State University of New York Press,
State University Plaza, Albany, NY 12246

Production by Christine M. Lynch
Marketing by Theresa A. Swierzowski

Library of Congress Cataloging-in-Publication Data

Countercurrents : on the primacy of texts in literary criticism /
edited and with an introduction by Raymond Adolph Prier.
    p.   cm. — (SUNY series, the margins of literature)
    Includes bibliographical references and index.
    ISBN 0-7914-0941-4 (acid-free). — ISBN 0-7914-0942-2 (pbk. : acid—
free)
    1. Criticism.   2. Literature, Modern—History and criticism—
Theory, etc.   I. Prier, Raymond Adolph.   II. Series: SUNY series,
margins of literature.
PN81.C777 1992
801'.95—dc20   91-13268
                                                                   CIP

10 9 8 7 6 5 4 3 2 1

CONTENTS

vii

ACKNOWLEDGMENTS

Seldom does an editor encounter so felicitous a combination of intelligence and congeniality in people as have I in my work on this volume. In addition to the contributors themselves, four must be cited with sincere praise: Mihai Spariosu, whose pressing understanding of the inhuman and antihumanistic state of textual exegesis presently in the West initiated this series; Carola Sautter, whose literary, theoretical, and linguistic expertise makes clear that at least one academic press in North America still possesses the powers of a broad and discerning humanism; Christine M. Lynch, whose time and steady hand helped all of us shape the manuscript into a book; and Lily Saade, whose sense of schedule and extraordinary devotion might well have kept more than one genius on line.

R.A.P.

INTRODUCTION:
Primacy, Criticism, and the Text

> En suma, el lenguaje es una condición de la existencia del hombre y no un objeto, un organismo o un sistema convencional de signos que podemos aceptar o desechar.
> Octavio Paz—*El arco y la lira*

The provocative title of the series in which the present volume appears is *The Margins of Literature*. Perhaps we should take it seriously, not in the sense that the following essays are not literature or about literature, but that they dare to address a once acknowledged, but now decidedly unpopular assumption: the primacy of texts in literary criticism.

Marginality, admittedly, is a rhetorical image or topos, its force traceable to the politics of master-slave in Hegel and Marx. Given any subversive agenda, it is negatively sophistic. But it also provides those "on the margins" the right to oppose the "center" or "centers," in short to say "no." It demands plain speech. Given the present imperialism of postmodern theory, moreover, the topos of Derridean marginality provokes a multitude of nonpartisan responses on the order of "your reading does not arise from the text," "you have lost the text in a proliferation of rhetorical self-interest," "your forced relativism of history as narrative emplotment rather than insight blinkers the reader," or, perhaps the most serious accusation, to which I shall return in conclusion, "your sophistry denies our experience, our education, and that of our students."

1

The essays in this volume suggest questions that devolve directly from the above issues: Has postmodernism deliberately effected a false relationship between itself and the past? (See Kaelin, Kennedy, Schildgen, Scaglione.) Do specific texts belie the postmodern, ultimately antitextual pose? (See Holdheim, Andrews, Schildgen, Prier). Is it possible to confront a text and adapt our own critical metaphors so that that text becomes a part of us and hence speaks on its own? (See Gillespie, Looney, Furst, Witt, Holdheim, Andrews, Nettels, Lorch, Mandelbaum, Prier.) Are there texts that are not "rhetorical agendas" but powers beyond or without words? In short is there a textual, non-postmodern syntax or grammatology? (See Witt, Kennedy, Schildgen, Nettels, Salm, Scaglione.) No one in this volume would deny the text some kind of aesthetic position, but a more penetrating question must be whether or not specific texts possess vital links to our perception, vision, and education. (See Kaelin, Looney, Holdheim, Schildgen, Salm, Lorch, Mandelbaum.) Finally, are there revealing historical junctures, conjunctive differences and similarities, that we must know before confronting any text from Homer to Handke? (See Looney and the last four essays that deal closely with the hyphen between Dante and Petrarch.)

But what is the underlying problem here? I should suggest that it is one of a text's ontology scuttled by the proponents of deconstruction, but in the end present if indeed we are present and responsible for our own education, and that of others. If there is no text in a class, there is no human being. The present, the human being, and the text are much more closely intradependent than some would have us believe.

There are, however, problems with the ontology of any phenomenon. It is not impossible to trace an unresolved ontological question in Parmenides or even in Homer. But what strikes me as unfortunate in the past decade is that, because of the seemingly philosophical nature of the issue, we have relegated the ontology of the text to either a more purely Aristotelian definition (the text might be primary, but it can be known or discussed only under the secondary category of metaphor) or a straight Heideggerian one (the text reveals itself in a muddle of fear, anxiety, chasms, and totalitarian authority). Derrida only argued he was avoiding the Heideggerian definition of the text; De Man and Bloom embraced such muddle. New Criticism might well be the best modern representative of the Aristotelian textual critique. There are also, because of Hegel's ultimately Aristotelian understanding of the pre-

Socratics, examples of a "mixed group": Ingarden and Iser, who combine Hegel with stricter Aristotelian principles. No category can exclude in praxis its opposite. Many other names will spring to the reader's mind, and I make no pretense of listing all the players in the modern-postmodern theoretical game, hence running the risk of detracting from the force of Kaelin's lead essay.

What I should like to propose, however, is an acknowledgment of a text's ontology apart from the psychologically negative hermeneutics of suspicion with which many postmodern exegetes of Nietzsche, Freud, and Marx, couch their pronouncements of disaster and utopia, parental abuse, and historical, linguistic, or gender-based slippage. Why maltreat the text in such unwholesome ways? It is time to acknowledge an authority shared between a text and its reader and, ultimately, among a text, its reader, and its author. To couch it in terms a young child might understand: we like texts and they like us. To hurt a text is to hurt ourselves. To turn away from it is to turn away from ourselves. (I use the pronoun accusatively.) It is unnatural (an adjective of which we should make more use in such cases) for a human being to fear a text, even if writing might indeed be equally unnatural. It is perverse when any particular person either denies the essential porosity between a text and oneself or, worse, denigrates its authority or primacy in the complex but essential peregrinations of human perception, reflection, and experience (a hermeneutic term, but one that is exploited much better by Dewey than Dilthey).

There is, I should be the first to admit, a distinct problem with the word "primacy" in the subtitle of this volume that must be resolved. Does it not take for granted an ontological primacy in the Aristotelian categorial sense of "primary being," in other words as a central focus that makes secondary the reader and the author? We are faced here with what, to my view, has always been the major difficulty with any kind of categorization, especially Aristotelian and, hence, Heideggerian: Do we want to relinquish authority to an "other" and run the risk of enslaving our self or ourselves, in this case, again, the reader, the author, or both? If we are open in experience and theory, have we no choice but to deny the logos, along with Derrida, or, even more paradoxically, deny the ethical *sensus communis* with Stanley Fish? We need to liberalize the postmodern rhetorical conservatives.

Neither Aristotle nor Thomas Aquinas placed the one "here." For them the demonstrative-locative position was "there." Both, however, established the proposition, inherent in language as the source of communication, that we could somehow know the one or One through the hermeneutics of rhetoric and belief. Heidegger, in the wake of Nietzsche, although considerably more negative in his explanation of the process, followed the same road. Ontological notions require epistemological enlightenment. With its rhetorical compulsion to exteriorize its texts "on the surface," postmodernism has failed to consider that no text, no reader, no author can or should be totally explained in such a fashion. Positing an inexplicable, existentially absurd underbelly to human perception and experience, the postmoderns have done their very best to explain it. "Primacy" has simply shifted to a self-deluding misuse of language.

But what is first is what is all, and if we are not to succumb to the divisive forces that dehumanize the world within and without academe, we must retrieve what eternally lies beneath the surface of the text, not as a rhetorical cliché, but as a mastering comfort in our ability to communicate with and among ourselves. (I use the word "divisive" as an attributive rather than subversively predicated adjective.) In short "primacy" lies in our shared participation in language. In this sense our texts do become primary. Hence to affirm the text is to affirm ourselves.

Another potential problem in the subtitle of this volume is the word "critical." Let us be honest. Can criticism be anything other than metaphor? Can it be anything other than rhetoric? The answer, once again, is "no." Language, texts, authors, and we are not intrinsically metaphors, although all possess the ability to be metaphorical. Our imagination, however, consists solely of metaphors, and nothing requires greater imagination *per se* than literary criticism, whether it run against the currents of postmodernism or, for that matter, spring forth as the original formulations of postmodernism itself. (I speak of Derrida but not the epigones of the eighties and nineties or, for that matter, any other period in the history of Western thought.) Then, too, rhetoric is essential to any presentation of language and, hence, to any text.

But, as Aristotle was quick to remind us in the first pages of his *Rhetoric*, there is rhetoric and then there is rhetoric, and, as Goethe noted in his musings on the Laocoön, there are metaphors and then there is direct metonymic experience. The key term, suppressed as irrelevant by the epigones, is *proairesis*, literally a stand "taken before." It comes to us as an "underlying agenda." And it is in this respect that, even if Aristotle's *Rhetoric* is closely tied to the *Organon*, it cannot be read without his *Ethics*. Too precipitously has Cicero's *De Officiis* fallen from the canon.

If a text, an author, or a reader, does not possess a positive, human ethical intent (*in-tendere*, "to stretch toward [Being]") or if, as Lorch so touchingly relates, we all do not stretch toward "the Mother," a text or we shall suffer beneath the contempt of the human condition. We cannot avoid the accusation of simply playing with words. Such is the immediate reaction of the human experience in us all. So Socrates would not consider banishment. So Protagoras in the dialogue of the same name queries the sanity of anyone willing to undergo such. In short a latter-day sophist leaves a very bad taste in the mouth to all but the perverse. Texts, authors, and readers, no matter how imaginative, will always be judged on positive or negative intentions. Intention, our desire toward the one, cannot be relativized. Why? Because it is the glue that keeps "here" our inter-est and experience. It is the metonymy of actual life that legitimizes literary, critical, in short, imaginative metaphors.

It is also the one sure proof of our own participation in language, communication, and being. It is the positive presence that legitimizes the necessarily negative rhetoric of any critical enterprise. It is our quick. It also guarantees a text's participation in the real.

What of "text?" One should not, I believe, deny the metaphors inherent in Barthes' expansion of "the text" beyond the narrow physicality of an artefact, of writing or print on paper. Certain contributors to this volume have not (see "Reflected Texts Beyond Words"). But neither was it Barthes' intention that multiple textuality be a license for sophistry, nor should it be ours.

As does anything that participates in an underlying or overarching ontology, a text might well be said to revel in its multiplicity. Correspondingly the reader is entirely within the province of meaningful experience to interpret texts in multiple, always interconnected ways: somewhat more theoretically ("The Theoretical Hyphen"), somewhat more narratively ("Lo, the Text Tells Its Tale"), somewhat more philosophically (Kaelin and "Appearing Texts"), somewhat more metaphorically ("Reflected Texts Beyond Words"), and especially somewhat more historically (Gillespie and again "A Cultural-Historical Hyphen"). Nothing in a text is invalid except the denial of validity. Such denial is little more than the modern critic's ignorance of

Parmenides' and Bergson's insistence that negation is an added, extra-experiential, non-essential category, in ancient Greek, for example, a prefix, a mere "alpha-privative" or *ouk*.

In its valid activity or ontology, moreover, a text must be inherently historical, despite postmodern attempts to make it otherwise. The recent inability to grasp what such a statement might mean, however, rests on the mistaken notion that a text may be adequately explained as a diachronic, linear narrative without an attendant synchronic, vertical link to our experience and that of its author. In short we are to agree with Derrida's blinkered reading of Saussure to the effect that we the readers can assert ourselves only in our marginality to any ultimately falsely posited text. Thence arises the nonsensical category of the "subjective reader" and the equally unfortunate reaction that demands a text reflect only what the reader has consciously but irrationally experienced. This putative value deflects rather than acknowledges the vital historicity of the text because it denies its making or creation in and for the present. Admittedly one may run into trouble emphasizing "the presence of the text," but no one with even a notion of the pragmatics of creating or reading a text can deny that all texts must be both made in the present and also read therein. This important human experience must be qualified as aesthetic.

The text's ontological historicity, however, lies in its reception from "sometime ago" (see Andrews, Schildgen, and Salm) and a thoughtful acknowledgement of certain outwardly different and inwardly similar socio-linguistic shifts or re-definitions (see Scaglione). A text, in its progressive tense, is also dependent on a perfect present of texts that "have been," that is of texts that leave open-ended the possibility of their re-creation now, wherever in the diachronic line "now" might be: Plato, Nietzsche, Derrida, or Kennedy; the Greek theater, Saint-Jean Perse, Andrews; Ovid, Dante, the death of a husband, Lorch. How inadequate, after all, is the term "resonance" for such a powerful chain and well of human experience. How inadequate much of the vocabulary we as humanists today are expected to employ in and for our own and others' texts. What means this postmodernist universe of privileging, foregrounding, marginalizing, relativizing, deconstructing, limiting, pulverizing, and materialized multiplicity without a center? Very little when compared to address, focus, actuality, answers begged or other-wise, genre, perception, eternity, value, the human condition, vision, visibilia, naming, the rose—in short THE TEXT. What, after all, are the metaphors of theory, narrative, appearance, reflection, and history without a text? More importantly what are the metonymies of our experience? Even less.

Does all this at best make a text and its ontology a necessary evil? The question is nihilistically perverse.

Look but a moment at the epigraphs that focus the texts of this volume. Each one reaffirms the essential historical nature of its subject, and each declares that text's ontological value: "En suma, el languaje es una condición de la existencia del hombre y no un objeto. . . ." "What distinguishes a man from a word?" "Compaignons, oyez vous rien?" "Vous créez un frisson nouveau." "What is the answer?. . .In that case, what is the question?" "A future is opened to us only as we become reconciled to the past." "Qui, non si narra!" "All our actions have a contingent character." "Dante ist sehr schön. . .und erst weit in der Allgemeinheit kannst Du Dich mit ihm treffen." "So io ben ch'a voler chiuder in versi / suo' laudi, fora stanco / chi più degna la mano a scriver porse." "Regina caeli, laetare, / Quia quem meruisti portare / Resurrexit. . . ." "What's in a name?"

What better bespeaks intention? What better implicates us in the anticipation of a new work, a new esperience?

With the exception, for calligraphic reasons, of citations from ancient Greek, I have asked that those epigraphs in modern European languages be left untranslated. This is not some elitist affectation, even though the demand requires of a reader the ability at least to parse French, German, Italian, Latin, and Spanish. It's a sincere token of respect to the original, archaic authority of language and text, a potent reminder that language is a condition of man's existence, not an object and that it remains the hidden yet shared resource upon which we all must draw: language and languages, its and their ontology, and its and their texts. The translations of this volume are an aid to rhetorical clarification; language, in any form, is a reminder of the ontological primacy of the text.

In short such a text does not stand as an obstacle to our life on this earth, even if the prevailing opinion within and without the walls of academe appears bound to posture otherwise. A text helps us along, gives us a hand, provides us a boost, and, with a child's metaphors exhausted, supplies an insight. Within these limits, a text provides a view of which we may or may not approve. After all, Pandora's trapped hope, Hesiod reports, is all-too-human. But the text remains, an inexhaustible resource.

But a resource for what? The better relative pronoun is "whom," of which we are the antecedent.

What now I am about to say in conclusion will appear to some the words of John Dewey, to some those of several nineteenth-century Germans, perhaps even to some those of a Javanese phrase, *jarwa dhosok*, supplied by a new colleague in our shared discussion of the archaic *Shield of Herakles* and signifying the "pushing" of old language into the present. Andrews begins his intrapenetration among Perse's seamarks of eternity with a citation of Nietzsche to the effect that we are not able to destroy that certain accommodation by which each new age measures itself by the past. For reasons that merit separate discussion in the future, Nietzsche must be said to reflect a telling position of an earlier philologist, Friedrich Schlegel, who, in addressing the parameters of knowledge, speculated that our relationship to the past must indeed be extremely modern: "Vielleicht muss man um einen transzendentalen Geschichtpunkt für das Antike zu haben, erzmodern sein" (*Athenäum Fragmente* 271).

Clearly the resource of the past is ours, but the Javanese, Nietzsche, and Schlegel direct our attention to its centrality as a process or experience, not as the dead, surd flotsam of *écriture* best suited to the anti-humanistic arguments of sophistic exegetes. Language and its texts are the instruments of our education, and those who would deny our positive, experiential participation in these texts deny what we are. To "marginalize" readers and authors from their texts denies participation in being, or, in a phrase that partakes less of Heidegger's onto-theological madness, in experience.

But what is experience except an active involvement in, as, and for a work of art? I am able to supply no clever, let alone penetrating, answer to why those of us whose priorities lie in our education and that of others have not explored more fully Jacob Burckhardt's pregnant notion when he spoke of Renaissance man and culture. Perhaps indeed we have not read our Dewey. Perhaps, as the latter states or implies, we have created of art and of ourselves objects to hang on museum walls, to stack on library shelves, to dangle in the nooses of totalitarian desires for power, whether such desires be within or without the walls of academe.

What remains constantly present, however, is the quick of our desire or intention to know. Its form and substance is aesthetic. It necessitates our construction of texts in the process of constructing ourselves. The answers and questions Furst demands of a text are much more than Socratic. They are logically, centrally, and ontologically human. "Ontology," by its stress upon a "logos," may arguably be "philosophical," just as the focus on a written text may be "literary" and ultimately a function within the litterae humaniores, the humanities. But the intentional desire for knowledge is human and the reception of another's text is a hands-on primary, critical, and textual creation of ourselves as a living, constantly self-developing work of fine art.

> . . . fine art consciously undertaken as such is peculiarly instrumental in quality. It is a device in experimentation carried on for the sake of education.
>
> John Dewey—"Experience, Nature and Art"

PART ONE
The Theoretical Hyphen

An American View of the Structuralist-Poststructuralist Controversy

E. F. KAELIN

> Ce qui vaut pour 'hymen' vaut *mutatis mutandis*, pour tous les signes qui, comme *pharmakon, supplément, différance* et quelques autres, ont une valeur double, contradictoire, indécidable qui tient toujours à leur syntaxe, qu'elle soit en quelque sorte *intérieure*, articulant et combinant sous le même joug, *uph'en*, deux significations incombatibles, ou qu'elle soit *extérieure*, dépendant du code dans lequel on fait travailler le mot.
> —Jacques Derrida.

> What distinguishes a man from a word?
> — Charles S. Peirce.

I

To begin my tale, I should like to talk about the hyphen between 'structuralist' and 'poststructuralist' in my title. Although Jacques Derrida has assured us this little mark is like a hymen—o *Hymen Hymenaee* (Catullus, LXI, LXI I) joining as it separates the inner sanctum of that holiest of spaces—, the two concepts (of events) this

13

hyphen unites even as it separates were in actuality hardly separated in time, if appearances are of the essence, for the change from the one tendency or movement in literary criticism to the other was so rapid that it transpired almost imperceptibly. Indeed, according to B'rer Jas' epithalamium, so rudely forced from a thought of Jacques Lacan, the most rapidly moving tongue twisted into a language could never come to join any signifier with a signified since, in the strictest structuralist theory, the hyphen-hymen is replaced by a slanted stroke, and a sign becomes written as it is interpreted, as 'Sr/Sd.'

Time is of the essence in the story for two reasons: first, the theoretical, which demands that the space of writing, created by the placement of differential signifiers, be joined by an indefinite deferral of any fulfilling signification that would end the play (the slippage, the polysemic references) of any author's language use; and the second, cultural, which indicates an epoch of our recent history. The time period thus uncovered spreads between 1949 and 1967, and itself constitutes another kind of Derridean "fold" he has found so intriguing to introduce into theoretical discourse about intellectual discourse of any kind whatsoever.

But not all recent linguistic theory has been so heavily charged with sexual imagery.

The first French edition of Claude Lévi-Strauss's *Les Structures élémentaires de la parenté,*[1] which imported into the study of anthropology the structuralist principles of Ferdinand de Saussure's general theory of linguistics, appeared in 1949. While Saussure's course in general linguistics had been taught at the University of Geneva three times in the first two decades of this century, the first edition of the *Course in General Linguistics* appeared in July, 1915, under the editorship of two of the students who had heard Saussure give the lectures.[2] Merleau-Ponty, of course, had already introduced the principles of structuralism into his general theory of expression, but that impulse faltered with the eventual publication of his *Prose of the World.*[3] When he died in 1961, existential phenomenology lost its most influential proponent and that philosophical movement began its eventual decline. But structuralism lived on in other forms, both as a theory of linguistics, i.e. as a general theory of sign interpretation, and as the ultimate butt of later critical appraisal. In 1967, Jacques Derrida published the three main volumes of philosophical criticism he brought against the structuralist program.[4]

American students of French literature and criticism were just getting the hang of the structuralist methodology when Professor Derrida's groupies, blinded by their teacher's brilliance, had the temerity to announce its recent demise. As a result of this phenomenon very few American critics mastered the subtleties of structuralist criticism. The time was simply too short for those, who, like Roland Barthes, found themselves in the rear of the avantgarde.[5] But, as explained below, Barthes at least made the transition.

It would be a mistake to explain this phenomenon as just another fad in a culture addicted to change so much that its politics has given us the very image of a self-defeating revolution, expressed in its own language as *"plus ça change, plus c'est la même chose."* One need not have been blinded by anyone's brilliance to perceive that.

Throughout the changes within the institutions—political or linguistic—the life of the French intellectual has gone on, whether we choose to describe it as a circle returning upon itself or as developing in a straight line. Whether the one or the other, the process will merely repeat an angle of 180 degrees. The same sort of musing, some of us remember, led Nietzsche to declare the eternal return as a matter of cosmological principle.

Let me begin by attempting to penetrate the hyphen between structuralism and poststructuralism leisurely, by supplying the historical background for the applications of the first of these hyphenated terms. I shall not dignify what I am about to do by referring to it as a "deconstruction"; it will only be an attempt to understand how the grip of historical circumstance has pushed contemporary critics into taking a stand on the nature of literary texts, written as they are as a series of writerly strategies, and interpreted, as they should be, as a set of disciplinary controls on readers' responses. In the fold between the strategies and the discipline lies a living, breathing text.

Before becoming a theory of literary criticism, structuralism was known by those intellectuals influenced by Saussure as a general theory of linguistics, which had as its object the living language of a people. A language is a tongue by metonymy, since without a biological tongue nothing can be said in any language. Studying a living language of a people, as codified, is only a limiting case of a more general science of semiotic, which, in his famous course of linguistic study, Saussure had called "sémiologie." And that ramification of Saussure's linguistics into a general theory of signs still flourishes under the same rubric.[6]

For the founder of structuralism, semiotic was an as yet unnamed science, a part of social psychology, which studied communication managed by a system of signs whose meanings are determined by the social responses of sign-users. Although linguistics in the narrower sense—the study of language as communication—is a necessary tool for elaborating the more general language of semiotics—communication as "language"—, whatever is said of signs in general will apply to words in particular. Rather than by comparing the phenomena of codified language use with the patterns of behavior in acts of communication by the use of any other signs to arrive inductively at the laws of semiosis, Saussure chose *la langue* (spoken and written language) as his subject, and mandated an "internal point of view" for its study.[7]

Internally, a language has two different aspects: a social one (the conventional meanings expressed in a living language) and an individual one, the uses of such meanings to express an individual intention. The social aspect defines a language properly so called, while the individual aspect defines an individual speech act. Corresponding to the two different aspects of a language, there are two differing dimensions: the synchronic and the diachronic. The synchronic dimension unites a signifier with a signified in a functional relationship; indeed, for Saussure, this dyadic relation constitutes the sign in its function as signifying. To visualize this synchronic relationship Saussure drew a set of superimposed waves, the upper one a fluid mass of "ideas" (images, concepts) floating over an equally fluid mass of phonic materials (sounds, phonemes) that are distinguishable only by marks differentiating one phoneme from another. In general, he says, language possesses nothing positive, only differences related to other differences.

Diachronic changes are instituted within the historical time spread defining the life of a living language by virtue of the characteristic uses individuals make of the system of just those structural differences unified by the code of the language as synchronically constituted. In later applications of the theory, both metonymy (reference to a whole by naming of a part) and metaphor (extension of a name proper to one thing to another resembling it) will be used to explain differential uses of the same signs.[8]

Saussure's structural linguistics furnished the foundation for two diverse cultural manifestations. Claude Lévi-Strauss turned the theory into a methodology for cultural anthropology in 1949 and later elaborated the doctrine in two volumes of *Anthropologie culturelle* (I, 1958; II, 1973).[9] And Roland Barthes, whose *Degré zéro de l'écriture*, published in 1953,[10] is judged by some to have initiated the change from the older New Criticism (the American school of formalism) to the newer New Criticism (la nouvelle critique) of France,[11] was here in the avantgarde.

Barthes' gambit, from this position, was to change Saussure's emphasis upon the spoken language to a careful consideration of its substitute, the written language, considered as art. Besides the express informative function of language, which constituted the crux of Saussure's linguistic, the poetic arts display an indirect mode of communication. Within literary narratives, words may be used to describe events, and those events themselves may divulge otherwise hidden structural significances—psychological, anthropological, mythological, or what have you: and when they do, signifieds become signifiers. And reading what these scribes have scribbled may instill within the sensitive reader the "pleasures of the text."

As a result of the earlier Barthesian description of writing as the inscription of a text within the history of a language—the material process by which a writer manipulates the signifiers and the signifieds of his or her language to create, rather than merely to record, significance, and thereby to enrich the language one has inherited—, the criticism which operated upon such assumptions became known as "structuralist," to distinguish it from the formalism of the American New Criticism.

Thus, the transition to poststructuralism was not without its preparation. Under the world-wide onslaught of Freudian psychoanalysis, French intellectuals began to question the hereditarian value of the Cartesian soul-substance, even though, for the most part, they had elected to ignore the work of Freud himself for as much as a half century or more. Lacan's famous continuous seminar on Freudian psychoanalysis as linguistics was instituted in 1953, while Freud's *Traumdeutung* was first published in 1899, and postdated to 1900.[12] Lacan's "writings," of course, are better known through the transcriptions of the proceedings of his free style dialogical seminar meetings than by a shorter collection of pieces assembled under the title of *Ecrits*.[13]

Although the theoretical purpose of his pedagogical dialogues was the rescue of Freud from the Freudians (particularly Melanie Klein and Erich Fromm, among others), the immediate and more practical end was to produce more effective French psychoanalysts. The method was dialogical because psychological practice is dialogical, and the seminar sessions themselves, in their seeming chaos, resembled the dialogue initiated between a patient and her analyst. Not forgetting his humanities, Lacan recalled Arthur Rimbaud's laconic "...Je est un autre,"[14] which is obviously as ungrammatical as it is insightful into the composition of the human subject. So much, one would suppose, for the supposed supremacy of grammar in the study of languages. The question to be determined is the relationship between a speaking unconscious id and a self that must be led to understand what has already been "expressed" in that speech when the speaking id and the addressed self are of the same person. In classical psychoanalysis that demands an interpreting physician's complicity in the intercommunication, in the same way that some texts need the complicity of an understanding critic.

Recalling Rimbaud's mot—textually directed against the romantic poets' preoccupation with and narcissistic love of their suffering souls as the inexhaustible source of human feelings—was itself a poetic tour de force. Lacan, however, calls Rimbaud a "poet," as indeed he was in another dispensation; but the sentence occurs in one of the poet's letters to Paul Demeny that begins with the telltale sentence, "—Voici de la prose sur l'avenir de la poésie...."[15] Lacan saves himself from the charge of essentialism with the polysemic reference to Rimbaud's plight: poets always say beforehand what a scientist later discovers to be the truth (the Viconian theory of language), although by force of the play between the self and the other, which is their unconscious, they do not of course know what they are saying—at least until they have said it. What speaks in any event, whether the voice is poetic or prosaic, is not the conscious self, but the id: in Lacan's linguistics, "ça parle."[16]

Primitive thought, for Lacan as for Claude Lévi-Strauss, is already a code of systematic, i.e. structural, references to an established order of significances:[17] for the anthropologist, to discover this code in the behavior of peoples; for the psychoanalyst, to discover the subjectivity of his subjects in the patterns of their speech. Language itself, in this scheme, is the play of signifiers always separable from their signifieds by the tissue of a hymen, as expressed by the vertical slash within the functional representation of a sign as Sr/Sd. In the sequel, I shall continue to probe the significance of this hymenal ligature.

Writing about the same time that Lacan was beginning his seminar, Michel Foucault's first book encapsulated his study of the concept of madness in psychology.[18] The very language used by psychiatrists to separate the mad from the sane in every alienated personality itself has been inherited under the influence of theoretical presuppositions— linguistic, historical, and social. In a book entitled *"Les mots et les choses,"* Foucault introduced the term *épistémè* to define the characteristic patterns of interpretation proper to a given culture or epoch of our developing history. As an *épistémè* changes, so do the patterns of significance noted in the resemblances and differences of things to each other. What is sane in a feudal world is insane for Don Quixote straddling the two worlds of feudalism and the burgeoning postfeudal society of the Renaissance.

The epochal folds and joints of history as occurrent events show the differences in the treatment of the mentally disturbed—from ostracism, imprisonment, and shackling, to contemporary psychoanalysis—, which depict the series of changing social evaluations of such a condition. In the same way as the traditional concept of man has changed—from that of a being composed of body and soul, which Descartes brought forward from the medieval age, to help establish the classical *épistémè* that was displaced by the modernism of the nineteenth century, and which has all but disappeared in our own postmodern views on the subject— so has the ideal of a well-constructed, algorithmic language to depict what goes on in our natural and social worlds. Our behavioral worlds are all historical. So, to Lacan's Freudianism, we must link Marxism and its theory of history to our understanding of human significance.

To further trace the dependence of the concepts we have of our objects upon the methods pursued to elaborate a science of those objects, it would be fruitful to compare Foucault's *Les mots et les choses* with W.V.O. Quine's *Word and Object*.[19] Should we accept this gambit, and should we at the same time choose Lévi-Strauss' concepts of *bricolage* and engineering as models of practical knowledge, it would be surprising to see who comes off as the engineer, and who the bricoleur in matters of metalinguistics.

Foucault's place in the transition between structuralism and poststructuralism seems assured on the basis of the structural differentiation he finds determining the differences between the successive *épistémès* of our own lived history, as by his insistence that language tends to follow this same system of differentiations. That he should claim his work is not structuralist merely emphasizes the point of this essay: that Foucault's method of "archaeology" falls clearly within the split between structuralism and poststructuralism, within two modes of theoretical inquiry joined by the hyphen of my title.

Not only does it fall within this split, it contains a theory of how such epistemological changes may fruitfully be studied—or, as it has been said, how the later movement illustrates the dis-semination of the first.[20]

For the third figure making his appearance on the hyphen, I refer once again to Roland Barthes, mentioned before as in the avantgarde of structuralist criticism. In an interview for the avantgarde journal *Tel Quel*,[21] he describes himself, not as a critie, but as a romance writer—not of novels, but of texts revealing the essence of the novel (*le romanesque*). The writer of the avantgarde obviously knows, claimed Barthes, what is already dead within the culture, and those in the rearguard of the avantgarde find themselves there for the love they bear for what has already died. The dead texts are the merely readable ones; those that live are writable.

In his *Le Plaisir du texte*, Barthes' appreciation of a written text finally comes to be expressed in an image of love. But the image is hardly scatological, only metaphorical and drawn without the least crudity or reprehensible degree of insensitivity. Where critics of the past dealt with the readability of a text—interpreting it, explaining its meanings, exposing the structures of lived significances found in the system of codified significations, after Lévi-Strauss and Lacan and Foucault they could only describe a text's "scriptibility." The users of a living language no longer enjoyed the privilege of being the center of a verbal communication; their own lives as writers and readers were themselves texts expressing an unconscious self as an "economy of desires." And, if two economies of desire came into contact through the medium of a written text—wherein each meets the other objectified as if as an image in a mirror—the experience is properly described as the blissful union of complementary intents of the consenting partners. Thus, reading a text for its scriptibility is an experience of (sexual) pleasure (*la jouissance*). But, in the process, the old fashioned text likewise has lost its readability: it is reduced to an intertext between two communicating economies of desire. Nowhere in recent French culture could one perceive so clearly how Descartes' substantial theory of the thinking, feeling soul had been so thoroughly traduced into a basically Freudian theory of the human ego as subtended by an unconscious field of libidinal drives—a motive introduced into that culture by Lacan's reading of Sigmund Freud.

For Barthes, the intertext flows in a circular pattern of images, like a flower unfolding into a newer pattern of existence, as image calls out image in the reader's response to the textual stimulation. In this way, an old fashioned "readerly" text, closed in its significance, becomes a current "scriptible" text that each reader completes in the unfolding of an intimate and personal intertext merely for the pleasure of the experience.

The new French criticism thus proclaimed itself as a theory of writing. And the impetus supplied the movement by Barthes was reinforced by the theoretical writings of Jacques Derrida, beginning with his 1967 proclamation that the book was dead, long live the act of writing.[22] His blitzkrieg shattered three fronts at once.

Against Saussure and the fixed functional relationship between signifier and signified understood by a society of language users he argued, with Heidegger and Foucault, that the temporal differences of human subjectivity are as important as the spatial structures of a human world reflected in a body's orientation to the one world of nature. In its efforts to write, the space for the writing had to be created. This space eventuates from the articulation of signifiers, uniting in their differences the space of·human subjectivity as described in the stretch between the unconsciousness of our pasts and the consciousness of being lost between some past and an as yet nonexistent future. The human subject, in this Heideggerian way, is hemmed in, not by a field of presence but by on open and indeterminate horizon of absence; and so, a source for a distinctively human communication is lost as the conscious self is lost in the depths of the unconscious. Writing is a way of discovering the what that writes. Since the personality of the writer has been decentered within the locus of communication, the initiating gestures of the writer—themselves a text wherein is inscribed the subject's unconscious mind—reveal themselves only as a set of linguistic signifiers.

And how does such a "person" understand what is written? Merely by substituting for the set of signifiers set down in the text of the writer's act another set of signifiers, which in a later, reflective, moment is another act of writing. In this process there is no signification brought to consciousness by an act of insight, not even an indefinite circular referral of image to image in an act of "reading," but only an indefinite deferral of meaning fulfilling conscious acts. When the two sorts of differences—those between the signifier and the signified as articulated in an act of writing and the moments of the first articulation of a set of signifiers and that of the second, which merely supplements the first, the word for the phenomenon of meaning should be spelt *différAnce* to encapsulate both senses of the term—the spatial separation of the signifiers and the temporal deferral of their signification.

Careful readers will observe that the words "sense" and "significa-tion" of the last sentence should be written under erasure (following Heidegger's writing of *Sein* in the same way to refer to Being, which, as applied to any and all entities indeterminately as to their differences, constitutes a concept that is identical to that of non-Being), since the lexical meanings of these terms are exactly what is being denied by the grammatological theory, i.e. that every expression of our language possesses either a sense or a sense and a signification as its fulfillment. A mere inconvenience, this, since the "logocentric" metaphysics of our Western tradition has chosen to close the infinite progression of sign supplementation by positing the existence of essences, ideas, or logoi to codify what is brought to awareness in acts of insight. Whether these acts are imaginative or perceptive, they constitute the two meaning-fulfilling attitudes of the Husserlian epistemology.[23]

In the older dispensation, discourse was logos, and closed, by its own ingathering, into an essential determination; in the new, it is always in the making, and open for a future determination in an act of creative speech. Again, writing is dis-semination: delogicized and germinating, blossoming forth and spreading into an indefinite future in continuous acts of textual supplementation.

Derrida's second front was a war against Husserlian phenomenology. He begins by asking the difference between signs that actually point to a signified and expressions as signs that merely symbolize what they signify. Is there some notion of sign that englobes them both, a genus for the two species? No, because the two senses of "sign" are not mutually exclusive. As Saussure had indicated, expressions of our language may be of the spoken or written variety, and if they are written they serve as a substitute for the spoken version in the same way that an indicating sign points to its signified. But please note: the visual signifier (the written morphemes), as a supplement, stands for the verbal signifier (the sonic phonemes).

We have in this reference the same system of supplementation that was described in the case Derrida brought against Saussure in *Speech and Phenomena*, a book in which he casts anathema upon the houses of structuralist and phenomenologist alike. The argument is clear: if Saussure's distinction between spoken and written signifiers is accepted we cannot distinguish our linguistic expressions from merely indicative signs: the written characters of a phonetic language indicate what sounds must be uttered to make sense of the expression. He did not say, though he might have, that this is one reason poor readers still move their lips when reading a text.

The case against Husserl continues with the assault upon subjectivity. As Lacan had already made clear in an alternative manner, Derrida mocks the Husserlian methodology by seeking an intuition for the phonic stuff fulfilling the function of a Saussurean signifier. Reflecting upon one's own use of the voice, a speaker does not intuit a sound, but an ideally recognized sound that is only the trace of the past real sound. Granting, then, that signifieds may be separated from the phonic signifiers, these signifiers themselves can be intuited only as a trace—a phenomenon, to be sure, but not one that yields the presence of what it is the trace of. A trace, as the form of the unformed (according to Plotinus, from whom Derrida draws this designation), only leaves a mark.

What is left, then, when one dispenses with the essences of the Western tradition that are signified by a "correct" use of language? Only a trace; and this, not of the absent signified, but of a signifier that evanesces, with the rest of our self-conscious selves, into the depths of our unconscious experiences. The crossing out of fixed concepts, then, comes to mean the actual disappearance of the signifier as such: not into an absolute void, since there remains a trace; and this trace is supplemented by a second expressive act wherein the first is criticized. Criticism in this process becomes the deconstruction of a pre-existent text, an examination of the traces left between its empty spaces wherein the undecidable marks constitute a fleeting presence that is more than present (*plus-que présent*) and hence not present at all. Once again, the emphasis is upon the reading, but only as revealing the temporal structure of the human subject doing the reading, not, as in Barthes, as revealing a qualitative slice of human experience.

In such criticism, a text is not so much explained as it is supplemented by another text. And this other text "disseminates" the first, since that first leaves its trace in the space and time of our collective cultures. Although I have not read another critic of Derrida refer to the polysemic significance of this "dissemination," the play upon the etymology of the word seems obvious. Whether we write the word as 'dissemination' or as 'dis-semination,' as I have done above to accentuate the obvious polysemy of the *graphe*, it too is to be written under erasure, since the original "sense" of spreading the word is intended, along with that other (clearer when the word is spelled 'dis-semination') which is likewise a double entendre: first, the removal of the source, biologically contained in the seed, indicating that the word mentioned above was seminal in its effect, and, next, the destruction of the *seme* as the unit of discursive semantic significance.

The discovery of such linguistic phenomena in the confrontation with a written text might very well be the source of some covert critical sexual jouissance, but like, Roland Barthes, we should have to situate ourselves ever so slightly to the rear of the avantgarde to experience the thrill. Texts, dead or alive, readerly or newly and plainly writerly, need the effective presence of an interpretive consciousness to establish the evidence of their palpable conditions. But of this, more later, where the American voice supplements the Gallic strains of contemporary criticism.

The third prong of the Derridean offensive is to establish a science of the *gramme*, of that language before language which is neither written nor spoken, but which like the missing link in evolutionary biology has more lately become both spoken and written, both the apes and man. To achieve this aim Derrida deconstructs the essays of Rousseau on the "Origin of Language."[24]

Repeating the gambits of the poststructuralists outlined above, he shows that there is no origin of the Northern (written) languages from the Southern (the spoken), no significance on the "outside" of an expression that is different from that already apparent on the "inside," no primacy of the spoken over the written language. The *gramme* of this primitive language are supplied by the traces or marks inscribed within the life experiences of individuals becoming conscious of themselves as they become conscious of their placement in a world. As we remember our Heidegger, that was the experience of a primal opening given in an act of circumspection, which is the source of all our felt worldly significance. What gets disclosed to a worldly individual in such felt significance arrives, through the act of interpretation, into the ordered figures of speech that communicate what he or she already knows of the experience. All else, he said, was idle chatter—or, as our intrastructuralists would object, the sometimes pleasant play of our polysemic tongues against the folds of historical circumstance. And this can be understood even if all our concepts to express this fact are left behind the cloak of words written under erasure.

II

I shall begin the Americanization of my thesis with an account of Peircean semiotics. Just what stance does this particular theory permit our literary critics in search of a method? Unfortunately, there can be no question of mapping the various linguistic or semiotic theories that were argued before, during, or after the hyphen uniting structuralist criticism of recent memory with the predominant poststructuralism of the present day. Space and time are both lacking. I shall in what follows attempt to indicate what a thoroughgoing understanding of Peirce's semiotics, considered as an aesthetic theory,[25] might offer to avoid some of the easier of the criticisms brought against both structuralism and its alterego.

What the two critical theories sketched above have in common as the likeness in their difference is a dyadic account of a sign. The difference by which they constitute the dual of one another is the presence or the absence of a clear signified or set of signifieds functionally related to a set of articulated signifiers in a given literary text. Peirce's triadic notion of a sign as it signifies is the functional relationship between sign-vehicle, its object, and an interpretant. Along with his ceno-Pythagorean categories (ontological structures, these, of an attentive consciousness), which he chose to denominate firstness, secondness, and thirdness, and which denote either quality, fact, and law on the side of things known; or feeling (sensation), resistance (perception), or habitual action (conception) on the side of the knowing consciousness; such a theory of a sign's functioning certainly disposes of a number of pseudo-problems associated with the scientific or ontological pretensions of Peirce's competitors.

Why, for example, is it a scandal that structuralism offers no explanation of a thinking subject? We can replace the certainty of Descartes' cogitating soul with a Freudian unconscious self if we like;

but the risk is to exchange one kind of spurious certainty for an overinvestment in a quantity or quality essentially unknown and unknowable. A feeling of desire, even of conflicting desires, is still only a firstness, which, considered in itself, means nothing outside itself. We can, of course, make any feeling an object (and therefore a second) by intending it in an act of reflection. Of course, it will in the process become mediated as reflected upon, and in this state of secondness even be designated by the symbol 'feeling,' as the legisign for all similarly isolated conscious states.

But, it does not follow from the fact that a searchlight-like transcendental ego cannot be brought into self-presence that nothing is known; only a fool would deduce from this fact that there were no feelings in the world, or that a sighted person cannot see, or that human beings cannot initiate gestures that become habituated responses to recurrent appearances of things or their qualities, as we do whenever we form concepts. Although Peirce is concerned that this account resembles too strongly the Hegelian description of a completely reflexive consciousness,[26] he admitted to Lady Welby that he could offer no better phenomenological account of the matter. Firstness, secondness, and thirdness are irreducible characteristics of a human awareness.

Derrida—God preserve his metaphysically skeptical soul—should have known better: even Heidegger distinguished the mode of being of things and tools from the mode of being of existent subjects. For Heidegger, the being of a human being is a manner of being related to a world—caring, as he explains it; and the meaning of this caring is temporality—the stuff (under erasure) of which our souls are made. Heidegger had written *Being and Time* in the language of ontology peculiar to himself, using a method of hermeneutics that would be recognized for what it is if we called it a consistently applied set of interpretant symbols to the phenomenon of being in a world.

The being of a human being gets interpreted as caring for the entities it finds in its world; it is not, as Jean-Paul Sartre claimed for the being of consciousness,[27] always present to itself. For this reason, the metaphysics of presence has nothing to do with the meanings of our linguistic expressions, since these are signs which need only some kind of interpretant to fulfill their function, and which, when experienced as signs are always already interpreted. Such would be the Peircean view on the matter, had Heidegger's ontology been his own. Heidegger's "existentials" (human ontological categories) are, for an interpretant, structural components of a living conscious body temporalizing its spatiality in a distinctive way. Like any other categorial expression they denote the most general characteristics of the entities so characterized.

And along with the metaphysics of presence, so goes the so-called "logocentrism" of Western epistemology. Both are red herrings, confusing the linguistic issues of human intersubjectivity. Nothing-determinate follows from the abandonment, in our postmodern *épistémè*, of a substantial soul; that was, in the first instance, merely a sense without a reference; in Husserl's language, a meaning intention that went unfulfilled. Husserl merely replaced that useless notion with his own of an intentional act; and Lacan, with still another, the libidinous id. We have in these differences of concept three distinct philosophies of mind. If, for our part and in our own perversity, we should feel driven to replace these intentional acts with a set of linguistic functions, we would find our minds in our words, particularly in those words used to interpret the relationship between a sign and its object, just as Peirce had indicated we always do.

Some of our references, to be sure, will still misfire, and go by their referents; but if they do, the reason will be that we have failed to observe carefully what there is that can be referred to, a phenomenon of secondness, or to have exercised sufficient care to frame the concepts to sort out what can be referred to, a phenomenon of thirdness. As for the phenomena of firstness, that is the concern of Peircean aesthetics.[28]

An aesthetic sign, as a rhematic, iconic, qualisign refers only to itself as a possibility of precisely that quality it is perceived to be when we let ourselves go to the play of its "text," i.e. when be begin to make our interpretations by associating signifiers (signs) with their signifieds (the objects signified). As an act of the reading consciousness, signs and their objects are related by an interpretant; ultimately, in the aesthetic mode, the interpretant of a sign is the felt tension of the relationship between the sign and its object as registered in the behavior of any reader willing (and able!) to submit him or herself to the disciplinary actions required by the text.

The relationship between an aesthetic sign and its object is iconic because the sign-vehicle (an interpreted text) resembles its object (a possible qualitative experience) by virtue of a similarity in structure.

I realize that above I have only sketched out a Peircean criticism of structuralist linguistics. There is much more to this metacritical approach than a simple substitution of a dyadic for a triadic relational structure. For example, we still have to learn how Peirce's semiotics constitutes a full blown philosophy of mind, obviating the need for the Freudian basis of Lacan's and Barthes' and Derrida's linguistics. At the same time we must be led to see how the same semiotics, along with that philosophy of mind, which owes so much to Hegel for the cenoPythagorean categories (firstness, secondness, thirdness) with which he interpreted human sign behavior, can be turned into an interpretive tool for demonstrating the aesthetic pleasures of a literary text.

Although Peirce was distrustful of the grand Hegelian synthesis of the stages in mental development, as described in the *Phenomenology of Mind*, and as traducing the empirical study of logical relatedness in the larger *Logic*, he admitted to Lady Welby, his partner in the study of "significs," to use her word for semiotics, that he could find no better way to characterize a reflective self-consciousness.[29] At least his terms for the categories of consciousness were value-free and descriptive, rather than theoretical and normative.

In this contrast of semiotics and grammatology, one thing seems already apparent: it is not the openness or the closedness of a narrative plot that determines the qualities of a literary expression—that too is a red herring obscuring the contemporary debate concerning structural significance. Some pieces of writing, as scriptible as you please, have no plot at all, and yet are full of the tensions between an expressing surface and an expressed depth; the new French novel is a case in point.[30] And the experience of the relationship between the surface and depth of a text (the signifiers and the signifieds, phenomenologically interpreted) is that quality which stands for the possible feeling it represents. The overuse of sexual metaphors by structuralist and poststructuralist alike tends to debase this feeling by universalizing, and thereby overly sanitizing our actual sexual responses. That, after all, is a consequence of treating all literature as metaphor; if Peirce is right, a literary work is an icon of a definite, particular feeling. And not every *jouissance* has the same determinate character; not every hymeneal, the same singing of the spirit actually expressed in feeling. How songs become spirited is yet to be clearly explained.

We can make such functional relationships as those between the surface and depth of a literary expression apparent, provided that we first feel the tension (which should not be so difficult, since in reading we *are* that tension, a quality of feeling in itself a mere possibility (or first), actualized by a perception of syntactic structures (as perceived, a second), in relationship with the field of semantic references deployed as a matter of habit (a third) before our imaginations in the act of attentive reading. After all, calling a literary text a "rhematic iconic qualisign"— as I insist we ought to—is merely one way of saying that it is something to be read for the feeling that experience affords. And the secret of enjoying the pleasure having such feelings may occasion is to learn how to live in such worlds.[31]

There can be no play in the experience of a set of signifiers, no pleasure in supplementing one such set by another, unless an interpretant sets the play in motion. That is what the completer notion of the sign-function guarantees—at the same time it places human "subjectivity" back into the structures of significs. The poststructuralists have failed to make complete sense (even when this word is written under erasure) because they committed the impardonable gaffe of accepting Saussure's incomplete notion of the sign. For this reason, apparently, a poststructuralist is only a structuralist "*qui s'ignore,*" i.e. one ignorant of his own condition, but still linked by a hyphen within the flow of time to an apparently incoherent past.

What, precisely, are the differences between a semiotic reading of a text and a poststructuralist one? Perhaps only two or three.

First of all, the semiotician finds his readings structured by the signs of his text; but since all interpretants may themselves become signs for further interpretation, each is capable of an indefinitely extensible fine tuning that permits closer and closer approximation to exactness of expression. As always, here the criterion of "correctness" is supplied by the synchronic dimension of the written language as conventionally used by a society of interpreters who may introduce novelty into the code by various figures, such as metonymy or metaphor. Since these two figures make their appearance in the structuralisms of both Saussure and Lacan, there is no difference here between a structuralist and a Peircean semiotic theory. Only Lacan's doctrinaire dismissal of a signified justified the claim to a difference between the two. But he was talking about a signified self. And Roman Jakobson introduces the same terms as seminal meaning generating categories in his own general linguistics.[32]

A semiotician accepts the reality of a text; the poststructuralist, through the arrogance of his theory, insists upon supplementing a text he claims never to have existed with a text of his own—even though he is consistent enough to admit that his own text, in its turn, is to be supplemented by still another. But the process by which the supplementation of signifiers is carried to infinity in poststructuralist theory is more adequately motivated by Peirce's triadic account of the sign: all interpretants need further interpretation, as the grounds establishing them come under further investigation. Meaning, like truth, is never just given; it is something to which we approach ever so asymptotically.

Next, besides the controlled reading of a text, perhaps the most salient difference between European structuralism and American semiotics is the resultant corrigibility of a reading—not with respect to a purely subjective intention of a writer, or the reactions of an implicit reader,[33] but by virtue of the systematic code embodied within a living language. Saussure had already referred to this code as the ''collective consciousness'' of a society of language users, while we would, perhaps, refer to the same phenomenon as the intersubjectivity of the communication mediated by the systematic usage of a set of signs. Variations from the code, by either metonymy or metaphor, bespeak the mind of an individual author.

Between an author and his or her text, there is no third, connecting entity or process, just as there is no need of a supplement to the text offered us, if only we have learned how to read. When speaking of a text and its author, we are not speaking of two entities, but only of one: the language of the text. There is absolutely nothing outside the text, not even an economy of desires, that may guide the reading of a written text; indeed, as Peirce had said, there is nothing to the very concept of man, but the signs men and women use to express themselves.[34]

These texts are always already interpretants of other signs; and they become aesthetic only as their unfolding yields a quality that is interpreted as an icon of itself, merely as a possibility, which is the ontological counterpart of the cenoPythagorean category of firstness, i.e. a feeling unconnected to anything beyond itself.

What would have been the case had Lacan read Peirce and Freud, instead of Saussure and Freud? Perhaps a more insightful reading of Hegel would have made the difference between his structuralist linguistics and a phenomenological semiotics more clear. Adding Freud to either Saussure or Peirce is simply not enough to cover the facts of aesthetic communication through the effects of sign interpretation.

Scientists, like the anthropologists and the psychoanalysts we have been discussing, invent concepts, in the order of thirdness, to communicate to us what a human being is; artists, like the writers criticized in *la nouvelle critique*, use language to create the myths by which they create themselves in the order of firstness. And that, as we reflect upon it, is a matter of fact, in the apparent order of secondness. So, what is all this talk about logocentrism and the ubiquitous metaphysics of presence? Apparently, in the interpretant, an erroneous order of thirdness. But such is the fate of all thinkers who would attempt to refute a fact with some pet theory or another. When the facts of the case are trimmed to match our theory, we are dogmatists; when our theories are trimmed to match the facts, our inquiries may be said to be sensible.

But, then, what is a theory that is constructed with nonconcepts? Itself a myth for which there is no accounting without the creation of another myth. Every pharmacon is double barreled; every drug, a remedy and a poison, depending upon how it is used. And for that I have the word of Jacques Derrida.

For a third and final difference between the two theories, try the seriousness of their framers. That too is a quality of language use, and is palpable to any curious reader of the theoretical texts—to which, by these presents, I direct anyone interested in investigating the aesthetic properties of literary texts.

The cure for any malfunctioning theory is successful metatheory, and it is not yet clear to enough practicing literary critics that the road to theory passes through metacriticism—where linguistic theory and aesthetic theory both have a role to play. The hymen-hyphen between these two conscious functions seems grounded in a single phenomenon by Peirce, while the theoretical metacriticism of poststructuralist linguistics must import its connection to aesthetic theory from outside its linguistic context.

For that reason alone—for the rational preference of simplicity over complexity—the one seems superior to the other. From within the standpoint of the Peircean semeitoic theory of aesthetic signs, literary metacritics are themselves the hymenal tissue that unites and separates aesthetic and discursive uses of language. As interpreters of signs interpreting texts their responses must be grounded upon that feeling of tension between the signifiers and the signifieds by which those texts are structured. Why? Because, as written, texts are the results of rhetorical strategies; and, as read, they are reconstructed according to the discipline governing the intent of the work. And it is for this reason that a critic's "job of work" is to concern him or herself with the work, the whole work, and nothing but the work—as a system of signs referring to nothing other than their own potentiality to become, in interpretation, the icon of a definite feeling.

The Florida State University, Tallahassee.

NOTES

1. Claude Lévi-Strauss, *Les Structures élémentaires de la parenté* (Paris: Presses Universitaires de France, 1949).
2. Ferdinand de Saussure, *Cours de linguistique générale*, eds. Ch. Bally, Albert Sechehaye, Albert Riedlinger (Paris: Payot, 1949). New edition.
3. Maurice Merleau-Ponty, *La Prose du Monde* (Paris Gallimard, 1969). Posthumous text established by Claude Lefort.
4. The three texts of that year are: *L'Ecriture et la différence* (Paris: Editions du Seuil, 1967); *De la grammatologie* (Paris: Editions de Minuit, 1967); and *La Voix et le phénomène* (Presses Universitaires de France, 1967). For a comparison of Derridean deconstruction and Peircean semiotic, see John K. Sheriff, *The Fate of Meaning: Charles Peirce, Structuralism, and Literature* (Princeton: Princeton University Press, 1989).
5. From an interview reported by Jean-Luc Chalumeau, *La Pensée en France de Sartre à Foucault* (Paris: Edition Fernand Nathan, 1974), 131.
6. For the most fully developed approach to semiology, see the two works of A.-J. Greimas, *Sémantique structurelle* (Paris: Larousse, 1966) and *Du sens: essais sémiologiques* (Paris: Editions du Seuil, 1970).
7. See Ferdinand de Saussure. op. cit., p. 33. The course had been taught by Saussure at the University of Geneva in 1906-7, 1908-9, 1910-11.
8. For the exploitation of these phenomena in the the theories of Claude Lévi-Strauss, see his *La Pensée sauvage* (Paris: Plon, 1962); of Jacques Lacan, see his *Séminaire XI*, course transcription by Jacques-Alain Miller (Paris: Editions du Seuil, 1973), 172. And for the importance of these same two rhetorical tropes in the linguistics of the school of Russian formalism, see Roman Jakobson, *Essais de linguistique générale*, (Paris: Editions de Minuit, 1963), *passim*.
9. Claude Lévi-Strauss, *Anthropologie structurale*, (Paris: Plon, 1958), and *Anthropologie structurale, II* (Paris: Plon, 1973).
10. Roland Barthes, *Degré zéro de l'écriture* (Paris: Editions du Seuil, 1953).
11. For an account of this movement, see Chalumeau, op. cit.
12. See Sigmund Freud, *The Interpretation of Dreams,* trans. James Strachey, 3d printing (New York: Basic Books, 1958), pp. xi-xii.
13. Jacques Lacan, *Ecrits* (Paris: Editions du Seuil, 1966).

14. See Arthur Rimbaud, *Oeuvres complètes* (Paris: Gallimard, Bibliothèque de la Pléiade, 1951), 254. For Lacan's commentary, see his *Séminaire II*, 16, and *Ecrits*, 116–20.

15. See Rimbaud, op. cit.

16. See Lacan, *Ecrits*, 413.

17. See Lacan, *Séminaire XI*, 172, where the parallel between his own psychonalytical theory and the anthropological analyses of Lévy-Strauss is emphasized.

18. See his *Maladie mentale et psychologie* (Paris: Presses Universitaires de France, 1954); for his concept of the changing concepts of alienation, see his *Histoire de la folie à l'age classique* (Paris: Plon, 1971).

19. Foucault, *Les mots et les choses* (Paris: Nouvelle Revue Française, 1966); Quine, *Word and Objects* (Cambridge, MA.: MIT Press, 1960). Quine's explanation of the "First Steps of Radical Translation," 26–30, is purely imaginary (as many theoretical constructs are), and point out the close affinity between the mythological and the truly "scientific."

20. See Derrida, *La Dissémination* (Paris: Editions du Seuil, 1972), 319–407.

21. See Chalumeau, op. cit., 130–31.

22. See *De la grammatologie*, which opens with the theme of the death of the book.

23. See Edmund Husserl, *Logische Untersuchungen*, sixth edition (Tübingen: Niemeyer Verlag, 1980), vol. II, 2, 49–64.

24. When I asked him which of his earlier books was the best introduction to his critical work, Derrida replied with *De la grammatologie*, which contains a deconstruction of Rousseau's two essays on the origin of language.

25. For an account of Peirce's "aesthetics," see my "Reflections on Peirce's Aesthetic," *The Relevance of Charles Peirce*, ed. Eugene Freeman, (La Salle, Il.: The Hegeler Institute, 1983), 224–37.

26. See *Semiotic and Significs: The Correspondence between Charles S. Peirce and Victoria Lady Welby*, ed. Ch. S. Hardwick (Bloomington and London: The Indiana University Press, 1977).

27. Jean-Paul Sartre, *L'Etre et le néant*," (Paris: Gallimard, 1943), 115–21.

28. Loc. cit.

29. See his correspondence with Lady Welby, *Semiotic and Significs*, 25.

30. The French new novelists include such authors as Alain Robbe-Grillet, Michel Butor, Nathalie Sarraute, and Claude Simon, with Robbe-Grillet as the chief theoretician. The *Tel Quel* group, with which Derrida collaborated at one time, bring to literature the same radical tendencies they brought to politics. For an account of these two groups and their effect on the new (French) criticism, see Chalumeau, op. cit.

31. See my "L'Etre-dans-un-monde-littéraire," in *Analecta Husseriana*, XXIII (1988), 407–31.

32. Op. cit.

33. For these two modes of phenomenological reading, see Wolfgang Iser, *The Implied Reader: Patterns of Communication in Prose Fiction from Bunyan to Becket* (Baltimore: The Johns Hopkins Press, 1975) and *The Act of Reading: A Theory of Aesthetic Response* (Baltimore: The Johns Hopkins Press, 1978).

34. See Peirce, "The Reality of Mind," and "The Identity of Man and His Language," *Collected Papers*, eds. Ch. Hartshorne and Paul Weiss (Cambridge, Mass.: The Belknap Press of Harvard University, 1978–9), Vol. V, sections 313–14.

Address as Focus:
Plato, Nietzsche, and Postmodernism

WILLIAM J. KENNEDY

"Mit Nietzsches Eintritt in den Diskurs der Moderne verändert sich die Argumentation von Grund auf."
Jürgen Habermas (753)

Whatever postmodernism may be, its advocates seem to agree on the dominance of rhetoric over logic in all discursive practices and upon the role of Nietzsche as a forerunner of its own critical procedures (Habermas, 753). These procedures seek to undo every form of rigid identity or totality, genealogical causality, essentialism, continuism, analogism, and teleologism, comprehensively subsumed in the concept of "metanarrative." One of its influential theorists, Jean-François Lyotard, in fact defines postmodernism as an "incredulity toward metanarratives" (xxiv). Unravelling binary oppositions that in the name of purity, unity, order, and hierarchy eliminate human difference, postmodern criticism directs its energies toward conferring an idiosyncratic primacy upon texts and especially upon the local diction, figures of speech, and tropological structures of discourse in those texts. In so doing, however, it burdens rhetoric with a false, or at least illusionary, problematic. Does rhetoric entail nothing more than the invention of figures and tropes? Does rhetorical analysis require nothing more than a demonstration of their incompatible, self-contradictory effects? Does rhetoric engage no substantive concerns that transcend surface attention to local diction? As it turns out, Nietzsche's own enabling concepts of rhetoric suggest a strongly positive answer. They assert the importance of address as a focus for each utterance, a focus that incorporates principles of rhetoric enacted in Plato's *Phaedrus* and that helps to resolve aporias uncovered by deconstructive criticism in *The Birth of Tragedy*.

Nietzsche's lecture notes entitled *Description of Ancient Rhetoric [Darstellung der antiken Rhetorik]* were prepared for a course at Basel in 1874 that never took place, and they apparently overlap with notes for a course on "The History of Greek Eloquence" that Nietzsche gave in 1872–73. The *Description*, published for the first time in its entirety in 1989, offers sixteen chapters mostly on technical divisions of rhetoric, figures of speech, and discursive genres, along with an appendix on the history of eloquence and Aristotle's writings on rhetoric. Both the descriptive classification of figures and its history derive largely from authoritative nineteeth-century studies by Richard Volkmann, Gustav Gerber, and Friedrich Blass, among others. Nietzsche, however, interjects his own understanding of the importance of rhetorical address and its effect upon speech acts and discursive practices. That understanding, as one might expect, reveals a healthy skepticism about taxonomic concepts of rhetoric prevailing in his own day (Goth, 27).

Nietzsche models his view of language upon the Platonic Socrates's premise about its conventionality (*Cratylus*, 431–436), but he erases completely Socrates's vestigial nostalgia for a natural relationship between words and things, "that words should as far as possible resemble things" (*Cratylus*, 435c). Nietzsche drives it instead towards an anticipation of Saussure's principle of the arbitrary nature of the sign as a "means of expression used in society... based, in principle, on collective behavior or—what amounts to the same thing—on convention" (Saussure, 68). For Nietzsche, but not for Saussure, language does not point toward any transcendent truth about the nature of things; it instead expresses its speaker's perception of reality. Thus it enables a speaker's auditors to share that perception. Its essence is not to explain the nature of things but rather to transfer or to convey a subjective impulse or assumption about them.

The reason why language does not convey essential truth is that human beings, the makers of language, do not apprehend such truth themselves; instead they receive impulses from things, and they process these impulses only on the horizons of their own understanding: "Man, who forms language," Nietzsche claims, "does not perceive things or events, but impulses [Reize]: he does not communicate sensations, but merely copies of sensations" (21). As a result, the language that human beings fashion bears no necessary or complete relationship to the reality that it expresses. At the most it is rhetorical and conveys only a perspective on some truth. "There is obviously no unrhetorical 'naturalness' of language to which one could appeal; language itself is the result of purely rhetorical arts" (21). As Nietzsche earlier asserts, the *telos* or *officium* of rhetoric may be to teach or to persuade, but teaching or persuasion do not define the nature of the speech act "because the effect is not the essence of the thing, and furthermore, persuasion does not always take place even with the best orator" (5).

Nietzsche's understanding of rhetoric frames the act within the consciousness of a speaker. The perspective of this consciousness, and not reality itself, motivates what the speaker apprehends and what he or she says. How the speaker stands towards reality determines his or her expression of it. "It is not the things that pass over into consciousness, but the manner in which we stand toward them" (23). At the same time the speaker's perspective on the audience and how he or she may stand towards it can motivate the way the speaker puts his or her expression into words. Nietzsche emphasizes not only the process of transference but also its focus, the others to whom one's impressions are conveyed: "Language does not desire to instruct, but to convey to others [*auf Andere*] a subjective impulse and its acceptance [eine subjektive Erregung und Annahme]" (21). Rhetoric is a social act. The Greeks cultivated it as a republican art to express their opinions about public issues; the Romans, as a hegemonic art in order to impose their fictions on others. Agonistic competition among individuals defines its contours in the ancient world (37). Here as elsewhere Nietzsche regards agonistic competition as a spur to the highest Hellenic values (Spariosu, 73).

Nietzsche's emphasis on this social dimension makes of the speaker's interaction with the audience an external goal of rhetoric. Hence the focus of rhetoric becomes an interaction between the mode of address and the manner of its direction. "It is a matter of importance to observe for whom, and among whom, one speaks, at which time, at which place, and for what cause" (33). Here the very nature of the rhetorical situation, the dynamic and dramatic relationship between the speaker and the cess of human understanding. Dialectic entails a double "that of perceiving and bringing together in one idea the rticulars, that one may make clear by definition the particular he wishes to explain; . . . [and] that of dividing things again where the natural joints are, and not by trying to break any d–e). Human beings enter into dialectic not in isolation but ugh a process of interaction that rhetorical address brings Such a rhetoric does not require the speaker or writer and e to be present to each other. It does require, however, an f forms, concepts, signs, symbols, or speech between the e other.

media of exchange, however interiorized, bear marks of a to the outer world. They are constructions of a social reality eir users into contact with other users, no matter how solitary al, individual or institutionalized they may be. Socrates shows tic analysis as a prelude to dialectic must emphasize the social ions of meaning and hence what Foucault designates as the conditions of discursive practice (135–38). For example:

TES. When one says 'iron' or 'silver,' we all understand the ing, do we not?
RUS. Surely.
TES. What if he says 'justice' or 'goodness'? Do we not part y, and disagree with each other and with ourselves?
RUS. Certainly.
TES. Then in some things we agree and in others we do not.

is analysis dialectic itself must deal with modes of circulation, , attribution, and appropriation that affect both the focus and the construction of meaningful truth.

Phaedrus at 260a asserts that the rhetorician "does not need at is really just, but what would seem just to the multitude," e presses upon a raw nerve and exposes the social character he functional conditions of any discursive practice do not lter truth, nor do they make even a provisional truth out anifestly untrue. They do, however, situate the perception an area of contestation. Rhetorical address confers a focus erception by summoning a cluster of pertinent responses.

audience is of paramount concern. In Nietzsche's view, as in Aristotle's (*Rhetoric*, 2.12, 21; 3 16), the speaker must actively adapt to the specific situation at hand. However unfamiliar that situation might be, the speaker contrives to make his or her share in it appear appropriate. Language furnishes the speaker with material to fashion a particular role: "Here he practices a free *plastic* art [eine freie *plastische* Kraft]; the language is his material which has already been prepared [ein bereites Material]" (35). This process partakes of the dramatic art in which a speaker constructs an image of a role to present himself or herself to an audience in an appealing way. "What is remarkable about him is that, through art [durch Kunst], through an interchange of persons [durch ein Vertauschen der Personen], and through a prudence which hovers over them, he finds and turns to his advantage what the most eloquent lawyer of each person and each party, namely egoism, only is able to discover" (35).

The transference of identity here is double. The speaker relays one identity for another in assuming a persona for the audience to accept, "ein Vertauschen der Personen" ("an interchange of persons"). This very interchange requires the audience to surrender its own belief in the speaker's identity as a stable construction. When it enters into this game of masks, the audience transforms its own identity, too. It plays a complementary role that will permit an exchange of egos with the speaker, "eine Vertauschung des ego" ("an exchange of egos") (35). The rhetorician contrives this situation just as the dramatist contrives a play, requiring speaker and audience alike to perform complementary roles.

An interaction between the speaker and audience is also crucial in Nietzsche's "On Truth and Lies in the Extramoral Sense" ("Über Wahrheit und Lüge im aussermoralischen Sinne") which he composed during this period. There Nietzsche calls into question any criterion for "correct perception." Irrational animals perceive the world differently from humans. The question of whose perception has a greater claim to truth as "the adequate expression of an object in the subject" is "ein widerspruchsvolles Unding" ("a self-contradictory absurdity") ("Truth" 252/"Wahrheit" 267). Each is adequate only to its respective subject. The relationship between two so absolutely different spheres can be only "an *aesthetic* stance": "I mean an allusive transference, a stammering translation into a completely foreign medium" (252/267). By analogy this "allusive transference" sets in motion an interchange of persons and an exchange of identity. Each spectator must project himself or herself into the situation of the other so as to apprehend the world from the other's point of view. For humans this "freely fictionalizing and freely inventive middle sphere and middle faculty" is the power of imagination (252/267). Among those who exist within a shared community it is available also through language. Through language one person communicates to another his or her perspective on the world: "What, then, is for us a law of nature? It is not known to us as such, but only in its effects, i.e., in its relations to other natural laws, which in turn are known to us only as relations" (253/268). Instead of defining the essence of a thing, we articulate the relationships and effects that circumscribe it.

These relationships and effects determine all we know and all we say. Likewise our relationships to them constitute an important perspective. To the extent that we are mindful of this perspective when we speak, we fashion our words to others with a focus on their potentially different horizons of understanding. In consequence our address to others provides a focus for what we have to say, however indirect the act of communication must be. Only in this way can Nietzsche resolve what one critic of postmodernism apprehends as a tension "between the critique of knowledge and the desire to give us knowledge about a life that escapes concepts and critique" (Kolb, 42). A shattered narrative and destabilized frame may impede the transmission of some fancied or imagined absolute truth, but the focus of address allows for a sharing of attitudes towards some undetermined truth.

The sense of a shattered narrative and destabilized frame nonetheless bothered Western consciousness long before Nietzsche and post-modernism. Nietzsche himself understood it as an animating force in Plato's dialogues and he construed it as a crucial issue in Socrates's discussion of rhetoric in *Phaedrus*. There Socrates offers no assurances that any preconceived metanarrative grounds ideas in a stable synthesis. To demonstrate his own rhetorical skill in that dialogue Socrates articulates a highly compromised metaphorical account of the immortality of the soul, the awakening of love, and the subjugation of appetite. The narrative implied in this account is hardly univocal. Part of our uneasiness about it is caused by a general confusion in our concept of narrative introduced by Plato himself when he discusses *diegesis* 'description' in the *Republic* (392d–397c). There narrative has an important epistemological function associated with the narrator's rhetorical powers

(Prier, 162–69). Modern and postmode
emphasize this function in linear and disj
than in quantitative and concrescently
Though Socrates's narrative begs to be
Socrates and Phaedrus discuss possibilitie

In their discussion Socrates rebuke
provenance of each utterance: "But to yc
who the speaker is and where he come
only whether his words are true or not"
the reader's distance from the author of a
to question the latter's identity. For S
address is already clear and establishe
regardless of its origin or its medium
is not formally inferior to spoken tru
falsehood. Written truth remains tr
misunderstanding, and, although the
error, it also invites rereading and henc
dramatizes this advantage when he as
of Lysias's written speech (262d, 263

Socrates, moreover, dismisses trea
attention to diction and arrangement (26
Instead he urges Phaedrus to concen
audience's response. The physician m
properties of various treatments but al
the quantity of the prescription (268b).
more than the stylish properties of di
the psychological properties of his or h
must analyze a nature, in one that of t
the soul" (270b). This privileged und
object of address converts address itse

Theoretically Socrates subjects hi
and its focus of address to his episten
(271c–d). In that way he resists psy
depends as much upon the speaker's
audience's responses to an utterance.
arguments based upon probability and
a "likeness to truth," it therefore requ
truth (273d). Rhetorical truth is, more
the audience believes to be true, but,

to the pro
procedure
scattered p
thing whic
by classes.
part" (265
rather thro
into focus.
the audien
exchange
one and th

These
relationship
that bring t
or commun
how seman
determinat
functional

SOCRA
same th
PHAEI
SOCRA
compar
PHAEI
SOCRA
(263a)

In light of t
valorizatio
of address

When
to know wh
he therefor
of truth. T
change or
of what is
of truth in
upon this

For instance, in Kenneth Burke's sense of "identification," they cause the audience to associate its interests with those of one group and against those of another (Burke, 19-29; 45-46). They activate the audience's potential for distrusting these identifications, its sense that the speaker can manipulate the focus of address by appealing to certain aspects of socialization and faction rather than to others. The problem for the writer is how to control the circulation of rhetorical address in the written text.

Contrary to what Derrida suggests in his questioning of Plato's logocentrism (*Dissemination*, 117-20), Socrates in the *Phaedrus* mounts no full-scale attack on the written word. To the contrary, he attributes productive strength to its indeterminacy and he appropriates that strength in his own rhetorical performance. Early on Socrates asserts that "writing speeches is not in itself a disgrace. . . . But the disgrace, I fancy, consists in speaking or writing not well, but disgracefully and badly" (258d). The poor writer fails to control the frame of discourse if he or she misunderstands its focus of address. A reader incurs disgrace if he or she reads badly. A deficient reader fails to control the text's spread of meaning (Holdheim, 259). Inattention to the focus of address undoes the act of reading, as Socrates implies in his account of the cicadas' hum. It lures ordinary listeners to distraction and avoidance of any interpersonal exchange, until they find themselves "not conversing at mid-day, but, like most people, dozing, dulled to sleep by their song because of our mental indolence" (259a). No audience, and certainly not a reading audience, can afford to let itself be seduced by an insignificant sound of words. The audience overcomes seduction only when it concentrates on the focus of address.

Socrates himself offers several paradigms for rhetorical address. The first concerns his own role as an addressee in the reading of earlier texts: "I certainly must have heard something, either from the lovely Sappho or the wise Anacreon, or perhaps from some prose writers" (235c). Here Socrates internalizes a focus of address from these texts, a focus that enables him to approach truth from the perspective that it offers. The second paradigm concerns Socrates's role as a rhetor who addresses several audiences in his own set speeches. These audiences include the fictive "boy" whom Lysias sought to convince (237b); then Phaedrus whom Socrates invokes for reassurance in the middle of his first speech: "Well, my dear Phaedrus, does it seem to you, as it does to me, that I am inspired?" (238c); and finally in his second speech the divine Eros, whom he endeavors to assuage for any affront in his earlier discourse: "There, dear Love, thou hast my recantation, which I have offered and paid as beautifully and as well as I could" (257a). This final address appeals to a transcendent power to valorize the speaker's capacity for truth. Such valorization comes with a heavy price. It implies that only an essentialized, universalized deity can survey the truth and focus on its essential, universal meaning.

To be sure such an appeal is the whipping boy of postmodernist rhetoric, but does not the alternative carry an even heavier price? It would imply that concrete historical personages like Phaedrus project themselves into the focus of any address in a forever tentative, always unsettled way. The living presence of an audience in the company of an oral speaker does not guarantee an unbroken transmission of ideas from that speaker to his or her listener. The functional conditions of discursive practice continue to erode the stable identifications of speaker and audience even in their presence to each other. Systems of dependence governing the circulation, valorization, appropriation, and control of discourse unsettle spoken as well as written discourse. In their written form the dialogues as a whole sustain at least a relative immunity to these variations by lending themselves to rereading. Perhaps this explains why Plato wrote them (Ferrari, 220–22). As the *Phaedrus* shows, address as focus requires the audience to analyze not only the formal mechanisms and expressive power of a given discourse, but also its mode of existence, the controls and limitations that modify its appearance, distribution, and variation. Socrates's concept of rhetoric tries bravely to apprehend the workings of these systems.

So too does Nietzsche's concept of rhetoric. Nineteenth-century conditions of production and distribution were enormously more complex than those of ancient Greece, but they challenged Plato's rhetorical model only upon a secondary level of technological application. A formidable obstacle to Nietzsche's ideas, however, was the legacy of Kant and the Enlightenment with its sharp distinctions between "art" and "reality," its epistemic inclination toward formalism and internal consistency, and its strong convictions about universal beauty and truth (Megill, 340–41). In Kant's view rhetoric veers toward an immoral form of persuasion. Routed from science, law, politics, and religion, it acquires legitimacy only in the realm of sublime aesthetics (Kennedy). Nietzsche, on the other hand, reinstates rhetoric within all these domains. With his own inclination to distrust empty formalism and false consistency and his equally strong convictions about the particularity of beauty and truth, Nietzsche blurs the boundaries of art and reality.

Nietzsche's most celebrated earlier text, *The Birth of Tragedy* (1870–71, 1886), examines Greek tragic rhetoric precisely from this point of view. It seeks to define the address of Greek tragedy to its particular audience as a way of understanding the nature of its reality and ultimate truth. To ask the question "What is Dionysian?" (*Birth* 20/*Geburt* 9) is to ask "What does the Greek audience believe about the Dionysian spirit? What does the Dionysian spirit mean to that audience, and how does Greek tragedy address its audience with respect to that meaning?" At the same time *The Birth of Tragedy* situates itself before its own contemporary audience whose perspective it examines as well as its own. *The Birth of Tragedy* comes into focus through two forms of address: the first, vaguely defined as "my friends," appeals to a readership with general as well as specialized scholarly interests in antiquity and Greek tragedy; the second, more precisely defined, appeals to those with an interest in contemporary German culture, to artists themselves, and specifically to Richard Wagner. This second group comprises, therefore, a readership immersed in modern culture but unconscious about the limits, modifications, and conditions of its own understanding. Nietzsche's divided audience and his split focus of address reflect a mixed mode of argument unfolding in the text (Stern and Silk, 188–96).

Nietzsche's principal argument to accommodate the modern understanding of art to the ancient rests upon his theory of "objective" art. The ancients, he claims, expressed a single tragic perspective on the nature of truth and reality through the interpenetration of two contrary ones, the Apollonian and the Dionysian. In that way they embraced the sum of relations in as nearly an objective fashion as possible. All art aspires to this objective condition as it seeks to capture and express the fullest possible range of multiple perspectives. The subjective art that records experience from only one perspective amounts to bad art: "We know the subjective artist only as the poor artist" (48/38–39).

At this point Nietzsche boldly revises the status of lyric poetry that some nineteenth-century writers had associated with self-expression: "Hence our aesthetics must first solve the problem of how the 'lyrist' is possible as an artist—he who, according to the experience of all ages, is continually saying "I" and running through the entire chromatic scale of his passions and desires" (48/39). As René Wellek correctly notes, classical standards prevail over Dionysian exuberance in Nietzsche's literary judgments (4.346). Lyric poetry becomes art only when the "I" of the lyric poet takes on a fictive otherness that brings objectivity to the representation of consciousness. It can be recuperated, *in nuce*, only when it approaches the mode of drama.

> The lyric genius is conscious of a world of images and symbols—growing out of his state of mystical self-abnegation and oneness [aus dem mystischen Selbstentausserungs- und Einheitszustande]...so he, as the moving center of this world, may say 'I': of course, this self is not the same as that of the waking, empirically real man, but the only true existent and eternal self resting at the basis of things, through whose images the lyric genius sees this very basis. (50/40)

The creation of a rhetorical voice and the shaping of a fictive "I" save lyric poetry from blind self-indulgence. They enable lyric poetry to announce its vision as a fusion of perspectives, and thereby to frame its articulation in a space of heightened consciousness.

Just as poets create a rhetorical voice, so they fashion a rhetorical address that puts these multiple perspectives into focus for the receiving audience. Nietzsche's inquiries into the role of the Greek spectator, into his or her relationship to the tragic chorus, and into Euripides's downgrading of the chorus as the ruin of Greek tragedy pursue the question of address as the ground for such a focus. Tragic drama insists upon articulating the position of its audience and inviting the spectator to share a rhetorical perspective on the play's action. The agency for this operation is the chorus. Here Nietzsche discards A.W. Schlegel's formulation of the chorus as "somehow the essence and extract [den Inbegriff und Extract] of the crowd of spectators—as the ideal spectator" (57/49). To replace the chorus with the spectator as Schlegel does would effectively result in "the spectator without the spectacle" (57/50) and thereby eliminate the play itself. Instead Nietzsche evokes Schiller's idea of the chorus "as a living wall that the tragedy constructs around itself in order to close itself off from the world of reality and to preserve its ideal domain and its poetical freedom" (58/50). The chorus's explicit address to the audience articulates drama as a fusion of perspectives, a contest of ideas whose warring views summon an authentic reality cleansed of all illusions. The chorus challenges the audience's belief that its perspective on reality is the only one. In this way the audience participates in what Nietzsche calls the primary dramatic phenomenon, *das dramatischer Urphänomen*: "to see oneself transformed before one's own eyes and to begin to act as if one had actually entered into another body, another character" (64/57). By responding to the chorus's address the audience finds itself in the chorus.

Nietzsche claims that he articulates his argument just at the moment when German imagination is surrendering its leadership to mystified and mystifying claims "under the pompous pretense of founding a *Reich*, a leveling mediocrity, democracy, and 'modern ideas'!" (25/14). In the Preface to Richard Wagner dedicated in December 1871 Nietzsche straightforwardly asserts "what a seriously German problem is faced here and placed right in the center of German hopes, as a vortex and turning point" (31/20). He reproves readers who might dissociate his reflections from their serious goal (31/20). The conclusion appended to the text in 1886 iterates this argument in the form of a rhetorical address: "I know that I must now lead the sympathizing and attentive friend to an elevated position of lonely contemplation, where he will have but few companions, and I call out encouragingly to him that we must hold fast to our luminous guides, the Greeks" (137/143). A conclusion implied earlier about the decline of Greek civilization returns in amplifed form:

> On the heights we encounter the same overabundant lust for knowledge, the same unsatisfed delight in discovery, the same tremendous secularization, and beside it a homeless roving, a greedy crowding around foreign tables, a frivolous deification of the present, or a dully dazed retreat—everything *sub specie saeculi*, of the "present age." And these same symptoms allow us to infer the same lack at the heart of this culture, the destruction of myth. (138/144–45)

The rhetorical function of Nietzsche's double address in *The Birth of Tragedy* establishes two coordinates for this argument. On the one hand the thesis directed towards students of Greek culture proposes that the celebrated achievements of fourth-century B.C. Athens—the development of logical reasoning, scientific inquiry, and theoretical optimism—are symptoms of distemper and fatigue. Nietzsche formulates this thesis against the Socratic position, and it activates a "highly complicated, deeply equivocal relationship" with the latter (Nehamas, 24). On the other hand, the argument directed towards producers and consumers of contemporary culture proposes that the same goals define our civilization, too, and likewise portend its doom. Nietzsche's own discursive argument, itself a product of logical reasoning, scientific inquiry, and at least some theoretical optimism, would seem to self-destruct at the point it devalues the efficacious rational power of language in favor of the tumultuous irrational power of music.

Paul de Man has asked, "Why, then, if all truth is on Dionysos's side, is Apollonian art not only possible but even necessary?" (92). The question is a powerful one, but the answer to it may not be so undecidable as the deconstructive aporia makes it appear. De Man sought to indicate in the text "all the trappings of the statement made in bad faith: parallel rhetorical questions, an abundance of clichés, obvious catering to its audience" (97) and to conclude that

> the narrative falls into two parts or, what amounts to the same thing, it acquires two incompatible narrators. The narrator who argues against the subjectivity of the lyric and against representational realism destroys the credibility of the other narrator, for whom Dionysian insight is the tragic perception of original truth. (98)

The difficulty here announced posits an incompatibility between these two perspectives, as though one were wholly and exclusively Apollonian in its rationality, the other wholly and exclusively Dionysian in its forceful consequences. The deconstructive approach has made the issue too simple and too pat.

The difficulty issues from an exiguously verbal analysis of the text that tries unsuccessfully to distinguish between its performative and constative functions. The reason for paralysis is that neither of these functions, considered separately, accommodates the frame of Nietzsche's argument or defines its focus. His framing of the argument is best associated with the rhetorical construction of a speaker's voice: its qualifications, complications, modifications all unfold not as symptoms of bad faith but as tokens of an active rhetorical inquiry open to contestation, refutation, and further argument. Nietzsche's focus is best identified with a speaker's rhetorical mode of address to an audience that includes a wide range of prospective opponents, proponents, adherants, antagonists, and participants in the debate. Only in this manner can separate perspectives on the argument comes into play as separate propositions. For each proposition the use of language remains neither uniformly constative nor uniformly performative in any rigid way, but rather, as speech act theorists assert, it varies according to the context and occasion of each utterance. The bearer of meaning is no longer the word, but the sentence as a whole. The interaction of utterances will uncover an extended and complex argument.

J.L. Austin notes a particular use of language in which a statement with a "perlocutionary" form—one that tries to produce certain consequential effects upon the audience—turns out to be doing something else:

> For example, if I say 'Go and catch a falling star,' it may be quite clear what both the meaning and the force of my utterance is, but still wholly unresolved which of these other kinds of things [joking, 'acting a part,' or 'writing poetry'] I may be doing. . . . The normal conditions of reference may be suspended, or no attempt made at a standard perlocutionary act, or no attempt to make you do anything. (104)

In Austin's analyses every locutionary act involves simultaneous multiple action, so that the intended effects are only congruent possibilities, perhaps completely unachieved.

Derrida admires Austin's project because "the performative is a 'communication' which does not essentially limit itself to transporting an already constituted semantic content guarded by its own aiming at truth" (*Margins*, 322). He endeavors to clarify this issue by bracketing both intention and context from Austin's speech acts. For Derrida both the transparency of an intentional meaning and the presence of a total context constitute "a teleological and ethical determination," "a philosophical 'ideal' " whose privilege is open to question (325). To circumvent such a determination, he analyzes in different contexts the graphemic possibility of iteration with no single intention—a possibility encompassed within the action of *différance*. In so doing he necessarily concentrates upon "the structure of *locution* (and therefore before any illocutionary or perlocutionary determination)" (322). According to this model, however, the process of communication entails a unilateral flow of words from the speaker to the audience. Its hidden assumption is that the structure of communication enables a "transport or passage of a content of meaning" (321). Yet doesn't this model belie the complexity of the speech act? Doesn't the hypostasizing of pure locution constitute exactly the sort of philosophical reduction that Derrida seeks to avoid: the determination of a philosophical and teleological ideal? The disputed terms of speech act theory may still provide a clue to Nietzsche's use of language that can unravel de Man's deconstructive aporia in *The Birth of Tragedy*. If we take note of Nietzsche's modes of address we can begin to resolve the seeming contradiction within his argument and to clarify its changing focus. In *The Birth of Tragedy* Nietzsche is fashioning an address as though it were a perlocutionary act, but he everywhere retracts its claim to have a universalizing, univocal, essentializing effect. By construing his audience as multiple from the start, by refracting its membership among those with a specialized scholarly interest in antiquity and those with a particular interest in contemporary European culture, he implies that some members of his audience may greet some parts of his argument with enthusiasm, others with contempt, still others with amazement. Nowhere does he assume that the argument will affect all in the same way. The result is a perspectival approach that invites any member of his audience to register his or her own response in the light of his or her own position. It also implies an awareness of the possible variety of positions occupied by other members of the audience.

One of Nietzsche's perspectives concerns an analysis of the ancient Greek audience. Its attitudes, experiences, and expectations enabled it to reconcile Apollonian to Dionysian with no apparent contradiction. It did not, according to Nietzsche, assign exclusive truth to either Apollo or Dionysus. Nietzsche noted that "All that exists is just and unjust and equally justified in both" (72/66). The Greeks saw that whatever exists in Apollo and Dionysus is both true and untrue and equally verified in both. The distortion occurs with us when we assign the exclusivity of "all truth" to either Apollo or Dionysus. This distortion—itself resurrected when de Man begs the question by hypothesizing "if all truth is on Dionysos's side" (92)—is a modern one, exactly as Nietzsche tells us, the product of a modern perspective on truth. Our perspective, after all, defines truth as the adequation of mental images to things. Modern and postmodern discursive practice insists on associating truth with this adequation, even though, as Nietzsche repeatedly insists, Kant shattered such an illusion by demonstrating the utter conventionality of mental images in iconic schemata: "Kant showed that these [mental images] really served only to elevate the mere phenomenon [die blosse Erscheinung], the work of *maya*, to the position of the sole and highest reality, as if it were the innermost and true essence of things" (112/114). Since most moderns, and all postmoderns, see only the veil of Apollo, they assign truth only to Apollo's victory. Some moderns, on the other hand, are able to understand Dionysian truth. To these few Nietzsche addresses his caution that Dionysian truth is not exclusive either. An interaction between Apollo and Dionysus is fundamental.

Nietzsche's concern with the audience as a focus of address, then, rewrites Plato's dominant concern with address itself. A postmodern, deconstructive approach heightens the extremes of Plato's concern with this focus by asserting Socrates's distrust of writing, his privileging of the spoken word, his metaphysical assumption of presence as self-evident to itself. This approach burdens Plato's text with all the consequences of logocentrism, rigid identity, essentialism, analogism, and teleologism that the assumption of presence entails. This extreme interpretation itself results from the kind of hyper-logical reasoning and theoretical optimism that Nietzsche interrogated. The fact of this matter is that the same uncertainties that Socrates attributes in the *Phaedrus* to written discourse apply also to spoken discourse in an exacerbated form. In contradiction to the deconstructionist reduction, for Plato and Nietzsche the focus of address provides an important measure of tentative determinacy for both spoken and written discourse. Throughout Plato's dialogues, and especially in the *Phaedrus*, Socrates demonstrates the effectiveness of this focus. Nietzsche does no less. The interaction of rhetoric and dialectic that Plato sought became a goal for Nietzsche, too. Inscribed in both written and spoken discourse through the focus of address, the interaction of these human modes of language undoes those aporias of figure and trope that have arisen as red herrings in recent critiques of both Plato and Nietzsche.

Habermas is partially correct: with Nietzsche's entrance into the discourse of postmodernism, the question of rhetoric is radically transformed. One must add, however, that this has occurred only through Nietzsche's engagement with the rhetorical practices of ancient Greece.

Cornell University

WORKS CITED

Austin, J.L. *How To Do Things With Words*. Cambridge, Mass.: Harvard UP, 1962.

Burke, Kenneth. *A Rhetoric of Motives*. Berkeley: U of California P, 1969.

de Man, Paul. *Allegories of Reading*. New Haven: Yale UP, 1979.

Derrida, Jacques. *Dissemination*. Tr. Barbara Johnson. Chicago: U of Chicago P, 1981.

Derrida, Jacques. *Margins of Philosophy*. Tr. Alan Bass. Chicago: U of Chicago P, 1982.

Ferrari, G.R. *Listening to the Cicadas*. Cambridge: Cambridge UP, 1987.

Foucault, Michel. *Language, Counter-Memory, Practice*. Tr. Donald F. Bouchard and Sherry Simon. Ithaca, NY: Cornell UP, 1977.

Goth, Joachim. *Nietzsche und die Rhetorik*. Tübingen: Max Niemayer, 1970.

Griswold, Charles. *Self-Knowledge in Plato's Phaedrus*. New Haven: Yale UP, 1986.

Habermas, Jürgen. "Der Eintritt in die Postmoderne." *Merkur* 37 (1983): 752–61.

Holdheim, W. Wolfgang. *The Hermeneutic Mode*. Ithaca, NY: Cornell UP, 1984.

Kennedy, William J. "Voice as Frame: Longinus, Kant, Ong, and Deconstruction." *Media, Consciousness, and Culture*. Ed. Bruce Gronbeck and Thomas Farrell. Newbury Park, Ca.: Sage, 1991.

Kolb, David. *Postmodern Sophistications*. Chicago: U of Chicago P, 1990.

Lyotard, Jean-François. *The Postmodern Condition*. Tr. Geoff Bennington and Brian Massumi. Minneapolis: U of Minesota P, 1984.

Megill, Allan. *Prophets of Extremity: Nietzsche, Heidegger, Foucault, Derrida*. Berkeley: U of California P, 1985.

Nehamas, Alexander. *Nietzsche: Life as Literature*. Cambridge, Mass.: Harvard UP, 1985.

Nietzsche, Friedrich. "*Über Wahrheit und Lüge im aussermoralischen Sinne.*" In *Werke. Kritische Gesamtausgabe.* Part 3, Vol. 2.Ed. Giorgio Colli and Mazzino Montinari. 15 vols. Berlin: de Gruyter, 1967-.

Nietzsche, Friedrich. "On Truth and Lies in the Extramoral Sense." In *Friedrich Nietzsche on Rhetoric and Language.* Ed. and Tr. Sander L. Gilman, Carole Blair, David J. Parent. New York: Oxford UP, 1989.

Nietzsche, Friedrich. *Die Geburt der Tragödie.* In *Werke. Kritische Gesamtausgabe.* Part 3, Vol. 1. Ed. Giorgio Colli and Mazzino Montinari. 15 vols. Berlin: de Gruyter, 1967.

Nietzsche, Friedrich. "Description of Ancient Rhetoric." In *Friedrich Nietzsche on Rhetoric and Language.* Ed. and Tr. Sander L. Gilman, Carole Blair, David J. Parent. New York: Oxford UP, 1989.

Nietzsche, Friedrich. *The Birth of Tragedy.* Tr. Walter Kaufmann. New York: Vintage-Random House, 1967.

Plato. *Collected Dialogues.* Ed. Edith Hamilton and Huntington Cairns. New York: Pantheon, 1961.

Plato. *Phaedrus.* Ed. and Tr. Harold North Fowler. Loeb Classical Library. Cambridge, Mass.: Harvard UP, 1921.

Prier, Raymond Adolph. *Thauma Idesthai: The Phenomenology of Sight and Appearance in Archaic Greek.* Tallahassee: Florida State UP, 1989.

Spariosu, Mihai. *Dionysus Reborn.* Ithaca, NY: Cornell UP, 1989.

Stern, J.P., and M.S. Silk. *Nietzsche on Tragedy* Cambridge: Cambridge UP, 1981.

Wellek, René. *A History of Modern Criticism.* 6 vols. New Haven: Yale UP, 1955-86.

Theoretical Dreamwish and Textual Actuality: The Polyglot Renga by Paz, Roubaud, Sanguineti, and Tomlinson

GERALD GILLESPIE

> "Compaignons, oyez vous rien? Me semble
> que je oy quelques gens parlans en l'air, je
> n'y voy toutesfoys personne. Escoutez."
> Rabelais, *Gargantua and Pantagruel*, IV, 1v

During a few intense days in April 1969 in Paris, the Mexican Octavio Paz, the Englishman Charles Tomlinson, the Frenchman Jacques Roubaud, and the Italian Edoardo Sanguineti composed a European variety of the Japanese *renga* or a chain of linked poems.[1] Their chain grew from a starting collaborative sonnet in a standard sequence of two quatrains and two tercets. Each traditional part of the sonnet was couched in a distinct modern tongue (in order: Spanish, English, French, Italian). Bolder prosodic and generic experimentation rapidly ensued, the four primary languages began to interpenetrate one another, and the native utterance of each poet became shot through with reminiscences from their larger, crosshatched literary repertories, thus with fragments of other languages such as Greek, Latin, Provençal, and Japanese. Cross-cultural allusiveness and polyglot punning emerged with an inevitability dictated by the poets' striving for cosmopolitan interchange. Several streams of Occidental and Oriental thought reached a confluence in their attempt to celebrate poetic communication as ongoing and communal, even anonymous. It is not my purpose to argue for or against their view

52

of poetry in our day. However, the way the experiment was presented to the world public raises interesting issues and clues for translation theory and criticism.[2]

The French edition of the multilingual sequence with a facing French version appeared in 1971 under the title *Renga: poème*. Presumably Roubaud acted as translator of the verses; the prefatory essays by Claude Roy and Roubaud were originally in French; the French renditions of the essays by Paz and Tomlinson are unattributed. Keeping the format of the French volume, Tomlinson published the same collection of twenty-seven multilingual poems in the same year with a facing English translation, explicitly by his own hand, under the title *Renga: A Chain of Poems*. He is the implicit translator of all non-English prefatory matter. In 1972, the Mexican edition, *Renga: un poema*, followed suit. Paz translated the verses into the facing Spanish text, while Salvador Elizondo and Joaquín Zirau Icaza are named as translators of the French and English prefatory matter.

In Tomlinson's edition, the title mirrors itself in a mini-translation more accurate than Roubaud's or Paz' general term "Poem." All the editions employ the same typographical convention of textual mirroring. The body of the multilingual source text is printed in italic to distinguish it from the body of the target text in roman. Reciprocally, foreign locutions or passages in the source text appear in roman, while such materials appear in italic in the English translation. A chart as headnote in each volume indicates that both the polyglot and the monoglot set of a Westernized *renga*, which we are about to read, consist of four subcycles of seven poems each, and that the fourth and final subcycle is defective, thus symbolically "open." Each facing set, whether the source or the target text, supposedly can "be read in either of two ways, the first horizontal and the second vertical" (Tomlinson, 39). In so reading, we encounter discontinuities and transformations of the sonnet form, which the poets have elected to treat as their analogue to the Oriental tanka. Since the tanka has been cultivated in Western languages for many decades, and since tanka competitions in the West predate their experiment, the four poets deeply condition the possibilities of composition and reception by clinging to a venerable European form.[3] Even the possibility of moving either vertically or horizontally in a logodaedalia is familiar, starting at least in the sixteenth century with the brooding conceptualist poet Jean de Sponde. In this respect, Paz and his colleagues seem to exhibit a strain of postmodern mannerism that relives impulses from the late Renaissance.[4]

I shall return to some of the historical dimensions behind the choice of the sonnet, but one curious point about Tomlinson's and any similar effort ought to be spelled out. His act of translating appears to reverse the sense of a polyglot collaboration, because it is a stepping backwards out of multilingual into unilingual culture. As mentioned, prefatory essays by Claude Roy, Paz, Roubaud, and Tomlinson on the original collaboration and its Oriental model bolster the facing multilingual source and the unilingual target text; an interpretational discourse thus swaddles the infant experiment. In effect, this one of three virtually simultaneous "first" editions pulls the European flow toward one of its component currents, English. The containing format of the book betrays the actual status of lyrical interplay in four main languages as a game of high culture. The actual shaping gainsays in great measure Tomlinson's belief that "One still found oneself speaking with a communal voice" (37), at least in any older sense of the folk, people, or masses, despite the eagerness of the four sophisticated, cosmopolitan poets to function as bardic channels in the postmodern age.

I do not detect any explicit or implicit commentary by Tomlinson that allows us to ascribe some "predictive" force to his use of English as the absorbing language into which the polyglot flow directs itself in the case of his translation. That is, he does not seem to stress the actual historical position of English in the twentieth century as the major global lingua franca and/or the special evolution of English as a maccaronic medium, as a locomotive and harbinger of some convergence of languages already underway in Europe. That question would require our pursuing the thematic complexities of *Renga: A Chain of Poems* as a joint composition, over against the three separate unilingual translations thereof—a forbidding task under space restraints. A further dimension would be the contrastive features appearing in the Romance texts, over against the (Germanic) English. Instead I shall concentrate on selected questions of interliterary mediation posited by André Lefevere in his book *Translating Poetry* and by contributors to the volume *The Manipulation of Literature* in regard to single languages, and shall widen them for their potential applicability in a multilingual situation. Toward that end, permit me an excursus with obvious sociological overtones.

Let us imagine we are enjoying a "spaghetti" Western. A Scots cowboy, who—so the dialogue or flashback reveals—is of a recusant Highland family and has earlier learned Spanish during aborted studies for the priesthood in Salamanca and sign language among the Sioux of the upper Great Plains, encounters an Arapaho in the territory of New Mexico. The canny paleface and wary redskin employ slightly variant styles of North American Indian signs. Then, discovering that Castilian and Mexican can serve them as a working language, cowboy and warrior switch to a mixture of rough Spanish and Indian signs. On screen as in real history a new lingua franca comes into existence. The Italian source text in which the Spanish is embedded is perhaps flavored with an Italian version of a Scots and Arapaho brogue. Now since *"we"* happen to be viewing the film in Germany, a version dubbed into the local non-Romance language, that sticky moment when the two men of quite separate cultures communicate in Spanish will have a very different effect if their speech is rendered in two actual varieties of Spanish (perhaps accompanied by German subtitling), rather than being absorbed into the dubbing and flattened in a cardboard *cinecittese*. The problem for an Iberian distributor, then, would be how to convey the special contextual nuances of such a North American use of Spanish in what is a derivative "spaghetti" scenario.

Just as the sonnet was first imported *from* Italy into England, France, Germany, Spain, etc., the conventions of the film genre called Western were once an exotic import *into* Italy but have long since been assimilated into the horizon of the Italian audience and are being reexported in their Italianate transmogrification. Expense aside, the optimal solution in Spain and Latin America might be to dub the hypothetically English speeches as Scots English with its dialect color, the Arapaho as Arapaho, with Spanish subtitling. The Hispanic distributor might well keep the Mexican and Castilian passages steeped in foreign accents for their exotic flavor.

Any movie fan could suggest other cases, but the general analogy between cinematic practice and Tomlinson's English rendition of the joint *renga* should be fairly obvious. Film makers often employ mixed casts in joint ventures, have the actors perform in their native or quasi-native languages, and selectively redub, with auxiliary subtitling as required, for the specific market. For whichever specific pragmatic reasons, Tomlinson certainly resembles a performer who assumes directorial functions and dubs his fellow poets for outlet in an important market.

Tentatively then, we can label Tomlinson's English version of the total *renga* in line with Gideon Toury's descriptive framework. It legitimately constitutes a primary object of attention because at least a section of the "target or recipient culture" has served "as the initiator of the decision to translate and of the translating process" and the translation exhibits the "facts" of the "target system" (*Manipulation,* 18f.). However, we quickly discover the at least equal attractiveness of returning from the English version to the polygot source and of treating the two facing ledgers as expressions of two interactive literary systems—in line with José Lambert's and Hendrick van Gorp's descriptive scheme, furthering notably Itamar Even-Zohar's ideas of polysystemic analysis (*Manipulation,* 42–53). Tomlinson's juxtaposition of the quatrilingual and unilingual texts stresses the dynamic relationship between the systems to which they pertain. His unilingual text also meets Lefevere's "prescriptive" test insofar as it concentrates on the "totality" of the source text, not just one aspect (*Translating Poetry*, 99). This is hard going since linguistic polyphony created by the fluctuation among languages underpins the communicative value and sense of the source text, and unilingual continuity tends to threaten that experience. On another level, to many observant readers (whether or not they are acquainted with the Romance languages), the juxtaposed texts seem interlaced because the cross-over of passages in English from the multilingual and unilingual side binds the two ledgers together. Roubaud's and Paz' translations of the source into French and Spanish establish a similar horizontal interweaving and a sense that the *renga* has been drawn into the literary tradition of each of these languages in turn. These translations, too, were published with the same prefatory materials rendered unilingually into or in each of the two respective target languages. I shall reserve the special relationship among the Romance languages for separate treatment, and regrettably it exceeds the scope of this analysis to comment on similarities and dissimilarities vis-à-vis the English in either the French or Spanish.

But we may generalize about the peculiar complicating feature that in each instance the translator of the multilingual collaboration is also one of its authors. In the case of the English version it is indeed an author of the high qualification defined by Lefevere, since Tomlinson is "familiar with the literature written in his own language, as well as with the evolution of one or more other literatures" (*Translating Poetry*, p. 105). The existence of several poets of that caliber, revealed in their collaboration on a cross-cultural poem which each potentially could reframe in his own native idiom, is powerful evidence that their shared polysystemic understanding is a fundamental component of European poetic consciousness per se. That is, whether or not we knew we were reading a documented translation, we would be likely to notice and respond to traits that exhibited the embedding of foreign locutions and allusions in any unilingual version of this *renga*; the English version fits harmoniously into the tradition of Pound, Eliot, Joyce, et al. for reasons that transcend English, even though the majority of its readers will remain bound or limited to English as the medium of communication.

Like so many other twentieth-century poets, Tomlinson explicitly acts both as a primary reader of the cosmopolitan super-elitist source system and as a mediating reader in the rather demanding target system. Certain old-fashioned English readers might well complain that his mediation is ostentatious. Some of these readers might be less piqued over swatches of borrowed or imitated foreign poetry in Pound's *Cantos*, so long as no facing text of foreign fragments oppressively reminded them of that realm. Let us now imagine that a lost manuscript of the *Cantos* is brought to light in which Pound converts virtually every non-English locution into English. Should we deem his unilingual cycle to be a translation of his own and others' utterance or an in-between category? In this light many modernist works can be viewed as "rewrites" that are second cousins to literary criticism and cultural history. Whether we regard Tomlinson's replication of his own original English passages as a kind of translation will depend to some extent on our analysis of all his other specific acts of keeping as English the English fragments embedded within the non-English passages of the source text, and of rendering into English non-English fragments embedded either in English passages or in the other main languages. Tomlinson's actual practice bears out Lambert's and van Gorp's caution against rigid one-directional approaches to the relations between source and target text, when complex relations obtain.

Tomlinson's treatment of single words in key positions illustrates this principle, as the following two examples show by contrast. His own original English in line 11 of the multilingual sixth sonnet of cycle three reads: "*Inventamos?—decipher, rather: text.*" Without the standard inverted question mark before *inventamos*, the Spanish word is en route toward English. (Dealing with the same sonnet III.6, Paz omits the inverted question mark in the English part on the multilingual side, but as translator restores it on the Spanish unilingual side, while keeping Tomlinson's interpolated Spanish verb as part of his own Spanish.) Tomlinson subsumes the several syntactical nuances of the first-person plural verb *inventamos* ("let's invent?"/"shall we invent?"/"do we invent?") in the neutral infinitive form of English and writes: "Invent?—decipher, rather: text." does this minimal step of switching one cognate term yet amount to an act of self-translation?

Let us compare this with switching terms on behalf of a fellow poet. Closing off the first subcycle in the polygot original, Paz gathers numerous thematic threads in a wholly Spanish sonnet (I.7) that reflects self-referentially on the joint work in progress, on the *renga* as an ultimately anonymous participation in dream and death, serpentine wandering, and rebirth. The interplay between an "I" and "thou" are sounded in the octet. The sestina then culminates in a pointed reference to the "reader" who is linked to the "no-one" in the depths of the unconscious. These two tercets read:

> *No hay nadie ya en al cámara subterránea*
> *(caracola, amonita, casa de los ecos),*
> *nadie sino esta espiral somnilocua,*
> *escritura que tus ojos caminantes,*
> *al proferir, anualan—y te anulan, tú mismo*
> *caracola, amonita, cuarto vacío, lector.*

Tomlinson turns this into English thus:

> There is no-one now in the underground room
> (seashell, ammonite, house of echoes),
> no-one save for this somniloquent spiral,
> script that your traveling eyes,
> in uttering, annul—and you they annul, yourself
> seashell, ammonite, empty room, *lecteur.*

There are no foreign terms in Paz' lines and yet a foreign term appears as capping word in the punch-line on the English side.

Why the move here into French? The exhibition of the primordial evolutionary code in the emptied spiral forms "seashell" and "ammonite" leads to exhibition of the social-anthropological code in the "empty room." In the pan-European vocabulary descended by way of Romantic poetry, "room" signifies the space of the self. Symbolist art has meanwhile witnessed the death of the self but also has been haunted by the structures of the self. Tomlinson is so convinced that Paz is probing this nexus that he avoids the ordinary English term "reader" and prefers the French "*lecteur*"—most probably not because it has matching prosodic dimensions as a Romance cognate of "*lector*," but because it reinvokes the theatrical flourish in Charles Baudelaire's "Au Lecteur," introducing *Les Fleurs du Mal*. In *Renga* sonnet I.5, Baudelaire is imagined as if with the poets in their hotel. Hence Baudelaire's confrontation with the "reader" is a value that still resonates in "the house of echoes" of line 10 of sonnet I.7. This "house" corresponds to the "city," the post-Romantic realm which Baudelaire examined and which furnishes the four poets of the *Renga* with important imagery and the metaphor of poetry's multiple organ. Tomlinson reads a Baudelairean allusion in Paz' "*lector*" which competent English readers will recognize more swiftly as a French quotation.

I pass over the question whether, in the polygot source, Paz' metaphor of an *écriture* (Spanish "escritura") that undoes and reconstitutes itself is a postmodern statement catching the new drift of terminology in Derrida or Barthes. Most likely it is. In any event, Tomlinson's choice of the cognate "script" (with a more biblical and theatrical undertone) rather than the contemporary codeword "writing" looks back toward the age of Shakespeare and Calderón. Since "utter" is commonly more associated with "voice" than with "writing" in English, the phrase "in uttering" for "*al proferir*" blunts a postmodernist inference even though it conveys the interaction between "writing" and "reading" or "speaking" and "hearing" as the relationship "proferring" and "receiving."

Tomlinson's English rendition of sonnet I.6 is odder but amusing. His own part of the multilingual original is the second tercet which occurs in a sonnet that is undergoing metamorphosis by inversion of its parts. The poem now consists of an inverted sestina followed by an octet minus one line. Sanguineti leads off in Italian; Tomlinson chimes in next to round out the sestina; and finally comes the defective seven-line octet by Paz and Roubaud in Spanish and French. Tomlinson's part reads in the source text:

O Sade, Rousseau—utopies sexuelles—
Avec un requin, oui, Mais, mon cher Lautréamont
(O mathématiques sévères!) on ne peut s'accoupler avec un éléphant:

Except for the "English" names Sade and Rousseau, this spate of pornographic whimsy appears in roman on the polygot side where roman means "non-standard" language. However, by a doubling of the rule, italic here may also indicate the introduction of foreign locutions within the (expected) "English." Sade and Rousseau technically both are and are not "English" in the multilingual register. Tomlinson converts this totally overwhelmed "English" part into the identical French words on the facing page in the unilingual English register, but he uses italic throughout, thereby depriving Sade and Rousseau of some momentary status as naturalized British. (Roubaud restores their French identity by switching to roman throughout on the French unilingual side.) The jest in the multilingual chain is that English becomes French under certain circumstances. Tomlinson's translational solution for handling this joke is to treat the passage as if it is indeed English, and so French crosses over to—and appears word for word in—the unilingual English chain. There is no trace unless Sade and Rousseau *are* the trace. Why Tomlinson exempts Lautréamont as unambiguously French on both sides is not transparent. French functions here somewhat as it does in the risqué climax of part five of Thomas Mann's novel *Der Zauberberg* when Hans Castorp woos Clawdia Chauchat. Just as a French translation cannot fully represent the contextual setting and effect of French in *Der Zauberberg*, so a French unilingual version of this polyglot *renga* faces a special problem at this indelicately delicate juncture.

The above examples of switching illustrate the very high value placed on the modern poet's role as a cultural critic and interpreter. Not only does the Englished work *Renga: A Chaim of Poems* thematize the collapsing together of the creative writing function and the interpretative reading function; we can also have recourse to Paz' own "Introduction" for clues. (Presumably all the collaborators were privy to or shared the terms in which he interprets or paraphrases himself.) Typical today, Paz says, is:

—A feeling of voyeurism: I see myself manipulating sentences, I see them come together, fall apart, come back into shape. [. . .] Writing is reading and erasing written signs in a space which is within and outside us, a space which is ourselves and in which we cease to be ourselves in order to be what or who? (Tomlinson, 23)

Translation practice demonstrates such an attitude in an age when English is sometimes French. Lefevere's citation of the example of Paz in 1975

(*Translating Poetry*, 5) is astute, because indeed a new openness to translation as a significant area of contemporary literary life, and hence of Comparative Literature, is flourishing. In my view, actual works of poetry, and not merely philosophical currents, have conjured this nurturing climate. There is nothing paradoxical in saying that Paz' own practice should make us skeptical about Lefevere's more radical rejection of literary interpretation or "rewrites" in his stimulating essay included in the Hermans volume.[5]

The impossibility of a "pure" or "perfect" translation tells us something. Any rewriting entails change and some (often a high) degree of randomness and uncertainty. With regard to our Europeanized *renga*, for instance, if we look at the source text, we may well ask: Why has Paz written not *lecteur* but *lector* (I.7)? He is as francophone as Tomlinson and in all probability the French allusion carries as much weight with him, yet he sticks with the cognate in his main idiom, Spanish. Our curiosity is stirred because in the first tercet of another inverted sonnet on the multilingual side (IV.5), Paz cites Rimbaud directly in French within his own Spanish ("U vert")

> *Decia* (A noir, E blanc, I rouge, V vert. . .): "O equals
> X-ray of her eyes; it equals sex." *Omega azul (digo):*
> *cero rebosante, gota de tiempo diáfano, presencia sin reverso.*

But is should be emphasized that I cite the tercet above from the American edition where there is a slight "flaw" in Paz' version of Rimbaud on the multilingual side, a flaw which exactly follows the French edition. Anticipating the word "*vert*" phonetically and visually, the Mexican poet appears to revert playfully to the ancient Roman V lodged in his cultural memory. It is striking, then, that as translator, on the Spanish unilingual side, Paz overrides both the French and the English material which as author he himself interpolated in his own presumptively original version of lines 1–3. In contrast, the French and the American editions carry his highly interpretive, even whimsical V. The slightly later Mexican edition stands alone in taking the double step of restoring Rimbaud's U on both the multilingual and unilingual sides. Most likely to avoid confusing the competent English reader who is presumed to know some French, Tomlinson eschews the playful touch and restores the U on the unilingual side *only*:

He said (*A noir, E blanc, I rouge, U vert*...): "*O equals*
X-ray of her eyes; it equals sex." Omega azul (I say):
brimming zero, iota of diaphanous time, Presence without reverse.

The English quotation interpolated by Paz appears duly in italic on the
English side.
Tomlinson amplifies the Greek basis of much of the Spanish
vocabulary by recasting "*gota*" as the rhyme "*iota*." This is a stronger
interpretive touch than visually raising the term "presence" to conceptual
prominence in English by capitalization, unless perhaps he detects an
underground association with the architectural doublet *guttae* for the
decorative waterdrops on classical temples, and therefore the capital
duly appears in a cryptic manner. Tomlinson seems to make larger
demands on his readers. The English translator consistently carries more
material from all the Romance languages in his English than Paz carries
French or Italian—not to speak of English—in his unilingual Spanish
version. Since Paz is fluent in French and English, the question arises
whether the Mexican poet exercises restraint out of belief or pleasure
in Spanish or out of worry that the Spanish-speaking readership does
not possess a high degree of cosmopolitan sophistication.
　　Because Tomlinson by and large respects the interpolation of one
language within another, readers may wonder why in another inverted
sonnet (IV.1) he differentiates between the treatment of mixed locutions
in the opening tercet and closing quatrain. Lines 1–2 and 11–14 of the
source passage read:

1 rouge (*nella mia nebbia*); *dolce; 4* noir(s): (*severe!*), *inverno, tempo:*
mia neve, e inferno, inferma: in ferma, in decente, tu, materia;
[...]
o sweet ciego rojo limp al punto de la rota
quand, plus-de-bleu plus-de-noir toi séquence de céréales
nombre du puits des feuilles ouvres en tremblant (tremor
at pitch of neve) *ta lueur de louve* (aloof!) *sémillante*

Tomlinson maintains Sanguineti's French terms in lines 1–2, it is
reasonable to assume, for their Rimbaudian referentiality that also covers
Oriental chromatics; and though less of the word play comes through,
he captures some of the sound play:

1 *rouge* (in my mist); sweet; 4 *noir(s)*: (severe!) winter, weather:
my snow, and inferno, infirm: in you, firm, seemly matter;

But does Tomlinson cave in when languages alternate in virtual free association in lines 11–14? Unaccountably he fails to maintain even the visual crossover, that is, to italicize Roubaud's interpolated English; and he scraps Roubaud's interpolated Spanish and Italian entirely:

sweet, blind and limp at the center of the wheel
when, no-more-blue no-more-black you, cereal sequence,
number of the well of leaves, opens (trembling) (tremor
at snow pitch) your sheen of a she-wolf (aloof!) spilling life:

This late in the game we might well expect instead something like the following:

o *sweet ciego rojo limp al punto de la rota*
when, no-more-blue no-more-black you, cereal sequence
number of the well of leaves, open trembling (*tremor*
at pitch of neve) your sheen of she-wolf (*aloof*!) spilling seed.

Converting the second-person verb "ouvres" into a third-person singular that picks up the appositions "*séquence*" and "*nombre*" is a minor shift, whereas the unitary English quashes Roubaud's initial mixture of English and Spanish and later mixture of English and Italian. Paz may be more adroit in providing the cognate of the second-person verb ("abres"), but he is less successful in conveying the magical luminosity of the she-wolf:

oh dulce ciego rojo lacio en en centro de la rueda
si, ya-no-más-azul ya-no-más-negro, tú, secuencia de cereales,
número de pozos de hojas abres temblando (temblor
agudo de la nieve) tu claridad de loba (¡lejos!) vivaz

As if his own nerve fails, Roubaud, too, domesticates his own quatrain for home consumption in French:

doux aveugle et gourd au centre de la roue
quand, plus-de-bleu plus-de-noir toi séquence de céréales
nombre du puits des feuilles ouvres en tremblant (*tremblement*
aigu de la neige) ta lueur de louve (et *loin*!) sémillante

A ''unitary'' unilingualism in the English, French, and Spanish here, in general, imposes an inteligibility that violates the pulsating *sacre du printemps*, overlaid upon the other seasons, in the original multilingual form of this quatrain.

Translation may seem, to a polyglot, to make the ''horizontal'' level of contemporary differences among languages even flatter. But, for the monoglot, this means that, through translation, the actual palimpsest is only hidden from view. Nonetheless, it may be felt, vaguely or hauntingly, beneath the unilingual surface. A similar principle is eternally at work tending to blunt the ''vertical'' dimension of differences among languages over time. One language absorbs values or impulses from another, and these remain present on or below the surface in varying degree of cultural intensity. The several unilingual renditions of the final tercet of sonnet I.3 of *Renga* illustrate how layers of language ultimately flow into a copresence. The original multilingual version reads:

> [*Commentaire (1180: Arnaut: ''pois floris la seca verga...(etc...)''*
> *et plus loin ''*son Dezirat c'ale Pretz en cambra intra...'' (*et Dante*
> *''comme se noie une pierre dans l'herbe...''*) (kokoro no kami—
> *l'obscurité du coeur!*)]

Here, in sequence, are the translations. First Tomlinson's English:

> [Commentary (1180?): Arnaut: ''since the dry rod flowered'' (etc.)
> and further on: ''his *Désirée* whose price brings her into the bedroom...''
>   (and Dante:
> ''as a stone is drowned in grass...'') (*kokoro no kami*—the heart's obscurity!)]

Paz' Spanish:

> [Comentario (1180): Arnaut: ''después floreció la verga seca...(etc.)''
> y más lejos: ''su Deseado tiene precio para entrar en al quarto...'' (y Dante:
> ''como se ahoga una piedra en la hierba'') (*kokora no kami:* ¡la obscuridad
>   del corazón!)]

Roubaud's French:

> [Commentaire (1180?): Arnaut: ''depuis qu'a fleuri la Verge aride...'' (etc.)
> et, plus loin: ''sa *Désirée* qu'entre en chambre son Prix...'' (et Dante:
> ''comme se noie une pierre dans l'herbe...'') (kokoro no kami—l'obscurité
>   du coeur!)]

The numerous small diffferences in the treatment of punctuation and of italicizing reveal the myriad important acts of interpretation that go into unilingual attempts to smooth out the palimpsest that results from cultural sharing. Whether the multiligual version cites bits from Arnaut's influential sestina "Lo ferm voler q'el cor m'intra" acurately, or merely paraphrases or rewrites them, is a topic worth separate consideration, but it is rendered moot in our context, because the point here is that the Provençal words of this high point of *trobar clus* "disappear" from view through translation. We experience reoccultation: enter into, or yearn to enter, a new poetic enclosure and "darkness." The sexual and psychological parallel, as usual, pleases the modern poets. The tercet takes for one of its themes the primary act of interpretation and of writing as an act of response to earlier writing (love as a response to love). It illustrates this by citing the influence of Arnaut on Dante, and thus openly acknowledges that our current single language (the momentary embodiment) *is* the palimpsest. In reinstating the values in the original languages, the tercet virtually digests them and converts them into the tension-ridden "flatness" of today's language—a surface that throbs with the mysteries it enfolds (if we "enter" the chamber for the "prize"). The fragments of Provençal disappear rather easily into the bodies of the Romance cousins. The Japanese quotation, however, retains its own form and sonority; it is still too exotic a lump, and we are invited to sense its magic potency. In all three cases (English, Spanish, French), a straight act of translation releases some of the power and begins the process of absorbing the alien locution. Curiously, Paz uses an ambiguous masculine for what is "desire(d)," and by being closer to the Provençal his term thus sounds more abstract, whereas both Tomlinson and Roubaud give this desire explicitly a feminine name, one tinged with irony because it reminds of cheap erotic tales. Yet the religious double entendre shines through in all three unilingual versions: we are directed to the Virgin and the rod that bears the supreme Rose (Jesus) as symbols of the miracle. Dante, who has digested Arnaut, appears himself as a poet whom the French have meanwhile digested. The Spanish- and the English-speaking readers are invited to treat Dante as someone whom their language stream has thoroughly imbibed, too, and shares.

Authorial compromises in mediating between traditions such as Spanish and English will seem justifiable or overdone or unwarranted according to the target reader's horizon of literary experience. But the same principle governs intra-textually, that is, when poets internally construct or reconstruct bridges to other traditions or earlier phases of their own tradition. Approximations of generic and prosodic features within a tradition or between traditions seem to obey the same underlying law. The four *renga* poets foreground the resemblance between inter- and intra-textual switching on the plane of form. After Rilke and many others, experimentation with the structures of the sonnet is quite familiar to contemporary readers of European languages. Paz, Roubaud, Sanguineti, and Tomlinson choose an inherently conservative pathway by moving toward structures of the tanka through structures of the sonnet. Line 14 of the inaugural sonnet conveys, on one level, a reassurance that the Western vehicle and voice are capable of mediation. Tomlinson translates with a clever pun ("I was relique and clepsydra through the panes of the West:") the window metaphor in the Italian of the multilingual side (*"ero reliquia e clessidra per i vetri dell'occidente:"*). The use of alternating languages highlights the internal characteristics of the constituent quatrains and tercets and eases the way for the flipflop that occurs in I.2, I.4, and I.6 where the traditional octet and sestina are reversed. Round one becomes two interwined strands of regular and inverted sonnets. Of these, I.6 provokes by its defective or deviant final quatrain lacking one line, and I.7 surprises by restoring the standard form in a single language, Spanish.

Sonnet I.6 proffers a kind of magical slippage or syncopation in the octet that reveals internally the fundamental tension between a quatrain and a tercet. It is this juxtaposition which on a larger scale a full sonnet exhibits. This result of much older experiment remains, even though the sonnet took its start from a general musical and prosodic structure, the medieval *canzone*. In Paz' view, the inherent tension of the form also shadows the classic Japanese tanka consisting of three lines followed by two lines (Tomlinson, 25). Hence the reversals of octet-sestina order in the sequence of sonnets tactily imitate the "3/2, word/echo, question/reply" pattern of the tanka, when this "proliferates" producing the *renga* chain or "3/2/3/2/3/2/3/2 . . ." pattern. The mirrored sonnets become something different from an older European sonnet cycle, even though tentatively I.7 reaffirms the European form. The series of transformations in round one prepares the subtler twist in the second round. This shift is announced when the opening sonnet (II.1) starts not with an octet but with a tercet followed by a quatrain; and the restatement or variation occurs when this reversed modified octet is paired not with a sestina, but with a couplet followed by a tercet. Out of the self-mirrorings of the sonnet, a tanka-like structure slips forth in reverse order, the pattern 2/3. This however is a relationship that appears in an encatenation of tankas. Hence now, in II.2, the generative tanka structure of three lines followed by two can make its debut in place of the normally expected octet. The effect is that sonnet and tanka constructs appear to interflow effortlessly; the thematized underlying kinship of structures appears visibly on the formal plane.

It is my contention that their practice in spinning intertextual threads to link up with the tanka resembles experimentation with the sonnet in its own right inside the cultural space of one or several European languages. It is clear these four poets have been astute in their choice of forms which can readily be harnessed to their special themes. The sonnet has ceased to *belong* to any single linguistic tradition within the family of European languages. In that respect it had taken on a kind of communal existence as common property shared across temporal and cultural divides, somewhat as the tanka was and is common cultural property. The English, French, Italian, and Mexican co-authors who claim to write depersonalized, denationalized poetry when they "translate" back and forth between the structural idiom of the tanka and sonnet certainly are aware that, besides Japanese models, they have European predecessors. Their experiment has its roots in the activity of medieval troubadours who switched languages, who occasionally wrote poems with each strophe in a different Romance tongue and capped in the international binding idiom of Provençal.

We do not think of later poets such as Góngora or Hölderlin as being primarily "translators" when, in their experiments in their native language, they assimilate, alter, and naturalize "alien" Greek syntax and prosody. But at a certain point their experimentation may approach or become primarily translation. The *Renga*, then, is another interesting reminder of just how porous the boundaries of poetry in a distant tradition can become. In real history, elements are constantly passing through the membrane that appears, from the inside perspective, to contain and shape one's own culture. However, the examples of single authors like Joyce or collaborations like that of the four *Renga* poets confront us with the challenge of elaborating a polysystemic approach, because anything less will prove inadequate in dealing with the convergence of myriad elements streaming in, into, and from the cultural container of European modernism.

Stanford University

NOTES

1. It seems typical that even good accounts of work and thought of the individual collaborators—e.g., Jason Wilson, *Octavio Paz: A Study of his Poetics* (Cambridge: Cambridge University Press, 1979)—pass over this non-individual work with a mere mention.
2. It is not my aim to erect any theoretical scaffolding when I start from the observation that contemporary translation theory entertains the notion of a polysystemic analysis but tends to focus on binary sets of relations such as those between a source text in one language and a target text in another language. Rather, I shall ramble over pathways marked by four poets who attempt to work through their own consciousness of being writers in a polysystem.
3. An authoritative study of the *renga* tradition is Earl Miner, *Japanese Linked Poetry: An Account with Translations of Renga and Haikai Sequences* (Princeton, N.J.: Princeton University Press, 1979); the reception of *renga* in English is treated by Hiroaki Sato, *One Hundred Frogs: From Renga to Haiku to English* (New York and Tokyo: Weatherhill, 1983). The Paz-Roubaud-Sanguineti-Tomlinson collaboration is not cited in either of these studies.
4. On verbal labyrinths in the sonnet, see my remarks in *Garden and Labyrinth*, 322; and on mannerist affinities in postmodernism, ''From 'Baroque' Michael Drayton to 'Enlightened' Ebenezer Cooke: (Re-)Debunking the American Golden Age,'' in *Erkennen und Deuten*, 326–334.
5. It is not farfetched to think of Paz' verse contributions to the *Renga* as a ''rewrite'' of his prefatory prose text, or to consider his prose text as a ''reading'' act that constitutes, in his eyes, a translation across the least substantial boundary, that of genre. Again, I am only reporting a general viewpoint which some will dismiss as a nugatory paradox. ''Postmodern'' poets like Paz suggest that our rigorous neo-positivistic modes of devising theoretical models of the operations of the bundle of subsystems called literature amount to ''rewrites,'' too. If we privilege exclusively the very competent translation, as Lefevere wants to do, then any theory of translation (such as his own) must be included among other suspect ''secondary'' genres.

WORKS CONSULTED

Even-Zohar, Itamar. ''The Position of Translated Literature within the Literary Polysystem.'' *Papers in Historical Poetics*. Tel Aviv: Porter Institute for Poetics and Semiotics, 1978.

_____. "Polysystem Theory." *Politics Today* 1, nos. 1–2 (autumn 1979): 287–310.

Gerald Gillespie. "From 'Baroque' Michael Drayton to 'Enlightened' Ebenezer Cooke: (Re-)Debunking the American Golden Age." *Erkennen und Deuten: Essays zur Literatur und Literaturtheorie, Edgar Lohner in memoriam.* Berlin: Erich Schmidt, 1983: 326–34.

_____. *Garden and Labyrinth of Time: Studies in Renaissance and Baroque Literature.* New York, Berne, Frankfurt a.M., Paris: Lang, 1988.

Lambert, José, and van Gorp, Hendrik. "On Describing Translations." *The Manipulation of Literature: Studies in Literary Translation.* Ed. by Theo Hermans. London and Sydney: Croom Helm, 1985: 42–53.

Lefevere, André. *Translating Poetry: Seven Strategies and a Blueprint.* Assen: Van Gorcum, 1975.

_____. "Why Waste Our Time on Rewrites? The Trouble with Interpretation and the Role of Rewriting in an Alternative Paradigm." *Manipulation:* 215–241.

Paz, Octavio, et al. *Renga: A Chain of Poems by Octavio Paz, Jacques Roubaud, Edoardo Sanguineti, Charles Tomlinson; with a Foreword by Claude Roy, Translated by Charles Tomlinson.* New York: George Braziller, Inc., 1971.

_____. *Renga: poème par Octavio Paz, Jacques Roubaud, Edoardo Sanguineti et Charles Tomlinson; presenté par Claude Roy.* Paris: Gallimard, 1971.

_____. *Renga: un poema de Octavio Paz, Jacques Roubaud, Edoardo Sanguineti y Charles Tomlinson; presentado por Claude Roy.* México: J. Moritz, 1972.

Toury, Gideon. "A Rationale for Descriptive Translation Studies." *Manipulation:* 16–41.

PART TWO

Lo, The Text Tells Its Tale

The Misshapen Beast:
The *Furioso*'s Serpentine Narrative

DENNIS LOONEY

denique sit quod vis, simplex dumtaxat et
unum.

Horace, *Ars poetica*, 23

Così il Trissino *E* qui ha peccato quel
grandissimo poeta che io non nomino per
veneratione, ma il suo peccato gli sarà
perdonato dal giudice il più severo se fosse
ancora un Dracone perchè ha partorito tante
maravigliose e divine bellezze.

Torquato Tasso's gloss on Horace[1]

To criticize Ariosto's *Orlando Furioso* for its multiple plots Torquato
Tasso evokes an image from canto XXV of Dante's *Inferno*, the canto
that depicts robbers being metamorphosed unendingly into snakes. In
the second of the *Discorsi dell'arte poetica*, Tasso criticizes romance
poems in general, although the context of his remarks makes clear that
he specifically has in mind the *Furioso*: "'. . . the interposing and mingling
of their parts, one with another, is monstrous, resembling that beast
Dante describes for us:

> Ellera abbarbicata mai non fue
> ad arbor sì, come l'orribil fera
> per l'altrui membra avviticchiò le sue;

73

> Ivy was never so rooted
> to a tree as the horrid beast
> entwined its own limbs round the other's;

and in the passage that follows.''[2] Tasso adduces the snakelike creature wrapped around a man in the second half of the tercet as an example of radical unnaturalness. It is analogous to the *Furioso*, a gargantuan fusion of multiple plots worthy of an unnatural beast.[3] Since Tasso is a resourceful critic, one should not be surprised at an occasional allusion to the *Inferno* in the service of his criticism. This particular borrowing from Dante, however, is telling, for this same image of the snake-man monster that threatens Tasso's critical sensibilities plays a prominent part in Ariosto's poem.[4] In fact, a sequence of snake similes that partially derives its significance from allusions to *Inferno* XXV organizes the *Furioso*'s narrative.[5]

The same can be said of the ivy simile in the first half of the Dantesque tercet. Ivy on a tree as a symbol of fastness is a familiar, even trite, image in the classical repertory behind *Inferno* XXV,[6] although Dante does invigorate his vernacular version with the words ''abbarbicata'' and ''avviticchiò.'' Tasso surely appreciated this moment of innovative imitation in which Dante did his models one better.[7] But what was the critic in him thinking when he trotted out this tercet to gloss the *Furioso*'s lack of narrative continuity? Like the sequence of snake similes important to the perception of the *Furioso*'s internal unity, there is a sequence of ivy ones, again linked to the passage in *Inferno* XXV, which unifies the poem's narrative. In other words, the Dantesque tercet that bears Tasso's emblem of the misshapen narrative is twice contradicted by the actual text of Ariosto's poem. Two images, then, through which Tasso criticizes the *Furioso* for its lack of unity had been used by Ariosto to unify his poem.

What led Tasso to ignore these unifying textual details in the *Furioso* but at the same time prompted him to reclaim them subversively as symbols of the poem's narrative disproportion? Why the ivylike snake-man as a figure for Ariosto's multi-storied narrative? Does this suggest that Tasso didn't or couldn't read the *Furioso* very well? Did institutional pressures impinge on his interpretation of the poem, blinding him to inherent unities in Ariosto's narrative? Or—a final possibility—did Tasso understand exactly his resort to paradox when in a single stroke he simultaneously criticized and praised Ariosto's organization of multiple plots into a single narrative?

I reserve a final opinion until the conclusion of this essay. I need first to set Tasso's reaction to the *Furioso* in the context of his narrative theory and his own long poem, the *Gerusalemme Liberata*. Here Tasso's problematic position toward the ivy and the snake becomes acute. I shall then focus on the object of Tasso's criticism, the *Furioso* itself, especially on the simile of the snake that provides a running commentary on the madness of the poem's titular hero, Orlando. It shapes the *Furioso* into anything but the misshapen beast to which Tasso objects.

Tasso's comparison of Ariosto's *Furioso* to an infernal creature bespeaks a complex relationship to the poem and the poet, who was his major predecessor at the Este court in Ferrara. Ariosto (1474–1533) had long since died when in the 1560s Tasso worked out the critical positions expressed in the *Discorsi*, but the *Furioso*, already published in over thirty different editions, was very much alive. No one was more aware of the *Furioso*'s extraordinary popularity, of its success as a sixteenth-century bestseller, than the young Tasso who used the composition of his *Discorsi* to chart ever so tentatively a critical course that would negotiate the shoals of neo-classicism and post-Tridentine Christianity without forfeiting the fame and profit Ariosto's poem was accruing. At the theoretical level Tasso's *Discorsi* reflect an uneasiness in the young poet's dismissal of Ariostan romance in favor of a dogmatically classicizing poetic propriety. This uneasiness is perhaps nowhere more present than in the passage on the relationship between plot and narrative construction. Here Tasso formulates his ideas on plot and narrative into a theory that he puts into practice in the *Gerusalemme*.[8] The poem, for its part, constantly challenges and frequently undermines many of the theoretical positions that are articulated in the *Discorsi* against the typical romance narrative, e.g., Ariosto's "misshapen beast." Much is at stake in Tasso's critical negotiations with the literary precedents set by the *Furioso*.

This becomes apparent when one sees how Tasso works out the *Discorsi*'s criticism of romance narrative in the *Gerusalemme*, where various episodes composed of romance-like narrative threaten the poem's epic plot. In the passage from the *Discorsi* cited above, the aspect of romance narrative that specifically elicits the comparison to Dante's beast is "the interposing and mingling of their parts"—"il traporre e mescolare le membra."[9] The verb "traporre" (here used substantivally) translates a technical term that derives from the Latin rhetorical tradition:

"interponere" in a narrative context means to interrupt a continuous narrative with a digression.[10] In Latin and Italian the verb means literally "to place between," and it suggests the placing of one narrative within another in order to interrupt the continuous flow of the prior narrative. Tasso sets this theoretical verb in a dramatic context in the opening canto of the *Gerusalemme* when he describes God's vexation with the Christian crusaders for delaying their attack on Jerusalem. Gabriel, the angelic interpreter, addresses Godfrey, the leader of the Christians, paraphrasing God's message:

> Goffredo, ecco opportuna
> già la stagion ch'al guerreggiar s'aspetta;
> perché dunque *trapor* dimora alcuna
> a liberar Gierusalem soggetta?
> Tu i principi a consiglio omai raguna,
> tu al fin de l'opra i neghittosi affretta.
> Dio per lor duce già t'elegge, ed essi
> *sopporran* volontari a te se stessi.[11]
>
> (I, 16)

Godfrey, behold the season now is ripe that is waiting for you to go to war. Why then *interpose* any delay in liberating captive Jerusalem? Assemble the princes at once in council, hurry the slothful on to the end of the task. Now God elects you as their leader, and *they will* willingly *subject* themselves to you (emphasis mine).[12]

Military strategy is not the only information transmitted in the divine message to Godfrey. God, the divine artificer, suddenly becomes very much like a poet, an Italian one no less. But here the similarity does not depend on the usual humanistic commonplaces about poetic creativity, which often derive from Neoplatonic teachings on the mysteries of inspiration.[13] Rather, the view of God conflates in this passage with the perspective of the poet and highlights two contradictory methods of constructing the poem's narrative. The verbs "trapor" (16.3) and "sopporran" (16.8) suggest modes of narrative construction associated with romance, on the one hand, and epic, on the other. God is concerned lest his Renaissance Christian epic degenerate into a medieval romance.

The form "trapor" is a syncopated infinitive from "traporre," the key verb in the passage of the *Discorsi*. To build a narrative around this verb would be to write a romance made up of narratives within a narrative, a poem full of delays and delights, which would never achieve the thesis of liberating the holy sepulcher of Christ, announced in the poem's programmatic opening stanza. In sharp contrast to the meaning of "trapor" is the syncopated form "sopporran," an irregular future from "sottoporre," which suggests not only an appropriate tactical strategy for taking Jerusalem but also the necessary compositional formula for a successful epic plot. Only when Godfrey's peers willingly "put themselves under" his leadership can the teleological machinery of the epic bring the plot to its close. Only when the divided Christian camp is reconstituted as a single fighting unit can Jerusalem be taken and subsequently defended.[14]

Readers of the *Gerusalemme* know that this concession to Godfrey's authority is long in coming. Finally in canto XVIII, Rinaldo, the last prince to submit to Godfrey's leadership, dutifully chops down a tree in the enchanted wood and thus rids the forest and the poem of its romance magic. Of course this cannot happen without one last example of narrative deferral (the poem after all manages to postpone its inevitable conclusion for twenty cantos). As Rinaldo prepares to chop down the enchanted tree, Armida, the magical pagan temptress, suddenly reappears, her actions marked by the verb of narrative interposition:

> Vassene al mirto; allor colei s'abbraccia
> al caro tronco, e *s'interpone* e grida
> "Ah non sarà mai ver che tu mi faccia
> oltraggio tal, che l'arbor mio recida!..."
>   (XVIII, 34.1-4)

He approaches the mytle; whereupon she embraces the trunk and *interposes herself* and cries: "Oh it will never be that you do me such outrage that you cut down my tree..." (emphasis mine).

The image of Armida in front of Rinaldo hugging the tree parodies an earlier moment in their romance when the young couple lay entwined in each other's arms shaded by entangled vines (XVI, 11). But now things are different. Rinaldo, who has "put himself under" the authority of Godfrey, does not succumb to Armida, although she has interposed herself ivylike between the hero and his goal. Her transformation into a figure of ivy (and then into that image of romance *par excellence*, a monstrous giant with enlarged parts, XVIII, 35) is one of the final non-epic touches in the *Gerusalemme*'s narrative and as such alludes nostalgically not only to earlier passages in the poem but also to several passages in the *Furioso* in which the narrator uses the image of entwined ivy to describe the amorous configurations of lovers.

There are, however, some noticeable differences in Ariosto's version of the ivy simile despite its function as a mediating text between Tasso's Armida in XVIII, 34 and the Dantesque tercet of the infernal snake-man. In Ariosto's rewriting of Dante's simile the configuration of lovers does not produce a monster. The embrace of Ruggiero and Alcina, the wayward Christian hero and the pagan temptress in Ariosto's poem, is marked by a reflexive verb:

> "Non così strettamente edera preme
> pianta ove intorno abbarbicata s'abbia,
> come si stringono li due amanti insieme."
> (*Furioso* VII, 29.1–3)[15]

Ivy never clung so tightly to the stem round which it was entwined as did the two lovers cling to each other.[16]

With a similar emphasis on amorous reciprocity the Ariostan narrator describes the ivylike embraces of Angelica and Medoro in the grotto of ivy where the lovers appropriately leave an entanglement of inscriptions, in Arabic and Italian, as a graphic imitation of how they passed the time (XIX, 36 and XXIII, 103–06). When Ricciardetto, a minor character in the poem, recounts how he and Fiordispina embraced, he predictably calls on the by-now-familiar image of the clinging plant:

> Non con più nodi i flessuosi acanti
> le colonne circondano e le travi,
> di quelli con che noi legammo stretti
> e colli e fianchi e braccia e gambe e petti.
> (XXV, 69.5–8)

Never did twisting acanthus entwine pillars and beams with more knots than those which bound us together, our necks and sides, our arms, legs, and breasts in a close embrace.

The figure of ivy in the *Furioso* is not directly associated with the misshapen beast as it is in Tasso's scene of Armida, but for Ariosto the image is nevertheless problematic. The erotic embrace, for example, deters the Ariostan characters from fulfilling their various duties. Love continually comes between the protagonist and his or her duty in the *Furioso*, much as it does in the *Aeneid*, interposing itself and as a result creating new narrative possibilities. Ruggiero escapes Alcina's clutches in canto VII only to fall back into the deferred episodic narrative of romance at the end of canto X where he attempts to rape Angelica. This is in contrast to Rinaldo in the *Gerusalemme* who, once set right, dispatches his duty without further delay: "Ma pur mai colpo il cavalier non erra, / né per tanto furor punto s'arresta" (XVIII, 37.5). (But yet the knight never misses a stroke, nor stays a moment for all that madness.)[17] It is as if Tasso's character were finally able to free himself from Ariostan "furor," from a literary model cast in the mold of romance. Like the character in his poem, Tasso is finally able to resist the temptations of episodic romance by canto XVIII of the *Gerusalemme* whence the poem hastens to a suitable epic ending. But, then too, overcoming the threat of romance in Rinaldo's decisive meeting with Armida hardly discounts the ongoing dalliance with romance narrative in the better part of the *Gerusalemme*.

The inclusion of romance elements in Tasso's poem depends in part on the poet's ambiguous relationship to the *Furioso*'s narrative. But his recourse to ivy as a sign for the narrative interposition of romance is contradicted by the same symbol in Ariosto's poem. The three examples of the ivy simile in the *Furioso* do not threaten to disrupt the narrative; on the contrary, they contribute to its unity by establishing a network of anticipated allusions within the text and beyond it to Dante's *Inferno*. The contradiction between Tasso's theory and Ariosto's praxis is greater and even more apparent in the *Furioso*'s sequence of snake similes in which the snake-man rears his misshapen head.

These similes in cantos I, XXIII, XXXIX, and XLII, are textual markers that signal Orlando's move in and out of madness and point to Angelica as the prime cause for the hero's fall.[18] By alluding to one another within the text, the four similes establish an "*intra*textual" continuity that helps the reader negotiate the vast distance from the beginning of the poem to canto XLII near its end. At the same time, the similes' allusions to other texts beyond the *Furioso*—classical, biblical, and vernacular—provide a sort of commentary on Ariosto's treatment of literary models that also contributes to the poem's unity. The simile in canto I, for example, alludes to *Inferno* XV and, through

Dante's poem, to the New Testament, Vergil's *Aeneid*, and Ovid's *Fasti*. These various allusions (and others) are repeated in different ways each time the simile returns over the course of the narrative, with Ovid's *Fasti* in particular serving as a base for Ariosto's "*inter*textual" poetics. The snake simile becomes a kind of *crux* in the *Furioso*, an intertextual crossing point where many and differing texts are brought together through the poet's imitation.

Consider the first example of the simile in which Angelica, the Oriental princess, object of many knights' desires, flees the snake:

> entrò in un bosco, e ne la stretta via
> rincontrò un cavallier ch'a piè venia.
>
> Indosso la corazza, l'elmo in testa,
> la spada al fianco, e in braccio avea lo scudo;
> e più leggier correa per la foresta,
> ch'al pallio rosso il villan mezzo ignudo.
> Timida pastorella mai sì presta
> non volse piede inanzi a serpe crudo,
> come Angelica tosto il freno torse,
> che del guerrier, ch'a piè venia, s'accorse.
> (I, 10.7—11.8)

> Entering a wood and following a narrow path, she came upon a knight who was approaching on foot. He wore a breastplate, and on his head a helmet; his sword hung by his side, and on his arm he bore his shield; and he came running through the forest more fleet of foot than the lightly-clad farmer sprinting for the red mantle at the village games. Never did a timid shepherd-girl start back more violently from a horrid snake than did Angelica, jerking on the reins the moment she saw the armed man approach on foot (adapted from Waldman, 2).

Ariosto departs from the tradition of chivalric romance in Boiardo's *Orlando Innamorato* and Niccolò degli Agostini's continuation of Boiardo precisely where Angelica flees the Christian camp. She manages to escape on horseback just as the Saracens overcome the Christian army encamped in the shadow of the Pyrenees. No sooner has Angelica entered a wood—Is this perhaps a figure for the narrative of Ariosto's poem itself?— than she encounters a knight whom we eventually discover is Rinaldo. The repetition of the qualifying phrase, "ch'a piè venia" (10.8 and 11.8), calls the reader's attention to something unusual about this knight: he has no horse. The poem will frequently fix on the paradox of the horseless equestrian, indeed the theme of the "cavalliere" without his "cavallo" that is introduced in these lines will contribute to the resolution of its multiple plots as the poem ends.[19]

In stanzas 10 and 11 of the opening canto, the knight who approaches Angelica wears a full suit of armor, as if to make up for the lack of a horse. Here the text signals another paradox, this time not through repetition but through a playfully serious pun, the first of many in the *Furioso*. The knight's armor does not impede him, quite the contrary: "e più leggier correa per la foresta, / ch'al pallio rosso il villan mezzo ignudo" (11.3–4). He is like a country runner in speed and agility (indeed he is faster than a racer). The pun on "più leggiero," which here has the sense of "more gracefully" but literally means "more lightly," suggests that Rinaldo runs fast despite his armor. The pun works in that his armor actually makes him heavier (not lighter) than the comparison implies. This emphasis on the dress of the knight makes the subsequent focus on the vehicle of comparison, the "villan" as "mezzo ignudo," rather curious; for this knight is, if anything, overdressed. In fact, the reader sees him (through the eyes of Angelica) as a horseless suit of armor, emphasized piece by piece: first the cuirass, then the helmet, then the sword dangling at his side, and finally shield in hand (1–2).

Why then does the poet compare the knight to the country racer? Surely not merely to focus on speed and dress. The allusion is to a passage from the end of *Inferno* XV, which describes Ser Brunetto racing back to join his particular group of sinners: "e parve di coloro / Che corrono a Verona il drappo verde / Per la campagna" (121–23) ("and [he] seemed like one of those who run for the green cloth in the field at Verona"—Singleton, 161). The Dantean source in turn alludes to a passage from the Second Letter to Timotheus (4:7–8), where Paul describes the Christian's experience of life as a race to the end with God as the ultimate judge. The Dantean allusion, with its sexual overtones (Ser Brunetto is a condemned homosexual) and with its foregrounding of the issue of winners and losers, calls to mind as well a contemporary event of Ariosto's Ferrara, the palio of San Giorgio, a public contest full of sexual coding.[20] Whether or not the poet alludes directly to this contemporary race, this depiction of the "villan" prepares the reader for later scenes of knights racing like naked "villani" in and out of the narrative picture.

The second half of stanza 11 portrays Angelica's reaction to Rinaldo in its juxtaposition of the knight as footracer to Angelica as shepherdess.[21] The two similes overlap in Rinaldo who metamorphoses from the "villan" into the frightening snake. The snake simile focuses not only on Angelica's fear but also on the speed with which she turns away and thereby generates the centrifugal movement for which the *Furioso*'s first canto is so famous.[22]

Angelica's deft retreat before the figurative snake alludes to a passage in the *Aeneid* which describes how a Greek, Androgeos, on the rampage inside Troy, mistakes a band of Trojans in the dark for his compatriots: "improvisum aspris veluti qui sentibus anguem / pressit humi nitens trepidusque repente refugit" (II, 379–80).[23] (Just as he who has squashed an unseen snake along some path of briars, when stepping on the ground, frightened suddenly pulls back.) Although Ariosto does not follow the model rigorously (his character manages to escape the snake whereas Androgeos is killed), an early commentator, Ludovico Dolce, made much of this allusion to the *Aeneid* in the poem's opening simile.[24] Dolce's agenda was to align the *Furioso* with the Roman epic so that the Venetian publisher, Gabriele Giolito, might capitalize on the public's association of Ariosto with Vergil—a successful marketing strategy which led to twenty–seven printings of the Giolito edition with Dolce's commentary between 1542 and 1560.

A late sixteenth-century commentator on the *Furioso*, Alberto Lavezuola, was the first to suggest another source for the simile of the snake, proposing Ovid's *Fasti* as the more likely model for the shepherdess and snake: "ut saepe viator / turbatus viso rettulit angue pedem" (II, 341–42). (As often a traveler / startled at the sight of a snake pulls his foot back in fear.) Lavezuola's response to the *Furioso* is conditioned by an agonistic reading of Dolce's commentary, which he hardly disguises in his account of the relation between Ariosto's text and the Ovidian simile.[25] Yet, having aggressively distinguished himself from Dolce (and from Girolamo Ruscelli who in 1556 published a plagiarized version of Dolce's commentary), Lavezuola then borrows an observation from the commentaries of his predecessors.[26] He notes, as do Dolce and Ruscelli, that the passage from *Aeneid* II is actually an important subtext for a later version of the snake simile in *Furioso* XXXIX, 31–32. This observation constrains him to develop Ariosto's use of the simile from its first example to its later version and to read horizontally, as it were, from cantos I to XXXIX as he accounts for the classical models that underlie vertically various passages of the modern text. Such a reading from cantos I to XXXIX reflects the essential nature of Ariosto's art of imitation, indeed of his poetics in general: namely, how an intratextual interpretation must combine with an intertextual reading of the poem.

Yet why did Ariosto draw on Ovid's *Fasti* at such a prominent moment in the *Furioso*'s narrative? And how might he have come to know it?

Like the *Metamorphoses*, the *Fasti* was part of Ariosto's humanist education.[27] Both Ovidian works were central tests in the curriculum of the Ferrarese *Studium*, the school founded by Guarino Veronese in the 1430s and run by his family during Ariosto's lifetime. Ariosto never attended the school but was in close contact with students who did and at least one of his private tutors taught there.[28] Once Ariosto began to read the *Fasti* he found in the work a repository of themes dealing with madness and desire that he would use later for the literal and figurative center of the *Furioso*'s narrative. I do not mean to argue that Ariosto encountered these various themes only in the *Fasti*, but rather to suggest that the numerous allusions in the *Furioso* to the Ovidian work document the Italian poet's dependence on that model and attest to its influence on several central episodes in the poem.

The *Fasti* purports to be a commentary on the days of the Roman calendar. It is, however, much more than a work of anthropological interest.[29] The poem reflects no lack of literary artifice, and its narrator is as subversive as his counterpart in the *Metamorphoses*. The passage Ariosto alludes to in his poem's opening simile is linked to the passage in *Fasti* II that deals with the festivals of February. Ovid proposes an etymology of the month's name that connects it with the theme of purification and the Luperci (an order of Roman priests) who purify the ground with strips of hide (*Fasti* II, 19 and 31–32). The stories that the narrator then recounts (and there are many) consistently set the issue of purification in the context of the problematics of desire. One particular narrative is that of Faunus to which the snake sequence in the *Furioso* alludes in structure and theme.

The story of Faunus is offered as a possible explanation for the curious custom of purification, one which, we shall see momentarily, may be a model for Orlando's behavior after he has gone mad. The gist of the Faunus narrative is as follows: once the woodland god saw Hercules returning to a cave with a beautiful woman, Omphale, whom he immediately began to desire. Later that night Faunus crept into the cave intending to have her while Hercules slept. He didn't know that Hercules and Omphale were purifying themselves for a feast of Dionysus the following day, that they were having a chaste night (their beds pushed apart to enforce this), and that oddly enough they had exchanged clothes. The outcome of the escapade is predictable: Faunus tiptoes past the guards; he reaches up to the first bed, feels the cloak of the Nemean lion, and recoils:

> ut saepe viator
> turbatus viso rettulit angue pedem.
> (*Fasti* II, 341–42)
>
> as often a traveler
> startled at the sight of a snake pulls his foot
> back in fear.

The narrative continues (343–50):

> Next he touched the soft drapery of the neighboring couch, and its deceptive touch beguiled him. He mounted and lay down on the nearer side. His groins were swollen harder than horn. Then he reached up under the tunics at the lowest hem. There he encountered legs that bristled with a thick rough hair. When he would have proceeded further, the Tirynthian hero suddenly thrust him away, . . . [30]

Everyone laughs, especially Omphale who looks at Hercules standing there, one assumes, with her tunics pulled up over his head, a caricature of a hero. From that day on, betrayed by garments, Faunus urges all followers to come to his rites undressed.

Faunus's solution to his problem is not to check his desire but to let it run rampant. When such a solution is applied to the world of the *Furioso*, however, it inevitably leads the typical heroic knight to abandon his proper station and go astray. It can produce an effeminate hero who resembles the Hercules of *Fasti* II (e.g., Ruggiero on the island of Alcina in canto VI). Or it can produce a madman like Orlando whose identity, sexual and otherwise, is totally confused. Indeed before Orlando can be identified with the wisdom of Silenus in *Furioso* XXXIX, he must pass through the bleak and (for him) very unhumorous experience of a Faunus. [31]

Later in the narrative in the vicinity of the snake simile's second version, Orlando initiates the travesty that will transform him into a wild version of the woodland god. In the lair of the snake, as it were, Ariosto foregrounds the issues of sex and sexuality:

In tanto aspro travaglio gli soccorre
che nel medesmo letto in che giaceva,
l'ingrata donna venutasi a porre
col suo drudo più volte esser doveva.
Non altrimenti or quella piuma abborre,
né con minor prestezza se ne leva,
che de l'erba il villan che s'era messo
per chiuder gli occhi, e vegga il serpe appresso.
(XXIII, 123)

Amid such bitter anguish the thought occurred to him that on this very bed in which he was lying the thankless damsel must have lain down many a time with her lover. The downy bed sent a shudder through him and he leapt off it with all the alacrity of a yokel who has lain down in the grass for a nap and spies a snake close by (Waldman, 280).

The interlacing of episodes from cantos XII to XXIII allows the paladin to arrive at the nuptial bed of Angelica and Medoro. In canto XIX the narrator recounts how the two fall in love, consummate their relationship, marry, and depart for Cathay on an extended honeymoon (XIX, 17–36). The narrative immediately thereafter provides a proleptic glimpse of Orlando gone mad when he encounters the couple as they travel to Cathay (XIX, 37–42). In any case by the time Orlando arrives at the grotto, the text has already provided the reader with an extensive tour of the ivied love nest. And should the reader have forgotten, the narrator reminds him that he has already seen this place (XXIII, 102.5).

As Orlando enters the grotto the narrative recalls the first instance of the snake simile in canto I:

Il merigge facea grato l'orezzo
al duro armento et al pastore ignudo,
sì che né Orlando sentia alcun ribrezzo,
che la corazza avea, l'elmo e lo scudo.
Quivi egli entrò per riposarvi in mezzo;
e v'ebbe travaglioso albergo e crudo.
(XXIII, 101.1–6)

A welcome breeze tempered the noontide for the rugged flock and naked shepherd, and Orlando felt no discomfort, for all that he was wearing breastplate, helmet, and shield. Here he stopped, then, to rest—but his welcome proved to be harsh and painful (Waldman, 278).

The breeze makes the setting pleasant for the flock, even at noon, and for the shepherd, who is described, curiously, as "ignudo" (2). This seemingly gratuitous adjective works in two ways: it foreshadows Orlando's discovery that nature made this a comfortable place in which to undress and it recalls the "villan mezzo ignudo" who earlier flashed into Angelica's view before quickly turning into a snake. The allusion to I, 11, is signaled by the repetition of two of the rhyming words from the stanza, "ignudo" and "scudo". Orlando's armor, whose enumerated parts recall the formulaic language of I, 11.1–2, keeps him from feeling the breeze.

What is of interest in XXIII, 101, is the poem's backward glance, its intratextual meditation on itself. This moment suggests that a troubled confusion of the sexes underlies the juxtaposition of the two similes in I, 11. The reference to "pastore ignudo" combines the two vehicles of the double simile in I, 11, the "villan ignudo" and the "timida pastorella." It turns the shepherdess, who sees the half-naked snake-man, into the naked shepherd. And this new metaphorical configuration stands as an indirect comparison to Orlando who is, for the moment at least, fully dressed.

The issue here involves gender and simile. In *Furioso* I, 11, Ariosto matches the gender of the vehicle to that of the tenor in each comparison: Rinaldo is compared to a racer and Angelica to a shepherdess.[32] The neatness of this division, this fastidiousness to gender, loses its superficial schematization in canto XXIII where a retrospective reworking of the problem of gender takes place.

In XXIII, as Orlando is haunted by a nightmarish image of his lady repeatedly giving herself to Medoro, the simile's vehicle is another "villan" (123.7), who like the "pastorella" of canto I reacts quickly to the image of the serpent: "né con minor prestezza" (nor with any less speed) (123.5). The ramifications of the figurative language increase as it works backward and forward in the narrative. At stanza 133 Orlando becomes the "ignudo villan" once he has ripped off his armor (again described piece by piece). This phrasing recalls Rinaldo, to be sure, but it also prefigures later scenes, in which Orlando, thoroughly mad, is repeatedly associated with the sphere of the "villan." In XXIV he invades the Arcadian world of the shepherds who try to fend him off with a "villanesco assalto" (attack of peasants) (8.8). When he arrives at Rodomonte's jousting bridge, he fails to abide by the proper chivalric codes and the offended Saracen calls him an "indiscreto villan" (reckless peasant) (XXIX, 41.7) and a "bestia balorda" (impudent beast) (42.2). By canto XXXIX just before Orlando retrieves his wits, the "villan" has regressed further along the rural chain of being into a bull, a horse, an ox, and a generic beast (45–54). Ironically, a snake of sorts comes to the rescue.

In canto XXXIX, just before Orlando bursts back onto the scene, the narrator describes how Rodomonte commissions a helmsman to ferry his prisoners across the Mediterranean, from France to Algiers:

> Quivi il nocchier, ch'ancor non s'era accorto
> degli inimici, entrò con la galea,
> lasciando molte miglia a dietro il porto
> d'Algieri, ove calar prima volea,
> per un vento gagliardo ch'era sorto,
> e spinto oltre il dover la poppa avea.
> Venir tra i suoi credette e in loco fido,
> come vien Progne al suo loquace nido.
>
> Ma come poi l'imperiale augello,
> i gigli d'oro e i pardi vide appresso,
> restò pallido in faccia, come quello
> che 'l piede incauto d'improviso ha messo
> sopra il serpente venenoso e fello,
> dal pigro sonno in mezzo l'erbe oppresso;
> che spaventato e smorto si ritira,
> fuggendo quel, ch'è pien di tosco e d'ira.
> (XXXIX, 31–32)

Here the helmsman, unaware of the enemy's presence, brought in his galley, leaving the port of Algiers, his intended goal, many miles astern, for a strong wind had got up and driven him beyond it. Now he imagined he was putting into a safe refuge, like Procne returning to her twittering nest. But when he noticed the Imperial Eagle, the Golden Lilies, and the Leopards close by, he blanched like a man suddenly aware that his incautious foot has trodden upon a horrid poisonous snake which has been slumbering torpidly in the grass: he recoils in a fright and flees from the angry, venomous reptile (adapted from Waldman, 469).

The mission fails, however, when the helmsman blown off course, lands in the midst of the Christian fleet in its preparation to attack Biserta. From the shore the soldiers recognize their companions on board the prison galley, many of whom are important fighters for the Christian cause. Their reunification enables the narrative to continue with the naval battle between Dudone and Agramante, the sack of Biserta, and, most importantly, the revival of Orlando, who appears just after the prison galley comes to harbor. It takes the combined force of the warriors on shore and those on the ship to restrain the mad Orlando while Astolfo prepares to purify him for the ritual of reawakening.

The snake simile comes into play in canto XXXIX to describe the helmsman's realization that he has sailed into enemy hands. Ariosto establishes the simile in this overtly political context by an allusion in stanza 31 to the myth of Procne, which he knew from another Ovidian source, *Metamorphoses* VI.[33] The Ovidian passage contains several parallels that contribute to the snake's third occurrence. In Ovid's version of the myth, a tale of betrayal and revenge, Tereus rapes his sister-in-law, Philomela, once he ferries her from Athens to Thrace. His actions betray his marriage vows to Procne as well as the trust of his father-in-law, Pandion. Once the plot is uncovered, Tereus, Procne, and Philomela are punished by being transformed into birds. The passage in the *Furioso* alludes to the plot of the myth in Ovid, but then immediately subverts it: the helmsman coming to shore with his prisoners is like the bird returning to the nest, or, in the terms of the myth, the helmsman is like Tereus bringing Philomela to shore. In stanza 32 we discover that the helmsman in the end is more like Philomela than Tereus; the helmsman becomes a prisoner himself. The key terms in this equation are "fido" and "credere" (31.7). Philomela trusts in Tereus just as the helmsman trusts in the place where he is about to land. But both are betrayed by faith.

Stanza 32 opens with an adversative conjunction "ma" that signals the helmsman's reinterpretation of what lies before him. Procne has flown into the claws of the Imperial Bird—one more allusion to the Ovidian Tereus compared to an eagle, "the bird of Jupiter" (*Met.* VI, 517). The helmsman sees the banners of the eagle, the lilies, and the leopard and suddenly knows that he is in the midst of the joint armies of the Holy Roman Empire, France, and England. But with a chivalric wind at his back, "vento gagliardo" (31.5), there is no retreat. Thus the familiar simile recurs as the helmsman is now likened to an indeterminate man (''quello'') who carelessly steps on a sleeping snake. The snake simile takes precedence over the formulaic reference to the helmsman as ''pallido'' (32.3), a topos usually associated with a ship on a stormy sea and the shipwrecked sailor.[34] Here, in the comparison between the helmsman and the man stepping on the snake, the knights awaiting the ship become that very creature. The figurative metamorphosis of Christian knights into a single serpent, into *the* serpent, registered by the linguistic shift from the ''serpe'' of cantos I and XXIII to the ''serpente'' of XXXIX, is significant.[35] On the one hand, it is the first time in the sequence of the simile that the snake itself is asleep. This provides an appropriate gloss on the Christian forces finally on the verge of awakening to dispatch the infidels. On the other hand, the image of the Christians as a serpent is pointedly ironic, especially because they have been such ineffective defenders of the faith heretofore in the poem. To compare them to the symbolic and archetypal enemy of Christian good exactly at the moment of positive Christian action reminds the reader of all that the narrative has postponed and left undone. The deviation of narrative plots characteristic of romance is about to yield to a more purely epic movement that is signaled by the Christians' attack on Biserta. And yet at this initial moment one encounters the archetypal image of deviation. Clearly Ariosto posits some difficulty in the poem's concluding ''epic'' cantos, and a hint of what is to come can be garnered from the full comparison proposed by the simile: the man who squashes the snake manages to escape while the Christians capture the helmsman whom they mercifully sentence to rowing duty on a prison galley. The snake, for its part, also escapes, only to resurface later in the poem's figurative language.

This scene of Rodomonte's helmsman precedes the salvation of Orlando by Astolfo, an act of purification that recalls the thematics of book II of Ovid's *Fasti*. As I have argued, Faunus is a model for the confusion of sexuality in Orlando's madness. Yet other details of the Lupercalia in *Fasti* II, 267ff., shed light on Orlando's subsequent behavior in later cantos of the *Furioso*, especially as it culminates in canto XXXIX before he regains his wits. Ovid recounts the following story: on the hallowed ground of the Palatine Hill where the she-wolf suckled Romulus and Remus, a group of priests, called Luperci, honored the wolfish origins of Rome. Once a year on February 15th, the priests raced around the hill wearing skins of sacrificed goats about their loins. With strips of the same goatskins, the racers would strike at anyone who crossed their path, singling out young women who accepted the blows as insurance against difficult births and infertility. The race around the boundaries of the Palatine Hill, the sacrificing of animals, and the symbolic beating of women of childbearing age were all part of a purificatory rite.

These Lupercalian moments correspond to ones in the *Furioso*, although they are recast in a negative light. The figure of a man racing naked or half-naked is highlighted, as we have seen, at the beginning of the poem. That racer prefigures Orlando at his most "furioso," as the insane wildman who rampages through the countryside randomly killing people and animals. His indiscriminate violence is a parodistic inversion of the proper mode of animal sacrifice at the Roman Lupercalia. The madness that leads Orlando to chase Angelica and to beat her horse to death may also be a satirical gloss on the festival's symbolic beating of women (XXIX, 67–71). A final detail from the Ovidian model perhaps arises in Ariosto's curious insistence that Fiordiligi, Brandimarte's wife, is the first to recognize Orlando in his rampage (XXXIX, 44). The woman, young and childless, is in the position of the Roman women on the Palatine Hill every February 15th. But Orlando's parody of the Lupercalian race does not render Fiordiligi more fecund; on the contrary, the hero's return presages the death of Brandimarte (as Fiordiligi's dreams portend) and thus her barren days as a widow.

The snake returns to the poem when Brandimarte dies. One could say that the snake kills him. The snake simile is directly involved with Orlando's shift from madness to sanity in XXIII and XXXIX.[36] Its final appearance in the narrative, however, marks a fall back into madness:

Qual nomade pastor che vedut'abbia
fuggir strisciando l'orrido serpente
che il figliuol che giocava ne la sabbia
ucciso gli ha col venenoso dente,
stringe il baston con colera e con rabbia;
tal la spada, d'ogni altra più tagliente,
stringe con ira il cavallier d'Anglante:
il primo che trovò, fu 'l re Agramante.
(XLII, 7)

As the Numidian shepherd will grasp his stick with frantic rage, seeing the horrible snake slither away once its poisonous fangs have slain

his child playing in the sand: so did Orlando rabidly grasp his sword
which was unmatched for sharpness. The first man he came upon was
King Agramant (Waldman, 497–98).

This octave contains a crucial variation in the simile's development:
for the first time the serpent actually bites the unsuspecting human. At
last Ariosto resolves the implications of *Aeneid* II, where the Greek,
Androgeos, is killed by the Trojan snake. Ariosto's imitation, however,
is more pointed in its phrasing than the Vergilian model. In canto XLII
a father sees a serpent bite his son who immediately dies: its "poisonous
fangs have slain his child" (7.4). The poet underscores the father's
pathetic plight by calling the serpent "orrido" and the child a
"figliuolo." There is no contest.

The simile glosses Orlando's anger at his realization that Gradasso
has killed his boon companion, Brandimarte, in the battle of Lipadusa.
It alludes not only to Vergil but also to a somber passage near the end
of Pulci's *Morgante* in which Charlemagne laments the deaths of his
heroes at Roncesvalle and is described as a pelican whose young have
been killed by a snake (XXVII, 213.1–5). Ariosto inverts Pulci's simile
by establishing Orlando as he mourns Brandimarte, in the authoritative
position of Charlemagne mourning Orlando in the *Morgante*. Ariosto's
Orlando does for another what Pulci's Charlemagne had done for him—a
macabre example of one poet out-imitating another.[37]

The realignment of Ariosto's imitative poesis from the Ovidian to
the Vergilian model indicates a change of tone in his intertextual poetics
from tragi-comic burlesque to epic grandeur. That he refracts this change
through Pulci, a poet known for his humorous anti-epic strain,
exemplifies Ariosto's uncanny ability to make the reader reinterpret the
poem's sources in ways that contradict the typical sixteenth-century
reception of those sources. Ariosto's final version of his simile takes
the narrative out of the realm of romance and into the sphere of epic.
But the excursion is only temporary, for the subsequent adventures of
Rinaldo, the "snake-knight" of canto I, are "steeped in a slithering
mass of serpent imagery."[38] In the following cantos the snake as simile
does not occur but there are many references to snakes. Rinaldo even
hears of a *bona fide* snake-man, Adonio in XLIII, 74–116. One of the
ways the *Furioso*'s return to romance in XLII–XLIII mocks the epic
thrust of the final quarter of the poem's narrative is to maintain the
thematics of the serpent established over the course of the poem.

When Torquato Tasso criticizes the *Furioso*'s narrative for its interposed episodes that disrupt the poem's continuity, he confuses the issue of the poem's construction by drawing attention to the snake simile and the snake-man. Indeed the repetition of that simile (and the associated one of ivy) unifies the poem in an intratextual and intertextual network. Repeatedly Ariosto's allusions to literary models create a narrative unity as they encourage the reader to expect their recurrence with each version of the simile.

Yet another passage in Tasso's criticism—this time outside the *Discorsi*—intensifies his ambiguous stance toward the *Furioso*: a gloss, the epigraph to this essay, found in his private copy of Horace's *Ars poetica*.[39] He notes in response to Horace's dictum that the work of art be "simplex dumtaxat et unum" (at least simple and uniform): "Così il Trissino E qui ha peccato quel grandissimo poeta che io non nomino per veneratione, ma il suo peccato gli sarà perdonato dal giudice il più severo se fosse ancora un *Dracone* perchè ha partorito tante maravigliose e divine bellezze" (emphasis mine). (Thus Trissino. And here has sinned also that very great poet whom I do not name out of veneration, but his sin will be pardoned him by the severest judge, were he even a Draco, because he has given birth to so many marvelous and divine beauties.)[40]

The gloss first addresses Trissino's *Italia liberata dai Goti* and its epic narrative that is consistent with neo-classical theory and practice. Tasso himself had already observed in the *Discorsi* (II: 26) that copies of Trissino's poem were buried in the libraries of Europe while readers of all sorts eagerly sought Ariosto's. So much for obeying the rules of Horace.

The second, much longer portion of the gloss, contrasts the multi-form nature of Ariosto's narrative to Trissino's. Ariosto, respectfully unnamed, "has sinned" by failing to create a poem that conforms to the Horatian rules of a simple and uniform narrative. The gloss's tone is strikingly Counter-Reformational: "his sin will be forgiven by the most severe judge." Tasso's comment concludes, however, with a literary cliché: seemingly he agrees with other sixteenth-century critics that in the *Furioso* Ariosto has given birth to "wondrous and divine beauties."

How does Tasso achieve this shift from a Counter-Reformational to a literary-critical tone? By way of a most curious observation in the mixed conditional: "[Ariosto] will be forgiven, were he even a

Dracone." What is this capitalized "Dracone"? Is it a proper noun referring to the Athenian lawgiver, Draco?[41] Or, in the context of Tasso's critical theory, is it the capitalized form of the Italian word for "dragon," from Latin "draco" ("serpent" or "snake")?[42] This latter possibility seems the more probable and it suggests once again the dimensions of Tasso's ambiguity toward Ariosto's achievement. Secretly in the margins of his Horace, in the private and confidential rhetoric of the annotator, Tasso metamorphoses Ariosto into the emblem of his narrative: a serpent. And he does so with a prophetic benediction: "...that greatest poet...will be forgiven." For the creator of the *Gerusalemme Liberata*, Ariosto, the *Furioso,* and the snake had become unbearably indistinguishable, unbearably meaningful—and unbearably successful.

University of Pittsburgh

NOTES

1. The passage from Horace and Tasso's unpunctuated gloss on the line are taken from Rudolph Altrocchi, "Tasso's Holograph Annotations to Horace's *Ars Poetica*," *PMLA* 43 (1928): 931–52. The line from Horace translates: "In short, be the work whatever you will, let it at least be simple and uniform" (trans. H. Rushton Fairclough, Loeb edition, 1970, 453). I discuss Tasso's gloss in some detail at the end of this essay.
2. I am adapting Lawrence Rhu's translation of Tasso's *Discorsi* (copyrighted typescript, 33), forthcoming from Wayne State University Press. For the passage from *Inferno* XXV, 58–60, I follow Charles S. Singleton's translation: Dante Alighieri, *The Divine Comedy: Inferno* (Princeton: Princeton University Press, 1977), 263. Translations in this essay not attributed to anyone are my own.
3. Giovanni Battista Pigna makes a similar observation about romance narratives in *I romanzi*... (Venice: Vincenzo Valgrisi, 1554), 45: "Ma che diremo di questo Romancio, che vien a essere un animale sproporzionato?" (But what shall we say of this romance that is like a disproportionate animal?) For several modern observations on Pigna's comparison, see Margaret Ferguson, *Trials of Desire* (New Haven: Yale University Press, 1983), 208, n. 2; and David Quint, "The Figure of Atlante: Ariosto and Boiardo's Poem," *MLN* 94/1 (1979): 85–87.
4. Tasso was very aware of Ariosto's allusions to the *Inferno*, as the annotations to his private copy of the *Divine Comedy* make clear. For example, in a gloss on the Pier della Vigna episode in *Inferno* XIII, Tasso accuses Ariosto of stealing the image of a soul encased in a tree from Dante for his episode of Astolfo in canto VI of the *Furioso*. The gloss reads: "furto dell'Ariosto" (theft of Ariosto). See Torquato Tasso, *Postille alla* Divina Commedia, ed. Enrico Celani (Città di Castello: Lapi, 1895), 57.

5. The *Furioso* makes at least eight direct verbal allusions to *Inferno* XXV: II, 5.4 and V, 62.3 allude to XXV, 31; VII, 29.1-2 alludes to XXV, 58-59; XI, 12.1 to XXV, 94-97; XII, 48.2-4 to XXV, 85-86; XV, 69.8 to XXV, 61; XVI, 75.6 to XXV, 27; XVIII, 36.5-6 to XXV 79-81. Cesare Segre classifies these allusions into different categories in "Un repertorio linguistico e stilistico dell'Ariosto: La *Commedia,*" *Esperienze ariostesche* (Pisa: Nistri-Lischi, 1966), 51-83.

6. Dante's ivy probably alludes most directly to Ovid's *Metamorphoses* IV, 361-65. For a thorough and witty discussion of the presence of Ovid in *Inferno* XXV, see Madison U. Sowell, "Dante's Nose and Publius Ovidius Naso: A Gloss on *Inferno* 25.45,'' *Quaderni d'italianistica* X, 1-2 (1989): 157-71. Sowell has also edited a volume on Dante's reading of Ovid: *Dante and Ovid: Essays in Intertextuality* (Binghamton: SUNY Press, 1991).

7. For a similar discussion of creative imitation in Dante, see Maristella de Panizza Lorch's essay in this volume—Ed.

8. While it is impossible to pin down the exact dates of Tasso's literary chronology, scholarship has determined that he wrote the *Discorsi* in the early 1560s and the bulk of the *Gerusalemme* in the decade from around 1565 to 1575. See C.P. Brand, *Torquato Tasso* (Cambridge: Cambridge University Press, 1965), chaps. 1 and 3. See also Guido Baldassarri, "Introduzione ai *Discorsi dell'arte poetica del Tasso,*" *Studi tassiani* 26 (1977): 5-38.

9. For the text of the *Discorsi*, see Torquato Tasso, *Prose*, ed. Ettore Mazzali (Milan-Naples: Ricciardi, 1959), 349-410.

10. The most lucid definition of the phenomenon is in Quintilian, *Institutio Oratoria*, IX, iii, 23: "interpositio," a grammatical figure of speech, "consists in the interruption of the continuous flow of our language by the insertion of some remark." I follow the text and translation of H.E. Butler, 4 vols. (1921; Cambridge: Harvard University Press, 1976), 3:458-59. Subsequent theoreticians who applied Quintilian's grammatical category to the discussion of narrative included Fortunatianus and Martianus Capella. See Heinrich Lausberg, *Handbuch der Literarischen Rhetorik*, 2 vols, (Munich: Max Hueber, 1960), 1:167 + 399.

11. I follow Lanfranco Caretti's text of the *Gerusalemme* in the edition of Marziano Guglielminetti (Milan: Garzanti, 1974).

12. I cite from the commendable translation of Ralph Nash (Detroit: Wayne State University Press, 1987).

13. This is not to belittle Tasso's Neoplatonism, for which see Annabel Patterson, "Tasso and Neoplatonism," *Studies in the Renaissance* 18 (1971): 105-33.

14. Sergio Zatti discusses the textual dynamics of the dispersal and retrieval of the Christian army in *L'uniforme cristiano e il multiforme pagano* (Milan: Il Saggiatore, 1983). David Quint, in a groundbreaking article, presents the historical and cultural problems to which Tasso's thematics of dispersal and retrieval refer: "Political Allegory in the *Gerusalemme Liberata,*" *Renaissance Quarterly* XLIII/1 (1990): 1-29.

15. I follow the text of the *Furioso* established by Debenedetti and Segre, as it is given in the edition of Emilio Bigi, 2 vols. (Milan: Rusconi, 1982).

16. In this passage and subsequent ones I use Guido Waldman's translation of the *Furioso* (1974; Oxford: Oxford University Press, 1983), 63.
17. I have adapted Nash's translation; see 390.
18. Albert Russell Ascoli has discussed some of the connections among these similes in *Ariosto's Bitter Harmony: Crisis and Evasion in the Italian Renaissance* (Princeton: Princeton University Press, 1987). Although Kristen Olson Murtaugh does not deal in detail with any of the examples of the snake simile, her essay has been a helpful guide: *Ariosto and the Classical Simile* (Cambridge: Harvard University Press, 1980). Surprisingly, Ariosto's great positivist readers do not have too much to say about the sequence: see Pio Rajna, *Le fonti dell'*Orlando furioso (1876; 1900; Florence: Sansoni, 1976), 549–50; and Augusto Romizi, *Le fonti latine dell'*Orlando furioso (Turin: Paravia, 1896), 90 and 97–98.
19. E.g., the Saracen ship that blows to shore just in the nick of time to provide the Christian triumvirate with weapons and a horse for the duel on Lipadusa (XLI, 23–29); Brandimarte dies in the subsequent gladiatorial duels because the horse was not an adequate defense (XLI, 79).
20. In the palio (or in Ariosto's spelling, "pallio"), prostitutes and Jews, similarly marginalized yet necessary elements of the civic fabric, were forced to race through town scantily clad. See Bigi's note on I, 11 (I:99), with its reference to the depiction of the runners in a detail from the fresco cycle in the Palazzo Schifanoia. I am reminded of Deanna Shemek's informative paper, "From Ritual Space to Picture: Feminine Good and Evil in Ferrara's 'Palio di San Giorgio' " (MLA Convention, Washington, D.C., 1989).
21. D.S. Carne-Ross (acknowledging Durling) has observed that the chiastic arrangement of the tenor and vehicle in the double simile has an Horatian elegance; see "The One and the Many: A Reading of the *Orlando Furioso*, Cantos 1 and 8," *Arion* 5/2 (1966): 201.
22. For a recent and excellent discussion of Angelica's place in the canto, see Peter V. Marinelli, "Shaping the Ore: Image and Design in Canto I of *Orlando Furioso*," *MLN* 103/1 (1988): 31–49.
23. I follow the text of R.A.B. Mynors (Oxford: Oxford University Press, 1969).
24. See his "Brieve dimostratione," first printed to accompany the *Furioso* (Venice: Giolito, 1542), and reprinted frequently in the sixteenth century.
25. *Osservationi...sopra il* Furioso *nelle quali si mostrano tutti i luoghi imitati dall'Autore nel suo poema* (Venice: Francesco dei Franceschi, 1584), 2: "Coloro...affermano l'Ariosto haverlasi presa [la comparatione] da quella di Vergilio...Ma non s'accorgono, che le parole dell'Ariosto non vi s'adattano puntalmente...Questa imitatione dunque si vede chiaramente esser fatta da quel distico d'Ovidio nel secondo de'*Fasti*." (Some [i.e., Dolce and Ruscelli] claim that Ariosto took the simile from Vergil...but they fail to realize that Ariosto's words don't exactly fit Vergil's text... This imitation then is clearly seen to derive from that distich in the second book of Ovid's *Fasti*.)
26. Daniel Javitch has noted that Dolce consistently highlights what he takes to be a principal source at the expense of any others whereas Lavezuola is usually attuned to the multiple allusions behind a given passage of the Furioso. He is more attuned

at least than Dolce to Ariosto's habit of imitating literary passages that in themselves are also imitations of previous works. See Javitch's "Sixteenth-Century Commentaries on Imitations in the *Orlando Furioso*," *Harvard Library Bulletin* 34 (1986): 221–50.

27. The curriculum of the school is discussed in Remigio Sabbadini's study of Guarino Veronese: *Guariniana: Vita di Guarino Veronese; La scuola e gli studi di Guarino Veronese*, 2 rpt. vols. bound in 1 with original pagination, ed. Mario Sancipriano (1891; 1896; Turin: Bottega d'Erasmo, 1969), 2: 35.

28. For an account of Ariosto's education see "Ludovico studente," in Michele Catalano, *Vita di Ludovico Ariosto* (Geneva: Olschki, 1930–31), 1: 86–103. Nicola Maria Panizzato, a lifelong friend to whom Ariosto refers in *Furioso* XLVI, 14.8, was a student and eventually became a teacher of Latin and Greek at the *Studium*. Ariosto was probably tutored from 1486 to 1489 by Luca Ripa who taught at the school during these years.

29. See Sara Mack's discussion of the *Fasti* as literary art in *Ovid* (New Haven: Yale University Press, 1988).

30. Ovid, *Fasti*, ed. and trans. Sir James George Frazer (Cambridge-London: Harvard-Heinemann, 1976), 57 + 59. I have adapted Frazer's expurgated translation, 83.

31. I would complement Ascoli's discussion of Orlando as Silenus with this view of the hero as a Faunus type. See the chapter in *Ariosto's Bitter Harmony*, "Oneness in Nonsense," 331–60.

32. Another early commentator of the *Furioso*, Oratio Toscanella, makes the obvious but nonetheless valid point that the double simile in the stanza respects the gender of each character: "...comparing the male to a person or thing that is masculine and the female to a person or thing that is feminine. Since Rinaldo's gender is male, he compares him to a masculine person, a half-naked farmer. And just below, coming up with a simile for Angelica whose gender is female, he compares her to a feminine person, a shepherdess." The Italian text reads: "il comparare il maschio, à persona, ò cosa maschia; et la femina; à persona, ò cosa feminile; essendo Rinaldo di sesso maschile, lo compara à persona maschile; cioè ad un villan mezo ignudo: et poco più giù comparando Angelica, che è di sesso feminile, la compara à persona di sesso feminile; cioè ad una pastorella..." In *Bellezzee del* Furioso *di M. Lodovico Ariosto; Scielte da Oratio Toscanella:...* (Venice: Pietro dei Franceschi, 1574), 11.

33. Ariosto alludes to this Ovidian episode in several passages of the *Furioso*, for example, when Bireno abandons Olimpia (X, 15.1–4), the poet editorializes by borrowing a comment from the description of Tereus (*Met.* VI, 472–74).

34. Ariosto is reserving the topos of the "pallido nocchiero" for a passage later in the narrative (XL, 29).

35. This is not to contest Elissa B. Weaver's observation that the snake in XXIII calls to mind the biblical serpent and the theme of problematic knowledge; that allusion is all the more present in XXXIX. See her "Lettura dell'intreccio dell'*Orlando Furioso*: il caso delle tre pazzie d'amore," *Strumenti Critici* 31 (1977): 384–406.

36. See Ascoli, 346–48.

37. The proem of *Furioso* XLII also borrows from Pulci (*Morgante* XXVII, 212). The Ariostan narrator reflects on the inevitability of revenge when a friend, a lord, or a relative is injured before one's eyes. The poem's appropriateness becomes clear immediately as Orlando, who holds Brandimarte even closer than a relative (15.8), avenges his death by killing Agramante. The threat of the serpent creates a curious sense of family: Sobrino, the remaining pagan warrior surrenders only to become like a relative (19).

38. Ascoli, 348. The two snake similes I have found in Boiardo's *Innamorato* are both used for Ranaldo, the precursor of Ariosto's Rinaldo: I xxiii 38.1–4 and I xxvii 13.1–4.

39. Altrocchi (see note 1 above) uses internal and external evidence to conclude that Tasso annotated his copy of Horace in the mid-1580s.

40. Altrocchi's translation, 935.

41. This is, one assumes, Altrocchi's interpretation, but as his note reveals he is not at all certain about it.

42. The proper Italian is "dragone" from the Latin, "draco," and from the Greek " *drakōn*"; "dracon" is a linguistic variant. The word is used, especially in the Christian tradition, as a synonym for "serpent"; e.g., Rev. 12:9: ". . . draco ille magnus, serpens antiquus. . ." (that great dragon, the ancient serpent).

Begging an Answer:
Kleist's *The Beggarwoman of Locarno*

LILIAN R. FURST

"What is the answer?...In that case, what
is the question?"

Gertrude Stein.

Am Fuβe der Alpen bei Locarno im oberen Italien befand sich ein
altes, einem Marchese gehöriges Schloβ, das man jetzt, wenn man vom
St. Gotthard kommt, in Schutt und Trümmern liegen sieht: ein Schloβ
mit hohen und weitläufigen Zimmern, in deren einem einst auf Stroh,
das man ihr unterschüttete eine alte kranke Frau, die sich bettelnd vor
der Tür eingefunden hatte, von der Hausfrau aus Mitleiden gebettet
worden war. Der Marchese, der bei seiner Rückkehr von der Jagd
zufällig in das Zimmer trat, wo er seine Büchse abzusetzen pflegte, befahl
der Frau unwillig, aus dem Winkel, in welchem sie lag, aufzustehn und
sich hinter den Ofen zu verfügen. Die Frau, da sie sich erhob, glitschte
mit der Krücke auf dem glatten Boden aus und beschädigte sich auf
eine gefährliche Weise das Kreuz, dergestalt, daβ sie zwar noch mit
unsäglicher Mühe aufstand und quer, wie es ihr vorgeschrieben war,
über das Zimmer ging, hinter dem Ofen aber unter Stöhnen und Ächzen
niedersank und verschied.

Mehrere Jahre nachher, da der Marchese durch Krieg und Miβwachs
in bedenkliche Vermögensumstände geraten war, fand sich ein
florentinischer Ritter bei ihm ein, der das Schloβ seiner schönen Lage

In the foothills of the Alps, near Locarno in Northern Italy, there used to stand an old castle belonging to a marquis, which can now, when one comes from the St. Gotthard, be seen lying in ruins: a castle with high-ceilinged, spacious rooms, in one of which the mistress of the house one day, out of pity for an old sick woman, who had turned up begging at the door, had bedded her down on the floor on some straw, which was spread under her. The marquis, who, on his return from hunting, by chance entered the room, where he was used to keeping his gun, unwillingly ordered the woman to get up from the corner where she lay and to remove herself to behind the stove. The woman, as [because] she arose, slipped with her crutch on the smooth floor and dangerously injured her back: with the result that she did manage to stand up with indescribable difficulty and to cross the room from corner to corner, as had been prescribed to her, and then collapsed behind the stove amid moans and groans and expired.

Several years later, when [because] the marquis had got into straitened financial circumstances as a result of war and poor harvests, a Florentine knight turned up who wanted to buy the castle from him

wegen von ihm kaufen wollte. Der Marchese, dem viel an dem Handel gelegen war, gab seiner Frau auf, den Fremden in dem obenerwähnten leerstehenden Zimmer, das sehr schön und prächtig eingerichtet war, unterzubringen. Aber wie betreten war das Ehepaar, als der Ritter mitten in der Nacht verstört und bleich zu ihnen herunterkam, hoch und teuer versichernd, daß es in dem Zimmer spuke, indem etwas, das dem Blick unsichtbar gewesen, mit einem Geräusch, als ob es auf Stroh gelegen, im Zimmerwinkel aufgestanden, mit vernehmlichen Schritten langsam und gebrechlich quer über das Zimmer gegangen und hinter dem Ofen unter Stöhnen und Ächzen niedergesunken sei.

Der Marchese, erschrocken, er wußte selbst nicht recht warum, lachte den Ritter mit erkünstelter Heiterkeit aus und sagte, er wolle sogleich aufstehen und die Nacht zu seiner Beruhigung mit ihm in dem Zimmer zubringen. Doch der Ritter bat um die Gefälligkeit, ihm zu erlauben, daß er auf einem Lehnstuhl in seinem Schlafzimmer übernachte; und als der Morgen kam, ließ er anspannen, empfahl sich und reiste ab.

Dieser Vorfall, der außerordentliches Aufsehen machte, schreckte auf einem dem Marchese höchst unangehneme Weise mehrere Käufer ab; dergestalt, daß, da sich unter seinem eignen Hausgesinde, befremdend und unbegreiflich, das Gerücht erhob, daß es in dem Zimmer zur Mitternachtstunde umgehe, er, um es mit einem entscheidenden Verfahren niederzuschlagen, beschloß, die Sache in der nächsten Nacht selbst zu untersuchen. Demnach ließ er beim Einbruch der Dämmerung sein Bett in dem besagten Zimmer aufschlagen und verharrte, ohne zu schlafen, die Mitternacht. Aber wie erschüttert war er, als er in der Tat mit dem Schlage der Geisterstunde das unbegreifliche Geräusch wahrnahm; es war, als ob ein Mensch sich vom Stroh, das unter ihm knisterte, erhob, quer über das Zimmer ging und hinter dem Ofen unter Geseufz und Geröchel niedersank. Die Marquise, am andern Morgen, da er herunterkam, fragte ihn, wie die Untersuchung abgelaufen; und da er sich mit scheuen und ungewissen Blicken umsah und, nachdem er die Tür verriegelt, versicherte, daß es mit dem Spuk seine Richtigkeit habe, so erschrak sie, wie sie in ihrem Leben nicht getan, und bat ihn, bevor er die Sache verlauten ließe, sie noch einmal in ihrer Gesellschaft einer kaltblütigen Prüfung zu unterwerfen. Sie hörten aber samt einem treuen Bedienten, den sie mitgenommen hatten, in der Tat in der nächsten Nacht dasselbe unbegreifliche, gespensterartige Geräusch; und nur der dringende Wunsch, das Schloß, es koste was

for its beautiful location. The marquis, who was eager to make the deal, told his wife to put the stranger in the above mentioned room, which was standing empty, and which was beautifully and sumptuously furnished. But how disturbed the couple were when the knight came down to them in the middle of the night, distraught and pale, and assured them long and loud that the room was haunted, in that something invisible to the eye had stood up in a corner of the room with a sound as if it had been lying on straw, had crossed the room slowly and laboriously, with audible steps, and had sunk down behind the stove amid moans and groans.

The marquis, frightened, without himself really knowing why, laughed at the knight with feigned jollity, and said he wanted to get up immediately and remain with him in the room for the rest of the night in order to calm him. But the knight begged to be allowed to spend the night in an armchair in the marquis's bedroom; at daylight, he ordered his carriage to be made ready, took leave and departed.

This incident, which caused an extraordinary stir, frightened off several buyers in a manner most unpleasant to the marquis; with the result that, when [as] the rumor spread among his own servants, strangely and incomprehensibly, that the room was haunted at midnight, he resolved, in order to scotch it with a decisive step, to investigate the matter himself that very night. Accordingly, at the approach of dusk he had his bed set up in the designated room, and awaited midnight without sleeping. But how taken aback he was, when he indeed heard the incomprehensible sound at the witching hour; it was as if someone rose from the straw crackling beneath him, crossed the room, and sank down behind the stove amid sighs and the death rattle. The marquise, the next morning, when he came down, asked him, how the investigation had gone, and when [as] he cast around with abashed and uncertain glances, and after he had locked the door, assured her that it was right about the ghost, she took such fright as never before in her life, and begged him, before letting the matter get about, to subject it to a further coldblooded examination in her company. But together with a faithful servant, whom they had taken along, they in fact heard in the following night the same incomprehensible, ghost-like sound, and only the urgent desire to get rid of the castle, at any price, enabled them, in the presence

es wolle, loszuwerden, vermochte sie, das Entsetzen, das sie ergriff, in Gegenwart ihres Dieners zu unterdrücken und dem Vorfall irgendeine gleichgültige und zufällige Ursache, die sich entdecken lassen müsse, unterzuschieben. Am Abend des dritten Tages, da beide um der Sache auf den Grund zu kommen, mit Herzklopfen wieder die Treppe zu dem Fremdenzimmer bestiegen, fand sich zufällig der Haushund, den man von der Kette losgelassen hatte, vor der Tür desselben ein; dergestalt, daß beide, ohne sich bestimmt zu erklären, vielleicht in der unwillkürlichen Absicht, außer sich selbst noch etwas Drittes, Lebendiges, bei sich zu haben, den Hund mit sich in das Zimmer nahmen. Das Ehepaar, zwei Lichter auf dem Tisch, die Marquise unausgezogen, der Marchese Degen und Pistolen, die er aus dem Schrank genommen, neben sich, setzten sich gegen elf Uhr jeder auf sein Bett; und während sie sich mit Gesprächen, so gut sie vermögen, zu unterhalten suchen, legt sich der Hund, Kopf und Beine zusammengekauert, in der Mitte des Zimmers nieder und schläft ein. Drauf, in dem Augenblick der Mitternacht, läßt sich das entsetzliche Geräusch wieder hören; jemand, den kein Mensch mit Augen sehen kann, hebt sich auf Krücken im Zimmerwinkel empor; man hört das Stroh, das unter ihm rauscht; und mit dem ersten Schritt: tapp! tapp! erwacht der Hund, hebt sich plötzlich, die Ohren spitzend, vom Boden empor, und knurrend und bellend, grad als ob ein Mensch auf ihn eingeschritten käme, rückwärts gegen den Ofen weicht er aus. Bei diesem Anblick stürzt die Marquise mit sträubenden Haaren aus dem Zimmer; und während der Marchese, der den Degen ergriffen, "Wer da?" ruft und, da ihm niemand antwortet, gleich einem Rasenden nach allen Richtungen die Luft durchhaut, läßt sie anspannen, enstschlossen, augenblicklich nach der Stadt abzufahren. Aber ehe sie noch nach Zusammenraffung einiger Sachen aus dem Tore herausgerasselt, sieht sie schon das Schloß ringsum in Flammen aufgehen. Der Marchese, von Entsetzen überreizt, hatte eine Kerze genommen und dasselbe, überall mit Holz getäfelt wie es war, an allen vier Ecken, müde seines Lebens, angesteckt. Vergebens schickte sie Leute hinein, den Unglücklichen zu retten, er war auf die elendiglichste Weise bereits umgekommen; und noch jetzt liegen, von den Landleuten zusammengetragen, seine weißen Gebeine in dem Winkel des Zimmers, von welchem er das Bettelweib von Locarno hatten aufstehen heißen.[1]

of their servant, to repress the horror they felt, and to ascribe the incident to some trivial and fortuitous cause, that could surely be discovered. On the evening of the third night, when [as] both of them, in order to fathom the matter, went up the stairs to the guest room with beating hearts, the house dog, who had been unchained, turned up by chance before the door of the room: so that both of them, without specifically consulting each other, perhaps in the unconscious intention of having some third living being with them, took the dog with them into the room. The couple, with two lights on the table, the marquise not undressed, the marquis with the dagger and pistols, which he had taken out of the cupboard, beside him, each sat down around eleven o' clock on their beds; and while they endeavored to divert themselves as best they could with conversation, the dog lies down, head and legs curled up, in the middle of the room, and goes to sleep. Then, at the moment of midnight, the terrible sound is heard again; someone, invisible to the human eye, rises on crutches in the corner of the room; the straw crackling under him can be heard; and at the first step, tap! tap! the dog awakes, suddenly rises from the floor, pricking his ears, and gnarling and barking, just as if a person were advancing toward him, retreats backward toward the stove. At this sight the marquise rushes out of the room, her hair standing on end; and while the marquis, who had seized his dagger, shouts ''Who goes there?'' and as [because] no one replies, like a madman lunges in the air in all directions, she has the carriage made ready, determined to leave for town immediately. But even before she had rattled out of the gate, after collecting a few possessions, she already sees the castle all around going up in flames. The marquis, overwrought by the horror of it, had taken a candle and set it alight in all four corners, panelled in wood as it was, and he being weary of his life. In vain the marquise sent people in to save the unhappy man, he had already perished in a most miserable way, and to this day his whitened bones, gathered together by the local people, lie in that corner of the room, from which he had ordered the beggarwoman of Locarno to arise.[2]

The Beggarwoman of Locarno was written in 1810, just one year before Kleist's suicide at age thirty-four. He was at that time living in Berlin, where he had founded the *Berliner Abendblätter,* the first daily newspaper in German. This story may well have been intended for that publication, although it actually appeared in the two volume collection of Kleist's *Novellen* put out in 1810 and 1811.

Certainly the brevity and the dramatic quality of *The Beggarwoman of Locarno* would make it ideal material for a newspaper. It is best known nowadays as the shortest *Novelle* in German; yet despite its shortness, it is of an extraordinary complexity. It is distinguished, above all, by its capacity to beg an answer, to leave both protagonists and readers to face an enigma that defies resolution. This uncertainty arises not so much from lack of information as from the kinds and amounts of information both given and withheld. In the many details more is offered than is needed or can be coherently accommodated in any reading. The legalistic precision of the discourse with its tight syntax and its compressed, almost spastic constructions, is a cover for the essentially problematic nature of what is told. The ample documentation of the attendant circumstances fashions an illusory surface of factuality which conceals, at least temporarily, the central motivational ambiguity. Kleist's artfulness has created a tale that is brief, gripping, tantalizing, and ultimately beyond interpretation.

At first glance, *The Beggarwoman of Locarno* seems a classic ghost story. The recurrent irruptions at the witching hour of midnight of the invisible but audible phantom provide the structure of the tale. The pattern is one of repetition with three hauntings on three successive nights and with three discrete witnesses, apart from the marquis: the Florentine knight, the servant, and the marquise, with the dog for good measure. Always it is basically the same phenomenon, although with slight variations of emphasis: the mysterious sound of someone laboriously crossing the room and the crackling of straw. All three episodes are directly and obviously derived from the incident related in the opening paragraph. The repetition is deliberately intensified by the modifiers attached to "Geräusch" ("sound"): on the first occasion it stands alone: on the second, the adjective is "unbegreiflich" ("incomprehensible"), to which is added the third time "gespensterartig" ("ghost-like"), while on the fourth it turns into "entsetzlich" ("terrible"). The repetitiveness is manifest in other instances too, for instance in the flight of the Florentine knight and the marquise, when the same phrase about ordering the carriage to be readied heralds the panic stricken departure. The story, indeed, reverberates to its own internal echoes, even linguistically: the "Aber wie betreten" ("But how disturbed") is reiterated in heightened form in the "Aber wie erschüttert" ("But how taken aback"). These resonances and reprises not only lend unity but also underscore the rising tension in the movement from the relatively low-key beginning to the shattering climax of the end. The switch, at the critical moment, from the past tense to the present (in the final vigil with the dog) further enhances the narrative's vividness and punch.

But *The Beggarwoman of Locarno* goes beyond the normative limits of the ghost story in the moral question it implicitly raises. A casual reader might easily suppose that this is a parable of crime and punishment, in which an evil deed is followed by retribution. Kleist's discourse at once fosters and subverts such a reading. The question implied is not the simple one as to either the presence or the identity of the ghost, both of which are posited with an unusual degree of certainty. What is at issue, rather, is the more complicated matter of the likelihood of a cause and effect link between the death of the beggarwoman and that of the marquis. Many of the elements of the plot seem to point quite strongly to an association between the misadventure that befalls the beggarwoman and the misfortunes that beset the marquis. The castle had not been haunted before her appearance; the ghost is described in such a way as to leave absolutely no doubt as to its model; here the circumstantial detail plays a crucial role—the tapping of the crutch, the crackling of the straw, the moans and groans all characterize the beggarwoman. In the closing sentence the marquis is again closely linked to her when we learn that "his whitened bones, gathered together by the local people, lie in that corner of the room, from which he had ordered the beggarwoman of Locarno to arise." That creates a highly dramatic, almost melodramatic ending to this eerie story, and one might well ask what would be the point of including it were it not to reinforce the connection between the treatment accorded to the beggarwoman and the ruin of the marquis and the castle. I am not questioning the existence of such a connection, but I am asking whether it is justifiable to envisage it as a cause and effect sequence. Through hints and suggestions the narrator leads readers on toward the supposition that the beggarwoman is claiming vengeance on the marquis. This is easy enough to assume. However, ultimately Kleist's discourse thwarts any such univalent reading because of its multiple ambivalences.

The seeming simplicity of *The Beggarwoman of Locarno* is in fact quite deceptive.

This is immediately illustrated in the opening paragraph. The appearance of precision is conveyed at the outset through the initial naming of the geographic location: "Am Fuße der Alpen bei Locarno im oberen Italien" ("In the foothills of the Alps near Locarno in northern Italy"); the placing is actually kept fairly vague, just sufficiently specific to evoke the illusion of reality, but not so concrete as to dispel the aura of romance suggested by the old castle. The temporality of the narration is from the outset dualistic in the contrast between the castle's proud past and its present derelict condition. By this oblique means readers' curiosity is immediately aroused as the story's pivotal question is adumbrated: how did the castle come to fall into its present ruined state? The second half of that immensely long opening sentence, since it follows a colon, leads readers to expect an amplification of the statement made in the first half. But that expectation is disappointed, although the latter half of the sentence does continue the motif of the castle by elaborating on its former splendor.

Then, still in that gargantuan first sentence, the narrative seems to take a great leap from its primary theme, the destruction of the castle, to the apparently trivial incident of the old beggarwoman who is given shelter by the mistress of the house. Interestingly, there is no syntactic fracture: the transition from the castle to the old woman is accomplished via a subsidiary clause referring to one of the rooms in the castle. Kleist's prose is, as Staiger has described it in a perspicacious article on *The Beggarwoman of Locarno*, "eine Prosa, die bis ins Letzte gegliedert, deren Teile mit schärfster Logik gefügt und auf einander bezogen sind"[3] ("a prose that is articulated throughout, whose parts are fused and related to each other with incisive logic"). The syntactic interlacement is incontestable, not only here but throughout the narrative. But it does not correspond necessarily to a CONCEPTUAL connectedness. On the contrary, the syntatic continuity serves to conceal the cognitive discontinuity. Here in the very first sentence readers encounter the paramount disjuncture that haunts their reading of the story: what is the nature of the conjunction between the two halves of the sentence, between the two happenings recorded, the advent of the beggarwoman and the ruination of the castle? Is there a direct, causal connection between them, or are they fortuitously adjacent events? The grammatical structure, despite its tightness, does not afford any decisive clues. What is more, the gap is overlaid by a plethora of subsidiary information, such as the castle's geographic location, the size of its rooms, the straw spread under the woman. While this last detail about the straw will later prove significant in the plot development, the other facts are largely redundant. Only the phrase "aus Mitleiden" ("out of pity") stands out in this description because it is the sole denotation of motive. Since the marquise's motives in giving shelter to the beggarwoman are wholly benign and disinterested, the ethics of the situation are thereby further complicated.

The second, considerably shorter sentence is sandwiched between the two long ones with which the paragraph begins and ends. If the first sentence contains the crucial enigma, the second encompasses the critical act, and it, too, is highly perplexing in both motivation and presentation. The marquis, on his return from hunting, "by chance" ("zufällig") enters the room where he is accustomed to keeping his gun. There is a grammatical contradiction here: the word "pflegte" underscores the habitual aspect, the customariness of his action: in other words, it was predictable that he would enter the room, so that "pflegte" contravenes "zufällig" ("by chance"). And WHY does he order the beggarwoman to move? This is another unanswerable question that countervails the surface impression of conjunction stemming from the immaculate syntax. Equally puzzling is the floating adverb, "unwillig," attached to the marquis. Does it refer to the tone of his command or to his entire attitude toward the beggarwoman? Luke and Reeves[4] translate "unwillig" as "angrily," while Greenberg[5] opts for "irritably." If these are correct interpretations, then the marquis's stance could neatly be set off against his wife's for she took the woman in "out of pity." On the other hand, "unwillig" most commonly means "reluctantly"—in which case, the question as to why he asks her to move becomes even more impenetrable. From the way in which the narrative is presented, an answer is beyond even hypothesis. As an impersonal, though at times quite knowledgeable narrator, Kleist adopts a reportorial tone that permits an occasional glimpse of a situation from a protagonist's point of view but no extensive probing of inner states of mind. In this respect Kleist's use of indirect discourse is the opposite to that of Flaubert and the modernists who derive from him. Whereas for Flaubert indirect discourse is the means for slipping into the perspective and the mentality of the persona, for Kleist it is the method for maintaining his detachment as an external observer who records, often visually, what happens.

The third and final sentence of this opening paragraph recounts the beggarwoman's accident. Again the disposition of the narrative is ambiguous. In this instance the crux of the dilemma resides in the conjunction "da" which English translators render by "as." In German, however, "da" has a dual potential, for it can denote either a consecutive, temporal or a consequential, causal link. At this point in *The Beggarwoman of Locarno* the interpretation of that "da" is crucial: did she slip AS she arose, or BECAUSE she arose? The temporal is, as the translators have assumed, the more likely. Nevertheless, the mere existence of the alternative in German is extremely important insofar as it would permit a direct relationship to be established between the woman's rising in accordance with the marquis' command and her fatal accident. This strategy of equivocation is highly significant, not least because the conjunction "da" recurs six other times in *The Beggarwoman of Locarno*, frequently with the same dualism of the temporal and the causal. The discourse is poised in such a manner as to preclude the explicit reading it seems at first sight to invite. Its ambivalences are screened by the patina of its rigorous grammatical cohesiveness: the interlocking syntactical entities with their abundance of precise but peripheral information clothe a story riddled with controversy. The close-knit surface of Kleist's discourse is a blind and a decoy.

Lest the ulterior potential of "da" encourages the ascription of the beggarwoman's accident to the marquis' command, it must be noted that her fall is categorically presented in the active tense: "glitschte mit der Krücke...und beschädigte sich" ("slipped with her crutch ...and dangerously injured her back"). It is she who injures herself, as the reflexive verb in German makes evident. Her fall is not attributed to any factor other than the smooth floor. Legally, presumably, the marquis would be responsible—but then he would be covered by homeowners' insurance. At any rate, what is at stake here is not the legal but the moral responsibility. Yet the second half of the sentence, beginning with the typically Kleistian construction "dergestalt daβ" ("with the result that"), again carries a suggestion of consequentiality. The situation is far from clear in this packed sentence as it rushes onwards with utmost urgency to its astonishing concluding phrase: "und verschied" ("and perished"). This climax is something of an anti-climax in the sparseness of its formulation after the involutions of the previous clauses. There has been a concessive "zwar noch" ("although"), a lengthy encapsulated phrase: "wie es ihr vorgeschrieben war" ("as had been prescribed to her"), a precise indication of her trajectory, "quer" ("from corner to corner"), and a duplicative auditory description of her arrival by the stove "unter Stöhnen und Ächzen" ("amid moans and groans"). These various physical details will form the basis for the recognition of the ghost in its haunting returns. But in stark contrast to this feast of explanatory documentation of "how" things happened, there is a famine of silence on the "why." Did the beggarwoman die of this additional injury, or was she already dying anyway? Probably a combination of both, but we simply cannot know. These major lacunae in our knowledge are in strangely antagonistic alliance with the plethora of circumstantial information placed before us. Questions of motivation, responsibility, and causation are inevitably raised in our minds, but remain forever without answer. That is a cardinal source of the endless fascination exercised by Kleist's narratives.

Throughout the rest of the story the same syntactical, lexical, and narrational strategies recur constantly. The paratactic, hyperstructured sentences, without parallel in German except in Kafka, seem to represent, through their super-rationalism, a strenuous, desperate effort to keep the irrational at bay. The recourse to the emphatic "dergestalt daß" ("with the result that"), for instance, conjures up the semblance of utmost logic. This taut intertwining of motifs is apparent too in the reiterated suggestive echoes and foreshadowings of words as well as phrases: "niederschlagen" (of the marquis' resolve to scotch the rumors of haunting) is reminiscent of the beggarwoman's "niedersinken," while the crackling of the straw that signals the ghost's visitation, "knisterte," might point forward to the crackling of the fire that consumes the castle. When the marquis confirms to his wife "daß es mit dem Spuk seine Richtigkeit habe" (the ambiguity here is virtually untranslatable: that the business about the spook had its rightness [?]), does he mean merely that the prospective buyer was right in complaining about the existence of the ghost, or, furthermore, that the ghost is right in its haunting of the castle? Finally, when the marquis, "von Entsetzen überreizt" ("overwrought by the horror of it"), sets the castle alight, is it legitimate to maintain that his death is caused by the ghost, or is this just a precipitating contributory factor? Is he "müde seines Lebens" ("weary of his life") because of the ghost, or because of his financial and property worries, or are these too attributable to the beggarwoman? As always, so at the end, in compensation for this central uncertainty, there is massive peripheral detail: that he lit the fire with one of the candles they had brought up for their vigil, that the room was panelled in wood, and then he set it alight in all four corners—perhaps another ironic geometric reference to the beggarwoman's movement from corner to corner, like the consuming fire.

The Beggarwoman of Locarno is a text in which, as Staiger put it, "alles oder gar nichts der Erklärung bedürftig [ist]"[6] ("everything or nothing [is] in need of explanation"). Is, for instance, the recurrent adjective "unbegreiflich" ("incomprehensible") to be taken as an irony? Since the ghost is evidentially that of the beggarwoman, the haunting, if it is deemed "incomprehensible," must be so for moral rather than physical reasons. Similarly, the adverb "zufällig" ("by chance") appears twice: first in the reference to the marquis's entry into the room where the beggarwoman lies, and again about the dog, who had been unchained and happens to turn up in front of the door to the room. "Zufall" is a favorite word and concept in the Kleistian world, in which incomprehensible things often, literally, "fall to" the protagonists. But whether such chance represents the sport of fate or has other recondite mainsprings remains open to speculation.

The outcome of this simultaneously communicative and reticent mode of narration is that we, as much as the marquis, are puzzled readers of an insolubly enigmatic situation. His dilemma is paralleled by ours, and, as it were, transferred onto us. If, as Todorov insists, "A text always contains within itself directions for its own consumption,"[7] then those directions in The Beggarwoman of Locarno are patently self-contradictory. Our interpretive processes are repeatedly thwarted by the absence of assured exegetic models within the text. But, as Wolfgang Kayser has asserted in his essay on Kleist: "Die paradoxe Wertung ist ein typischer Stilzug dieses Erzählens"[8] ("Paradoxical evaluation is a typical trait of this mode of narration"). Through his eschewal of definiteness within the text Kleist withholds from us reliable prototypes to guide our meta-exegetic tactics. Or rather, the system into which readers are intitiated is essentially one of indeterminacy. Again our position as readers is very similar to that of the marquis in his role as a fictive reader of his predicament. Just as he hesitates in his confrontation of his experiences, so we are made to hesitate in confronting his hesitancy.

In *The Beggarwoman of Locarno* Kleist has taken the familiar, almost trite features of a ghost story, and instilled into them an entirely new dimension. The physical phenomenon of the haunting has been invested with a moral, indeed metaphysical undercurrent. And we as readers are challenged to beg the question long anterior to the unattainable answer.

University of North Carolina, Chapel Hill

NOTES

1. Heinrich von Kleist, *Sämtliche Werke und Briefe*, ed. Helmut Sembdner. 2nd. rev. ed. (Munich: Hanser, 1961) II: 196–198.
2. This translation is my own. I have deliberately sought to convey the tone and pace of the original rather than to write a polished Engiish version.
3. Emil Staiger, "Heinrich von Kleist: *Das Bettelweb von Locarno:* Zum Problem des dramatischen Stils," *Heinrich von Kleist: Aufsätze und Essays,* ed. Walter Müller-Seidel (Darmstadt: Wissenschaftliche Buchgesellschaft, 1967), 117.
4. Heinrich von Kleist, *The Marquise of O- and Other Stories*, trs. David Luke and Nigel Reeves (Harmondsworth and New York: Penguin Books, 1978), 214.
5. Heinrich von Kleist, *The Marquise of O- and Other Stories*, trs. Martin Greenberg (New York: Ungar, 1960), 187.
6. Emil Staiger, *op. cit.*, 116.
7. Tzvetan Todorov, "Reading as Construction, *The Reader in the Text*, ed. Susan R. Suleiman and Inge Crosman (Princeton, N.J.: Princeton Univ. Press, 1980), 77.
8. Wolfgang Kayser, "Kleist als Erzähler," *Heinrich von Kleist: Aufsätze und Essays,* ed. Walter Müller-Seidel (Darmstadt: Wissenschaftliche Buchgesellschaft, 1967), 234.

Narrative, Genre, and Mode: Pirandello's "La Patente"

MARY ANN FRESE WITT

"Qui, non si narra!" Pirandello,
"Sei Personaggi in cerca di autore"

THE NOVELLA	THE PLAY
I	**I**
Vedere, non aveva potuto vedere molte cose, il giudice D'Andrea; ma certo moltissime ne aveva pensate, e quando il pensare è piu triste, cioè di notte.[1]	*Resta un po' assorto a pensare, poi suona il campanello...*[2]
II	**II**
E al giudice D'Andrea, quando si faceva giorno, pareva una cosa buffa e atroce nello stesso tempo, ch'egli dovesse recarsi al suo ufficio d'Istruzione ad amministrare—per quel tanto che a lui toccava—la giustizia ai piccoli poveri uomini feroci.	*...apre lo sportellino della gabbiola e fa passare da questa nella gabbia grande un cardellino.* D'ANDREA. Via, dentro! . . . Zitto adesso, al solito, e lasciami amministrare la giustizia a questi poveri piccoli uomini feroci. (607)

112

THE NOVELLA	THE PLAY
I	**I**
He couldn't have seen many things, Judge D'Andrea, but he had certainly thought many, and thought them when thinking is the saddest, that is at night.	[Judge D'Andrea] remains somewhat absorbed, thinking. Then he rings the bell. . . .
II	**II**
And to Judge D'Andrea, as the day dawned, it seemed at once comic and atrocious for him to have to go to his judicial office to administer—however briefly—justice to poor little fierce men.	*. . .he opens the door of the small cage, takes a goldfinch from it and puts it into a large cage.* D'ANDREA Come on, go in! . . .Be still now, as usual, and let me administer justice to these poor little fierce men.

III

Era veramente iniquo quel processo
là: iniquo perché includeva una
spietata ingiustizia contro alla quale
un pover uomo tentava disperatamente
di ribellarsi senza alcuna probabilità
di scampo. C'era in quel processo una
vittima che non poteva prendersela
con nessuno. Aveva voluto
prendersela con due, il in quel
processo, coi primi due che gli erano
capitati sotto mano, e— sisignori—la
giustizia doveva dargli torto, torto,
torto, senza remissione, ribadendo,
cosi, ferocemente, l'iniquità di cui
quel pover uomo era vittima.

IV

Ahimè, è proprio vero che è molto
piu facile fare il male che il bene.

V

Il Chiàrchiaro s'era combinata una
faccia da jettatore, ch'era una
meraviglia a vedere. S'era lasciata
crescere su le cave gote gialle una
barbaccia ispida e cespugliuta;
s'era insellato sul naso un pajo di
grossi occhiali cerchiati d'osso, che
gli davano l'aspetto d'un cigno,
aveva poi indossato un abito lustro,
sorcigno, che gli sgonfiava da
tuttle le parti.
    Allo scatto del giudice non si
scompose. Dilatò le nari, digrignò
i denti gialli e disse sottovoce:
—Lei dunque non ci crede?

III

Ecco qua, signori miei, *prende dalla
scrivania il fasciolo del processo
Chiàrchiaro* io debbo istruire
questo processo. Niente di più
iniquo di questo processo. Iniquo,
perché include la più spietata
ingiustizia contro alla quale un
pover'uomo tenta disperatamente di
ribellarsi senza nessuna probabilità
di scampo. C'è una vittima qua,
che non può prendersela con
nessuno! Ha voluto, in questo
processo, prendersela con due, coi
primi due che gli sono capitati
sotto mano, e—sissignori—la
giustizia deve dargli torto, torto,
torto, senza remissione, ribadendo
cosi, ferocemente, l'iniquità di cui
questo pover'uomo è vittima.

IV

D'ANDREA. Ma si, carina!...Ma
voi sapete: è molto più facile fare
il male che il bene.

V

*Rosario Chiàrchiaro s'è
combinata una facciada jettatore che
è una meraviglia a vedere. S'è
lasciato crescere su le cave gote gialle
una barbaccia ispida e cespugliuta;
s'è insellato sul naso un pajo di grossi
occhiali cerchiati d'osso che gli danno
l'aspetto d'un barbagianni; ha poi
indossato un abito lustro, sorcigno,
che gli sgonfia da tutte le parti, e
tiene una canna d'India in mano
col manico di corno. Entra a passo
di marcia funebre, battendo a terra
la canna ad ogni passo, e si para
davanti al giudice....* CHIARCHAIRO
*(senza somporsi minimamente allo
scatto del giudice, digrigna i denti
gialli e dice sottovoce);* Lei dunque
non ci crede?

III

It was truly unjust, that case: unjust because it included an impious injustice against which a poor man was desperately trying to rebel, but without any hope of escape. There was in this case a victim who couldn't lay the blame on anyone. He had intended to blame two men, in this case, the first two he had happened to fall upon, and— yes gentlemen— justice had to judge him wrong, wrong, wrong, without remission, thus corroborating, fiercely, the injustice of which this poor man was the victim.

IV

Alas, it is really true that it is much easier to do harm than good.

V

Chiàrchiaro had made himself up into a *jettatore* that was a wonder to see. He had grown on his hollow yellow cheeks a shaggy, bushy beard; he had saddled his nose with a pair of huge glasses encircled with bone which made him look like a swan, and he had put on a shiny, mouse-colored suit that flattened him out everywhere.

At the judge's outburst, he did not lose his composure. He flared his nostrils, ground his yellow teeth, and said *sottovoce*, "So you don't believe in it?"

III

Here it is, gentlemen. *He takes from the desk the file of the Chiàrchiaro case.* I have to prepare this case for trial. Nothing more unjust than this case. Unjust because it includes the most merciless unfairness against which a poor man is desperately trying to rebel, but with no probability of escape. There is a victim here who can't lay the blame on anyone! He intended, in this case, to blame two men, the first two he happened to fall upon and— yes, gentlemen—justice must judge him wrong, wrong, wrong, without remission, thus fiercely corroborating the injustice of which this poor man is the victim.

IV

D'ANDREA Of course, my dear!. . . But you know, it is much easier to do harm than good.

V

Rosario Chiàrchiaro has made himself up into a jettatore *that is a wonder to see. He has grown on his hollow yellow cheeks a shaggy, bushy beard; he has saddled his nose with a pair of huge glasses encircled with bone which make him look like a barn owl, he has put on a shiny, mouse-colored suit that flattens him out everywhere, and he holds in his hand a bamboo cane with a horn handle. He enters at a funeral march, beating the cane on the gound at each step, and he presents himself before the judge . . .*
CHIARCHIARO (*without in the least losing his composure at the judge's outburst, grinds his yellow teeth and says* sottovoce: "So you don't believe in it?"

VI

E il giudice D'Andrea infrontò
gl'indici delle mani per significare
che le due vie gli parevano opposte.
　Il Chiàrchiaro si chinò e tra i
due indici cosi infrontati del
giudice ne inserì uno suo, tozzo,
peloso e non molto pulito.

VI

D'ANDREA. . .Già l'una e l'altra,
scusate, sono tra loro cosi.
*Infronta gl'indici delle due mani
per significare che le due vie gli
sembrano in contrasto.*
CHIARCHIARO Nossignore. Pare a
lei, signor giudice.

VII

E ansimando, protese il braccio,
battè forte sul pavimento la canna
d'India e rimase un pezzo
impostato in quell'atteggiamento
grottescamente imperioso.
—La patente?
　Il Chiàrchiaro protese di nuovo
il braccio, battè la canna d'India
sul pavimento e, portandosi l'altra
mano al petto, ripetè con tragica
solennità:
—La patente.

VII

D'ANDREA (*alzandosi*) La patente?
CHIARCHIARO (*impostandosi
grottescamente e battendo la
canna.*) La patente, sissignore!

VI

And Judge D'Andrea crossed his index fingers to signify that the two ways seemed opposed to him.
Chiàrchiaro bent down and between the judge's two crossed fingers inserted one of his, stumpy, hairy, and not very clean.

VI

D'ANDREA ... The two ways, excuse me, are to each other like this. *He crosses his index fingers to signify that the two ways seem opposed to him.*
CHIARCHIARO No, sir. It seems so to you, your honor.

VII

And gasping, he extended his arm, beat the bamboo cane hard on the floor, and stayed for a while fixed in that grotesquely imperious attitude.
"The license?"
Chiàrchiaro again extended his arm, struck the bamboo cane on the floor and, lifting his other hand to his chest, repeated with tragic solemnity, "The license."

VII

"The license?"
CHIARCHIARO (posing grotesquely and beating the cane) "Yes sir, the license!"

The above text is taken from Luigi Pirandello's *La Patente* (*The License*), the novella of 1911 and the one-act play of 1918, and represents one of several such adaptations at the hands of the Sicilian. Unlike many writers who have tended to abandon one genre to assume another, Pirandello, although in his maturity heavily involved with the theater, continued to write stories. A master of both the epic and dramatic modes, but perhaps never completely satisfied with either, Pirandello has provided critics interested in the comparison of genres with a number of test cases.[3]

What interests me in Pirandello's work in both genres (and indeed in some of the theoretical works such as the preface to "Six Characters") is the dialogic tension between modes of narrating. Thus if one can speak of a "theatrical vocation" in novelle written almost entirely in dialogue such as "The Man with the Flower in his Mouth", it is also possible to discern what might be called a nostalgia for narration in the many literary stage directions in the plays, often taken word for word from the story on which they are based, or in characters such as the Father in "Six Characters" who seem obsessed with a monologic desire to control the telling of the story by their own narratives. The Father's soliloquies prompt his antagonist the Stepdaughter to scream the words cited above as epigraph "Qui non si narra!"—No narrating here! (i.e. on stage). But dramatic characters *do* narrate, thus raising the problem of point of view in the dramatic text. I have argued elsewhere, in regard to *Six Characters*, that the distinction made by Gérard Genette between *qui parle?* and *qui voit?* (not necessarily the same person) in his discussion of point of view in narrative fiction may be applied to the dramatic text as well.[4] In performance, the two types of point of view may even be taken more literally, since it necessarily becomes clear which character is speaking and which one is watching, whether or not they are the same person.

Although a possible or actual, mental or physical performance can probably never be entirely excluded from the analysis of dramatic texts, we would do well to acknowledge that these texts are also *read* and that it is legitimate to speak of a reader as well as (or instead of) a spectator when dealing with drama. Thus a third question on point of view may be added: *qui lit?* To the reader (who may also be a director or an actor) reading a play, the *didascaliae* (everything in the written text except the dialogue) may appear to contain a narrative voice identical to that of an "epic" narrator.[5] For the spectator, on the other hand, this voice is silent, or semiotically represented by gestures, props, scenery, etc. Here I wish to concentrate on the *written* dramatic text and the problems of narration and point of view as they appear in both the short story and one-act play versions of *La Patente*. Arguing that the mimetic and diegetic modes are crucial to both forms, I hope to illustrate a permeablility or elasticity in the barriers between genres. I shall also attempt to demonstrate that the texts in question may be read as metanarratives about one of Pirandello's central preoccupations, the self-reflective question of how to tell a story.

A basic plot line—a very Sicilian one—is common to both story and play, although the latter has added elements. D'Andrea, a judge, meditates on a difficult case. A man named Rosario Chiàrchiaro, reputedly a *jettatore* (one who possesses the evil eye; a jinx), has instigated a libel suit against two men in his town (in the play, one is the mayor's son). The complaint? They have reacted publicly with the usual exorcisms as he passed by: the sign of horns, touching an amulet, etc. The judge reasons that, although the poor man is innocent, he will lose the case because his adversaries can hardly be condemned for reacting to him in the same manner as everyone else in town, including his fellow judges. He thus summons the man himself, hoping to convince him that the suit can only be harmful to him. In the story, the narrator warns the reader of possible problems with D'Andrea's intentions by pronouncing the theme: "It is easier to do harm than good" (see IV above). In the play, Chiàrchiaro's daughter Rosinella comes to see the judge when she learns that he has summoned her father, and describes the family's past and present miseries. D'Andrea tells her that he wants to help, not hurt, but pronounces the same axiom. When Chiàrchiaro enters D' Andrea's office, the judge is shocked to see him sporting a beard and dressed in a manner that confirms his image as a stereotypical *jettatore*. The judge crosses his index fingers to show that the libel suit and Chiàrchiaro's appearance are working in opposition to each other. Chiàrchiaro, however, undertakes to demonstrate that the judge's attempts to help and befriend him make the judge his "worst enemy." If he loses the libel suit, he will become in the eyes of the townspeople an officially sanctioned *jettatore*. The negative decision will thus in effect grant him a "license" analogous to the judge's diploma. As a "licensed" conveyer of the evil eye, the unemployed Chiàrchiaro will be able to earn his living by collecting fees from the townspeople for staying away from their places of business. Judge D'Andrea, reduced to silence by this controversion of his liberal, rational, humanistic sentiments, can only utter "La patente?" ("the license?") to which Chiàrchiaro responds, triumphantly, "La patente." The story ends here, but the play has a final scene. A bird cage containing D' Andrea's pet goldfinch, "as if moved by the wind" (617) falls to the ground, killing the bird. Three judges and D'Andrea's clerk Marranca (characters in the play but not the story) enter, asking what has happened. D'Andrea is only able to respond, "The wind...the window...the goldfinch..." but Chiàrchiaro explains that it was he, not the wind, and that with his powers he can make them all die. The judges, convinced by the demonstration, offer him money, and the *jettatore* exclaims, "I am rich!"

Represented in both the play and the story is the struggle of a fundamentally diegetic or epic mode with a fundamentally mimetic or dramatic mode, ending with the triumph of the latter. The problem then becomes how to represent the two modes in the form of either story or play. The key lies in Pirandello's characterization of his two antagonists, one—the introspective D'Andrea—who is fundamentally a "narrative" character and the other—the flamboyant Chiàrchiaro— who is fundamentally a "dramatic" character.

The first half of the novella is dominated by the narrator's "voice" and D'Andrea's "view"[6] while the second half, almost entirely in dialogue, is dominated by Chiàrchiaro's voice and view. In the introduction the narrator describes Judge D'Andrea in relation to the racial mixture of his Sicilian ancestors—for example his "Negro hair"—telling the reader that it is "necessary to imagine" the "monstrous" interweaving of races over the centuries in order to understand the "human product" that is D'Andrea. The narrator characterizes the judge with two paradoxes, each of which contains a physical and a moral term: the judge has poor vision but deep moral insight; his thin, bowlegged body is deformed but his sense of rectitude is irreproachable. The reader thus envisages the judge both in a certain historical perspective and as a subjective, reflective personality. An insomniac and a thinker, he has the habit of gazing at stars and thinking long into the night. In the second didascalia of the play, the narrator's voice tells us simply that he is "thinking"—a direction rather difficult to render exactly in performance (see I).

In the play, Pirandello attempts, not entirely successfully, to convey the judge's reflective, inward nature through the theatrical sign of the pet bird. It is to the bird that the judge pronounces a kind of prologue to the action—"let me administer justice to these poor little fierce men"—perhaps an echo of the last lines of *Paradiso* XXII in which Dante gazes down from heaven at the insignificant earth, termed "l'aiuola che ci fa tanto feroci" ("the flowerbed that makes us so fierce (ravenous).") In the story, these words (as if from "on high") are conveyed through the narrator's voice but D'Andrea's view ("it seemed to the judge", II above). Almost immediately after the "prologue" in the play, the three judges tease D'Andrea about his "childish" pet bird, but he tells them that it is "the only remaining memento of my [recently deceased] mother" (610) and that he speaks to it in its own language. The relationship between judge and bird thus suggests a regressive imitation of pre-Oedipal babble between mother and child. (It might also echo the relationship between mother and child in *Paradiso* XXIII. See Maristella de Panizza Lorch's essay in this volume.) Thus the bird, like the descriptions in the story, but less fully, suggests the judge's interior, private life: both its reflective, moral aspect and its emotional, pre-verbal one. It is this rational and instinctive monological "I" that perceives a problem in the *jettatore*'s suit, pities the poor fellow, and decides to help him.

D'Andrea's moral sentiments about the "poor victim" along with his intellectual rebellion against a system of justice that must condemn the innocent in the case before him are conveyed in the story by indirect discourse and in the play by a speech he makes to the three judges during the scene in which he tells them about the bird (III above). The repetition "torto torto torto" (wrong, wrong, wrong), echoing an earlier reference to his gasping for breath ("aria aria aria"—"air, air, air"), evokes the judge's emotional reaction while the adverb "ferocement" ("fiercely") suggests the Dantean reference produced by his nocturnal (or bird directed) reflections. The reader's sympathies lie with D'Andrea. In both the play and the story it is his voice and view, in this first part, that command our perception of the matter at hand.

Another way of looking at D'Andrea is to see him as a parallel to the "author" before whom the "characters" appear in the various narratives from which *Six Characters in Search of an Author* emerged.[7] Thus D'Andrea is *writing* at his desk when Chiàrchiaro arrives but throws his papers in the air when he sees him, thereby suggesting that the new dramatic "character" will not fit into his own narrative. Indeed, Chiàrchiaro's initial *appearance* states his non-conformity to the judge's previously articulated notion of his motivations. In the novella, the *jettatore*'s theatrical posing and costuming are described through the narrator's voice and D'Andrea's view ("a wonder to see"). In the play, they are conveyed by the narratorial voice in the didascaliae, with the addition of a description of the character's manner of entrance to the step of a funeral march (See V above). Certain descriptions taken directly from the novella, in particular "he grinds his yellow teeth," would be impossible to realize effectively in production. With Chiàrchiaro's first words in both play and story, "So you don't believe in it?" the voice becomes his but the view remains D'Andrea's with whom the reader shares surprise and shock at this highly theatrical apparition. As if exteriorizing his inner musings, D'Andrea crosses his index fingers— a *theatrical* sign that may also suggest that he, too, if unconsciously, is exorcizing the evil eye. In the story Chiàrchiaro counters the sign by inserting his own finger in the judge's cross—a *theatrical* gesture—and in the play he does so with the words "Pare a lei, signor giudice" "It seems so to you, your honor"—a questioning of *narrative* point of view (see VI above). In any case, here lies the crux of the common plot, for here the tables begin to turn. The judge's small gesture can hardly compete with the consummate theatricality of the tossing of the head, the beating of the cane, the posing, and, in the play, the miming of the "licensed" *jettatore*'s future plans. (See VII above).

The narrative voice with its monological point of view that has dominated the discourse in play as well as story becomes at this point displaced by the theatrical creation: telling gives way to showing and reflection to illusion. Once Chiàrchiaro has explained *his* point of view on the case, D'Andrea literally as well as literarily loses his voice. In the play, the narrator in the didascalia informs us: "D'Andrea, compreso di profonda pietà, è rimasto veramente come balordo a mirarlo" ("D'Andrea, overcome by deep pity, has become as if stupified watching him"—617). In the story, he tries to speak, but "la voce non volle venir fuori" ("his voice wouldn't come out"—576), and he can only embrace the man he hoped to help. The pose that Chiàrchiaro assumes is described by the narrator in both story and play as "grotesquely imperious" (see VII above). The oxymoron reveals the desperate "loser wins" logic of the marginalized victim turned actor. More cognizant of human nature than the idealistic judge, the outsider understands the necessity of privileging *Schein* over *Sein*. (A few years later, Mussolini would successfully impose a grotesque-imperious mode over a humanistic-rational one in Italian politics.) The final words of the story—"La

Patente!'' pronounced by Chiàrchiaro confirm the replacement of the diegetic by the mimetic mode of the triumph of theatricality over both rational discourse and individual compassion. The outcome prefigures the loss of control that Pirandello in his author persona will experience with theatrical ''characters'' (see the preface to *Six Characters*) as well as his increasing preoccupation with the elusiveness of ''reality'' and the necessity of illusion.

The play's final scene, almost an epilogue, in which the *jettatore* gives the illusion of using his powers to kill the judge's pet bird, is, perhaps, anticlimactic but it does underline the outcome of the conflict. Whether or not Chiàrchiaro really possesses the evil eye is not at point: he must *seem* to have it. It is this power of illusion that destroys the bird, the sign of D'Andrea's interior life. D'Andrea's attempt at explanation, which he is unable to formulate in a coherent sentence, ''Il vento...la vetrata...il cardellino'' (''The wind...the window ...the goldfinch''—617), is to no effect before the *jettatore*'s ''demonstration'' and triumphant confirmation, ''Ma che vento! Che vetrata! Sono stato io''' (''What wind? What window? It was I!''—617).

In both novella and play we have, then, a tension between diegesis and mimesis in which the inner ''truth'' value attributed to the former is displaced by the exterior illusion as means of social survival ascribed to the latter. In neither version does anything really ''happen'' in the present: rather it is a question of the reader's being informed of prior events by the voice of the narrator and of D'Andrea, and of Chiàrchiaro's bizarre demonstration of his future vocation. Even the play's final *coup de théâtre* is a revelation of a decision already taken. The effect of the *jettatore*'s decision to pursue the license depends on the reader's having previously adopted the point of view of the judge. Thus functions normally attributed to the diegetic mode—description, narration, and what I have called view and voice contribute to the dramatic as well as to the novelistic test.[8] Mimetic functions such as gesture, mime, costume, and dramatic monologue, however, also contribute to the resolution of the story as well as to that of the play. Thus in both texts one may speak of a permeability of genre, or of modes within genre. The two texts are also on one level metanarratives in that they pose the questions of whose story and what story will be told as well as of the relations between author, character, and reader. The struggle between the mimetic and diegetic modes, as well as that between the two characters that embody them, represents not only the painful liberation

124 MARY ANN FRESE WITT

of a dramatic "character" from a narrative "author" but also a struggle
for the consensus of the reader.

North Carolina State University

NOTES

1. Luigi Pirandello, "La Patente" ("The License"), in *Novelle per un anno*, vol. I,
   Milan: Mondadori, 1985, p. 567. All references to this novella in the text will be
   from this edition. All translations are mine.
2. Luigi Pirandello, "La Patente" ("The License") in *Opere di Luigi Pirandello* vol.
   5, Milan: Mondadori, 1981, p. 607. All references to this play in the text will be
   from this edition. All translations are mine.
3. The comparison has certainly not gone unnoticed in Pirandello criticism, but such
   studies tend either to demonstrate how the dialogue in Pirandello's short stories
   evidences his "dramatic vocation", or to show how he successfully adapted one
   genre to the requirements of the other, or to argue that one form of a particular
   plot is more successful than the other. See for example Ulrich Leo, "Luigi Pirandello
   zwischen zwei literarischen Gattungen, *Romanistisches Jahrbuch*, XIV (1963),
   133–169; Nino De Bella, *Narrativa e teatro nell'arte di Luigi Pirandello*, Messina,
   1962. The essay by Olga Ragusa, "Pirandello's *La Patente:* Play and Story," in
   Olga Ragusa, *Narrative and Drama: Essays in Modern Italian Literature from Verga
   to Pasolini,* The Hague: Mouton, 1976, analyzes in some detail differences between
   play and story and argues for the importance of "La Patente" in the context in
   Pirandello's entire work.
4. "Six Characters in Search of an Author and the Battle of the Lexis", *Modern Drama*,
   September 1987, pp 396–404. Genette's discussion appears in *Nouveau discours
   du récit*, Paris: Seuil, 1983, and is taken up by Cesare Segre in "Punto di vista
   e polifonia nell'analisi narratologica", *Teatro e romanzo: Due tipi di communicazione
   letteraria,* Torino: Einaudi, pp 86–101. Neither apply the notion to the analysis
   of drama.
5. For a discussion of the narrative function of *didascaliae* see Michael Issacharoff,
   "Texte théatral et didascalecture," *Le Spectacle du discours,* Paris: Corti, 1985,
   pp 25–40. I differ from him here in that I postulate a *narrator's* voice, rather than
   the *author's* voice in the didascaliae.
6. I will use "voice" and "view" as the equivalent of Genette's division of point of
   view into "qui parle?" and "qui voit?"
7. This is suggested by Olga Ragusa in "Pirandello's *La Patente.*"
8. The questions of "narration" and "point of view" in drama raise important
   theoretical questions that have not yet been resolved. Is the dramatic "world" to
   be distinguished from the epic one, as Keir Elam states, in that the former is observed
   in the present and in the making "without narratorial mediation" (*The Semiotics
   of Theatre and Drama,* London: Methuen, 1980, p.111) whereas the latter is

recounted by a narrator in the past? Or can a narratorial voice be discerned in *written* drama in the *didascaliae* and other elements that contribute to the reader's, as opposed to the spectator's, reception of the dramatic text? Finally, even limited to dialogue, is it legitimate to speak either of "point of view," or of what Peter Szondi, in *The Theory of Modern Drama* (trans. Michael Hays, Minneapolis: University of Minnesota Press, 1987) calls an "epic I" in drama? I would argue that the "world" of the dramatic text is not clearly separate from other fictional worlds.

PART THREE
Appearing Texts

Sartre's *La Nausée* and the
Aesthetics of Pure Perception

W. WOLFGANG HOLDHEIM

> Vous dotez le ciel de l'art d'on ne sait quel
> rayon macabre. Vous créez un frisson
> nouveau.
>
> Victor Hugo à Charles Baudelaire,
> le 6 octobre 1859

Jean-Paul Sartre's early novel *La Naus*ée (1938) is particularly rich in poignant, virtuoso episodes that could be included in anthologies of prose writing. The best known of these is the protagonist Antoine Roquentin's nauseating confrontation with the root of a chestnut tree in the *jardin public,* an "extraordinaire passage" in Georges Poulet's words), "peut-être le plus celèbre dans la littérature contemporaine, avec celui de la madeleine de Proust" ("extraordinary passage, perhaps the most famous one in contemporary literature, together with the one of Proust's madeleine").[1] The statement is justified, and yet the careful reader (at least this particular reader) cannot quite ascribe the passage's undisputed prominence entirely to its literary value. Roquentin's Sunday walk is more brilliant as a piece of writing; so is his visit to the Bouville museum; as for his remarkable rumination on the Cartesian *cogito ergo sum,* it is more original in execution and probably richer in its philosophical implications. No doubt the public garden scene has moved to the foreground for thematic reasons: it has been widely perceived as the

129

focus of the young Sartre's philosophical preoccupations and of the message of his book.

There are reasons for this reaction. First of all there is the novel's title, although this may be misleading, since the title was chosen by the publisher who had rejected the author's original suggestion; the publisher's choice, of course, reflects his own perception, and perhaps even more his expectation of a positive impact on a reading public that had been suitably pre-nauseated by Céline. Secondly, we have been influenced by what we know about the actual elaboration of the book: its original inspiration was a projected "factum" (a meditation) on contingency which was then progressively narrativized over the years.[2] But the prime reason is the pre-eminent status of the episode in the finished product. Occurring late in the diaristic novel, it is nevertheless prepared from the very outset. The early entries set the theme: Roquentin encounters objects (a pebble, a door knob, an acquaintance's face and hand, a khmer statuette, a glass of beer, a piece of paper) that have somehow changed their nature, are losing their familiar meanings, increasingly impose themselves in a mode of sheer objectality.[3] Roquentin, registering their modifications in a mood of disgust or even nausea, tries to understand his bizarre experiences. His obsession reaches crisis proportions when his own face, viewed in a mirror, seems to lose its human characteristics (30–31). This dehumanizing defamiliarization is highlighted by stylistic feats of surrealistic metamorphosis. The protagonist panics when he feels that objects lose their identity and might at any moment turn into anything at all (112–14). The next stage comes when he realizes that he himself exists in the same gratuitous way as the objects (122), and his key crisis overcomes him when he grasps the fact of his own contingency (172–74). He flees by jumping into a streetcar, where he has to face a bench that loses its identity before his very eyes (177–78). He runs into the public garden, where his nausea (together with his education) culminates in the crucial confrontation with the tree (178–91).

Here, in short, is the message that emerges from those pages: "...L'existence s'était soudain dévoilée" ("existence had suddenly unveiled itself") (180), writes Roquentin; "...j'avais trouvé la clef de l'Existence, la clef de mes Nausées, de ma propre vie" ("I had found the key to Existence, the key to my attacks of Nausea, to my own life") (182). The lesson of his personal experience claims universal validity. "L'essentiel c'est la contingence" ("the essential thing is contingency")

(185): Nausea reveals the utter gratuity of existents, of existence. Objects (the tree root, for example) are simply there, without rhyme or reason: "le monde des explications et des raisons n'est pas celui de l'existence" ("the world of explanations and reasons is not the world of existence") (183). The obscenely nude, unmitigated existence of things cannot be exorcised by any function: "La fonction n'expliquait rien. . . .Cette racine, avec sa couleur, sa forme, son mouvement figé, était. . .au-dessous de toute explication" ("function explained nothing. . .This root, with its color, its form, its arrested movement, was. . .beneath any explanation") (183). Nor can existents be placed in any meaningful context: "*De trop:* c'était le seul rapport que je posse établir entre ces arbres, ces grilles, ces cailloux. . .Chacun d'eux s'échappait des relations où je cherchais à l'enfermer, s'isolait, débordait" ("*Superfluous*: that was the only relationship I could establish between those trees, those gratings, those pebbles. . . .Each of them escaped from the relationships in which I tried to enclose it, isolated itself, went beyond" (181). Furthermore, objects can no longer be fixated by verbal determinations; they are unnameable, outside of language: "Je ne me rappelais plus que c'était une racine. Les mots s'étaient évanouis et, avec eux, la signification des choses, leurs modes d'emploi" ("I no longer remembered that this was a root. The words had faded away and, with them, the meaning of the things, their uses") (179). The result is that "la diversité des choses, leur individualité n'était qu'une apparence, un vernis" ("the diversity of things, their individuality was only an appearance, nothing but veneer") (180); things on the level of pure thereness are bound to lose any well-defined identity. And their sheer presence is at every instant a sheer present; there can be no transitions, no real process of becoming: ". . .le monde était partout présent, devant, derriére. Il n'y avait rien eu *avant* lui" (". . .the world was present everywhere, in front, behind. There had been nothing *before* it") (190). Finally I myself, supposedly a consciousness, exist on the same level of contingency, and there is no difference between the "subject" and the object: "Nous étions un tas d'existants gênés, embarrassés de nous-mêmes, nous n'avions pas la moindre raison d'être là, ni les uns ni les autres. . ." ("We were all of us a heap of clumsy existents, useless to ourselves, we didn't have the slightest reason to be there, any of us. . ." (181). Roquentin has become one with his Nausea (179), has at last realized that he also is *de trop*. He has acceded to a philosophy of the absurd (182).

I have just restated an argument that is by now quite familiar, as it should be; after all, it has been repeated by virtually every critic with minor variations. The critics have based themselves on the indisputable and seemingly unambiguous evidence of the text. Indeed this reading is but barely an interpretation, for Roquentin/Sartre has already done the interpreting on his own. In fact the scene in the public garden, as the quotations above should indicate, is largely and surprisingly discursive.

Surprisingly, for there is a strange disparity here. The scene is supposed to present an irrational or extra-rational state of mind, a kind of mystic vision—immediate, irresistible, and beyond words. This lyrical evocation, however, tends at every moment to turn into a highly verbose discourse that drives home the situation's philosophical significance. The narrator, for that matter, seems to be aware of the contradiction. Emphasizing that he writes in retrospect (at 6 p.m. of that day), he notes on two occasions that it is only his temporal distance that enables him to formulate:

> Le mot d'Absurdité naît à présent sous ma plume; tout à l'heure, au jardin, je ne l'ai pas trouvé, mais je ne le cherchais pas non plus, je n'en avais pas besoin...(182)

> A vrai dire, je ne me formulais pas mes découvertes. Mais je crois qu'à présent, il me serait facile de les mettre en mots. (185)

> The word Absurdity presents itself, as I am writing; earlier, in the garden, I did not find it, nor did I look for it, I did not need it then....

> Frankly, I did not formulate my discoveries to myself. But I believe that now I would find it easy to put them in words.

Both sentences sound almost like (somewhat clumsy) apologies, especially since both are followed by particularly lengthy philosophical disquisitions: on absolute (as opposed to merely relative) absurdity in one case, on contingency in the other. The reader still feels that extra-rational experience is paradoxically presented in the form of philosophical ratiocination. It is understandable that an early critic objected that Sartre's novel, subordinating literary to philosophic inspirations, has too much of a *roman a thèse*.[4]

Understandable but not quite correct. It is undoubtedly an artistic flaw that such an impression is created, but matters are more complex at second sight. Why indeed should Sartre in the late 1930s propagate a philosophy of the absurd? We may assume with some plausibility that Roquentin's philosophical generalizations do correspond, more or less, to the notes on contingency which the young Sartre took with him when he went to Berlin on a scholarship in 1933. But in Berlin, and thereafter, his philosophical development moved in a different direction. It is not certain that he was familiar with Heidegger (who was to loom large in *L'Etre et le Néant* in 1943) by the time he gave its final form to *La Nausée*,[5] but it is sure that Roquentin's ratiocinations could not (or no longer) have reflected his philosophical convictions even then. Yet it seems to be widely believed that they did. Sartre grappled with Husserl's phenomenology throughout the 1930s, and it has become almost a cliché that Roquentin's confrontation with pure objects is somehow "phenomenological" in nature. Nothing could be further from the truth. True, Sartre himself has contributed to such a view in two studies written during the early 1940s. In "Une Idée fondamentale de la phénoménologie de HUSSERL: *L'Intentionnalité*," he stresses the phenomenological thesis about the outer-directedness of consciousness, in contrast to all psychologistic conceptions of interiority.[6] And in a lengthy and well-known study about the poet Francis Ponge, "L''Homme et les choses," Sartre states that Ponge's *chosisme* applies the basic axiom of phenomenology: "zurück zu den Sachen" ("back to the things").[7] It is dangerous, however, to overinterpret such passing remarks: the latter is a scanty ad hoc statement, the former a polemical oversimplification in a brief essay that reads like an anti-Proustian manifesto. Consciousness, in the perspective of phenomenology, is certainly not outer-directed in the sense that it dissolves into the object, taking intentionality with it; the study of intentionality always remains a "study of correlation," a parallel investigation of the act of cognition and its object. Nor is that object ever perceived as a sheer existing thing: on the contrary, its *existence* is precisely what the phenomenologist brackets, treating the object as a pure phenomenon posited by consciousness. And finally, that object is not even necessarily a "thing"; in the exhortation "zurück zu den Sachen," the word "Sache" (like *res* in Latin) has a broader meaning: it can refer to a question or an issue. What the Husserlian imperative demands is a concentration on the objects and issues to be clarified, freed not from meaningful referential and linguistic contexts but from obscurantist sedimentations and conventional clichés.[8] Roman Ingarden, a leading exponent of classical phenomenology, attacks the epistemological presuppositions of "naive-empirical" or "positivistic realism," which believe that we can have commerce only with objects that are real and that we find ready-made, so that we merely have to gape at them. Above all, the assumption that sensory perception may be not an activity but just a matter of passive gaping is opposed to the phenomenological theory of knowledge.[9] Roquentin's public garden experience, viewed through phenomenological eyes, would (if anything) be a narrative enactment of naive-empirical realism—its *reductio ad absurdum*, as it were.

In the context of the novel, however, a different interpretation imposes itself. During the 1930s, Sartre was preoccupied with the problem of the Cartesian *cogito*. This concern found expression in the important *cogito* episode in *La Nausée,* where the proposition "I think, therefore I am" disintegrates in a nightmarish interior monologue.[10] Roquentin's vision in the public garden, on the other hand, is a *cogito* turned inside out. Descartes descends into the depth of selfhood; Roquentin gapes at sheer otherness, to the point of self-annihilation. Descartes grasps existence through the evidence of a spiritual, transcendental *res cogitans* and proceeds to establish the existence of the *res extensae;* Roquentin, in a contrary movement, must first yield to the "aveuglante évidence" ("blinding evidence") (173) of the existence of a purely material and contingent *res extensa* (an evidence that is less a clear and simple idea than a clear and simple sensation), and is thereafter led to extend its mode of existence to the subject (himself) as well. His vision is an *anti-cogito,* and stands in a contrapuntal relation to the earlier rumination, which was a parodistic enactment of the *cogito.* We have on one hand a parody, on the other a reversal of the founding act of modern philosophy, which placed subjectivity and consciousness into the very center of being and knowledge. Discussing the *cogito* scene, I have demonstrated elsewhere that both ego and consciousness refuse to be supplanted and end up by rebounding with a vengeance.[11] One might keep this in mind in evaluating the public garden episode.

It seems clear that Roquentin's philosophical elucubrations, even where they look too didactic for comfort, cannot simply be equated with a thesis propounded by the author. In fact the contrapuntal interplay between the two crisis scenes is distinctly a literary procedure. It behooves us to adopt a less purely philosophical perspective and to view the public garden episode in the context of modern literature.

In the literary tradition, we find another (somewhat earlier) narrative treatment of contingency. I am referring to André Gide's *Paludes*, the first of that author's three *soties* (parodistically self-conscious novels or anti-novels).[12] "Treatise on Contingency" was the subtitle in the first edition of the book; "*dic cur hic*" ("say why here") remains its burlesque epigraph; and the protagonist at one point discusses contingency with a philosopher who, having a vested professional interest in necessary relations, denies that such a thing exists.[13] *Paludes,* like *La Nausée,* is a narrative in diary form, written in the first person singular by a writer-protagonist (we may call him André) who leads an empty and humdrum life which he experiences as absurd. Like Roquentin, he hankers for adventure and spends much time preparing for privileged moments that fail to materialize. There is even an important garden scene, set in the Jardin des Plantes in Paris, though what is here emphasized is the artificiality of the park's seeming naturalness:

> Grâce à des surveillances continuelles ces bassins ne sont pas soignés; de l'eau coulant sans bruit les alimente. Il y pousse les plantes qu'on y laisse pousser; il y nage beaucoup d'insectes. (*Pal.*, 35)

> Thanks to continual care, these basins appear uncared-for; they are nourished by soundlessly flowing water. The plants that grow there are those that are allowed to grow; many insects swim around.

The hero's calm contemplation of this deliberately orchestrated disorder, which (to be sure) *seems* a far cry from Roquentin's irresistible merger with an unadulterated natural object, inspires him to write his book, *Paludes*. That ongoing creation, as carefully excogitated as the basins, is set in the tradition of pastoral, with the sedentary Virgilian character Tityrus as its protagonist. André conceives Tityrus as a lonely fisherman surrounded by swamps (note that *La Nausée* is set in a place called Bouville, "Mudtown"), and the disconsolate monotony of his paludal landscape is meant to be the symbolic expression of André's life.[14]

As the projection of a mood, André's *Paludes* is lyrical in inspiration. Considering the nature of the mood, this is a kind of lyricism in reverse: *Paludes* is the counter-idyll of boredom, the expression of the contingent and the absurd. It is the perfect embodiment of a negative mood (as it were) that has been brilliantly described in paragraph 29 of Heidegger's *Sein und Zeit:* the "sustained, monotonous and pallid moodlessness" in which *Dasein* encounters the diluted horror of everyday existence.[15]

We know that this existential condition (an antipoetic state of mind, a poetic moment reversed into negativity) has its place in the literary tradition. Under the name *ennui*, it has played an important role in romantic and postromantic literature; in a self-conscious and largely parodistic form, it makes its culminating appearance in Gide's *Paludes*.

Is Sartrean nausea simply an intensified form of *ennui*? The terminological evidence in *La Nausée* is inconclusive. Words such as *écoeurement* and *dégoût* ("loathing" and "disgust") are used in the earliest entries. There is only one reference to *ennui*, which occurs in connection with the khmer statuette. The term "nausea" appears for the first time when Roquentin, recalling his experience with the pebble, describes it as "une sorte de nausée dans les mains" ("a kind of nausea in my hands") (22). But soon thereafter, nausea grips him with a vengeance: "je l'ai, la saleté, la nausée" ("I've got it, that dirty nausea") (32). It could possibly be argued that *ennui* is the earlier form (the experience with the khmer statue is reported ex post facto: it was actually what impelled Roquentin to break off his travels several years before), and that it gradually escalated into nausea. Or one could point out, probably with greater plausibility, that the passing remark in the statue scene ("Je m'ennuyais profondément," ["I was deeply bored"], 15) is too vague and general to be built up into romantic *ennui*. Moreover, while all those references have to do with a sense of contingency and absurdity, they are without exception expressly brought on by an unusual encounter with an object. "Ce moment fut extraordinaire" ("this moment was extraordinary"), writes Roquentin about his vision in the public garden (185). *Ennui* is more diffuse and would seem, precisely, to exclude the extraordinary. "Si j'insiste ainsi," . .says André as he is telling an endless and supremely boring story, "c'est pour bien vous faire comprendre à quel point cette nuit était ordinaire" ("if I insist as I do, it is to drive home just how ordinary that night was") (*Pal.*, 91).

Above all, *ennui* (a much more inclusive term than the English "boredom") is spiritual and subjective; nausea is more physical, material, outer-directed. *Ennui* stands to nausea exactly as feeling stands to sensation. In fact, sensation plays a shadowy role in *Paludes*. It is what constantly hovers in the background, what is sought without ever materializing. For contingency, in *Paludes*, is two-pronged, it can engender a dual response. Realizing the gratuity of his existence, man can fold back on himself and founder into boredom and acedia. But gratuity can also invite freedom, liberation from all constraints—social, professional, moral; it can become a challenge to sensory and sensual enjoyment of every fleeting moment, an ecstatic acknowledgment that external reality exists.[16] André, unlike Tityrus, is not content in his solipsistic staticity; he teaches restlessness, departure, dynamic contact with the outside world. But he is a sorry prophet who does not practice what he preaches. His timid efforts towards a breakthrough end in failure. When he tries to leave, he gets no farther than the suburbs. When he opens a window early in the morning to let the world flow in, this supreme gesture of openness and receptivity (Gide's famous *accueil*) does not provoke a fervent fusion of subject and object but peters out in a senseless succession of trite occurrences (*Pal.*, 95). Roquentin's ongoing quest for an adventure—for a privileged experience that is to come to him (*advenire*) without his doing, from the outside, makes him very much a successor to André.

We know that the lesson André tried to teach was to remain a Gidean preoccupation, and that *Paludes* was in effect an ironic preface to *Les Nourritures terrestres* (1897). That vitalistic paean to departure and sensation was still a veritable bible of liberation at the time when the young Sartre was writing *La Nausée*.

Like Roquentin, the narrator of *Les Nourritures terrestres* believes that the external world *exists*. What he seeks and preaches is total openness to that world as it happens to present itself.[17] The ideal is the joyful (the fervent) fusion of subject and object in a fulfilled moment— many moments—of total presence. While this contact takes place through all the senses, its privileged medium (or rather the medium that stands for all sensory perception) is the eye. "Regardons tout avec une égale insistance . . . Regardons! Regardons!" ("Let's look at everything with equal insistence . . . Let's look! Let's look!")—already André had exclaimed in the open widow episode (*Pal.*, 95). In the *Nourritures,* the ecstatic glance that takes *in* reality expresses the power of lived experience: "Que *l'importance* soit dans ton regard, non dans la chose regardée" ("Let the *importance* be in your look, not in the thing looked at").[18] Total presence is also total presentness, rejecting memory and expectation, excluding the other dimensions of time. Succession, therefore, is no longer a process of becoming but a juxtaposition of presents, a cumulative addition of privileged instants. Yet we find that there is an unexpected development in the *Nourritures*. The subject, all too passive, is invaded by the world, flooded and overwhelmed by the objects, finally to the point of depersonalization and disintegration.

"Que ton oeil soit la chose regardée" ("let your eye be the thing looked at") (*Nourritures*, 47), we suddenly read: the displacement towards the object is palpable. So is the movement away from fervor, until we end up with a hankering for unconsciousness, reification—a veritable flight from intentionality: "Abandon à l'oubli des vagues; volupté du renoncement; être une chose" ("Abandonment to the oblivion of the waves; pleasure of letting go; to be a thing") (*Nourritures*, 150). Paradoxically, Gide's cult of sensation opens up toward a *chosisme* of its own.

There are other parallels between *Les Nourritures* and *La Nausée,* striking precisely because they go together with a difference in tone and spirit that could hardly be more radical. Thus in Roquentin's central experience as well, eyesight is increasingly important. Already the Indochinese work of art becomes vaguely disquieting when Roquentin looks at it intensely: "Je fixais une petite statue khmer...La statue me parut désagréable et stupide..." ("I looked fixedly at a khmer statuette ...The statue seemed disagreeable and stupid to me...") (14–15). Later, a glass of beer turns into a veritable threat: "...Voilà une demi-heure que j'évite de *regarder* ce verre de bière" ("...for half an hour now I have been avoiding to *look* at that glass of beer"), writes Sartre's protagonist (19, his emphasis), finally deciding to exorcise the menace through an exact but banalizing visual description. Later his face, viewed in a mirror, becomes a nondescript "chose grise" that loses all meaning and humanity: "...J'approche mon visage de la glace jusqu'à la toucher. Les yeux, le nez et la bouche disparaissent: il ne reste plus rien d'humain" ("I bring my face close to the mirror, to the point of touching it. My eyes, my nose and my mouth disappear: there is nothing human left").[19] And the final scene with the tree is aggressively visual: "Et tout d'un coup, d'un seul coup, le voile se déchire. J'ai compris, j'ai *vu*" ("and suddenly, with one stroke, the veil tears apart. I have understood. I have *seen*.") (179). Seeing is a traditional metaphor for understanding. Here, however, the metaphor is in some way reversed: understanding is contracted into a visual "illumination" (179) that is the result of an obsessive stare.[20]

It would seem that Roquentin's defamiliarizing gaze has little in common with Gide's (or Gide's hero Menalcas') concupiscence of the eyes. And yet again there is an unexpected similarity. In *La Nausée,* defamiliarization is not distantiation, and Roquentin does not keep the object at bay. It invades him in all its strangeness and appropriates him,

until he too feels like a thing among things. This paradoxical correspondence between two seemingly dissimilar works is further strengthened
when we consider what happens to Roquentin's experience of time. In
a remarkable passage in *La Nausée* (49–50), we see the sense of temporal
processuality disintegrate under the protagonist's disgusted gaze. He
sees time as he watches an old woman walking, advancing step by step
with tantalizing slowness:

> "du train dont elle va, elle y mettra bien dix minutes, dix minutes
> pendant lesquelles je resterai comme ça, à la regarder, le front collé
> contre la vitre. Elle va s'arrêter vingt fois, repartir, s'arrêter.

> "at her speed, it will take her ten minutes, ten minutes during which
> I will stay like this to look at her, with my face against the window
> pane. She will stop twenty times, start again, then stop"

As he watches, the flow of becoming falls apart into its component
individual moments. Time is expectation, projection of the future, but
"je ne sais plus où j'en suis: est-ce que je *vois* ses gestes, est-ce que
je les *prévois*?" ("I no longer know what the story is: do I *see* her
gestures or *foresee* them?"). In the mode of sight, expecting becomes
fore-seeing, which is a variety of seeing. The future, accordingly,
becomes a particular form of present: "Je *vois* l'avenir. Il est là, posé
dans la rue, à peine plus pâle que le présent. Qu'a-t-il besoin de se
réaliser? Qu'est-ce ça lui donnera de plus?" ("I *see* the future. It is
there, sitting in the street, scarcely any paler than the present. Why
does it have to come into being? What will it gain by that?"). Before
his very eyes, movement in time thus transforms itself into a nauseating
cumulation of presentnesses. "C'est ça le temps, le temps tout nu, ça
vient lentement à l'existence, ça se fait attendre et quand ça vient, on
est écoeuré parce qu'on s'aperçoit que c'était déjà là depuis longtemps"
("That's what time it is, time in its nakedness, it slowly comes into
existence, it keeps us waiting, and when it comes, we are nauseated
because we notice that it had actually been there all along"). The
experience is recognizably (and, I believe, deliberately) anti-Proustian.
And by the time of the public garden scene, time has evolved entirely
into a juxtaposition of thing-like presences, without transitions or "temps
faibles" ("weak moments"), with every trace of processuality removed
(186-87).

In the *Nourritures* as well, time becomes a succession of present moments, but there parataxis is a cause for exultation: all instants are equally valuable, and each is experienced in its entire plenitude. In *La Nausée,* the (so to speak) qualitative result is quite the opposite: everything is irremediably *there*, nothing really comes into being; time is stale and empty; novelty itself is "du neuf terni, défloré qui ne peut jamais surprendre" ("a stale and deflowered novelty that can never create surprises") (50). Here as elsewhere, Roquentin's experience is the mirror image of Menalcas', its reversal into a negative mode. The fullness of sensation has turned into the surfeit of nausea, the exuberance of gratuity into the disgust of the *de trop*. Nausea is the intensified boredom of the extraordinary occurrence, an event (and a moment) that is no longer privileged but degraded. Roquentin is an André who, even when torn away from the everyday banality of his existence, cannot rid himself of his *ennui*.

But is he really torn away? André squarely remains a *littérateur* on the margin of life who does not follow his own teaching: "Cela m'est égal, parce que j'écris Paludes" ("I don't really care, because I am writing Paludes") (*Pal.*, 33). Not so Roquentin, it seems, who after all abandons his biography of the marquis de Rollebon, and whose major crises occur precisely after that abandonment. Unsheltered by the phony pursuit of a literary enterprise, he is forced to face the world directly— like Menalcas, who has also broken away from writing. This, at least, is the pretense. But in his practice, the putative sensualist of *Les Nourritures terrestres*, who rejects literature in theory, remains an uncommitted aesthetic dilettante, writing didactic books and (not unlike André) experimenting with carefully selected poetic moments.[21] And Roquentin, in so many ways Menalcas' photographic negative, is not any more authentic in the public garden scene. Here indeed lies the key to the discrepancy, diagnosed earlier, between his supposedly wordless experience and the didactic verbosity of his account. For he is not separated from his experience merely by the lapse of several hours: he is never totally a part of it, but always remains the detached observer who writes it down. His consciousness is never overpowered by the invasion of the subject.[22] Intentionality is never in danger of dissolving, indeed it is conspicuously shifted to the object: "Arrivé a la grille, je me suis retourné. Alors le jardin m'a souri" ("having reached the grating, I turned around. Then the garden smiled at me") (190). The garden, in fact, had smiled at him before, at the beginning of his Sunday walk (63). Another reversal: the subject is no longer assimilated to the dehumanized status of the objects; on the contrary, the natural object (supposedly a raw piece of material facticity) is now endowed with human characteristics. Who can fail to recognize the pathetic fallacy, a well-worn literary technique and a clear reminiscence of romantic poetry?[23] Roquentin has not renounced literature at all. He leaves the garden expressly to *write down* what he has experienced (191). Has he perhaps formed, or inflected, his experiences after literary models? And could that smiling garden, consciously or not, be a reminder of the "poetic thought" which inspired André in the Jardin des Plantes: "Tityre sourit" (*Pal.*, 36, 57)?

Roquentin emerges, therefore, as an artist as much as a philosopher. I must repeat that as a philosopher, he is emphatically *not* to be equated with Jean-Paul Sartre. He certainly bears little resemblance to the somewhat later Sartre, the one who wrote the study on Francis Ponge. Sartre there points out that Ponge tries to realize the old human nostalgia to exist in the mode of an *en-soi,* a self-enclosed and self-sufficient object stripped of intentionality—and makes it very clear that this is impossible.[24] Surely the stricture must apply to Roquentin as well. Elsewhere in the same essay ("L'Homme et les choses," 257–58), Sartre specifically refers to the Heideggerian analysis of *Vorhandenheit,* which is indeed the authoritative response to *chosisme* of any kind.

Zuhandenheit ("instrumentality," "availability" or possibly, "serviceability") is the mode, according to Heidegger, in which we primarily encounter entities in the world. They present themselves as objects endowed with meaning, ready to serve a certain purpose. *Vorhandenheit* (the fact that they are there, their sheer existence or presence) is usually but a subordinate aspect of their availability that is taken for granted but remains unobtrusive; it becomes noticeable only when the serviceable objects are in some way deficient, or when there is an obstacle to their use. To begin with, things are always embedded in certain contexts, in a *world*; it is only when *Vorhandenheit* moves to the foreground that the world recedes and that the object emerges as a decontextualized entity. The important point is that *Vorhandenheit* is not a pristine experience (as Roquentin would have us believe); it is essentially secondary—the effect (as Sartre puts it) of a deliberate neutralization to which the observer has subjected himself ("L'Homme et les choses," 257). That neutralization is completed through the act of staring: the observer gapes at the objects as mere things that are simply there.[25] What comes to mind is Ingarden's critique of the epistemology of passive gaping. As we have seen, Roquentin is such a gaper. However, he is not as passive as he pretends. "Si tu te regardes très longtemps dans la glace," an aunt had told him, "tu y verras un singe" ("If you spend a long time looking at yourself in a mirror, what you will see is a monkey") (30), and he proves it by staring fixedly into a mirror until his face is totally transformed. It is his intense and prolonged gaze that makes the objects lose all meaning and identity.

Absurdity, then, seems to be less the result of an unadulterated vision of the truth than that of a certain kind of perception—not at all a direct intuition but a derivative thing. Are Roquentin's raw bits of facticity perchance in reality ideal objects of some kind? In describing Roquentin's perception, one critic has noted its similarity to certain procedures in the work of Kafka and to the vision of the Proustian painter Elstir.[26] The comparison may at first glance seem surprising, for while we can easily associate Sartre's absurdist hero with Kafka, his connection with an aesthete is unexpected. But upon closer considaeration, it must strike us that virtually all aspects of Roquentin's experience can be viewed in specifically aesthetic terms. His stare defamiliarizes it objects, and defamiliarization ("making strange" or *ostranenie*) is the very essence of a poetic vision, in the view of the Russian Formalists. Such an aesthetic perception, precisely, views the object in a new light by isolating it, removing it from its ordinary contexts, from the pragmatic universe of referential relationships. The object ceases to be instrumental, serviceable, useful (in short: *zuhanden*) and indeed becomes gratuitous, *de trop*. It bears its significance in itself, and *in extremis* one can even say that it is devoid of meaning; in a well-known essay, Susan Sontag (from a perspective that is not absurdist but aestheticist) assails the quest for literary meaning and the desire to interpret, declaring that "in place of a hermeneutics we need an erotics of art."[27] The work of art needs (and sustains) no explanation, has no function; being simply *there*, it is in effect an extreme of *Vorhandenheit* (Heidegger) or *être-en-soi* ("being-in-itself") (Sartre). Foreign as it is to the meaning-bestowing human project, such being exemplifies the dehumanization which characterizes Roquentin's experience, which Sartre expressly associates with Ponge's *chosisme*, and which had previously been proclaimed as the quintessence of modernist aesthetics in Ortega y Gasset's famous essay "The Dehumanization of Art."[28] In a well-known study on *L'Étranger*, Sartre argues that Camus drives home his absurdist message through the stylistic trick of breaking up his protagonist's actions into its component parts.[29] He could have been talking about Roquentin, who behaves as an artist even when he pretends to speak as a philosopher. And there is a strong hint as to the artistic nature of his original inspiration: the khmer statuette, the first indigestible object he encountered, is after all a work of art.

The statuette impressed him as "désagréable et stupide" (15), and the epithets are telling. Beauty, in its complacent self-enclosure, may well strike us as "stupid": Flaubert liked the term to describe such an effect. As for the "disagreeable" part, it inflects the self-sufficiency of the thing of beauty in the direction of a different aesthetics. The statuette, after all, does not stand in the Greek Apollonian tradition of harmonious idealization. And the "things" that take its place in Roquentin's successive experiences, up to the public garden scene, represent an art of the horrible that had in itself become a major tradition, running from Baudelaire ("Une Charogne" ["A Corpse"]) to authors such as Céline.[30] Roquentin's striking reversal of the privileged poetic moment (as in Proust's *petite madeleine* episode) into a fit of nausea is also an important contribution to the aesthetics of the *frisson nouveau*.

Overall, we are dealing with an instance of what may be called the "aesthetics of pure perception," a variation on the ontology of *Vorhandenheit* that Heidegger had impugned. In art as well, this aesthetics is not the only one—be it in its "stupid," be it in it "disagreeable" form. Historically, it is a rather extreme form of modern (and modernist) aestheticism. Hans-Georg Gadamer deals with it in the section of *Truth and Method* devoted to a "Critique of the Abstraction of Aesthetic Consciousness."[31] The critique is directed against the "aesthetic differentiation," which wants to abstract an autonomous "purely aesthetic" domain cut off from the concerns and contexts of life. Gadamer finds its most systematic expression in the aesthetician Richard Hamann's formula for aesthetic perception as "significant in its own right" (*eigenbedeutsame Wahrnehmung*)—a vague "auto-significance" that in reality amounts to a suspension of the very concept of meaning. Referring to both the Gestalt psychologists and Heidegger, Gadamer argues that perception can never be passive mirroring, that it always (be it aesthetic or not) apprehends its contents *as* something, so that meaning is inevitably installed at its very core. Gadamer's important analysis also covers Roquentin's *jardin public* experience—a scene (I have tried to show) at the confluence of many philosophical concerns and literary traditions, but ultimately an extreme case of the aesthetic differentiation built up into (and merged with) an absurdist conception of life.

What would be its alternative? Clearly, a more broadly based aesthetics that would transcend the limitations and reductions of modernist aestheticism with its expulsion of human concerns, its suspension of human meanings, its staticizing disintegration of human time. That alternative, in fact, appears on the horizon of *La Nausée*. It emerges in the constant nostalgia for adventure, which is nothing else than a meaningful unfolding of time. That nostalgia is both literary and existential. On the literary level, it is the quest for an aesthetics of narrative, diametrically set against the static aestheticism of lyrical (or anti-lyrical) moments. On the level of life, it is a search for personal salvation, rescuing Roquentin's past, filling his present and assuring his future. At the end, he decides to write a novel. One hopes that artistically and existentially, he may succeed.

Boca Raton, Florida

NOTES

1. Georges Poulet, " 'La Nausée' de Sartre," in *Le Point de départ* (Paris: Plon, 1964), 229. All translations are my own.
2. For a detailed account of what we know about the genesis of *La Nausée*, see the remarks of Michel Contat and Michel Rybalka in the Pléiade edition of Sartre's *Oeuvres romanesques* (Paris: Gallimard, 1981), 1657–78.
3. See Jean-Paul Sartre, *La Nausée* (Paris: Gallimard, 1938), 9–10, 13, 15, 19, 20–22. Future page references in the text without further identification will refer to this edition.
4. See Claude-Emonde Magny, "Sartre ou la duplicité de l'être: ascèse et mythomanie, in *Les Sandales d'Empédocle: Essai sur les limites de la littérature* (Neuchâtel: Editions de la Baconnière, 1945), 166. Maurice Blanchot defends Sartre by arguing that his thesis is totally integrated in the novel, which is doubtful; see "Les romans de Sartre," in *La Part du feu* (Paris: Gallimard, 1949), esp. 207, 210. Both critics agree, however, that a Sartrean thesis is being propagated.
5. I rather think that he was not. I was told by Henri Peyre that Sartre had told him he came across Heidegger's work quite late.
6. The essay is to be found in Jean-Paul Sartre, *Situations I* (Paris: Gallimard, 1947), 31–35. Note its briefness.
7. See *Situations I*, 262–63.

8. The study by Geneviève Idt, *La Nausée: Sartre* (Paris: Hatier, 1971) is a repository of all the conventional philosophical assumptions about Sartre's novel. Among others, she expresses the thesis of Sartre/Roquentin's practice of "phenomenological description" with particular clarity (49, also 47–48). Few critics who have written about *La Nausée* have resisted the temptation of using the adjective "phenomenological."

9. See Roman Ingarden, *Vom Erkennen des literarischen Kunstwerks* (Tübingen: Niemeyer, 1968), paragraph 9, 17–18.

10. 141–47. See W. Wolfgang Holdheim, "The *Cogito* in Sartre's *La Nausée*," in *The Comparative Perspective on Literature: Approaches to Theory and Practice* (Ithaca & London: Cornell University Press, 1988), eds. Clayton Koelb & Susan Noakes, 179–94.

11. See Holdheim, "*Cogito*," 192–94.

12. The other two Gidean *soties* are *Le Prométhée mal enchaîné* (1899) and *Les Caves du Vatican* (1914).

13. See André Gide, *Paludes* (Paris: Gallimard, 1926), 58. I have analyzed *Paludes* in detail in W. Wolfgang Holdheim, *Theory and Practice of the Novel: A Study on André Gide* (Geneva: Droz, 1968), 171–89.

14. Note that a character in the *Voyage d'Urien*, an earlier novel by Gide (1893), already reads a "Traité de la Contingence," and that the second part of that symbolist book is in many ways a prefiguration of the atmosphere of *Paludes*. See Holdheim, *Theory and Practice*, 182, ft. 7.

15. "Oft anhaltende, ebenmässige und fahle Ungestimmtheit"; see Martin Heidegger, *Sein und Zeit* (Tübingen: Niemeyer, 1972), paragraph 29, 134. See also W. Wolfgang Holdheim, "A Revaluation of André Gide's *Paludes*," in *The Hermeneutic Mode: Essays on Time Literature and Literary Theory* (Ithaca & Cornell: Cornell University Press, 1984), esp. 88 and 91.

16. The dual character of contingency does not come out clearly in my previous two studies on *Paludes*. I am happy to correct the omission here.

17. The following interpretation of the *Nourritures* appears in greater detail in Holdheim, *Theory and Practice*, 21–34.

18. André Gide, *Les Nourritures terrestres et Les Nouvelles Nourritures* (Paris: Gallimard, 1947), 21.

19. See the whole passage in *La Nausée*, 30–31.

20. About the broadness of the concept of "seeing," see Heidegger, *Sein und Zeit*, paragraph 31, 147. The "j'ai vu" is a clear reminiscence of Rimbaud's poem "Le Bateau ivre." The Rimbaldian connection is pointed out by Edward J. Ahearn in "Negative Ecstasy: Experience and Form in the 'Jardin Public' Passage in *La Nausée*, in *Fiction, Form, Experience: The French Novel from Naturalism to the Present*, ed. Grant E. Kaiser (Montreal: Editions France-Quebec, 1976), 144.

21. See Holdheim, *Theory and Practice*, 31–34: "... savons-nous quelles sont les choses importantes? Quelle arrogance dans le *choix*!" ("How do we know what is important? How arrogant to *choose*!"), writes André in the open window episode in *Paludes* (95), but when he makes his excursion the next morning, he reminds himself: "Ne noter du voyage rien que les moments poétiques—parce qu'ils rentrent

plus dans la caractère de ce que je le désirais" ("only note the poetic moments of the trip—for these are more in line with what I wanted") (97). It is interesting that Sartre mentions Gide in the essay "L'Homme et les choses" (262), opposing Gide's aestheticism to Ponge's presumed faithfulness to nature.

22. "*J'étais* la racine de marronnier. Ou plutôt j"étais tout entier conscience de son existence. Encore détaché d'elle—puisque j 'en avais conscience—et pourtant perdu en elle, rien d'autre qu'elle" ("I *was* the root of the chestnut tree. Or rather: I was entirely the consciousness of its existence. I was still separate from it—since I was aware of it—and still I was lost in it, was nothing in my own right") (185–86). A consciousness and yet a thing? Is this a prefiguration of the *en-soi-pour-soi* existence which the philosopher of *L'Etre et le néant* will declare to be man's impossible dream? Here it sounds like a form of the same discrepancy that characterizes the entire passage.

23. In *A Preface to Sartre* (Ithaca: Cornell University Press, 1978), Dominick LaCapra notes the paradox of this displacement of intentionality from the subject to the object and comments on it at some length (111–12). LaCapra also sees the discrepancy between the wordlessness of the experience and the wordiness of its description (although he is more concerned with the metaphoric than with the discursive verbosity of Roquentin's account; see 110–11). However, he does not offer much of an explanation or analysis, except for the more or less programmatic statement that opposites can never be satisfactorily determined and that ambiguity always reigns supreme. It is the strength of deconstructive criticism that it occasionally makes us see genuine contradictions; it is its frequent weakness that this determination of contradictions tends to become significant in its own right.

24. Sartre, "L'Homme et les choses," 288.

25. For Heidegger's discussion of *Vorhandenheit,* see *Sein und Zeit,* paragraph 31 and particularly paragraph 16, esp. 73–74.

26. See David I. Grossvogel, *Limits of the Novel: Evolutions of a Form from Chaucer to Robbe-Grillet* (Ithaca: Cornell University Press, 1968), 246–47, 204.

27. Susan Sontag, *Against Interpretation and Other Essays* (New York: Dell, 1964), 14 (in the essay "Against Interpretation").

28. In José Ortega y Gasset, *The Dehumanization of Art and Other Writings on Art and Culture* (Garden City: Doubleday, 1956). On the aestheticism of abstract materiality, see also W. Wolfgang Holdheim, *Die Suche nach dem Epos: Der Geschichtsroman bei Hugo, Tolstoi und Flaubert* (Heidelberg: Winter, 1978), 135–38 (à propos of Flaubert's *Salammbô.*).

29. Jean-Paul Sartre, "Explication de *L'Étranger*," in *Situations I,* 116.

30. There are other Baudelairian echoes in *La Nausée.* Note the nightmarish vision of vegetation invading and overpowering the city (218–19). Roquentin is afraid of leaving the city for that reason. (Gide's André wants to leave the city but gets no farther than the suburbs).

31. See Hans-Georg Gadamer, *Truth and Method* (New York: Continuum, 1975), esp. 80–83.

Painting the Seamarks of Modernity: Toward a Poesis of Integration in Saint-John Perse

MARK W. ANDREWS

Nicht zu erschöpfen ist die immer neue
Akkomodation jeder Zeit an das Altertum,
das Sich-daran-Messen.
Friedrich Nietzsche, *Wir Philologen* 7

We expect from a modern text a "writing of our world." In this its past or classical aesthetic can be obscured as it affirms its own present inscription. Contemporary French critic-philosophers and their epigones have tended to maximize the ahistorical "presence" of the text at the expense of its past or classical resonance. They have been quick to point to the arts to illustrate and exemplify modernity: artists and writers similarly preoccupied with the modern creative principle have not always insisted upon a radical noninvolvement of classical and modern "texts." To the contrary they have worked from the fruitful interdependence of the two. Sometimes the artist knows what Nietzsche only thought: "Always to be renewed is the constantly-new accommodation each age makes with antiquity, to measure itself by the other."

Saint-John Perse is not a modern poet in the sense that he resists the collapse of classical identity, unity, and integrity threatened by a fragmentary and circumstantial apprehension of the human condition; he is profoundly modern in his epic acceptance of the challenge laid down by his time, as he seeks to build anew upon the wasteland of the

147

present and retrieve the underpinnings of an integrated *ontos* using only the cultural shards and flotsam available to a latter-day Crusoe.[1] The charge of modern poetry, as set out by him in his Nobel Prize acceptance speech in 1960, *Discours de Stockholm,* is to strive toward a fully integrated way of life.[2] Bound by its destiny and free of contemporary ideologies, poetry is embarked upon a self-sufficient mission: to explore and illuminate the mysteries of the human soul, its expression no less rigorous than that of scientific discourse. Perse legitimizes the poetic enterprise by referring to Einstein's conception of scientific discovery as an artistic vision. Just as modern physics has arrived at a crossroads with intuition and imagination, so modern poetry, in turn, is informed by the clear light of reason, and the poet is our link to permanence, unity, and harmony

Yet today's poet must also attend to the present moment, and to the drama of the widening split between temporal and atemporal values in the twentieth century. The poet is portrayed as fighting a rearguard action against the materialistic *techné* of the modern age. Perse questions whether spiritual energy can compete with nuclear energy: "Face à l'énergie nucléaire, la lampe d'argile du poète suffira-t-elle à son propos?—Oui si d'argile se souvient l'homme" ("Facing nuclear energy, will the clay lamp of the poet be sufficient for its purpose?—Yes, if man remembers clay") (*Disc.*, 447). Perse's response is conditional but affirmative. It leads him to conclude his Nobel address by prescribing the role of spiritual gadfly for the poet, content to prick the uneasy collective conscience of his age.

Perse's poem *Amers* selects the sea as the site of predilection for an ultimate expression of man's secret vocation to transcend materialism and the fragmentary nature of modern temporal concerns. In his commentary, "Note pour un écrivain suédois sur la thématique d'*Amers*" ("Note for a Swedish Writer on the Thematics of *Amers*"), Perse sides with Einstein for timeless order against the fluctuation of quantum theory. "Si j'étais physicien, je serais avec Einstein pour l'Unité et la Continuité contre la philosophie 'quantique' du hasard et du discontinu. Si j'étais métaphysicien, j'accepterais allègrement l'illustration du mythe de Shiva..." ("If I were a physicist, I would be with Einstein on the side of Unity and Continuity against the 'quantum' philosophy of chance and discontinuity. If I were a metaphysician, I would agree with alacrity to illustrate the myth of Shiva...") (*Note*, 570). Shiva, the destroyer, presides as Mahakala over the annihilation of the cosmos, but appears in turn as his opposite, Mahadeva, the creator, who reciprocally restores the obliterated. Hence arises synthetic harmony, characterized by the dissipation of illusion and by the serenity born of turbulence. It is Perse's conviction that modern poetry can aspire to the embodiment of an integral, undivided whole, even as it mirrors man's double vocation: his quest for ultimate spiritual values, and his immediate temporal concerns. In its modernity Perse's poetry issues, however, from a proximate source: it is turbulent action and deals in shifting perspectives and concrete images. It is the antithesis of serenity, stasis, and abstraction, even as it strives to achieve universality and quintessential meaning. Perse's poetry is modern in ways which recall Baudelaire's definition of modernity as poetic in *Le peintre de la vie moderne*. Modernity is the ephemeral and contingent in art, the poetic distillation of the heady, bitter wine of life. It is one half of art, the counterpart to what is eternal and unchanging.

For Baudelaire modernity can be bizarre and excessive, even violent, but the portrait of his singular artist M.C.G. which most exactly foreshadows Perse's poetic persona is that of the solitary voyager whose goal lies beyond the barren contingent universe through which he travels:

— this solitary [man], gifted with an active imagination, ceaselessly journeying across the great human desert has an aim loftier than that of a mere *flâneur,* an aim more general, something other than the fugitive pleasure of circumstance.[3]

This seeker after modernity strives to discern in the latest fashions the poetry of an historic essence, a process which Baudelaire sums up as extracting the eternal from the transitory.

Perse's endeavor privileges a conceptual difficulty which has preoccupied proponents of modernity since Baudelaire: the retrieval of the whole from the fragment, history from the present, the invisible from visibilia, poetry from scientific precision, and greatness from alienation. Perse's goal is the total reintegration of man's complementary halves in a nihilistic age where man has passively accepted the contingency of matter and has abandoned the quest for absolute spirit and epic achievement. Exiled from its classical origins, dispossessed of its divine heritage, poetry must construct a home anew upon the shifting sands and spindrift of a schizophrenic modernity, its dislocated halves re-membered and re-written.

The recuperation of the classical aesthetic is not a project to be allied with the philosophical concerns for modernity, in which classical knowledge is taken to proceed from a long dominant, repressive, hostile mode of inscription. In a short address entitled "Re-writing Modernity," Jean-François Lyotard summarizes the split between classical and modern recording of the past as that opposition which separates, respectively, the writing from the re-writing of modernity. He illustrates the distinction by alluding to a shift which occurred in Freud's thinking from the quest for origins, the "remembering" (*Erinnerung*) of a primal scene, to an emphasis on free association designed to generate from the past the elements for a new scene, a "working through" (*Durcharbeitung*).[4] How peripheral Lyotard's theory is for the reader's appreciation of Perse's test, however, can only be assessed once the tests are read.

Perse's epic march toward the sea, *Amers,* succinctly encapsulates the tension between local and global semiosis, between fixity and movement, between the punctual and the universal in its ambivalent title. The etymological play on *amers*, signifying both seamarks and brine, is a remarkable choice by Perse, because it harnesses the potential for an exchange fundamental to Perse's poetics. The word, like the place it designates, occupies a space of shifting, migratory associations and allegiances, defining new synthetic relationships while preserving and reaffirming its original division of meaning.

The title of the poem, as Wallace Fowlie makes clear by his translation, *Seamarks*, refuses the spurious transcendence offered by the conventional poetic lexicon of the sea, preferring the concrete referents of nautical terms. *Amers*, used for the fragments of the poem which the *Nouvelle revue française* published in January and February of 1953, was first translated by Fowlie as *Brine* and corrected to *Seamarks* by Perse himself.[5] His translation is derived from the word's Scandinavian origin, *merki*, which conveys the sense of a beacon or coastal reference point for navigational aid or warning, and not from a perhaps obvious association with the Latin, *amarus*, which is the source for "brine" and also "bitters," Baudelaire's oenophilic preference for describing modernity.

The universal Being, "l'Etre universel" (*Note,* 571), with whom Perse identifies the sea in his note, is here transformed by the corrected translation into precise locations, objects recorded upon the pilot's chart and situated upon an elevation or salience, a promontory cape, or rocky eminence.

Perse's attraction to different categories of transitional space is pervasive in his poetry, and has particular significance for his poetics of the *écart*, the gap or marginal space of the border which delimits a territorial boundary. Such irregular elevations are more than particular referents for poetic musing and high ceremony in Perse's opus. It has been demonstrated how the angular ambiguity which links and combines the properties of different spatial dimensions also links this function of local topography to a general economy of signification circulating within Perse's poetry. High plateaus, overlapping waves, steps of various kinds manifest kindred morphological traits when they appear as frontier terrain. Images of time, stone, minerals, birds, fire, lightning, storms, and the printed word constitute thresholds which perform a dual function, opening reverie to the past and to the future, especially reverie which centers upon woman, the sea and the poem itself: "tout seuil se donne à lire à la fois comme origine et ouverture, et surtout ces objets où se concentre la rêverie de ce seuil: la femme, la mer, le poème" ("every threshold is to be read both as an origin and as an opening, especially those objects where the reverie of this threshold is concentrated: woman, sea, and poem").[6]

Perse's cycle of poems *Exil*, reveals that the painting of seamarks is a task reserved for the most exalted of navigators. The author of the seamark, that sign which assigns particular spits or headlands to points and angles on the geometrical grid of the navigator's chart, appears in *Exil* as a prince for whom the poem bears a superfluous message: ("Ceux-là sont princes de l'exil et n'ont que faire de mon chant") ("Those are the princes of exile: they have no need of my song") (*Exil*, 134). His role is a projection of that of the poet himself, and as such he needs no initiation into the secrets of the universe. The prince is a navigator, a seafaring nomad, who keeps the company of secular pilots or spiritual light-house keepers:

celui qui prend logement, pour la saison des pluies, avec les gens de pilotage et de bornage—chez le gardien d'un temple mort à bout de péninsule (et c'est sur un éperon de pierre gris-bleu, ou sur la haute table de grès rouge)

he who takes lodgings for the rainy season with pilots and coastline crews—with the guardian of a dead temple at land's end (on a spur of grey-blue rock or on a high table of red sandstone) (*Exil*, 132).

He spends his time in the standard navigational pursuits of maintaining signals buildings, charting cyclones, sounding the ocean depths, and even adjusting compasses for the recreational sailor. The navigator's ordinary activities are undifferentiated one from the other; like an exile he drifts between lesser and greater tasks with no sense of order or priority, yet the apparent aimlessness of his existence contrasts sharply with his privileged status as a repository of princely wisdom. He possesses the esoteric knowledge of the star-gazer, the dreamer-astronomer to whom are revealed the hidden laws and great sidereal routes of migration. He is introduced as a painter of signs, but his artistry is that of a sculptor of dreams, visiting the highest places, and also the most profound:

> Celui qui peint l'amer au front des plus hauts caps,
> celui qui marque d'une croix blanche la face des récifs;
> ...celui qui quête à bout de sonde, l'argile rouge des
> grands fonds pour modeler la face de son rêve

> He who paints the landmark on the brow of high headlands,
> he who marks with a white cross the face of high reefs;
> ...he who, with lead, gathers the red mud of the deep
> to model the mask of his dream (*Exil*, 132–33).

Paint and clay are the terrestrial media which represent the divine furor of poetry. To "remember the clay," Perse's admonition in his Nobel speech, is here enacted as the process of re-inscription in the Baudelairean sense of extracting the eternal from the transitory. Human clay reverses its separation from the divine, taking on the aspect of a spiritual intoxication. *Pluies* concentrates its torrential downpour around images of clay and paint: the wearer of the clay mask drinks of the divine draught, "Tel s'abreuve au divin dont le masque est d'argile" ("He drinks of divinity whose mask is of clay") (*Pluies*, 149), dreams are fever-painted, "Nos fièvres peintes aux tulipiers du songe" ("Our fevers painted on the tulip-trees of dream") (*Pluies*, 146). The lofty rains of the sisters of the warriors of Assur conjure up the painted image of Cortez' wife, drunk with clay: "Comme l'épouse de Cortez, ivre d'argile et peinte, entre ses hautes plantes apocryphes..." ("Like Cortez' wife, heady with clay and painted, among her tall apocryphal plants...") (*Pluies*, 143).

The figure of the classical Author, a persona within the drama, takes on a similar appearance in *Amers* as he faces the approach of the motley assembly of seafaring characters who make up the recitation in the sixth canto of the "Invocation": "Récitation en marche vers l'Auteur et vers la bouche peinte de son masque" ("Recitation marching towards the Author and towards the painted mouth of his mask") (*Amers*, 265). The Author dons the greasepaint of the theater to become a protagonist; his presence on stage serves to orient the itinerary of the chorus. He stands as a histrionic seamark, a catalyst for the conversion of sea into stone.

The staging of the poem *Amers* offers a robust counter to the de-hellenization of representation deplored by Perse in modern life and poetry. As a modern poet, rather than a physicist or metaphysician, Perse chooses to return to the antipode of antique Greek drama to structure his exaltation of mankind's march to the sea in *Amers*. The setting is provided by the classical theater itself, and the action by the ritualized celebration and ceremonial chants of the choric ode.[7] Perhaps we are to view the stone theater as an angular space of geometrical transformation, acting as a poetic vessel for the accumulation of the spiritual energy of the sea. Perse completes the portrait of the exchange in his own commentary upon the poem.

In the note on the thematics of *Amers*, provided for a Swedish translation of the poem, Perse explains his choice of the sea as a mirror of man's destiny, of his physical and moral integration, "sous sa vocation de puissance et son goût du divin" ("in his vocation for power and his taste for the divine") (*Note*, 570). The sea is described as a Janus-faced entity, construed both as a theater for man's accomplishments, and source for his ultimate spiritual illumination:

> lieu de convergence et de rayonnement: vrai 'lieu géométrique' et table d'orientation, en même temps que réservoir de forces éternelles pour l'accomplissement et le dépassement de l'homme, cet insatiable migrateur
>
> a place of convergence and of radiance: a true 'geometrical locus' and benchmark,[8] as well as a reservoir of eternal forces for the fulfillment and the surpassing of man, that insatiable migrator" (*Note*, 570).

The sea juxtaposes the concrete and abstract, and Perse underscores the fact in the paratactic image of the poem's erection *qua* seamark. The bare outcropping is represented as contiguous to the sea, facing rather than overlooking its imposing nightscape: the vertical darkness of the ontological cleft of being is flattened out by the night, and appears as a backdrop for the cinematographic projection of man's destiny taking its course: "C'est l'intégrité même de l'homme... que j'ai voulu dresser sur le seuil le plus nu, face à la nuit splendide de son destin en cours" ("It is the very integrity of man... that I wished to erect on the barest threshold, facing the splendid night of his unfolding destiny") (*Note,* 569–70).[9]

Perse presents a corollary image of the theater as a storehouse of divine inspiration from the deeps of the sea in the poem's opening stanza, when he announces the sea's theatrical conformation at its shores. The celebratory lapping of the waves is petrified into an endless chant that achieves a reciprocal balance between the poem's solid structure and its watery subject:

> La mer en fête sur ses marches comme une ode de pierre: vigile et fête à nos frontières, murmure et fête à hauteur d'hommes—La Mer elle-même notre veille, comme une promulgation divine...
>
> The Sea, in celebration of its steps, like an ode of stone: vigil and celebration on our frontiers, murmur and celebration to the height of men—The Sea itself our vigil, like a divine promulgation...
> (*Amers,* 259).

The paratactic coincidence of theater and sea occurs at the privileged periphery of their approaches, the vigilant frontiers of space populated by the solitary lookout or player, who provides beacons for navigation and arenas for the crossing of the image. The figure of the classical Author, framed by the play in which his is the pivotal role, appears as a metonymy for stone and sea, whose conjunction envelops seamark and painter, ode and actor, assimilating their functions into the transference which is taking place. Just as the sea becomes our lookout so the stone takes on the shape of the ode.

The word seamarks designates the space of the poem itself as theater and stages a liminal zone where opposites collide and paint each other with new colors. An unstable system of shifting contrasts and fluctuating hues permeates *Amers*. Imagery is suffused with color, and with a stylized color blindness, as it oscillates between reds and greens, linking the four elements in prismatic play throughout the spectrum: "comme le sel violet de mer aux flammes vertes des feux d'épaves..." ("like

the violet salt of the sea in the green flames of burning wrecks...'')
(*Amers*, 294).[10]
The antagonistic play of color bleeds paronomastically into the
surrounding text, offering antithetical variations on nouns containing
the color rose. The black reeds, ''roseaux noirs'' (*Amers*, 299), of the
Patrician women contrast with the white rose gardens of summer:
''roseraies blanches'' (*Amers*, 315). This heady play on words generates
the inebriation of the young women prophetesses, who, bound at the
foot of the capes, press the bitters from the sea, relaying the vinous
message of the gods. The spray-soaked acrimony and sedition of their
words reflects their dipsomania: ''ivres d'un vin de roseaux verts!...''
(''drunk on a wine of green reeds!...'') (*Amers*, 310).

The brush of the poet codes navigational signals, painting seamarks
according to a logic of displacement which is triggered by an often
paradoxical attribution of contour and color to one element by another.
Evocation of a pale sky is followed by that of white birds, an unsurprising
metonymy, yet both sky and birds are engaged in the displaced activity
of a demarcation of terrestrial features, rendering visible the vanished
contours which define the boundaries of their environment: Un ciel pâle
diluait l'oubli des sigles de la terre...Les oiseaux blancs souillaient l'arête
des grands murs'' (''A pale sky diluted the oblivion of earth and its fields
of rye...White birds soiled the ridge of the high walls'') (*Amers*, 273).[11]
Birds and sky remain balanced in contradistinction, soiling and washing
the earth as a complementary process of alchemical inscription.

Birds thus serve as navigational aids, and function as painters of
seamarks, possessing the capacity to individuate the character of their
environment. They participate in an alchemy of transmutation which
restores missing color and conjures visibility from absence. Their
intervention provides the occasion for a vast celebration in which light
and color accompany ritual offering and the exaltation of vision:

> Le Ciel qui vire au bleu de mouette nous restitue déjà notre présence,
> et sur nos golfes assaillis vont nos millions de lampes d'offrande,
> s'égarant—quand comme le cinabre est jeté dans la flamme pour
> exalter la vision

> The sky, turning to a sea-gull blue, is restoring to us our presence,
> and over the assailed gulfs our millions of votive lamps are straying,—
> as when cinnabar is thrown into the fire to exalt man's vision (*Amers*,
> 267).

The verb *virer* serves as a vehicle for paronomastic transformation.[12] Its secondary meaning of "to change color" is foregrounded by the primary sense of circling: Perse paints the sky by means of the synecdochic wheeling of the seagull's flight rather than through an implausible change in hue of the bird's achromatic plumage. He points to a similar possible transformation in the verb *s'égarer* when he refers it back to the literal scattering of the myriad lamps over the gulfs, mobile beacons which are a catalyst for heightened perception and which prompt the image of cinnabar, thrown into the flames to sublimate the senses. The verb's metaphorical signification of a loss of reason is here construed as an uplifting of vision. The appearance of color attends and dramatizes a paronomastic shift in meaning between a movement of dispersion and the enhancement of a state of mind from the everyday to the exalted: the shift occurs as the lamps distribute themselves across the gulfs like seamarks.

Seamarks, conveniently for the present reading of Perse's poetics, have the secondary meaning of "tidemarks" in English, the full seamark indicating the high tide line. Unlike the requirements of the classical theater, drama here needs no pretext for its staging of elemental collision, no paint for its tragedians' counterfeits: "nos paumes peintes comme des bouches, et nos blessures feintes pour le drame!" ("our palms painted like mouths and our wounds feigned for the drama!") (*Amers*, 289). Yet the theater of action remains the theater as well as the sea. The stone steps leading to the stage are identified with the sea's approaches in an insistent play on the word *marche*. Perse's choice of certain privileged terms as vehicles for the paronomastic exaltation of meaning bears strongly upon his expressed ambition that the modern poem be a beacon for man's full integration. Here his exploitation of the word's triple signification of steps, borders, and marches has the effect of creating a linguistic seamark which serves as a metonymic illumination of his poesis.

The festive marches of the sea which usher in the poem as a theatrical ode of stone are identified immediately as frontier territories. At the opening of the third canto of the "Invocation" the sense of borderlands then yields to that of a celebratory march which retains some of the associations of that word's initial sense of a boundary. This march corresponds to the circumambulation of the chorus about the stage's centerpiece, the altar of Dionysus: it is also an expedition around the periphery of the sea:

Poésie pour accompagner la marche d'une récitation
en l'honneur de la mer.
Poésie pour assister le chant d'une marche au
pourtour de la mer.
Comme l'entreprise du tour d'autel et la
gravitation du choeur au circuit de la strophe

Poetry to accompany the march of a recitation in
honour of the Sea.
Poetry to assist the song of a march around the
circuit of the Sea.
Like the ritual round the altar and the gravitation
of the chorus in the circuit of the strophe (*Amers*, 261).

The poetic circumscription of the sea becomes now a form of action. It elicits further parallels and identifications between the theater and the sea that center upon a third meaning of "*marche*" as a step, a sense implicit in the association between stone and sea at the poem's inception. The lapping of the waves, noted earlier, has the visual connotation of an overlapping of breakers, mirrored in the steps leading up from the orchestra to the proscenium where the drama proper is enacted. The approach of the recitation, a chorus of seafolk, "en marche vers l'Auteur," echoes the sea's approach to the drama's steps: "Et c'est la Mer qui vint à nous sur les degrés de pierre du drame" ("And it is the sea that came to us on the stone steps of the drama") (*Amers*, 265).

Stairways to the sea are an integral feature of the transitional architecture of the port, "Architecture frontalière" (*Amers*, 274), and as such participate in the transfer of space and identity. One such flight of steps provides the sonorous setting for the arrival of the tragediennes. As they mingle with the populace of the port and descend to the sea, their voices resonate throughout the stairwell as a choral antiphon, echoed in an invisible male counterpart: "Elles descendirent, et leurs voix mâles, les escaliers sonores du port" ("They descended, with their male voices, the echoing stairs of the harbour") (*Amers*, 289). The stairway transforms the stage into a metonymy for the port's male life, and as the tragediennes arrive the sea's edge there arises a sense of the port's failure coupled with a dissatisfaction with dramatic forms set in stone. The tragediennes' migration from the stage toward the sea takes on the aspect of man's return to the mythic space of his forefathers. The turn from land to seascape occurs in the poem through a paronomastic return from the broken line of the stairway to the angular ambiguity of the word *marche*: "Ah! nous avions mieux auguré de l'homme sur la pierre. Et nous marchons enfin vers toi, Mer légendaire de nos pères" ("Ah! we had augured better of man's stature on the stone. And at last we are walking towards you, legendary Sea of our fathers") (*Amers*, 289).

The stairway which distorts the sounds of the approaching troupe, promoting the breakdown of confidence in their performance, and, in a larger sense, the terrestrial accomplishments of man, is itself a projection of the erosion of the port, which has outlived its productive association with the sea: "Port d'échouage sur béquilles" ("Harbour for beaching on props") (*Amers*, 275). The stairwell too is broken, the poetry of its symmetrical lines reduced to alphabetic rubble: "où l'escalier rompu déverse son alphabet de pierre" ("where the broken stairway spills its alphabet of stone") (*Amers*, 275). The dilapidation of the port is the staging area for a poetic rebuilding, the paronomastic turn from steps to stepping out, that of a march, "*marche,*" towards a new theater of marine and maritime composition.

In his note to *Amers*, Perse affirms that it is the questing modern spirit that is illustrated by man's Promethean march toward the sea: "J'ai pris la marche vers la mer comme une illustration de cette quête errante de l'esprit moderne, aimanté toujours par l'attrait même de son insoumission" ("I have taken the march toward the sea as an illustration of that wandering quest of the modern spirit, always oriented by the very attraction of its own rebelliousness") (*Note*, 570). Perse subsequently confirms that the sea appeared to him as the classical stage itself: "l'arène solitaire et le centre rituel, 'l'aire théâtrale' ou la table d'autel du drame antique" ("the solitary arena and the ritual center, 'the theatrical surface' or the altar table of the drama of antiquity") (*Note*, 570). The sea copies the construction of the hellenistic amphitheater, but its repetition of a past model does not so much produce an imperfect copy as it does turn away from the ruined stones of history.[13] The route to the past lies, paradoxically, through the invention of a version for the future, capable of reintroducing the ancient epic into modern poetry.

Unlike the friable stone of which the original city was constructed, the poem chooses the ocean wave as the model for its poetics of modernity. The constant sameness of the sea's movement provides an antidote to the postmodern differential of reproduction which leads either to deteriorated copies of the past, or to the endlessly deferred genesis of a new order: "Une même vague par le monde, une même vague depuis Troie'' (''One same wave throughout the world, one same wave since Troy'') (*Amers*, 326)[14]. The sea remains identical to itself precisely because the formation of its waves possesses the same potential for a transference of identity as the seamark which paints the space-time coordinates from which we may observe the sea. So the sea both endlessly defines and is punctually defined by the coastal features it fashions, those points men designate to mark its confines and its power. At any given moment in history the sea also affords the potential for paronomastic exchange at the limits of human aspiration, offering the perspective of an integration of time and atemporality.

At this point it might behoove this exegesis to take seriously Michel Pierssens' provocative reading of *Amers* in his, ''Amère Amérique.'' There he studies the poetics of the gap, *l'écart*, which, he contends, invests Perse's poetry with a principle of coherency:

> La paronomase n' est pas un accident local, un hasard ou une rencontre. C'est la loi même d'une certaine cohérence où s'enracine la possibilité de la diction poétique—'l'initiative' (toujours Mallarmé) restant 'aux mots', qui font *texte* de ces jeux compliqués de la différence et de la répétition

> Paronomasia is not a local accident, a chance occurrence or an encounter. It is the law itself of a certain coherency in which is rooted the possibility of poetic diction—'the initiative' (still Mallarmé) remaining 'with words,' which make *text* of these complicated games of difference and repetition.[15]

Pierssens claims that the vertiginous propensities of the anagram provide a formula for poetic creation, and focuses upon the couple *Mer / Mère* (Sea / Mother) as a concealed key to Perse's poetics. Although his reading of *Amers* in particular is a contentious one, conforming in principle but not in practice to the integrative energetics of inscription we are seeking to elaborate, his perspective can serve to refine our own.

Pierssens proceeds from Perse's association of prosody with the sea to show that it is the play of *l'écart* which governs the action of the waves and provides the generative principle for the weaving of prosodic links. He juxtaposes the verse ''Mer magnanime de l'écart'' (''Magnanimous Sea of divergence'') (*Amers*, 376) to one which describes the caesura shared by classical meter and the female body, ''Etroite la mesure, étroite la césure, qui rompt en son milieu le corps de femme comme le mètre antique..." ("Narrow the measure, narrow the caesura, which breaks the woman's body at the middle like an ancient metre...") (*Amers*, 335), and views the dynamics of the sea's prosody as obeying a law of paronomastic or anagrammatic propagation. Pertinent to our purposes, the allusion to the caesura immediately follows the refrain considered above: "One même vague par le monde, une même vague notre course..." ("One same wave throughout the world, one same wave our course") (*Amers*, 334–35). The verse suggests a dynamics for paronomastic activity which competes with that proposed by Pierssens, basing its generativity on an image of undulation rather than procreation.

Throughout the poem, to be sure, the sea conjures up images of body parts and scents, and these are frequently, but not uniquely, identified with woman: "Mer au parfum d'entrailles femelles et de phosphore" ("Sea with the scent of female entrails and of phosphorus") (*Amers*, 268), "l'odeur de vulve des eaux basses" ("the vulva smell of low waters") (*Amers*, 276), or "tout ce parfum d'algue de la femme" ("all this seaweed perfume of woman") (*Amers*, 277). These references find their fullest articulation in a climactic evocation of those divine entrails glimpsed by man as he peers into the ancient sea from the remaining fragment of his last terrestrial bastion and views the prospect of open water, his universal consort:

Et l'homme chassé de pierre en pierre, jusqu'au dernier éperon de schiste ou de basalte, se penche sur la mer antique, et voit, dans un éclat de siècles ardoisés, l'immense vulve convulsive aux mille crêtes ruisselantes, comme l'entraille divine elle-même un instant mise à nu

And man hunted, from stone to stone, to the last spur of schist and basalt, leans over the ancient sea, and sees, in a flash of slate-coloured eternity, the immense convulsing vulva with a thousand streaming crests, like the divine entrails themselves laid bare for one lightning moment (*Amers*, 374).

The relation of man and sea is here antiphonal rather than homophonic, connubial rather than maternal, taken in the context of the jagged line of rock spur and wave crest. This reading is confirmed at the beginning of the following stanza by the apostrophe to the sea as a mature, licentious, and universal spouse. When the association of the sea with motherhood does occur earlier in the poem, it takes place during the protracted antiphon of love-making, "Etroits sont les vaisseaux" ("Narrow are the vessels...''). Perse centers our attention upon the birth of the lovers, first man, "né de mer" ("born of the sea") (*Amers*, 327), stretched out upon the strand of his partner's body, and later the woman's body, "De mer issu" ("Issue of the sea") (*Amers*, 345), born, like Aphrodite, from the sea, but where a thin rain takes the place of the foam, inscribing the legacy of the birth as fine tracery of bruises upon the sandy flank of the mother.

Thus the conflation of fecundity and sexual congress suggests a generalized eroticism; the roles of mother, lover, spouse, and whore combine to focus upon the narrow caesura dividing the woman's body as a locus for libidinous activity. (For the philosophical and theoretical power of this image, see Eugene Kaelin's essay in this volume.) The caesura functions in this context as a prosodic metonymy, a linguistic seamark for the antiphonal exchange between the ancient stones of the classical theater and the ageless waves of the sea which takes place in the poem. It characterizes the transfer between the projecting stone remnant and the restless waves as an act of love and concomitantly signals the poem's climax.

Pierssens' systematization of paronomastic play, on the other hand, is suspect in that it privileges a singular homophonic relation of the sea to the mother, a conventional instance of paronomasia not exploited in the poem itself. His interpretation also contradicts his own claims for a plural model of linguistic play. His reading is inconsistent in proposing a local, reproductive model of repetition which copies the original intertextual model of the sea as mother, while making a case for the opening of a general economy of germination within the text, a model which he explicitly refers to Deleuze and Lyotard (AA, 278). His reading is, therefore, exemplary of the pitfalls which attend a postmodern attempt to demonstrate a dialectical poetics of modernity, one which is inattentive to the poem's quest for synthesis and its poesis of integration.

Yet Pierssens implicitly realizes this when he argues for a more fundamental and abstract *"poétique des fronts"* ("poetics at the front"), (AA, 280), in Perse's poetry: "Le chant, toujours bifrons, naît sur la crête où se rencontrent l'ici et l'ailleurs, la mémoire et la marche, l'établissement et le voyage, l'ancien et le nouveau, l'Est et l'Ouest" ("The song, always facing both ways, is born on the crest where here and elsewhere, memory and march, settling and traveling, ancient and new, East and West meet'') (AA, 281). The birth of the poem referred to here requires, however, some further elaboration, since "la naissance de son chant" ("the birth of his song") (*Exil*, 125) is specifically announced in *Exil* as a future event, beyond the compass of the poem. The jagged space of lightning founds the poem in a way both spasmodic, "Les spasmes de l'éclair" ("The spasms of lightning") (*Exil*, 123), and syntactic, ". . . Syntaxe de l'éclair!" (". . . Syntax of lightning!") (*Exil*, 136). It phrases a prediction of itself as a pure language. The spasms which attend the poem's awakening occur as the amorous preliminaries of conception rather than the toils of labor; they are explained as the paroxysm of a "ravissement" (*Exil*, 123), which has the dual sense of "rapt" and "rapture."

Poetry in *Amers* is similarly convulsed in a syntactic exaltation at its ultimate threshold, beyond the coastal waters, at the edge of the open sea. The paronomastic generation of convulsing genitalia, "vulve convulsive," communicates an semiotic ecstasy which is parsed by the ensuing allusion to "l'entraille divine." The paratactic juxtaposition of the human anatomy and the divine body at the crest of a thousand waves does not primarily display the contractions of birth, but heralds an amorous *exaltation*, in the double implication of a spiritual elevation and a transportation of the human senses. It is in this ambivalent manner that the poem enacts its exaltation of the human drama, the goal of Perse's poem in his note and prefigured earlier in the cinnabar episode. The final sections of the "Choeur" witness the power of love to translate the sign into its referent, and into its own medium: "Et mots pour nous ils ne sont plus, n'étant plus signes ni parures, / Mais la chose même qu'ils figurent et la chose même qu'ils paraient" ("And words for us they are no longer, being no longer signs or adornments, / But the thing itself which they signify and the thing itself they adorned") (*Amers*, 378). The paint of the seamark is thus fused with the rock spur it marks and the wave crests it signals. It purifies itself into the reality of love it represents.

The poet achieves his integration with the divine. His task of creation complete, the word is inscribed in flesh. Yet it is clear that Perse as commentator upon the power of love remains focused not upon the *jouissance* (orgasm) of the final antiphonal fusion with the divine, but upon the *plaisir* (erotic play) of the march of mankind as an ongoing process of integration with the universal Being: "la Mer identifiée à l'Etre universel, s'y intégrant infiniment et y intégrant l'homme lui-même, aux limites de l'humain'' ("the Sea identified with the universal Being, infinitely integrating itself with it and integrating man himself with it, at the limits of what is human'') (*Note*, 571). Perse's response to the challenge of modernity is most clearly at work in his paronomastic conversion of the classical space of the theater into its antithetical modern counterpart, the sea, at that conjunction of cinerarium and beacon, of past and future constituted by the seamark: "ô laveuse de tombeaux à toutes pointes de la terre, ô leveuse de flambeaux à toutes portes de l'arène!'' ("O washer of tombs at all points of the earth, O bearer of torches at all gates of the arena!'') (*Amers*, 369). He has measured his text by the past and, in effect, rejected the modernist attempt to set aside the sources of his poesis.[16]

> Quel est ce lieu, quel est
> cet arbre sur la falaise
> Et qui ne cesse de tomber?
>
> —Edouard Glissant,
> *La terre inquiète* (1954)

Perhaps the most telling image in this regard is not that of the sea, but one which has become the chief target of thinkers such as Deleuze and Guattari, for whom the history of Western thought is dominated by the sorry likeness, "triste image,''[17] of the tree. In his overview of contemporary philosophy, Christian Descamps succinctly encapsulates Deleuze's riposte with the counterimage of the rhizome.

> A l'arbre de l'Occident, à la grande pensée majuscule—avec ses racines, ses rameaux et ses branches qui organisent un sens tout droit—le rhizome oppose son existence acentrée, ses voisinages, ses multiplicités, ses façons de prendre les choses par le milieu
>
> The tree of the Occident, the great thought in capital letters—with its roots, its twigs, and its branches organizing a direction/meaning which is dead straight—is opposed by the rhizome's acentered existence, its neighborhoods, its multiplicities, its ways of taking hold of things by the middle.[18]

The opposition is clear, if not straightforward.[19]

Perse turns with, rather than against, the metaphysics of linear history in his modern dramatization of the poetics of the gap, *l'écart*, in *Amers*. In *Amers* the tree and the rose occupy a crossroads, marking an intersection on the horizontal grid of invasion even as they symbolize a hierarchical order: "très grande rose d'alliance et très grand arbre hiérarchique—comme un grand arbre d'expiation à la croisée des routes d'invasion" ("a very great rose of alliance and a very great hierarchical tree—like a great tree of expiation at the meeting of invasion roads") (*Amers*, 301). As Édouard Glissant has pointed out in his *L'intention poétique*, memory of origins, prompted by the presence of trees, endures into the present.[20] As witnesses to the collapse of ancient order and the emergence of new order, trees represent remembrance and knowledge of the past, marking points of departure for new expeditions.

Painting the seamarks of modernity, the poet, navigator and seer, conqueror and pilgrim, revisits the linear order of the past to give direction and shape to a migratory exploration of the future, even as that future is decentered, expanding beyond the confines of the model. The seamarks of *Amers* occupy elevated locations where contiguous spaces coincide and fold upon each other; they merge the spreading territory of the future with the eroding map of the past, and animate anew the ruined stone of the classical theater, now informed by the rolling undulation of a modern liturgical drama of the sea.

The paronomastic activity of poetic creation affords to writing and to re-writing the prospect of an epic integration denied by the divisive practice of modern philosophy; it offers the princely spectacle of a triumphant wave poised to strike, like the royal conger or the cobra, at the frontier of past and future, love and death, of the human and the divine: "la haute vague courbe et lisse à gorge peinte de naja" ("the tall wave curving and sleek on its painted cobra's throat") (*Amers*, 337). *Amers* mirrors in its imagery of the sea a poetics of reconciliation between the sharp profile of randomness and fragmentation and the smooth contours of permanence and unity, painting a single serpentile crest from Troy to modernity, and from here, no doubt, to the unexplored reaches of the soul.

Vassar College

NOTES

1. Cf. Perse's earliest published work, *Images à Crusoé*, which first appeared in 1909 in the *Nouvelle Revue française*.

2. Saint-John Perse, "Discours de Stockholm," *Oeuvres complètes* (Paris: Gallimard, 1972). Further citation from this edition will be followed by a page reference in parentheses. All translations are my own except for the poetry of Saint-John Perse, where I have preferred to use the following translations in which Perse collaborated: Saint-John Perse, *Exile and Other Poems*, trans. Denis Devlin, Bollingen Series XV (New York: Pantheon, 1949); Saint-John Perse, *Seamarks*, trans. Wallace Fowlie, Bollingen Series LXVII (New York: Pantheon, 1958).

3. Charles Baudelaire, "The Painter of Modern Life," *The Painter of Modern Life and Other Essays*, trans. Jonathan Mayne (London: Phaidon Press, 1964), 12.

4. Jean-François Lyotard "Re-writing Modernity" *SubStance 54* (1987).

5. See Henriette Levillain, *Sur deux versants de la création chez Saint-John Perse* (Paris: Librairie José Corti, 1987), 203–204.

6. Mireille Sacotte, *Parcours de Saint-John Perse* (Paris-Geneva: Champion-Slatkine, 1987), 265. Constant allusion to limitrophe environments is a prominent feature of Perse's imagery pointed out by most of his critics. Sacotte's analysis in her chapter, "De l'angulaire à l'ambigu: la géographie des limites," pertains to the spatial frontiers of a range of privileged locations: "seuils et terrasses des maisons, remparts et portes des villes, rives des fleuves, rivages des mers, orée du désert" ("thresholds and terraces of houses, ramparts and gates of towns, riverbanks, seashores, the edge of the desert") (229). This penchant extends, she notes, to his correspondence, replete with descriptions of capes and elevations, inhospitable observation posts the relative inaccessibility of which is often accentuated, depicted as an extreme threshold at the intersection of two opposing elements and spatial domains, earth, sea, or sky. She reminds us that such locations are more than boundary signs; the extremity at which two zones coincide takes on the aspect of both regions. Signs assume an ambiguous form and point two ways. The solitary beings who frequent such places of high ritual and enigmatic revelation become privileged initiates, observers of the great movements of history (Sacotte's observation should be read in the light of Baudelaire's portrait of the solitary painter of modern life in order to retain a sense of the poet's involvement of history in modernity). Reflecting upon its accidented topography, Sacotte, like Jean Pierre Richard before her, (Jean-Pierre Richard, *Onze études sur la poésie moderne* (Paris: Seuil, 1964), 75 goes on to speak of angular space. She points to the geometrical character of the locale, and its potentially dual role as concrete marker and as an architectural abstraction at the limits of space and place. It is on this barren place of exile that the poet founds his reverie:

l'angle est ainsi une figure archétypale de la limite: son apparence géométrique, à la fois concrète (qu'on peut figurer) et abstraite, (qui simplifie et généralise le réel), plaît à l'esprit du poète qui y loge de nombreuses rêveries

the angle is thus an archetypal figure of the limit; its geometrical appearance, both concrete (which can be figured) and abstract, (which simplifies and generalises the real), is pleasing to the spirit of the poet, who lodges numerous reveries there (233–4).

7. See Arthur Knodel, *Saint-John Perse* (Edinburgh: Edinburgh University Press, 1966). In his review of *Amers,* Knodel emphasizes that the poem's structure is dictated by the space of the theater and the movements of the chorus rather than by the dramatic content of the ode *per se:* "Perse indicates how the central structure of his poem was suggested, not by the drama itself, but by the physical disposition of the Greek theatre" (132).

8. Cf. Paul Robert, *Le petit Robert* (Paris: Société du nouveau Littré, 1972), 1738: "table circulaire de pierre, sur laquelle sont figurés les directions des points cardinaux et les principaux accidents topographiques visibles du lieu où elle se trouve" ("a circular slab of stone, on which are inscribed the points of the compass and the principal landmarks visible from its location").

9. Cf. the juxtaposition of planetary and universal space in the *Discours de Stockholm* (445–446), where the image of poetry's embrace leads into that of its exploration and illumination of the night of the soul.

10. Henriette Levillain notes in this regard an absurd discussion between poet and translator who, working from different versions of the original, were unable to agree on whether red or green silk was intended (203).

11. The phrase "the oblivion of earth and its fields of rye" should read "the oblivion of the earth's outline." The word *seigles* (rye fields) was corrected to *sigles* (abbreviations, initials or stenographic outline) in a later version of the poem, thus accentuating the association with writing.

12. In rhetoric "antanaclasis" might more accurately designate a homonymic play on words: "synonymia," an amplification by synonym in any consequent analysis. "Paronomasia" is the more frequently used term in poetics: I use it here to denote the poetic space where coincidence of opposites and reciprocal transfer of attributes occur.

13. Cf. Jacques Derrida, *Dissemination,* trans. Barbara Johnson (Chicago: University of Chicago Press, 1981), 167–171. Unlike Derrida, Perse seeks to distinguish between two repetitions, between the "poison" of material reproduction and the "medecine" of ideality, emerging from the dialectics of "differance" to find the way back to a metaphysical poesis, to what Derrida calls "the forbidden intuition of the face of the father" (167).

14. See Carol Rigolot, "*Amers*—à la recherche d'une poétique du discours épique," *Saint-John Perse 1: l'obscure naissance du langage* (Paris: Minard, La Revue des lettres modernes, 1987), 105. She discusses the barrenness of modern literature decried by the narrators of *Amers,* and in examining their appeal for a new epic spirit, argues that the poem responds to its own entreaty, modeling itself upon the future poem it describes and heralds. In this context she points to the privileged mention of the ancient city of Troy in the poem, which appears as a variant in the often repeated refrain quoted here. To make Rigolot's point in a different way, it may be said that the verse itself encapsulates the transmission of the epic through the image of an endless wave traversing history.

15. Michel Pierssens, "Amère Amérique," *Espaces de Saint-John Perse 3* (Aix-en-Provence: Université de Provence, 1981), 278. Further page references to this work will appear in the text in parentheses accompanied by the abbreviation AA.

16. The project of remembering the past is taken by modernist philosophers to be classical in that it seeks to identify origins and discover hidden roots of today's ills. Lyotard, for instance, suggests that such a process involves a complicity with history which condemns the investigator to remain within the frame of his inquiry. Lyotard takes Sophoclean tragedy and Freudian analysis as cases in point, arguing that Freud presumably realized the trap when he later abandoned his hypothesis of the primal scene.

Postmodernity contains a similar pitfall, but from an opposite direction: utopian rather than edenic, its attitude is totalitarian in its craving for ultimate order. Yet here Lyotard is more circumspect. He speaks euphemistically of postmodernity as a presupposition of modernity, a compulsion to resolve itself into a "final equilibrium" (4). From this perspective Lyotard views postmodernity not as a threat but as "a promise with which modernity is pregnant definitely and endlessly" (4). When he faces the prospect of computerized systems capable of organizing the free flow of information and play of imagination, his response is to defer delivery of such postmodern technologies of inscription by denying that his metaphor may be coming to term with the conclusion that: "to re-write modernity is to resist the supposedly postmodern writing" (9).

The model of modernity delineated by Lyotard is noteworthy for the vexed sense of progress and imminent fruition which attends the endless process of re-writing. The work of Gilles Deleuze and Félix Guattari on schizophrenic desire is similarly problematic in this regard:

Dans le processus schizophrénique, les objets partiels, organes du désir, s'accrochent sur le corps sans organes. ... Ils [les organes-machines) s'inscrivent comme autant de points de disjonction entre lesquels se tissent tout un réseau de synthèses

In the schizophrenic process, partial objects, the organs of desire, cling to the body without organs.... They [the organ-machines] are inscribed as so many points of disjunction between which a network of syntheses is woven. (Gilles Deleuze and Felix Guattari, "La synthèse disjonctive," *L'Arc* 43 (1970), 57).

Yet the organizing principle of this network precludes a closure of meaning, since it is the affirmation of ongoing disjunctive activity which creates the conditions for synthesis.

17. Gilles Deleuze et Felix Guattari, *Mille Plateaux* (Paris: Minuit, 1980), 25.

18. Christian Descamps, *Les Idées philosophiques contemporaines en France* (Paris: Bordas, 1986), 21.

19. Derided as infinite play by John Ellis in *Against Deconstruction* (Princeton: Princeton University Press, 1989), 55, defended as a Foucauldian form of competition by Christopher Norris in *Deconstruction: Theory and Practice* (London: Methuen 1982/6), 87, Derridean deconstruction sets itself against the metaphysics of linear history, but not against the very notion of history, as shown by Barbara Foley in her "The Politics of Deconstruction, " *Rhetoric and Form: Deconstruction*

at Yale (Norman: University of Oklahoma Press, 1985), 131. Lyotard, Norris claims in *Derrida* (Cambridge: Harvard University Press, 1987), 161, goes further than Derrida in his postmodern pragmatism, expelling the principle of reason from the aleatory structure of the emergence of knowledge. Lyotard, on the other hand, will devote much space to the survival of the epic as a form of legitimation of modern forms of knowledge and power in *La condition postmoderne* (Paris: Minuit, 1979). Deleuze, for his part, will pay considerable attention to the evolution of navigation in *Mille Plateaux,* where he is principally concerned with nomadism as an ahistorical rhizomatic phenomenon. History survives in postmodern analysis, relegated to a lesser order of validity.

20. Edouard Glissant, *L'intention poétique* (Paris. Seuil, 1969), 122.

PART FOUR
Reflected Texts Beyond Words

The Endurance of Value:
El Ingenioso Hidalgo Don Quijote in Defense of the Canon

BRENDA DEEN SCHILDGEN

> "Most of the things about which we make decisions, and into which therefore we inquire, present us with alternative possibilities. For it is about our actions that we deliberate and inquire, and all our actions have a contingent character; hardly any of them are determined by necessity."
>
> Aristotle, *Rhetoric* Book I, Ch. 2

> "A future is opened to us only as we become reconciled to the past."
>
> Edward Schillebeeckx, *Jesus*

The current discussion about the canon directs itself against the exercise of power and privilege, whether it be of ideology, social and economic status, gender, or ethnic identity at the center of the critical choices which establish revered lists of books and how we read them. Although the criticisms are a necessary counterpart to a rote and unthinking recital of the conventional value of particular texts, to dismiss these works without reference to their own capacity to respond to these same ideological and theoretical concerns is to abandon historical value in favor of contemporary prejudice. While the corrections attempt to

171

re-historicize, that is re-think history and historical value, they simultaneously de-historicize, for on the basis of an ideological criticism,
they would deprive works vested with canonical status of their power,
without considering their historical legacy or their "enduring" aesthetic,
intellectual, or social value.

In focussing on Cervantes' *Don Quixote* in my defense of the canon,
I will argue that the author created a revolutionary literary work which
responded in its own time to social, political, and ideological concerns
as it continues to do. Cervantes was himself involved in this same
exercise of interrogating the "canon," probing historical value, and
satirizing contemporary fads. Cervantes and his novel stretch back over
two thousand years of western literary history, reach out to literary
developments in the Europe of his own time, and advance forward to
influence the shape and interests of the modern novel. Such a pattern
of retrieval and influence qualifies a literary work as "great," as does
its enduring capacity to reveal its multiple inner complexities. A "great"
literary work, in other words, has a conviction about its own exceptional
status that aligns it with previous works of a similar calibre, to establish
cultural continuity and sometimes to subvert and undermine its forbears'
literary authority. At the same time as "great" works associate themselves with literary and cultural traditions, they also break new aesthetic
or philosophical ground, shattering conventions of language, genre, tone,
and subject matter. "Great" works express passionate convictions about
their own times and about how humans experience them. Even more,
they remind us of the enduring power of art to confront us with the
"condition" of the "human" in the labyrinth of human institutions and
social constructions. *Don Quixote*, perhaps more than any other work
in the western tradition, possesses all these traits.

I base my argument for a "received" canon of literary texts using *Don
Quixote* as an example on the following points: 1) canons of respected
texts are created by authors rather than critics as Cervantes shows us
by his retrieval and deployment of the classical literary tradition, a
tradition in which he places his own work; 2) a text worthy of
"canonical" status had a major influence on later literary works; 3)
the work radically exposed, altered, or developed its contemporary
literary culture; 4) it responded courageously to the central questions
of its own times; 5) it addressed concerns which transcended its own
times by examining the problems, desires, and passions of the human

experience; 6) it continues to pose problems and expose conditions which are of interest to contemporary audiences. In addition to these aspects of the text itself, I would argue in the Aristotelian tradition, that reading or interpreting is "triadic" and that therefore it engages the author (and his or her historical and cultural circumstances), the text (a product of its times but also a connection to the past and a communication to the future), and the audience whose interests, ideologies, and tastes change through time. Appreciation and understanding of a literary artifact therefore challenges our capacity to negotiate among these equally demanding phenomena: the author, the text, and its audience.

In my defense of canonicity, I do not argue against the "margins"; rather I argue against the tyranny of the present, against fads and trends and the self-immersion accompanying them which lies at the heart of the abandonment of historical value. I realize that because of history's contingencies, it may be that we do not learn anything definite from it except that we have a history. But this fact alone, that is, our own awareness of the existence of a "history," provides the opportunity for the humble recognition that because "time" makes human efforts relative, it also makes vulnerable the egoism of any absolute convictions. But no matter how tentative our recapitulation of the past, despite the care and discipline of historians in the last two centuries, I will argue for the necessity of continuity in value, as history is "our yesterday, and we cannot understand ourselves without it."[1] History, by leaving us stories, teaches us judgment because it provides the possibility to consider our social and human failures; it also gives us models of the tyrannies which confiscate the careful balances between "liberty" and "equality," "personal freedom" and "social justice,"[2] the public and the private, the present and the past. Despite the absolutism of such a conviction, as I approach this subject, I am aware of the hesitancy which ought to characterize any convictions about historical models, canonicity, periods, "greatness," or "permanence." In other words, there is a necessary contingency in our sojourn with the past and its artifacts, as Umberto Eco wrote in the *Postcript to the Name of the Rose*. ". . . the past, since it cannot really be destroyed, because its destruction leads to silence, must be revisited: but with irony, not innocently."[3] In addition to irony, I would also propose that humility ought to characterize this visit, and a recognition that our own insight, just as the reconstruction of our past, is tentative, and that an awareness of the "otherness" of the past and the traditions which preserve it, deserve our best efforts to revitalize and restore it, because we are in continuity with its "otherness."

Cervantes' *Don Quixote* is a model for discussing the canon. First, it has always been widely recognized as the "greatest" work of Spanish literature. It is one of the few Spanish masterpieces that has reserved a place for itself in an international literary canon, no small achievement for a Spanish work since Spanish literature, like the culture of the Iberian peninsula in general, has been beyond the Pyrenees, isolated and marginalized.

Second, the novel was immediately popular. Written in the common language, Spanish, Part I appeared in 1605 and Part II in 1615. Thomas Shelton translated Part I into English in 1612 and Part II in 1620. It appeared in French, translated by Cesar Oudin (Part I) in 1614 and F. de Rosset in 1618, into German in 1648 by Pahsh von der Sohle, Lorenzo Franciosini into Italian in 1622 and 1625, and by Nicolai Osipov into Russian in 1769.[4] These translations guaranteed the novel's impact on the emerging prose fictions in European literature. It has since been translated into all the remaining European languages[5] and in the twentieth century into a number of Asian languages. As a testimony to its popularity in Spain, Avellaneda's spurious Part II, appearing in 1614, attempted to impose an ascetic-moralistic element on the supposed libertarianism of Part I.[6] The novel's influence on the European literary scene was instantaneous and widespread, its style and genre immediately and continuously imitated.[7]

Third, the novel's self-referentiality places it within literary traditions which retrieve classical texts and genres as models to be examined, imitated, parodied, or subverted. Also, Cervantes locates the novel in the environment of Renaissance literature and literary interests including popular genres and motifs, as for example the chivalric novel, Renaissance epic, pastoral, elegy, love poetry, Petrarchism, and Erasmism. All this points to Cervantes' sense of his relation as author to revered canons, contemporary canons, and hierarchies of genres, and to his deflation of hierarchies both of canons and genres. In addition to his literary innovation, his use of traditional literary models and motifs, and his collaboration with or satire of contemporary literature, his literary influence is without precedent because of his impact on the development of the novel in Europe and the Americas. Although he may not have undermined the position of the long narrative poem as first in the hierarchy of genres, he showed that the novel would replace it as the most widely read genre from that moment forward.

Finally, the novel is also historically and culturally provocative precisely because of its capacity to undermine boundaries between the established and the current, folk culture and literary culture, peasant and gentry, male and female, the powerful and the powerless, and madness and sanity. *Don Quixote*'s carnival atmosphere foregrounds its popular concerns, its non-aristocratic bearing, and its democratic consciousness.[8] The novel satirizes all the major institutions of Golden Age Spain, race relations, and colonialism, parodies pretensiousness, and exposes tyranny, all with a combination of irony, ambiguity, and humor. Cervantes' attention to the "enchanted" and blunted desires of Don Ouixote and Sancho Panza show their quests as both temporal and timeless.

The novel has been long considered a satire of the popular chivalric novel. It declares its connection to this genre[9] at the moment when Don Quixote, bored with life as a small town hidalgo and refreshed by the excitement of chivalry novels, sets out on a journey ostensibly to retrieve the once secure but illusory time when knights were virtuous and believed in the regenerative power of good deeds and altruistic action. But the novel, with a closer look, is far more a retrieval of an older and more revered literary tradition, the epic, in which a middle aged man sets out on a quest which is utopian in its vision (e.g. *The Odyssey, Divina Commedia, Pharsalia, Aeneid*).[10] Cervantes' use of the epic has been related to the classical, Medieval, and Renaissance epic tradition for at least a century.[11] The quests of the "failed" mid-aged men of the epic tradition restore them as they confront and overcome the violence, narcissism, failed heroism and exploits, and consequential waste and loss of their youth. Cervantes adopts the utopian quest and reduces it, to create his hero as a bored and deluded country hidalgo who abandons his mundane life in favor of possible regeneration. As in the older works, the main character, a hero whose weaknesses have been explicitly revealed, "is forced" into a journey, the meaning of which is inflated by the character's sense of mission and by the genre in which the journey is explored. In a true epic tradition, Cervantes appropriates all its standard motifs into his hero's journey, including the epic encounter with giants ("Aventura de los molinos"/ the windmill incident, I, 8);[12] the conversation with characters in hell ("De la libertad que dio don Quijote a muchos desdichados"/ the freeing of the galley slaves, I, 22); the descent into hell in the Cave of Montesinos (II, 22); *deus ex machina* converted to the Don's "enchantment" and "malign influence of the stars" ' to explain why reality does not resonate with his illusions (I, 48; I, 52, 455; II, 10 etc.); the epic hero's armor ("El yelmo de mambrino"/ the winning of Mambrino's helmet, I, 21, passim); the epic battle (I, 18); the epic roll call (I, 18); the epic omen ("Malum signum! Malum signum!"") (II, 73); *ekphrasis* (II, 71); its inflated language (e.g. I, 16; I, 17) and literary *topoi* like starting a chapter with the rising of the sun (I, 13); and even the polyonomasia: Quijada, Quesada, Quejana, Quixote, Juana Panza/Teresa Panza, etc.[13] All of these events and characteristics have direct parallels in the *Aeneid*. Cervantes deploys the epic armory of motifs, which like the "quest of the epic hero" he handles with irony and humor because his hero is a simple hidalgo with delusions of chivalric grandeur.

Cervantes also resurrects the pastoral tradition as represented in Virgil's *Georgics* and *Eclogues*. In Part I, he locates events in the "pastoral oasis,"[14] (I, 11) examines pastoral love, and praises the golden age in "De lo que le sucedió a don Quijote con unos cabreros" and "De lo que contó un cabrero" (Meeting with the Goatherds and the Goatherd's Story) (I, 11–13), and in the story of the beautiful Leandra and Anselmo, Eugenio and their friends who sojourn in "la pastoral Arcadia" (I, 51, 595). The classical antecedents for Cervantes' praise of the golden age are numerous and include Ovid's *Metamorphosis* as well as Seneca.[15] He also deploys the pastoral elegiac form (I, 14). In Part II, he contrasts country life and life at court, with Don Quixote rejecting "el regalo, la abundancia... banquetes sazonados y... bebidas de nieve" ("luxury and abundance... highly-spiced banquets and snow cooled drinks") in favor of "la campaña rasa, libre..." and "La Libertad" (II, 58, 470) ("open country, free..." and "Liberty") (II, 837).[16]

Pastoral motifs also undergird the social satire against the corrupt present time. Only in the country is it possible to redress the confusions and unhappiness created by society and its boundaries. Cervantes exposes the cruelty of abusive adherence to his society's ideas about status, class, and rank through Dorothea's adventures and explanations of them. Speaking of her parents, she reveals the complexity of social, racial, and economic relationships which characterize the present "Siglo de Oro": "'... son labradores, gente llana, sin mezcla de alguna raza mal sonante, y, como suele decirse, cristianos viejos ranciosos," (I, 28, 348);

("they are farmers, simple people without any taint of ignoble blood, and what is generally called 'rusty old Christians' ") (239). Speaking of the man who had successfully seduced her, she identifies their "desigualdad" ("inequality") (I, 28, 350), and the confusion over strict social roles that the new wealth of the period had bequeathed to Spain:

> "Deste señor son vasallos mis padres, humildes en linaje, pero tan ricos, que si los bienes de su naturaleza igualaran a los de su fortuna, ni ellos tuvieran más que desear." (I, 28, 348)

> ("My parents are tenants of this lord, people of humble birth, but so rich, that if their rank were equal to their fortune they would have nothing more to desire.") (239).

The narratives concerning Cardenio and Lucinda, and Dorothea and Don Ferdinand (I, 27; I, 28; I, 36), and particularly Dorothea's speech from which I have quoted, reflect pastoral's power to subvert convention and the arbitrary despotism of parents, social stratification, and custom. Furthermore, in the pastoral settings in Part I, characters come to confront or disengage themselves from their unreflective delusions that result from their "literary" self-conceptions.[17]

"De lo que le sucedió a don Quijote con unos cabreros" ("What happened to Don Quixote with the goatherds" I, 11) presents pastoral life uncontaminated by the corruptions and anxieties of the contemporary society. Describing the idyllic golden age of ancient tradition, it describes a world in which everyone lived in harmony with a perfect balance between need and availability and no separation between thine and mine. In Don Quixote's lofty speech, referring to the First and New Testament advocacy for protection of widows and orphans (Isa. 9:17 and Jas. 1:27), he announces his own mission "defender las doncellas, amparar las viudas y socorrer a los huérfanos y a los menesterosos" (I, 11, 157) ("to defend maidens, relieve widows, and succour the orphans and the needy") (I, 11, 87).[18] It serves as a critique of rigid social and class lines, created by expanding colonialism, an autocratic monarchy, and the disruption of the countryside during Cervantes' lifetime. The author also satirizes the pastoral motif with "false shepherds" and the "pastor estudiante," Grisóstomo, who dies of love (I, 12-13, 161-180).[19] After the defeat in Part II, the Don's decision to turn shepherd, and lament his love for Dulcinea while also writing poetry accompanied by "los instrumentos pastorales" (II, 67, 549) ("pastoral instruments") (903) further exposes literary pastoralism. Cervantes grounds his discussions of literary art in similar ancient discourses first advanced by Plato in the *Republic*, Aristotle in the *Poetics*, and Horace in *The Ars Poetica*, which find their place in *Don Quixote*. The themes of *utile-dulce* and *imitatio* are introduced in the prologue, "Sólo tiene que aprovecharse de la imitación en lo que fuere escribiendo..." "...esta vuestra escritura no mira a más que a deshacer la autoridad y cabida que en el mundo y en el vulgo tienen los libros de caballerías..." (Prólogo, 57) ("In what you are writing you have only to make use of imitation..." "...this book of yours aims at no more than destroying the authority and influence which books of chivalry have in the world and among the common people...") (30).

The implications of these somewhat ingenuous assertions about the "useful" intent of the book expand both through the "donoso y grande escrutino que el cura y el barbero hicieron en la librería de nuestro ingenioso hidalgo" (I, 6) ("Of the great and pleasant Inquisition held by the Priest and the Barber over our ingenious gentleman's Library") (I, 6) and in the developed discussion beginning with the Canon's statement that "...yo hallo por mi cuenta que son muy perjudiciales en la república estos que llaman libros de caballerías." (I, 47, 564) ("...my own experience tells me that so-called books of chivalry are very prejudicial to the commonwealth") (424). The Canon's critique, based on Horace, "que son cuentos disparatados, que atienden solamente a deleitar, y no a enseñar" (564) ("which are extravagant tales, whose purpose is to amaze, and not to instruct" (424) (Horace, *The Ars Poetica*, Epistle II.3, 333-4), makes a case for realism and argues against the fabulous and unrealistic. Much of his discussion is based on Aristotelian precepts that include a defense of the unities of time, plot, and place and literary art as an imitation of reality.[20] The ironic implications of the Canon's argument, a recital of similar classical discussions of literary art, reveal themselves when he takes these earlier defenses as rules, and makes a case for censorship on the basis of their violation, exercised by "una persona inteligente y discreta que examinase todas las comedias antes que se representasen" (I, 48, 572) ("some intelligent and judicious person to examine all plays before they are performed") (430). In addition, Cervantes' fictional author Cide Hamete Benengeli examines *Don Quixote* according to the Aristotelian-Horacian literary theories of the day which further contributes to the parody of the various literary theories. Cervantes may be exposing the Aristotelian-Horatian literary aesthetic, arguing instead for the liberation of art from mimetic functions.[21]

From this overview of Cervantes' ancient literary sources, we can appreciate that he works with a literary canon with which he establishes continuity. I realize I am not discussing the tone in which the author captures the past, but rather emphasizing the author's adoption of a canon of previously established readings that fall in line with his assumptions about a cultural tradition that he is at liberty to control in his own work.

Yet at the same time our author establishes continuity with this literary canon, he also shows his knowledge of the literary developments in continental Europe. Cervantes' incorporation of Renaissance philosophy and literary developments has been well-established. These include the impact of Renaissance Italian literature, Ariosto,[22] Tasso, Castiglione,[23] and Petrarch, of Erasmus,[24] and of the contemporary pastoral[25] and chivalric novels.[26] Petrarch, Petrarchism,[27] and the absurdity of unrequited male love of a real or imaginary woman are satirized in Don Quixote's adoration of Dulcinea, a love which eventually contributes to his melancholic demise, just as Grisistomo's unrequited love for Marcela destroys him. (I, 12–13). Marcela is the Petrarchan object of love, who unlike the silent Laura, speaks back in her own defense.

Montaigne's *Essais* echo in Don Quixote's invocation to the past golden age when "Todo era paz entonces, todo amistad, todo concordia" (I, 11, 156) ("All was peace then, all amity, all concord") (I, 11, 86). This emphasis on a concordant commonwealth recalls Montaigne's indictment of Europe, a continent he finds in sharp contrast with the "bonté, libéralité, loyauté, franchise" of the native people of the New World.[28] Cervantes' reference suggests his interest in the simple peasant life and the decimation of Indian civilizations in the New World during the present "Siglo de Oro." The Don's speech to the "Goatherds," moored in Montaigne's essay in praise of traditional societies, connects the herders' remote and uncluttered life to the "arcadian" golden age, both of which are in ironic contrast to the Spanish Golden Age.

The *Quixote* comments on the literature and politics of its own age, deploys ancient literary motifs and discussions, and it revolutionizes the novel. It functions like a hinge for the two main narrative forms, connecting the ancient and Renaissance epic to the modern novel. Galdós wrote in *Napoleón en Chamartin* that the *Quixote* was "la matriz de todas las novelas del mundo" ("the matrix of all the novels in the world"). Without doubt, the impact of the novel on prose fiction in the following centuries was powerful and central.[29] Its influence spans all realms of literary art from the many expanded possibilities for the novel form, social context, characterization, perspective, tone and style, language, and attitude, among other elements. Harry Levin, working on an insight of Georg Lukács in *Die Theorie des Romans* (1916) believed that the *Quixote* was the essential link in the history of narrative from ancient epic to the modern *Bildungsroman*.[30] René Girard in his *Deceit, Desire, and the Novel* (1961) maintains that Cervantes' masterpiece establishes the core terms of desire and imitation underlying the accomplishments of the modern novel. Marthe Robert's highly respected *The Old and the New*, by juxtaposing Kafka's *The Castle* and *Don Quixote*, shows the role of Cervantes' novel as paradigm for modern fiction.[31] Before *Don Quixote*, we cannot find a fictional *prose* work with an autonomous relationship between author, narrator, and audience, for the author constructs narrators and abandons direct control over the reader or listener, a condition which begins to characterize the novel from Cervantes onwards. In other words, Cervantes constructs a literary world in which the author and his narrators have an ambiguous relationship to their audiences. His influence, not only on the development of the form of the genre but on the subject matter, is found in the European and American novel of the 18th and 19th centuries, in Swift, Smollett, Sterne, Fielding, Stendhal, Daudet, Dickens, Dostoevsky, Flaubert, Melville, William Dean Howells, and Mark Twain.[32] That he also had a wide readership among women is suggested by Charlotte Ramsay Lennox's *The Female Quixote: or the Adventures of Arabella*, which appeared in 1752 and went through eight English editions. Gide, Proust, Conrad, Joyce, Virginia Woolf, Pirandello, Sinclair Lewis, Thornton Wilder, William Saroyan,[33] and Kurt Vonnegut in the 20th century all assimilated the influence of the *Quixote*. In Latin American literature, where the novel's influence is likewise widespread, Cervantes' impact appears in the work of Rubén Dario, José Fernández de Lizardi, and Jorge Luis Borges among many others.[34]

I have so far discussed *Don Quixote*'s literary sources and the influence of the novel in an effort to demonstrate the nature of "canonicity," and the place of a canonical work in a literary tradition which the author constructs in his or her own creative activity.

Critics of the canon will certainly object that despite all the novel's literary grounding and Cervantes' sense of his own "canonical" activity, that the novel has nothing to do with the issues, concerns, and passions of our own time. To this criticism first I would respond that interpretive activity ought to acknowledge at least four time zones: the historical time when the work was composed; the imaginary time in which the work is set; the present, that is, our own time; and finally the timeless zone, the space for concerns and insights which may transcend historical circumstance.[35] Also implicit is a fifth time zone because texts direct themselves to the future, the time that has yet to come. The act of writing, rather than connoting "silence" or "absence," on the contrary, is a serious effort to communicate with the present and the future. In contrast to speech, writing directs itself to the future to set up a connection and continuity with it. The work of the interpreter is to know these times intimately, however approximate they may be, if he intends to scrutinize and live with a text with any kind of understanding. The interpreter works to re-discover the historical time in its own integrity but with self-reflection and consciousness of the time in which he or she lives.

"Great" works exist within these temporal approximations. They cross time zones that alter their defined meanings. They speak coherently about their own times and construct fantasy times and circumstances. They show their adaptability to new times in their capacity to regenerate themselves for future readers. Finally, they synthesize concerns about the human condition: the nature, experience, and meaning of time, death, love, sex, freedom, loyalty, justice and injustice, human transcendence, and the ineffable. The ambiguity, humor, and irony in *Don Quixote* render the specifically Cervantine version of these "conditions of being human." The novel also focuses on contemporary concerns with Spanish institutions, colonialism, social stratification, women's plight, and the inquisition. For us, it suggests a contemporary resonance in social history, feminism, Marxism, radical religious doubt as well as religious bigotry, and the contingency of human effort and accomplishment.

A second point which critics of the canon might consider is that "canonical works" in themselves represent a traditional consensus and as a consequence are a buttress for historical value despite their own contingent status. This concept of contingency in humanistic production and inquiry which makes all our efforts, including the construction of "lists," subject to probability and reasoned chance, possesses almost a canonical status. Rather than an invention of post-modernism, "contingency" has been appropriated by the "new" in the mistaken belief that relativity is unique to the present intellectual age. A central tenet of ancient education in rhetoric was, as Aristotle emphasized, the existence of "alternative possibilities." In the first four centuries of Christianity, major struggles were waged over what texts to include in the biblical canon and why, and how these texts were to be interpreted. In these early centuries, Jerome and Augustine, both trained in Ciceronian rhetoric with its contingency presuppositions, fought vehemently over scriptural exegesis. Jerome, the philologist, defended the same kind of multiple interpretation as he applied to secular literature, and asked Augustine, to "play together in the field of Scriptures without hurting each other." (Letter 81, Jerome to Augustine). Augustine rejected the idea of "play" in interpretation. asking his friend to help him "toil up the mountain of Scriptures." (Letter 82, Augustine to Jerome).[36] The two central figures of the early Latin Church were, therefore, obliged to concede to probability, that is, contingency, rather than certainty on issues of canonicity and interpretation of Christian texts. To make decisions about the interpretation and canonicity of a text, they demurred to "historical value," or tradition, for they were obliged to depend on apostolicity (i.e. the authority of witnesses), catholicity (i.e. "universal" consensus), orthodoxy, and established usage, even though they recognized the relativity on which these decisions relied.

A third point is that as a canonical text, *Don Quixote* does offer itself to contemporary theoretical concerns, particularly those of reader-response, feminism, and social or psychological history and interpretation.[37] The novel's canonical validity is re-enforced by its openness to the concerns of contemporary discourse theory; to retain its canonicity, it must remain as open to ideological criticism as non-canonical works.

Don Quixote declares itself from the start to be a novel about reading: "Desocupado lector: sin juramento me podrás creer que quisiera que este libro, como hijo del entendimiento..." (I, Prólogo, 50) ("Idle reader, you can believe without any oath of mine that I would wish this book, as the child of my brain...") (26).[38] The author engages the reader in the interpretation of the work, and throughout the novel uses the subjectivity of readers as a tool to deal with his literary ambuscade. The novel explores this response from the moment Don Quixote is inspired to ride out for adventure in imitation of the chivalric novels he has read. Who are the "false shepherds," except students in pastoral dress who are inspired by pastoral novels? In fact, nearly every character in the *Quixote* reveals an affection for imaginative literature.[39] Thus Cervantes focuses on the nature and impact of reading and throws open the interpretive possibilities of his text: if his hidalgo could shift from knight errant to false shepherd, Cervantes implies that literary works have the power to direct human activity no matter how absurd their directives might become. Cervantes is also indicting popular chivalry and pastoral texts because they appeal to a limited imagination and readers' desires for false self-images.[40] Perhaps the spread of literacy and armchair reading in the Renaissance allowed Cervantes to appeal to a private "reader-response," but individual "subjective" interpretations also allowed him to skirt the keen eyes of the censors. B. W. Ife shows that the vehement attacks against Spanish prose fiction in the Golden Age were a response to its popularity due in part to the printing revolution and to the spread of private reading. In answer to the moral and metaphysical Platonic critique against fiction, Ife argues, Golden Age writers bring readers into their fiction through the first-person narrative, so that readers are actually exploited by the narrator and lose their own point of view; but, this engagement with the text turns out to be a source of strength, not danger (contra Plato) because if the reader works hard at his reading, he will encounter "contingency," and have to confront conflicting interpretations, and therefore to judge complex issues as well as his own validity as an interpreter.[41] Wrapping his social criticism in the activities of a mad-man and his somewhat dishonest "escudero," lovable as they may be, Cervantes liberated himself from the conclusions serious or frivolous readers might assume.

The novel also invites feminist analyses. Many of Cervantes' female characters possess personalities that show autonomy and independence from hierarchical restrictions. Some are ingenious, intelligent, courageous, sensible, eloquent, honest; others can be vindictive and capable of guile. They emerge, like many of the women of the *Odyssey*, able to take care of themselves and to direct males. However, they contrast with the silent women of the Petrarchan love poetry tradition. They talk back, and they react when they are threatened by male power assumptions. Don Quixote's lady-love Dulcinea, on the other hand, in his fantasy, is the perfect Petrarchan love idyll who inspires the Don even though he has never spoken to her and has only admired her from a distance. Of course, the Don fails to see that she is actually "moza de chapa, hecha y derecha y de pelo en pecho, y que puede sacar la barba del lodo a cualquier caballero andante..." (I, 25, 312) ("a brawny girl, well built and tall and sturdy, and she will know how to keep her chin out of the mud with any knight errant who ever has her as a mistress...") (209). Marcela, Maritornes, Dorothea, Juana/Teresa Panza, Altisodora, the three village girls, that is, many of the women Don Quixote encounters on his journeys, are the opposite to his fantasy and the silent Dulcinea or his niece and housekeeper, whose conservative adherence to cultural codes restricts them to the dull and repetitious life of a small town and its affairs. Cervantes' treatment of the other mature, self-confident women reflects an emerging gender-consciousness in the Renaissance, when women, who were financially vulnerable or secure in their own right, were in the act of choosing autonomous lives for themselves. Marcela and Juana/Teresa Panza are examples of this excursus into the realm of female autonomy.

Marcela, for example, appears in the novel like an Artemis, a virgin who rejects congress with men and asserts her own right to do so. When a young man dies of love for her, fulfilling the promises of the Petrarchan lover, reality grips poetry. Unlike the taciturn women of the Petrarchan tradition, whose iciness is a poetic construction, Marcela is a real woman with the politics of gender on her side:

> "Pues si la honestidad es una de las virtudes que al cuerpo y alma más adornan y hermosean, por qué la ha de perder la que es amada por hermosa, por corresponder a la intención de aquel que, por sólo su gusto, con todas sus fuerzas e industrias procura que la pierda? Yo nací libre, y para poder vivir libre escogí la soledad de los campos." (I, 14, 186)

> (Now if modesty is one of the virtues and the fairest adornment of the body and the soul, why must the woman who is loved for her beauty lose it to gratify the desires of a man who, for his pleasure alone, tries with all his strength and ingenuity to rob her of it? I was born free and to live free I chose the solitude of the fields.) (I, 14, 108–109)

Insisting on her right to female autonomy, Marcela responds for all the silent female objects of male Petrarchan infatuation. Her argument convinces Don Quixote because of its eloquence, but also because Marcela, as "false shepherdess," like the Don as false "knight errant," is living out literary fantasies. In his treatment of Marcela, Cervantes combines literary and social commentary.

Like Marcela, Juana/Teresa Panza, the peasant Sancho's wife, is of independent mind and has no hesitation to press her demands on her recalcitrant husband whose delusions about social climbing and financial advancement match his master's mad desire to "reform the world." She is sensitive and wise, seeing the world in which she lives without glitter. If Sancho Panza is a realist in relationship to Don Quixote, he becomes as mad as his master in contrast to his wife. Juana/Teresa, firmly grounded in her peasant roots and unpretensious reality, knows herself and her place. Nor does she envy those who lack her self-knowledge:

> Pues con todo eso, temo que este condado de mi hija ha de ser su perdición. Vos haced lo que quisiéredes, ora la hagáis duquesa, o princesa; pero séos decir que no será ello con voluntad ni consentimiento mío. Siempre, hermano, fui amiga de la iqualdad, y no puedo ver entonos sin fundamentos. Teresa me pusieron en el bautismo, nombre mondo y escueto, sin añadiduras ni cortapisas, ni arrequives..." (II, 5, 76)

> ("All the same, I'm still afraid that this countessing of my daughter's will be her undoing. But do as you like. Make her a duchess or a princess. But let me tell you that it won't be with my will and consent. I've always been a lover of equality, and I can't bear to see haughtiness with no foundations. Teresa they wrote me down at my baptism, pure and simple without trimmings or ornaments...") (500)

This dialogue between Sancho and Teresa, which the narrator claims was "por apócrifo" (II, 5, 73) ("apocryphal") (497), because Sancho's remarks are so "subtle that they seem beyond the range of his intelligence," is a sensitive revelation of the social and class layers of the Spanish Golden Age. The discussion probes the consequences of new wealth on established social coding and how these changes disrupt people's sense of social place. It is an elaborate analysis of the various aspects of the class system and its social and economic inequities in Spain in the 17th century, and as such appeals to contemporary social and cultural interests. The contrast between Sancho and the Don, the peasant proverb versus the Latin literary tradition, marriages based on social class rather than love, and the "Goatherd" incident in Part I among others, all show Cervantes' interest in the psycho-social implications of class distinctions which were in a state of flux in the Spain of the

Golden Age. These incidents and the themes and social conditions they imply are, of course, fertile possibilities for the current interests in social analysis.

Don Quixote's madness has been the subject of numerous studies,[42] and like other thematic characteristics of the novel, it also resonates with contemporary interests in social history and psychoanalytic theory addressed by Michel Foucault and Jacques Lacan. The nature of madness, the rights of society to impose its standards of sanity on its members, and the questions, "who is mad?" and "who is sane?" are all proposed in the novel, even if the answers are clouded in ambiguities and the irony of authorial detachment. Madness is Cervantes' subterfuge by which he can satirize his society and its delusions yet conceal his criticisms beneath the ravings of a mad man and other aberrant or inadequate characters.

The novel's openness to contemporary interests and literary methods demonstrates that its canonicity hardly restricts it to a conservative, aristocratic readership or prevents it from re-presenting itself to a future readership. To the contrary, its canonicity is precisely its ability to attract successive interpretations and its openness to ideological criticism.

In conclusion, canons of literary excellence exist, and authors construct them to direct readers to their own place in a continuous dialogue of literary exchange. History exists, and it divides itself into periods and dominant interests. It is the responsibility of the critic to know these concerns and their chronologies so that he or she might appreciate and make sense of the artifacts that inhabit the sweep of our present and past. Finally, "central" texts have something profound and "beautiful" to say not only at the moment they undergo human creation, but later as they adapt to "contemporary concerns," and during all this time, they also express timeless human concerns in aesthetic form.

This discussion of *Don Quixote* as a "canonical text" privileges the author's literary intentions, the persuasive medium of his text, and the audience who has become intimately involved with both. Cervantes' sources reveal his own literary intentions and set him in a revered literary tradition, but the text is, to be sure, an autonomous entity that itself unravels deeper textual complexities. It is a matter of course that such narrative intentionality would engage current critical interests. The crux of the matter lies, to my view, in its ability to engage temporal interest in the reader that is both horizontal and vertical, historical, contemporary, and timeless. Ideologues might indeed attempt to seize control of the text—there are reasons that such attempts should be made—but always their ultimate struggle will be with a powerfully triple human phenomenology: a text's author, its canonical power, and the full response of its audience.

University of California,
Davis

NOTES

1. I.F. Stone, *The Trial of Socrates* (New York : Anchor/Doubleday, 1989), 6.
2. For an expansion of this idea, see Paul Gagnon, "Why Study History? To protect our democracy, we must grasp its meaning and accept its burdens," *The Atlantic* (November, 1988), 43–66.
3. *Postscript to the Name of the Rose*, trans. William Weaver (San Diego, 1984), 67. Lee Patterson elaborates on this idea in a thought-provoking essay, "On the Margin: Postmodernism, Ironic History, and Medieval Studies," *Speculum* 65 (Jan., 1990), 87–108.
4. Miguel de Cervantes, *Don Quijote de la Mancha (Bibliografía fundamental)* III. Ed. Luis Andrés Murillo (Madrid: Clásicos Castalia, 1978), 27.
5. See Dana B. Drake, *Don Quijote in World Literature: A Selective, Annotated Bibliography (1894-1970)* Vol. III (New York & London: Garland Publishing, Inc., 1980), 233–243.
6. Alonso Fernández de Avellaneda, *El Ingenioso Hidalgo Don Quijote de la Mancha.* Ed. Fernando García Salinero (Madrid: Clásicos Castalia, 1971); Stephen Gilman, *Cervantes y Avellaneda, estudio de una imitación.* Prólogo de Américo Castro (Mexico: Colegio de México, 1951) proposes that the spurious part 2 was written by a Dominican priest who wanted to redress the moral lapses in Cervantes' *Don Quixote.*
7. See *Don Quijote in World Literature.* 3–31 for a bibliography of the influence of the Quixote throughout the centuries including translations, editions, and analysis of the nature of the impact.
8. See Manuel Durán, *"El Quijote a través del prisma de Mikhail Bakhtine: carnaval, disfraces, escatología y locura,"* in *Cervantes and the Renaissance.* Ed. Michael D. McGaha (Easton, Pennsylvania: Juan de la Cuesta, 1980), 71–86.
9. See Edwin B. Place, "Cervantes and the *Amadis,"* *Hispanic Studies in Honor of Nicholson B. Adams.* Ed. J. E. Keller and K.-L Selig (Chapel Hill: University of North Carolina Press, 1966), 131–140.
10. Michael D. McGaha in "Cervantes and Virgil" makes a convincing argument that "the parody of the novels of chivalry was in reality only a smokescreen intended to mask Cervantes' primary intention in *Don Quixote,* which was to imitate and improve upon Virgil's *Aeneid."* In *Cervantes and the Renaissance,* 34. See also Chester L. Wolford, "Don Quixote and the Epic of Subversion," in *Cervantes*

and the Pastoral. Ed. José J. Labrador Herraiz and Juan Fernandéz Jiménez (Cleveland: Penn. State University-Behrend College and Cleveland State University, 1986), 197–211.

11. L.A. Murillo, "Don Quixote as Renaissance Epic," in *Cervantes and the Renaissance*. 51–70.

12. All references to the Spanish text of *Don Quixote* are to Miguel de Cervantes, *El Ingenioso Hidalgo Don Quijote de la Mancha* I & II. Ed. Luis Andrés Murillo (Madrid: Clásicas Castalia, 1978). The English translations are from Miguel Cervantes, *Don Quixote*, tr. J.M. Cohen (Middlesex, England: Penguin, 1950).

13. Leo Spitzer discussed the polyonomasia of the novel in terms of identity instability and medieval origins in "Linguistic Perpectivism in the *Don Quijote*." Rept. in *Cervantes*. Ed. Harold Bloom (New York, London, and Philadelphia: Chelsea House, 1987), 9–35. I am suggesting that another possible source might be the epic where multi-naming is commonplace. Of course, as with all other epic traits and motifs, Cervantes is playing with the device and subverting it for his own literary purposes.

14. The term "pastoral oasis" is Renato Poggioli's term for a brief retreat or bucolic episode in a *locus amoenus*, which breaks the action and suspends the "heroic, romantic, or pathetic mood of the whole." He identifies these pastoral moments, like E.R. Curtius, with Virgil and Virgilian bucolic tradition. *The Oaten Flute: Essays on Pastoral Poets and the Pastoral Ideal* (Cambridge, Mass.: Harvard University Press, 1975), 9–10.

15. *Metamorphosis* I, vss. 89–112; Seneca, *Epistulae morales*, 90.

16. See Thomas R. Hart, *Cervantes and Ariosto: Renewing Fiction* (Princeton, New Jersey: Princeton University Press, 1989), particularly chapters V, "Pastoral Interludes" and VI, "Disprayse of Courtly Life," 73–114.

17. See Ruth El Safar, *Beyond Fiction: The Recovery of the Feminine in the Novels of Cervantes* (Berkeley, Los Angeles, and London: University of California Press, 1984) for an elaboration of this point, 47–80.

18. Both Hart, 74–75 and Poggioli, 202–203 remark that while Cervantes' pastoral converges in formal patterns with Tasso's golden age vision found in the drama *Aminta*, Cervantes' ideology is completely different.

19. Dominick Finello, "Shepherds at Play: Literary Convention and Disguises in the Pastoral Narratives of the *Quijote*," in *Cervantes and the Pastoral*, 115–127.

20. John G. Weiger, *In the Margins of Cervantes* (Hanover and London: University Press of New England, 1988), assumes Cervantes' primary source for Aristotle's *Poetics* was Alonso López Pinciano's *Philosophía antigua poética*, published in 1596. See his discussion, 35–36 and 80.

21. See Alban K. Forcione, *Cervantes, Aristotle and the Persiles* (Princeton: Princeton University Press, 1970), particularly Part II: "Cervantes and the Classical Aesthetic: *Don Quixote*," 91–166.

22. Thomas R. Hart, in *Cervantes and Ariosto*, asserts that Cervantes learned more from Ariosto's *Orlando Furioso* than from the Spanish chivalry novels, 4. See also Luís Murillo, "Don Quixote as Renaissance Epic."

23. Leonard Mades, *The Armor and the Brocade: A Study of Don Quixote and the Courtier* (New York: Las Américas Publ. Co., 1968); Joseph G. Fucilla, "The Role of *the Cortegiano* in the Second Part of *Don Quijote*," *Hispania* 33 (1960): 291–296.

24. A number of essays deal with the Erasmus/Cervantes connection. A. Vilanova wrote *Erasmo y Cervantes* (Barcelona: CSIC, 1949) and Bruce W. Wardropper discusses Cervantes' connection with Erasmus in "Cervantes and Education" in *Cervantes and the Renaissance*, 178–193; also, see Alban K. Forcione, *Cervantes and the Mystery of Lawlessness* (Princeton: Princeton University Press, 1984) for interspersed digressions on the connection between Cervantes and Erasmus. José Ramón Sampayo Rodríguez, *Rasgos erasmistas de La Locura del Licenciado Vidriera de Miguel de Cervantes* (Kassel: Edition Reichenberger, 1986) argues that "erasmism" was deeply embedded in Cervantes' imagination, 39–55.

25. *Cervantes and the Pastoral.*

26. Ramón Menéndez Pidal, *Cervantes y el ideal caballeresco* (Madrid: PCCC, Gráfica Comercial, 1948).

27. Joseph G. Fucilla, "Cervantes," *Estudios sobre el petrarquismo en España* (Madrid: RFE, 1960), 177–181.

28. "Des Coches," Livre III, ch. VI.

29. *Don Quijote in World Literature*, a selected bibliography published in 1980, nevertheless lists over 500 items showing the novel's influence in Europe, Asia, and the Americas from the seventeenth century to the present.

30. Harry Levin, "The Quixotic Principle: Cervantes and Other Novelists," in *The Interpretation of Narrative, Theory and Practice*." Ed. Morton W. Bloomfield (Cambridge, Mass.: Harvard University Press, 1970), 45–66.

31. *The Old and the New: From Don Quixote to Kafka.* Tr. Carol Cosman (Berkeley and Los Angeles: University of California Press, 1977).

32. Manuel Durán, *Cervantes* (New York: Twayne Publishers, Inc., 1974). See also Ludmilla Buketoff Turkevich, *Cervantes in Russia* (Princeton, N.J.: Princeton University Press, 1950).

33. Leo Spitzer, "On the Significance of *Don Quijote*," *Modern Language Notes* 77 (1962), 113–129.

34. Juan Uribe-Echevarría, *Cervantes en Las Lettras Hispano-Americanas* (Chile: Ediciones de la Universidad de Chile, 1949); "Don Quixote in Latin America" in *Don Quixote in World Literature*, 197–218.

35. L.A. Murillo in *The Golden Dial: Temporal Figuration in Don Quijote* (Oxford: The Dolphin Book Co., Ltd., 1975) touches on the mythic sub-structure of the novel.

36. Saint Augustine, *Letters*. Vol. I (1–82). Tr. Sr. Wilfrid Parsons, S.N.D (New York: Fathers of the Church, Inc., 1951).

37. I am using general notions about these theories as represented in Terry Eagleton's *Literary Theory: An Introduction* (Minneapolis: University of Minnesota Press, 1983).

38. Carlos Fuentes explored this issue in *Don Quixote: or The Critique of Reading* (Austin: Institute of Latin American Studies, University of Texas at Austin, 1976).

39. *In the Margins of Cervantes*, 73.

40. *In the Margins of Cervantes*, 93; *Beyond Fiction*, 47-80.
41. B.W. Ife, *Reading and fiction in Golden-Age Spain: A Platonist critique and some picaresque replies* (Cambridge: Cambridge University Press, 1985). See "Introduction," 1-23 and 172-173.
42. See Volume III, *Don Quijote de la Mancha: Bibliografia fundamental*, 98 for previous studies and Carroll B. Johnson, *Madness and Lust: A Psychoanalytical Approach to Don Quixote* (Berkeley and London: University of California Press, 1983).

Texts Within Texts:
The Power of Letters
In Edith Wharton's Fiction

ELSA NETTELS

They lay on the table before him like live
things that he feared to touch. . .At length
he opened the first volume. A familiar letter
sprang out at him, each word quickened by
its glaring garb of type. The little broken
phrases fled across the page like wounded
animals in the open. . .It was a horrible
sight...He had not known it would be like
this. . . .

Edith Wharton, *The Touchstone*

Edith Wharton titled one story "The Letter," another, "The Letters,"
but she could have given one title or the other to a dozen of her short
stories. In her longer fiction as well, the writing and the reading of letters
are crucial in the development of plot and the revelation of character.
From her first novella, *The Touchstone* (1900), to her last completed
novel, *The Gods Arrive* (1932), written communications—letters, notes,
telegrams—affect characters' lives as decisively as words spoken.

Two metaphors from the short fiction identify the most important
functions of letters in Wharton's narratives. Letters are touchstones,
revelations of the moral nature of the writer and the recipient. As
touchstones, letters may test one person's faith in another, as in "The

191

Confession''; they may test the sense of honor and loyalty in many persons, as in *The Touchstone*. Letters also contain a ''spring'' (the metaphor appears in ''The Blond Beast''), a spring that moves characters to act and effects results, usually ironic reversals of a character's intention.

The reading of a letter, or even the sight of a letter, may transform lives—may cause a woman and her lover to meet (''Roman Fever''), a ghostly presence to commit murder (''Mr. Jones''), a woman to lose her husband to his first wife, who sends him letters from the land of the dead (''Pomegranate Seed''). Letters may be instruments of manipulation and revenge, weapons to deceive, intimidate, terrify, or blackmail the recipient. Letter may be vehicles for confession and expression of love; they maybe commodities to be bought and sold, as in *The Touchstone* and *The House of Mirth*. Whatever their purpose, letters are the perfect instruments for the effects Edith Wharton sought in her fiction—the creation of doubt, irony, and paradox. Once the writer of a letter dispatches it, the writer cannot control its course or its effects. Often the letter produces results opposite to those intended by the writer. The recipient of a letter may doubt its authenticity. Whether or not a letter was actually written may be in question if its existence can never be proved.

Wharton's characters who compose letters are usually moved by the fear of loss or failure. They write to avert rupture with a lover (as in *The Children*) or to sustain the illusion of a relationship (as in *The Touchstone* and ''The Letters''). Characters write letters in the desire to transform daydreams into reality, as Pauline Manford in *Twilight Sleep,* threatened by her husband's affair with her son's wife, reassures herself by idealizing the family's life in a letter that ''gives her the feeling, to which she was always secretly inclined, that a thing was so if one said it was, and doubly so, if one wrote it down.''[1]

Letters have been compared to performance, the letter-writer to an actor who creates an identity to elicit the desired response from an audience.[2] In several of Wharton's stories, characters fabricate letters of actual or imaginary persons to advance their own interests or to gratify desires that life does not satisfy. In ''The Looking Glass,'' a masseuse and medium triumphs over a rival by concocting love letters that her employer takes as proof from the spirit world that a man she once desired had returned her love. In ''His Father's Son,'' a businessman confesses to his son that years ago, out of longing for romance in a mundane life, he initiated a correspondence with a famous pianist by writing letters of worshipful adoration in his wife's name. A novelist in "Full Circle" writes letters to himself, praising his latest novel, attacked by the critics, so that his secretary, whose job is to answer the fan mail, will think that the novelist is highly successful. Later the secretary, desperate to keep his job, composes letters to the novelist so that the novelist will continue to need the services of the secretary to answer the mail. The secretary is so successful in creating one correspondent, a young woman in Florida, that the novelist writes to request a meeting with her.

So accomplished are the letter writers—as skillful in impersonation as their readers are susceptible to flattery—that other characters learn of the deceptions only when the letter writers confess to them. Their stories thus magnify the double-edged nature of letter writing in Wharton's fiction. On the one hand, many of the letter writers are suppliants, psychologically or financially dependent on the favor of another person. More love letters are sent to characters who don't want to receive them than to those who do.[3] A number of characters display more moral strength in destroying letters than in writing them.[4] On the other hand, a letter can be so potent an instrument that it confers the importance of its potential power upon the writer. And whatever the motives of the writer, whatever the ultimate fate of the letter, the writer enjoys, however briefly, undisputed control of words, such as no other situation allows. For some characters, the exercise of the imagination in the writing of a letter affords greater satisfaction than any other experience.

Edith Wharton wrote no epistolary fiction like James's "A Bundle of Letters" and "The Point of View" or Howells's *Letters Home* and *Through the Eye of the Needle*. Her characters read or write letters at decisive points in their lives but more often than not the text of the letters is not given. In stories in which letters are the focal point—e.g. *The Touchstone,* "The Letters," "The Pomegranate Seed"—the reader, in the absence of a text, must imagine the words that exert so powerful an effect. When the text of a letter is given, it usually appears at the point of its receipt by the person addressed. His response (the recipient is almost always male) may be noted, but the thoughts of a writer as she composes a letter (the writer is usually female) are rarely given.[5] Her motives in writing must be inferred from the text of the letter, which may lend itself to different interpretations.[6]

Passages from characters' letters are reproduced in several novels—
The Age of Innocence, Twilight Sleep, The Children, and *The
Buccaneers.* In only one work, "The Muse's Tragedy," included in
Wharton's first collection of short stories, *The Greater Inclination*
(1899), does an entire section consist of the text of a letter. The writer
of the letter, an intelligent and cultivated woman who for years ministered
to the genius of a great poet in the vain hope of being loved by him,
foreshadows a number of Wharton's female characters. The use of a
letter to tell a character's story is not characteristic, however. The story
is something of a *tour de force,* an anomaly in Wharton's fiction. But
the text of the letter, which makes the story unique, also makes the story
the best illustration of the kinds of ambiguities letters create, the strategies
letter writers employ, and the sources of the power that letter writers
in the other stories and novels command.

The first two parts of "The Muse's Tragedy" are narrated in third
person from the perspective of a young literary critic, Lewis Danyers,
who by chance encounters the author of the letter, Mary Anerton, at
a hotel on the Italian lakes. At first he delights simply in meeting the
woman universally believed to have been the beloved mistress and muse
whom the revered poet, Vincent Rendle, commemorated in his *Sonnets
to Silvia,* which Danyers, at college, had analyzed in a prize essay. (The
narrator of James's "The Aspern Papers" comes to mind.) As his
acquaintance with Mrs. Anerton develops, Danyers falls in love with
her and rejoices that she values him not merely as a devotee of the dead
poet, that in their walks "they did not always talk of Rendle or of
literature."[7] He responds eagerly to her proposal that he write a book
about Rendle, "a complete interpretation," but only when she indicates
that she will help him, in effect, as she did Rendle, by "[laying] the
awakening touch on his spirit" (13). Part II ends as they agree to meet
in Venice six weeks hence to talk of the book she will help him write.

Part III is the text of Mrs. Anerton's letter, indicating a lapse of
some ten weeks. During that time, the first paragraphs of the letter make
clear, she and Danyers spent a month together in Venice but never spoke
of the book. He proposed marriage, she left Venice with the promise
to return in a week to give him her answer. (The reader may assume
that they had become lovers.) In the letter she makes a series of
confessions to explain why she did not return.

She admits first that she was not honest in her promise to Danyers,
that when she left him she knew she would not return to Venice and

would not marry him. "I was running away from you—and I mean to keep on running!" (14). The reason she offers is not the reason he might suppose, that having been loved by Rendle she can love no one else. The truth, she states, is that Rendle never loved her, that all the while that she had craved his love he had wanted from her only intellectual companionship and an appreciative response to his poetry. He was also happy to enjoy the comfort and security of her husband's and her well-ordered household. She had allowed the public to believe that she was Silvia, the poet's mistress, feeding on the myth to keep her own hopes alive. Even after the poet's death, when she prepared his letters to her for publication, she had sought to perpetuate the myth by inserting asterisks at suggestive points to imply the omission of intimate details, too sacred for the public eye. But, in fact, "the asterisks were a sham—*there was nothing to leave out*" (18). The sonnets were "addressed to Woman, not to a woman!" (18). She confesses finally that, obsessed by the fear that no man could love her, she had conducted a "psychological experiment" (23) upon Danyers to discover whether she could inspire love in him.

Critics have treated "The Muse's Tragedy" as an unambiguous story of a woman forced by social convention to sacrifice her own life and talents to the needs and the desires of the man she loves. In Elizabeth Ammons's reading, Mrs. Anerton suffers "bitter disillusionment" in discovering that "men cannot love her body and her mind; it must be one or the other."[8] According to Cynthia Griffin Wolff, Mrs. Anerton "had been the perfect, passive incarnation of femininity; she had inspired great art; and she had been reduced, in the process, to the status of a friend, at best, and a convenient object at worst."[9]

No one has written to question these readings or to suggest that the text of Mary Anerton's letter requires analysis. But the feminist emphasis on the victimization of the protagonist obscures questions raised by the letter that make the story more problematic than critics indicate. The letter stands alone in Part III, with no salutation or closing and with no context to indicate whether or not Danyers received the letter or whether Mary Anerton even sent it. She tells Danyers that he is the first to know her secret, that in confiding in him she assuages her sense of loneliness: "If you knew what a relief it is to tell some one at last, you would bear with me, you would let me hurt you! I shall never be quite so lonely again, now that some one knows" (15–19). But if she kept her secret until she met Danyers, why did she tell the one man most likely to write a biography of the poet? What did she believe or hope that Danyers would say about her relationship to Rendle? She admits that she falsified letters to mislead the public and sustain a false identity. Can the reader be certain that the desire to create a certain impression has not resulted in fabrication in this letter? If she was married to a man devoted to her, as the confidante, Mrs. Memorall, tells Danyers in Part I, was the husband such a cipher, was her self-esteem so fragile, that she had to have an affair to test her power to win a man's love? How reliable an informant is Mrs. Memorall, whose name (memory of all) invites the reader's acceptance of her statements but who is satirized by the narrator's witty comparison of her to a "volume of unindexed and discursive memoirs" containing "layers of dusty twaddle" (7)? No conclusive answers are possible, but the text of the letter is rich in implications, suggesting in the letter-writer a complexity of feeling and motive that illuminates a corresponding complexity in Edith Wharton's own view of erotic love.

Most readily apparent in the letter are Mary Anerton's conflicting feelings about Rendle. She insists upon her love for the man himself; her acknowledged longing for his love implies more than the egoistic need to believe him worthy of the years of her devotion. Also evident is an undercurrent of antagonism, a sense of injury in his use of her, resentment of his obtuseness that allowed him to profit from her friendship without awareness of her feelings and thus without remorse or a sense of guilt. She seems to accept, even to value as a gift to him, her service as a passive object: "my mind must have been to him (I fancy) like some perfectly tuned instrument on which he was never tired of playing" (16). But her sentence implies his extraction of a single part of herself for his gratification.

When she writes of his dalliance with another woman, she uses the satiric effect of punctuation and cliches to undercut them all—the woman, the poet, and herself:

> There was a girl once (I am telling you everything), a lovely being who called his poetry "deep" and gave him *Lucile* on his birthday. He followed her to Switzerland one summer, and all the time that he was dangling after her (a little too conspicuously, I always thought, for a Great Man), he was writing to *me* about his theory of vowel-combinations—or was it his experiments in English hexameter?" (19-20).

(Danyers will presumably appreciate the irony of the gift to the poet of Bulwer Lytton's popular sentimental poem, in which the title character, a woman of intellect, suffers because she *refuses* to sacrifice herself for a man who loves her.) Assuming that Mrs. Anerton intends to send her letter to Danyers, she is giving to a prospective biographer information that not only deprives her of her identity as the adored Silvia but shows the foolish and parasitic underside of the poet's genius.

The dominant tone of the letter, however, is not vengeful or vindictive. The writer's purpose does not seem to be to retaliate for past wrongs by diminishing the stature of the poet. Nor does the letter suggest that she sought retaliation on the male sex by manipulating another man's feelings. It is true that she claims to have used Danyers to test her powers, and she refers twice to the affair as an *experiment.* Her phrasing also suggests that the feelings he roused in her—"I liked you from the first—I was drawn to you" (23)—gave her less satisfaction than the feelings she roused in him: "How happy I was when I discovered that you were growing jealous of my past; that you actually hated Rendle!" (23).

But nothing in her letter suggests that she was ever a manipulator of Rendle's feelings. What the letter indicates is that she was capable of maintaining a pose and altering documents to protect her self-esteem and to conceal any hint of her failure. In her letter to Danyers, she may again be creating a role to assert control and protect herself from pity. To confess herself the perpetrator of a "psychological experiment," with its faintly Gothic overtones, is to assume a part that counters the impression of a lonely middle-aged woman, reduced to seeking love and companionship of a man young enough to be her son.

What then were her feelings for Danyers? What moved her to spend the month in Venice with him? Although Mrs. Memorall, like the rest of the world, believed that Mrs. Anerton might have married Rendle after her husband's death, she gives an explanation of her friend's interest in Danyers that is plausible as far as it goes: "her life is too empty" (6); she "was bored as well as lonely" (12). The letter cannot mirror the past, for the lapse of time, the act of writing that shapes, even creates, feeling as well as reflecting it, and the effect upon a letter of the writer's anticipation of the recipient's response—all work to create an unbridgeable gulf between the woman who writes the letter and the woman as she was weeks before. But one can define the attitude of the letter writer towards the man she has refused.

Proleptic statement ("You will be angry with me at first") is a rhetorical strategy familiar to writers who would forestall or counteract the reaction anticipated in the reader. But at the least, prolepsis in Mary Anerton's letter shows that Danyers is constantly present to her mind. That she should confess to him her loneliness and pain in unrequited love implies more than her wish to pay him the compliment of making him her sole confidant. Her letter shows that she values him as a person of sensitivity and imagination, worthy of her confidence. But her letter does not convey a feeling of deep attachment or painful sacrifice in giving him up. Throughout, her tone is that of a sophisticated woman who defines the situation and sets its limits: "We have had our month together in Venice (such a good month, was it not?) and now you are to go home and write a book—any book but the one we—didn't talk of !" (14). She acknowledges the sincerity of his professions of love and absolves him of the desire to capitalize on their affair, to court her for literary profit, "in the hope (the pardonable hope!) of turning me, after a decent interval, into a pretty little essay with a margin" (23-24). But the trivializing ironies in the "decent interval" and the "pretty little essay" may also be calculated to discourage him from doing what she declares he will not do. Such manipulation of tone identifies her as an experienced woman, wiser than he in the ways of young lovers, who knows what a liaison like theirs will soon mean to him: "It will be an episode, a mere 'document,' to you so soon!" (22).

As if to draw the sting from this wounding statement, she ends with an ambiguous profession of love, affirming that her affair with Danyers has revealed to her for the first time all that she was denied by Rendle's failure to love her. Her experiment, she confesses, "will hurt me horribly (as much as, in your first anger, you may perhaps wish), because it has shown me, for the first time, all that I have missed. . . ." (24). But even in this concluding sentence she protects herself by minimizing her importance to him—he will feel anger, not anguish. And in writing "all that I have missed" —not "all that I might have had"—she reveals that her emotional attachment is still to Rendle, what *he* might have been to her.

At several points in the letter, Mary Anerton places a fictional Danyers in dialogue with herself, imagining his response to her statements: "It was all a sham then, you say? No, it was all real as far as it went" (15); "*The Sonnets to Silvia,* you say? But, what are they?" (18). Paradoxically, the rhetorical device diminishes rather than enhances a sense of intimacy between the two characters. The absence of any salutation or formal conclusion to the letter detaches it from Danyers and transforms it into a meditation that might be addressed to anyone—to an imagined reader, to the departed Rendle, to an idealized listener within the writer's own mind. The effect of unfixed discourse is reinforced by the ellipsis at the end of the letter, implying that more remains to be said than can or will be put into words. One of Wharton's favorite devices, the ellipsis, like the asterisks Mary Anerton claims to have inserted in the letters from Rendle, here precludes a sense of closure, leading the reader beyond the confines of the visible text into the boundless realms of the unspoken.[10]

Mrs. Anerton's fear of being turned into a "pretty little essay" bespeaks her determination not to be again converted into a text, but her words, "essay" and "document," suggest what might be the primary purpose served by the letter. Ostensibly she writes to Danyers to explain her behavior, ask his forgiveness, and affirm her true identity by sharing her secret with another person. If she sends her confession to Danyers, she grants him power over her. But the one who confesses exercises power too, in shaping the confession to elicit the desired response.[11] To confess in a letter is to create a document, to enjoy the authority that the act of writing confers. Rather than being turned into a text, Mary Anerton writes a text that is as artfully composed as the two parts of the story that precede the letter. The letter does not represent a random outpouring such as a person in the tumult of conflicting emotions might write. It is carefully constructed, its rising and falling currents of feeling determined not by the impulses of the moment but by the requirements of the narrative that builds, with strategically placed pauses, to its ironic climax. To give perfect form to one's imperfect life may be the letter writer's ultimate satisfaction.

The letter in "The Muse's Tragedy" has the formal properties of a story; Mary Anerton is a narrator who can be placed with Wharton's other first person narrators (none of whom writes a letter that is reproduced). But the letter-text creates a unique connection between character and author that offers a perspective from which Wharton's other characters may be seen. Edith Wharton was, of course, herself the great writer, not the muse in service to another's genius. But she created in "The Muse's Tragedy" a character remarkably similar to herself as a letter writer. In Mary Anerton, who writes: "After my husband died—I am putting things crudely, you see— (20), one sees a resemblance to the self Edith Wharton presented in a letter to Morton Fullerton at the high tide of their love affair: "I who revise, who 'edit' every sentence as I utter it, and to whom, in the most rushing moments, words keep their sharp edges of difference!"[12] Mary Anerton's letter does not exhibit the formidable knowledge revealed in Wharton's letters, filled as they are with quotations, allusions, and references to scores of literary, philosophical, and scientific works in English, French, German, and Italian. But in "The Muse's Tragedy" she created a woman of culture, who, like her creator, can view her own poses with wry detachment, can mock herself in the role of Silvia grieving, "attitudinizing among my memories like a sort of female Tithonus" (14).

The most tangible link between author and character is the motto Mary Anerton quotes when she enumerates the qualities she maintained for Rendle: *"Il faut de l'adresse pour aimer,* Pascal says; and I was so quiet, so cheerful, so frankly affectionate with him, that in all those years I am almost sure I never bored him. Could I have hoped as much if he had loved me?" (19). The complexity of feeling reflected in her letter has its counterpart in the conflicting interpretations of the motto which Wharton analyzed ten years later in a letter to Fullerton: "Pascal's terrible 'il faut de l'adresse pour aimer' has a noble side if it means the exercise of tact, insight, sympathy, self-effacement; but it is the most sordid of counsels if it appeals to the instinct to dole out, dissemble, keep in suspense, in order to prolong a little a feeling that hasn't enough vitality to survive without such aids."[13]

Wharton's letter is itself an exercise of *l'adresse,* as is Mary Anerton's letter to Danyers. Both letters establish the writer's identification with the first rather than the second half of the definition, although Wharton asked more of Fullerton than the opportunity to be quiet, cheerful, and frankly affectionate—the qualities Fullerton apparently desired in the women who loved him.[14] Mary Anerton represents only a modest measure of Wharton's intellectual and emotional capacity. The fate of the woman who unites steadfast devotion in love with literary genius is revealed in *The Touchstone,* in which Wharton most fully represents the power of one person's letters in the lives of the writer, the recipient, and the reading public.

The Touchstone, published a year after *The Greater Inclination,* portrays a situation that in some ways almost uncannily foreshadows the course of Edith Wharton's relationship with Morton Fullerton. The central elements of the novella—a famous novelist escaping from a disastrous marriage; the lover, her inferior in mind and character, incapable of the devotion she craves; the termination of their relationship after several years; the survival of her love letters, sold and published after her death—these elements all conjoin in the history of Wharton's one passionate sexual attachment, revealed to the public only when her letters to Fullerton were first published in 1985.

The protagonist of *The Touchstone* is a New York lawyer, Stephen Glennard, whose most important act is to sell for thousands of dollars the letters written to him by a famous novelist, Margaret Aubyn, destined for fame and early death. At the time of their first meeting, years before the novella opens, Glennard had been an insecure young man who craved the approval of a gifted woman like Margaret Aubyn. She had just freed herself from an unhappy marriage to an abusive man and craved the admiration and tenderness that Glennard offered her. Eventually, however, his awareness of his intellectual inferiority to her moved him to terminate their relationship. She moved to London but continued to write letters to him, letters which preserved the "rarest vintage" (274) of her powers of thought and feeling. When she died, he had hundreds of her letters tied in packets.

For Margaret Aubyn, the letters were the means by which she kept passion alive, sustaining it and sustaining herself on it by converting it into words: "she fed on her own funded passion" (272). For Glennard, the letters of the dead woman become valuable as a commodity, which he can sell to a publisher and thus finance his marriage to another woman, Alexa Trent, whose intellect seems to pose no threat. By selling the letters he can also retaliate for the guilt he suffered in rejecting Margaret Aubyn. His marriage starts to disintegrate and his mental torment begins only when the letters are published and many people, including his wife, condemn the unknown person who sold them. Thus Wharton shows Glennard to be an ordinary mortal, tortured not so much by the knowledge that he has acted basely as by the shame of exposure. He must wait months to learn that his wife had long ago guessed the truth but had waited for him to confess and judge himself, that she pities him in his misery and will not sever herself from him. In her devotion to Glennard, she has become a kind of incarnation of Margaret Aubyn, as she bestows the final meaning upon his act. Through his suffering and confession, Alexa says, Glennard has at last been "given to himself"; the letters through which he betrayed Margaret Aubyn have become the instrument of his regeneration. They are "a gift from the grave," in the words of the title of the English edition of the novella. The letters of Margaret Aubyn are the touchstone, the measure of every character associated with them—a compositional center like the spoils of Poynton of James's novel published four years earlier. To Glennard, the letters with their treasures of feeling and intellect reveal his own deficiencies. The letters establish the moral superiority of both Margaret Aubyn and Alexa Glennard, whose unfaltering love of the undeserving man endows them with the supreme power denied to Glennard: the power of forgiveness. The appearance of the letters in two volumes reveals the nature of a reading public (mainly women) that relishes the two-fold pleasure of reading intimate documents and then condemning their publication. Only one character, Glennard's wife, ever mentions reading one of Margaret Aubyn's novels, one titled *Pomegranate Seed*. Thus a link is established between Margaret Aubyn and Edith Wharton, the author of the later story, "Pomegranate Seed," in which through letters a woman exerts her power beyond the grave.

In the absence of any quotations from the letters, Margaret Aubyn exists in the novella as a spirit, invisible but pervasive, like a ghostly aura. At the same time, the publication of her letters transforms her into an institution, a *"monument historique"* (307), as one of the men observes, whose private life, he argues, now belongs to the public. Wharton was probably wise not to allow Margaret Aubyn to speak in her own voice, although she could easily have incorporated passages from the letters in the scenes where Glennard reads them. Having claimed that the letters represent the "rarest vintage" of a great novelist's mind, Wharton in quoting them would have exposed them to the reader's judgment of whether they were in fact so remarkable as everyone in the novel claims them to be. As Henry James in "The Turn of the Screw" compelled the reader to imagine for himself the ultimate in monstrous evil by refusing to specify the motives of his "demon-spirits,"[15] so Wharton obliges readers to imagine the words that create the "immense literary value" (307) of the letters. In so doing, she avoids any appearance of complicity in the morally dubious act of publishing the letters. Likewise, readers, imagining the words of the letters instead of reading them, collaborate with the author instead of taking their place with the letter-readers in the novella, engaged in an act condemned by some of them as immoral.

Although (or perhaps because) no words are quoted, the letters acquire the vitality of living beings, inducing powerful feelings in the readers. To Alexa, the letters are shaming, like voices heard through a keyhole (318). To another woman, the letters are shocking: "the woman's soul, absolutely torn up by the roots" (304). To a third, talk of the letters infects the air: "one breathes it in like the influenza" (304). When Glennard finally opens a volume and in dread and shame glances at a page, the words seem to flee before his eyes like stricken prey: "A *battue* of helpless things driven savagely out of shelter" (311).

The violence of these figures creates the image of a woman hunted, exploited, violated—more the victim than Mary Anerton. It is true that the letters in *The Touchstone* give only pain or a voyeuristic pleasure to their readers. The narrator's description of the letters as "tragic outpourings of love, humility and pardon" (260) does not suggest a great novelist's joy in the exercise of her powers. We are told too little of Margaret Aubyn to know whether, for her, the triumphs of the writer outweighed the failures in love. But we know from Wharton's other works that letters were to her much more than occasions for "tragic outpourings" of a rejected woman or public documents belonging to "the general fund of thought" (306). Even in "The Letters," the story that most clearly mirrors her own anguish in Fullerton's failure for months to respond to her urgent pleas for letters—even in this story, the protagonist, Lizzie West, gets more pleasure than pain in the correspondence with a faithless lover. The few letters she receives from him give her "sensations more complex and delicate than [his] actual presence had ever produced."[16] When he stops writing, in self-defense she composes a letter which, to her sense, so successfully creates the image of a sophisticated woman, who holds her lover to no "sentimental obligations," that she finds "a spectral satisfaction in the thought of making her final appearance before him in this distinguished character."[17]

Edith Wharton's own letters are filled with expressions of pleasure in the writing and receiving of letters. She confides to Fullerton: "I vowed I wouldn't write you again until I had overcome my black mood—& I thereupon set to work to overcome it, *in order to write you.*"[18] Letters between lovers are "signs" to be prized because "these are the ways in which the heart speaks."[19] Letters in praise of one's work are needed sustenance: "Of course one lives by such things, and not by bread alone.''[20] To Bernard Berenson she expresses pleasure in his praise of her "epistolary art," so gratifying that "beginning a letter to you has the excitement of a literary adventure as well as the joy of communing with a friend.''[21]

For Wharton's characters as well, the writing of a letter may be a literary adventure, a speaking of the heart, a sustaining of the self, if not the other. Whatever the attitude of recipients, letter writers are not victims but creators of texts of unique power that can reach—although so many times they are withheld from the eyes of the reader— farther than the power of any other agent in Wharton's fiction.

College of William and Mary

NOTES

1. *Twilight Sleep* (New York: D. Appleton and Company, 1927), 303.
2. The relationships of the letter writer to the recipient and to the reader are analyzed by Homer Obed Brown, "The Errant Letter and the Whispering Gallery," *Genre* 10 (Winter 1977), 573-99; Ruth Perry, *Women, Letters, and the Novel* (New York: AMS Press, Inc., 1980); and Bruce Redford, *The Converse of the Pen: Acts of Intimacy in the Eighteenth-Century Letter* (Chicago: University of Chicago Press, 1986).
3. See, for instance, *The Touchstone, The House of Mirth,* "Pomegranate Seed," "The Letters," and *Twilight Sleep.*
4. Salutary letter burnings occur at the climax of several stories: "The Copy," "A Cup of Cold Water," and "The Confession." The most memorable letter burning is Lily Bart's destruction of Bertha Dorset's letters to Selden in *The House of Mirth.*
5. *Exceptions include not only Pauline Manford's letter to her son in Twilght Sleep* but also Charity Royall's letter to Lucius Harney in *Summer,* and Lizzie West's letters to John Deering in "The Letters."
6. Examples are May Welland's letter to Newland Archer in Ch. 13 of *The Age of Innocence* and Rose Sellars's letter to Martin Boyne in Ch. 24 of *The Children.*
7. *The Greater Inclination. The Touchstone* (New York: Charles Scribner's Sons, 1914), 12. Subsequent page references to this edition will be given in parentheses in the body of the essay.
8. Elizabeth Ammons, *Edith Wharton's Argument with America* (Athens: University of Georgia Press, 1980), 6.
9. Cynthia Griffin Wolff, *A Feast of Words: The Triumph of Edith Wharton* (New York: Oxford University Press, 1977), 103.
10. Wharton's use of ellipsis is fully analyzed by Jean Frantz Blackall, "Edith Wharton's Art of Ellipsis," *The Journal of Narrative Technique,* 17 (Spring 1987), 145-62.
11. See Dennis A. Foster, *Confession and Complicity in Narrative* (Cambridge: Cambridge University Press, 1987), 14.

12. Letter of June 8, 1908. *The Letters of Edith Wharton,* edited by R.W.B. Lewis and Nancy Lewis (New York: Charles Scribner's Sons, 1988), 151.

13. *Ibid.,* 152.

14. The history of Edith Wharton's relations with Morton Fullerton is traced by the Lewises in their introduction to *The Letters of Edith Wharton,* 11–17.

15. Henry James, *The Art of the Novel: Critical Prefaces,* with an introduction by Richard P. Blackmur (New York: Charles Scribner's Sons, 1934), 175.

16. *The Collected Short Stories of Edith Wharton,* 2 vols., edited and with an introduction by R.W.B. Lewis (New York: Charles Scribner's Sons, 1968), II, 186.

17. *Ibid.,* 190.

18. Letter of June 8, 1908. *The Letters of Edith Wharton,* 150.

19. *Ibid.,* 198. Letter to Fullerton, Winter 1910.

20. *Ibid.,* 256. Letter to Fullerton, September 22, 1911.

21. *Ibid.,* 268. Letter of March 14, 1912.

The Reflected Text:
Kafka's Modern Inferno

PETER SALM

Dante ist sehr schön...und erst weit in der
Allgemeinheit kannst Du Dich mit ihm
treffen. Und wie leicht oder wie notwendig
man dort ihn trifft.
To Max Brod, February 1918[1]

During and after the Second World War, the name of Franz Kafka began
to resonate through many languages, and even its adjectival form
occurred with sufficient frequency to qualify as a dictionary entry.
Eminent thinkers and writers generated ever new interpretations of
Kafka's works. Among them was an "Homage" by Thomas Mann,
an essay which served as an introduction to a complete English translation
of *Das Schloss (The Castle)*. Mann saw a kindred spirit in Kafka—
homage indeed—which gave life to characters who were indelibly
marked as artists and hence painfully removed from the normal
preoccupations of his fellow burghers: "...being dehumanized," Mann
wrote in reference to Kafka, "being 'stunted' by the passion for art,
is certainly remote from God; it is the opposite of 'living' in the true
and right."[2]

And Albert Camus, speaking to an even wider international public,
pointed to aspects in Kafka which exemplified the cardinal principles
of his own brand of existentialism: "This subtle remedy that makes

206

us love what crushes us and makes hope spring up in a world without issue, this sudden 'leap' through which everything is changed, is the secret of the existential revolution and of *The Castle* itself." And "Thus it is that Kafka expresses tragedy by the everyday, and the absurd by the logical."[3]

Underscoring Kafka's global importance, W. H. Auden spelled out his view in the influential pages of *The New Republic* and brought the names of Dante and Kafka into close proximity. "Kafka is important to us," Auden wrote, "because the predicament of his hero is the predicament of contemporary man," and raising him to the level of the most august poetic spirits, he asserted: "Had one to name that author who comes nearest to bearing the same kind of relation to our age as Dante, Shakespeare and Goethe bore to theirs, Kafka is the first one would think of."[4]

But it is one thing to pay tribute—as it were in one breath—to two great authors who lived seven centuries apart, and obviously quite another to speculate on topical or spiritual equivalences between them. Scholars have shied away from any head-on comparisons between Dante and Kafka in the face of the daunting distance between them. Dante's visionary pilgrimage on the one hand and the terrestrial busy-ness of the Kafkaesque world on the other, seem incommensurable. After all, the religious and logical certainties of the fourteenth century had long since given way to the sweeping doubts and vexing metaphysical questions of the twentieth.

And yet the fierce winds buffeting Paolo and Francesca in the second circle of the Inferno have not abated and continue to rage in our own time. For Dante and his contemporaries there existed as yet no gulf between perturbations of the soul and atmospheric upheavals. T.S. Eliot's formulation seems most apt here: "Dante's is a visual imagination...in a different sense from that of a painter of still life: it is visual in the sense that he lived in an age in which men still saw visions."[5] How much, however, does the text of Dante's vision appear to structure Kafka's own?

To be sure, certain perceived affinities between Dante and Kafka were touched upon and mostly made to serve current theories of the unconscious. Hellmuth Kaiser's crassly psychoanalytic foray of 1931 bears the title "Kafka's Inferno," alluding to the cliché that Kafka, along with K., Joseph K., Gregor Samsa and others, functioned—or malfunctioned—in a guilt-ridden psychic and spiritual hell, while keeping

Dante's funnel-shaped Inferno barely recognizable and at a safe distance. By way of an analysis of *The Penal Colony*, Kaiser wrote this about the prisoner's execution: "While tying down the fellow's right hand, the leather strap tears. Strap *(Riemen)*, however, is a vulgar expression for penis. The 'tearing of the strap' alludes to castration. Since the strap was intended to shackle the right hand...we can imagine that the castration threat was actually a prohibition against masturbation."[6]

While it was common practice during the early phase of the psychoanalytic movement to apply its methodology to literary texts—especially in Freud's own journal *Imago*—such efforts were primarily contributions to psycho-pathology, though literary criticism was bound to be enriched by them. To lay bare unconscious urges lurking beneath the written word perhaps produced a voyeur's *frisson* and at the same time afforded plausible notions concerning the psyches of invented characters or even, by extension, of their author.

More directly germane to its title and less in the thrall of psychoanalysis than Kaiser's essay is Donald Pearce's study "The Castle: Kafka's *Divine Comedy*."[7] Pearce was on solid ground when he pointed out that the *Divine Comedy* and *The Castle* are both quests toward an absolute realm where the goal for both is identical and where "the conditions and difficulties thronging it alone are changed" (pp. 165-166). Pearce tellingly wrote about the steep and arduous, but clearly marked, path to salvation available to medieval Christians and, on the other hand, about the absence of any reliable markers in Kafka's 20th-century labyrinthine environment. His arguments become less tenable, it seems to me, when he moves from a textual analysis of Kafka's prose into Jungian speculations. These, while ingeniously developed, provide no tangible basis for comparison, which we were, after all, led to expect from the title of Pearce's essay. Passages like the following provoke not much more than puzzlement:

> K.'s relations with the castle...are those between the conscious and the unconscious (earthly and heavenly) in a reflective person, one who, discovering no traditional external Absolute turns inward and seeks by rational self-analysis to reach an Absolute within himself (the extremity of Romanticism; the "God within" of Jung) (169).

The present essay endeavors to build on a few commonly perceived structural and spiritual images that Dante and Kafka share. This is not, however, an attempt to illustrate Freudian or Jungian views of the psyche, but to work with an intuition of a text "without," its meaning and power, and a phenomenological tradition that both Dante and Kafka built into their texts with their own respective uses of logic and style. The similarities between the texts of these two authors are, perhaps, obvious enough on the surface, but they bespeak a textual generality of which both were aware.

Joseph K. in Kafka's *The Trial* awakens to find himself arrested on the morning of his thirtieth birthday. Precisely one year later he dies at the hands of his two look-alike executioners. Most of Kafka's protagonists, Georg Bendemann, Gregor Samsa, Joseph K., and K. the Land-Surveyor, are at the apex of their lives when their crisis befalls them.

When Dante loses his way in the dark wood, he is "Nel mezzo del cammin di nostra vita" in keeping with the allotted biblical life span (Psalm 90). Since his visionary journey took place in A.D. 1300, the poet was 35 years of age both as the poem's protagonist and as the biographical Dante Alighieri, born in Florence in 1265.

While Kafka's identification with several of his protagonists is not explicit as Dante's is in the *Commedia* there is no question that Kafka's major characters are more or less distorted projections of himself, painful and nauseating for him as they are. The very sound of "K," the first letter of his family name, which was also the cipher used for two of his heroes, sickened Kafka. A diary entry jotted down while at work on *The Trial* read: "I find the letter 'K' ugly, almost nauseating, and yet I write it down; it must be very characteristic of me" (May 27, 1914). Kafka was thirty at the time, the same age as his hero of *The Trial,* a structural constellation quite similar to Dante's in the *Commedia* where the spiritual self has all but absorbed the biographic one.

Yet neither the congruence of author and protagonist nor their positions at the midpoint in their allotted life spans are in themselves far-reaching analogies. Twentieth-century novels are positively teeming with thirty-year-old heroes, as Theodore Ziolkowski showed in his remarkable essay.[8] One need only cite as examples Roquentin in Sartre's *La Nausée* (Nausea), Mersault in Camus's *L'Etranger* (The Stranger), and Oskar Matzerath in Günther Grass's *Die Blechtrommel (The Tin Drum).* Nor is it merely a twentieth-century fashion; the thirtieth year of life has for many centuries been regarded as a milestone. For Aristotle and Cicero it meant the realization of the full human potential, and indeed Jesus was about thirty when he began his ministry (Luke III, 23). Kafka had some knowledge of the *Commedia*. He was at least as conversant with it as could be expected of a Prague intellectual, and he may have known more. His library contained the annotated German translation by Streckfuss, and his responses concerning Dante addressed to his friend Max Brod were characteristic of one who had reflected at some length on Dante's great poem. A passage in one letter reads:

> ...[Beatrice] was lost to [Dante] by her death, but you, you let her die, inasmuch as you feel compelled to I renounce her. In this way, incidentally, Dante also renounced her and voluntarily married someone else, a fact which does not favor your interpretation.
>
> (Zürau, February 1918)

Less than a month later he wrote this to Brod: "Dante is very beautiful...but it is only in a distant general realm that you can meet with him. And how easy and how necessary it is to meet with him there!" (Zürau, February 1918).

The matter of sequential time affords another basis for comparison. In pursuing this line of thought, we are aided by Walter Sokel's insights in his important book on Kafka. Referring to *Metamorphosis* he writes:

> No time sequence exists here. Punishment does not follow on the heels of sin, but guilt itself constitutes the punishment. We are reminded of Dante's Inferno here...how punishment has become sin forever transmuted into its *Gestalt* (p. 84).[9]

The qualitative coalescing of sin and punishment is matched by a telescoping of time into an eternal presence. With respect to Dante, we can test this phenomenon with Paolo and Francesca, whom I mentioned earlier. The question one may ask is whether it is indeed on a particular day in the year 1300 that Dante, during his passage through the second circle of the Inferno, encountered the souls of the two sinful lovers. Is it on that day and at that hour that Francesca approached the living Dante Alighieri to tell him how she had broken her marriage vows and given way to her illicit passion for Paolo?

Paolo and Francesca are forever united in Hell, forever adrift in storms of passion, forever bemoaning their fate and reasserting their passion for each other. Their punishment is an extension and intensification of their sin, as well as its symbolization. While Dante's journey clearly must be understood to have taken place in time, the souls in the *Commedia* exist outside the temporal dimension. Their condition is eternal, and even while they communicate with Dante and Virgil within the temporal framework of human speech, they reveal their timeless condition of damnation. This is also true of Farinata and Cavalcante rising out of their flaming tombs upon seeing the living Dante and the soul of Virgil as they pass through the sixth circle; and of Brunetto Latini who, while walking over the burning sands of the region reserved for the Sodomites, discovers the living and palpable shape of his former pupil.

Dante's and Kafka's visions of time, on occasion, have an eerie similarity. The beetle in the *Metamorphosis* is the shape of Gregor Samsa's guilt. The transformation did not occur *in consequence* of a life without grace, but indicates the permanent, insect-like condition of such a life. This is so despite the meticulously recorded progress of time by the advancing hands on Gregor's alarm clock in the first part of the story. In the second and third sections, time dissolves from hours into days and months. The passing of the minutes in the beginning is a visible state of anxiety and not indicative of a temporal extension of events.

The "Whipper" scene in the fifth chapter of *The Trial* may be cited as a paradigmatic representation of Kafkaesque time. One night, behind a door along the corridors leading away from the bank offices, Joseph K. hears sighing and, seized by uncontrollable curiosity (*unbezähmbare Neugier*), tears the door open and finds the two warders who had once come to arrest him, being whipped by a third man. They engage in conversation; one of the two victims grotesquely complains that if things had gone well for him, he might by now have been promoted to the post of whipper. The next day Joseph K. cannot get the warders out of his mind. After business hours he opens the mysterious door again and is faced by exactly the same scene: the whipper with his raised rod, the warders waiting for the blow to fall and a candle still burning on the shelf. One knows that whenever Joseph K. happens to open the closet door, he will encounter the same scene.

Such a stasis of time (its aesthetics mastered in Sartre's *La Nausée:* see Wolfgang Holdheim's essay in this volume), exists throughout *The Trial*. There is no progress and no development either in the hero or in the resolution of his guilt. The stasis begins when Joseph K. awakens on his thirtieth birthday, and remains in effect as the narrative moves in the course of one year from a rented room to the bank, to the halls of the court, to Huld's and Titorelli's lodgings and to the cathedral. Ziolkowski rightly remarks, "...these areas, unrelated to one another, represent no progress at all."[10]

Kafka saw himself as an expert on the fall of man. Between 1920 and 1923 he wrote to Milena, his beloved friend: "...sometimes I believe that I understand Original Sin like no other man...."[11] This parenthetical remark is followed only a few days later by one of the proudest self-assessments that Kafka ever made:

> I am dirty, Milena, infinitely dirty, and that is why I set up such a hue and cry about purity. No one sings with more purity than those who are in deepest Hell; what we think of as the chant of angels, is their song.[12]

The fact that Kafka, unlike Dante, is unable to extend his journey beyond the confines of Hell does not mean that he denies the existence of an absolute realm of light and perfection. On the contrary, such an Absolute, totally beyond human comprehension, reigns just as surely as does the inaccessible Law in the "Cathedral" chapter of *The Trial* or the ultimate authority in *The Castle*. However, the *deus absconditus* is masked beyond recognition and is more inscrutable than the God of Job. For Kafka, the gates to Purgatory and Paradise are forever barred by man's innate inadequacy and his distorting and distorted vision. Erich Heller is disturbingly insightful when he observes that in Kafka's works "the conviction of damnation is all that is left of faith...."[13]

The craving for an escape from a state of guilt-ridden and infernal hopelessness may take the form of hunger for "the right food." In the *Metamorphosis,* after rejecting the bowl of pap set down in a corner of his room by his sister, the insect Gregor, who has not lost human perceptions and feelings, hears his sister playing the violin in the living room. "He felt," Kafka writes, "as if the way were opening before him to the unknown nourishment he craved" (p. 76).

Or when the overseer asks the "hunger artist" who after his record-breaking fast is all but forgotten by the sensation-hungry crowd: " 'and why can't you help it [fasting]?'...the hunger artist says, lifting his hand a little and speaking with lips pursed, as if for a kiss, right into the overseer's ear, so that no syllable might be lost,—'because I couldn't find the food I liked' " (p. 200).

Particular, transubstantial references to food occur in Dante's Paradiso. (See Maristella Lorch's essay in this volume). In the sphere of Mercury, still under some earthly influence, Beatrice admonishes Dante:

> però che 'l cibo rigido c'hai preso
> richiede ancora aiuto a tua dispensa.
> *(Par.* V.38–40)
>
> the food that you have taken was tough food—
> it still needs help if you are to digest it.[14]

And higher up, after all earthly encumbrances are left behind, Dante as teacher-poet steps out of his role as pilgrim and lover to address the reader:

> Messo t'ho innanzi: omai per te ti ciba,
> che a se torce tutta la mia cura
> quella materia ond'io son fatto scriba.
> *(Par.* X.25–27)
>
> I have prepared your fare; now feed yourself,
> because that matter of which I am made
> the scribe, calls all my care unto itself.

In Kafka there is a vain craving for a taste of the divine, while in Dante's Inferno, the realm without hope, divine food can have no place at all. There exists only the sodden and stinking fare of the gluttons. For Kafka, the rotting apple beneath Gregor Samsa's shell is food of the twentieth-century world. In the *Inferno,* the significance of the heavenly food—or manna—lies in its absence and its infinite distance from the human grasp.

In contexts that are reminiscent of the opening lines of the *Commedia,* there are Kafka's informal or conversational allusions to the "dark forest." One is from a journal kept by Gustav Janouch which records a chat that took place between 1920 and 1923. Kafka said to his young and admiring friend:

> One who is afraid should not go into the wood. But we are in the wood. Everyone in a different way and in a different place.[15]

A further reference to "the forest" is contained in an undated letter to Milena:

> ...but basically...I belonged nowhere but inside this forest, lived out in the open only through your grace, and without knowing it (for I had forgotten everything), read my fate from your eyes...you must...have recognized certain peculiarities which pointed to the forest, to my origin and true home....[16]

Dante's realm of anxiety seven centuries earlier had been just that. But tempting as it is to adduce such structural and spatial images for the purpose of making comparisons between the two authors, a broader view should be taken here. Dante's and Kafka's images can resonate with quite different timbres in other cultural contexts. Food, after all, has ever stood for a purely divine sustenance or "manna" and dark disorienting forests have long cast their spells through legends and fairy tales.

Of a similar general nature are evocations of "the Way" in both its mundane transcendent sense, for example in Kafka's parable *Gibs auf! (Give it Up!)* that is cited and wonderfully explicated by Heinz Politzer in his *Parable and Paradox*.[17] The minuscule narrative concludes with a policeman's uncomprehending question, "From me you want to find the way?," which he delivers before he removes himself from the scene in a sweeping, parabolic arc. A routine inquiry about the way to the railroad station, by a traveler walking the streets of a strange town, has elicited this majestic rebuff. The traveler has lost Dante's *diritta via* ("the straight way"). Any story of a quest, for example of *The Castle,* naturally raises questions about "the Way." But for such a journey the Land-Surveyor has no Virgil to lead him through the intricate corridors. He is a lone quester. In one of his fragmentary notes Kafka wrote: "There is only a goal, never a way. What we call 'way' is [actually] hesitation" (September 17, 1920).

Floundering in oppressive surroundings, seeking slight advantages here and there, waiting for a door to open to the antechamber of yet another questionable authority, have become projections of our twentieth-century predicament, with which Kafka's name will likely be associated for a long time.

Perhaps Fräulein Bürstner in *The Trial* has a Dantesque aura about her. Her appearance both near the beginning of the novel, and then again on the way to Joseph K.'s execution, gives a frame to the incomplete narrative. She is the only character who appears twice in two widely separated episodes, and I agree with Walter Sokel's assessment expressed in a letter to me: "[The comparison between Fräulein Bürstner and Beatrice] contains in a nutshell the whole world of difference between the fourteenth and twentieth-century journey."[18] The fact that Fräulein Bürstner enters the last scene as a kind of spectral figure, without preparation in the narrative and without a hint of her own motivation—quite aside from Joseph K.'s uncertainty whether it is actually she—seems to indicate that she is not a participant in the labyrinthine toils of human affairs. Kafka's usually matter-of-fact style shows signs of stress, as her appearance in the clause of which she is the subject is delayed to the last grammatically possible position, and the language rises briefly to a new level of mystery and allusiveness: "Da stieg vor ihnen aus einer tiefer gelegenen Gasse auf einer kleinen Treppe Fräulein Bürstner zum Platz empor."[19] ("There, from a low-lying alley, scaling a small stairway, Fräulein Bürstner arose before them on the square"— my translation.) Joseph K. followed her so that "he might not forget the lesson that she had brought into his mind." In the early scenes of the book, Joseph K. had behaved in a chivalrous manner toward his rooming-house neighbor to whom he had so ineffectually expressed his erotic desire. He had angrily defended her against the insinuations of the landlady to the effect that Fräulein Bürstner had failed to come up to the moral standards of her establishment: " 'Die Reinheit!' rief K. noch durch die Spalte der Tür, 'wenn Sie die Pension rein erhalten wollen, müssen Sie zuerst mir kündigen.' "[20] (" 'Respectable!' he had cried through a chink of the door, 'If you want to keep your house respectable, you'll have to begin by giving me notice!' ")

In the end Fräulein Bürstner becomes—for a brief moment—a true guide as she leads the way. But rather than leading her charge, Beatrice-like, to transcendent fulfillment, she goes with him toward the place of his execution. Bitter is this infernal irony. Elsewhere, Kafka acknowledged that the "female principle" exercised a kind of hegemony in the world, but he saw Woman's role suffused by a desperate ambivalence. He wrote to Max Brod: "I do believe in the leadership (*Führerschaft*) of the Female, as was demonstrated for instance in the story of the Fall, where she acted out a role for which in most cases she has been ill rewarded" (January 1918). Fräulein Bürstner's presence is like the flame of the candle in *The Trial's* cathedral scene: its feeble light serves only to intensify the darkness.

It is possible to argue, though with poor prospects of success, that scattered textual affinities, along with Kafka's notes and letters, are sufficient to make a case for a demonstrable Dantean influence on Kafka. But "influence" conjures up imitation, and it is clear that Kafka's narratives do not lean on Dante's poem, but are a direct literary expression of a self-lacerating creative mind which, to be sure, is nourished by a persistent Dantean presence. One feels that such a "metamorphosed," presence exists "weit in der Allgemeinheit"—in an all-encompassing realm that both authors shared. So did Kafka express it in a letter to Max Brod. The passage serves well as our epigraph.

Case Western Reserve

NOTES

1. Franz Kafka, *Briefe,* ed. Max Brod (New York: S. Fischer/Schocken Books, 1958). 234. The translation from the German of these letters and other passages from the secondary literature are my own, unless otherwise noted.
2. Franz Kafka, *The Castle* (New York: Schocken Books, 1958), ix-xviii. Translated passages from Kafka's novels and short narratives are by Willa and Edwin Muir, unless otherwise noted.
3. *The Myth of Sisyphus,* trans. Justin O'Brien (New York: Vintage Books, 1955), 94, 97.
4. W.H. Auden, "The Wandering Jew," *The New Republic* (February 10, 1941), 186.
5. T.S. Eliot, *Selected Essays* (New York: Harcourt Brace, 1950), 204.
6. Hellmuth Kaiser, "Franz Kafkas Inferno, eine psychologische Deutung seiner Strafphantasie" (1931), *Franz Kafka,* ed. Heinrich Politzer (Darmstadt: Wissenschaftliche Buchgesellschaft, 1973), 99-100.
7. Donald Pearce, "The Castle: Kafka's *Divine Comedy,*" *Franz Kafka Today,* ed. Angel Flores and Homer Swander (Madison: University of Wisconsin Press, 1958), 165-172.
8. Theodor Ziolkowski, *Dimensions of the Modern Novel* (Princeton: Princeton University Press, 1969), 258.
9. Walter H. Sokel, *Franz Kafka, Tragik und Ironie* (München: Albert Langen, 1964), 84.
10. Ziolkowski, p. 61.
11. Franz Kafka, *Briefe an Milena,* ed. Willy Haas (New York: Schocken Books, 1952), 199.
12. *Ibid.,* 207.
13. Erich Heller, *The Disinherited Mind* (New York: Meridian Books, 1959), 207.
14. Dante's Italian text and its translation are from Allen Mandelbaum's California Dante. (See Allen Mandelbaum's essay in this volume).

15. Gustav Janouch, *Conversations with Kafka,* trans. Goronway Rees (New York: New Directions, 1971), 156.
16. *Briefe an Milena,* 224.
17. Heinrich Politzer, *Franz Kafka, Parable and Paradox* (Ithaca: Cornell University Press, 1952), 1–22.
18. From a letter to Peter Salm February 14, 1971.
19. Franz Kafka, *Der Prozess* (New York: Schocken Books, 1946), 236.
20. *Ibid.,* 32.

PART FIVE
A Cultural-Historical Hyphen

Petrarchan Grammatology
And the Birth of Modern Texts

ALDO SCAGLIONE

So io ben ch'a voler chiuder in versi
suo' laudi, fora stanco
chi più degna la mano a scriver porse;
qual cella è di memoria in cui s'accoglia
quanta vede vertù, quanta beltade
chi gli occhi mira d'ogni valor segno,
dolce del mio cor chiave?

Petrarca, *Canzoniere* 29.50–56

It is somewhat paradoxical that the dynamic, even obsessive development of modern literary theory and criticism has been fed from the outside, as it were, in the sense that non-literary disciplines—philosophy, anthropology, linguistics, psychology, and even economics and sociology—have determined the orientation of literary activities.

Methodologically, modern literary scholarship has been conditioned by three intellectual traditions above all others. The first one, that goes under the common label of structuralism, derives in a complex way from a convergence of Saussurian linguistics and Russian formalism, which combined in the Prague Linguistic Circle and then merged in Paris with the structuralist anthropological school. The second tradition, this one more clearly identifiable as originating in German philosophy, is that of the phenomenological school, chiefly of Martin Heidegger (starting with his *Sein und Zeit* of 1927). Via Windelband and Wundt,

221

it shared a common Kantian-Hegelian ancestry with another German ingredient, that of Gestaltism, which came in from psychology. The third tradition has a more widespread ancestry, although it was most specifically inspired by the school of historiography that originated in 1929 in the Parisian journal *Annales d'histoire économique et sociale*, edited by Marc Bloch and Lucien Febvre.[1]

Heidegger's phenomenologism can be directly related to Jacques Derrida's and Paul de Man's deconstructionism through the doctrine of "phenomenological destruction" which canonized in abstract gnoseological terms the modern predicament of loss of specific positive faith. Heidegger lucidly explained how his rejection of the traditional values or, rather, refusal to identify his thinking with the categorization of any of the traditional values, did not entail a direct denial of their inherent consistency but simply a statement of their inadequacy for a description of the human predicament. Thus his philosophy, he averred, was "against" humanism, logic, values, and transcendence, just as it also affirmed the (Nietzschean) death of God and nihilism, not in the sense that it upheld barbarism, irrationalism, skepticism, immanence, atheism, and, precisely, nihilism, but in the sense that it sanctioned the tenability of all the above positive positions (as well as their negative opposites) as part of the existential perspectives of the human condition of being. Derivatively, deconstruction holds that language qua language, hence literature and art per se, do not explicitly affirm, express, or represent an objective, external referential reality but only their own inner world (a subjective perspective on experience).[2] Similarly, just as for Heidegger the most real aspect of Being is the ek-sistent consciousness of the human being experiencing life and the world, so does another one of the schools of thought that are related to these three main traditions, the hermeneutical school of Konstanz (*Rezeptionsästhetik*), go back to Heidegger through his pupil Gadamer for the basic idea of the consciousness of the reader as the most real experience in the life of the text.

The impact of the *Annales* has produced a differently focused and divergently slanted way of reading and interpreting that, instead of centering on the divergence between the message and the reference, the signifier and the signified, holds the relationship between the two—language and world, sign and outside reality, story and social setting—as the most valid index of the hardness of the communicative act, the necessary foundation for the collective consensus that alone makes the message intelligible.

Accordingly, modern critical theory has alternatively emphasized either the strictly formal, as in Russian Formalism, or the sociological content—two distinct orientations which can be seen as opposite and mutually exclusive and yet can be occasionally combined—just as Marxism and Freudianism can often be found together. In any event, more often than not modern theory has been applied to rather recent literature, say, after 1700, and only seldom to the study of ancient literature—except for such aspects of it as its mythological content, the interpretation of the nature of genre, or the use of the Aristotelian and Platonic critical categories. Medieval and Renaissance literature are only slightly more often the object of such experiments, although, for example, the New Historicism has verged almost entirely on the English Renaissance. This interesting method of analysis combines a broadly-gauged use of total history with a search for inner, often hidden motives—the critic often invoking cultural themes as masks for the search for power or as rhetorical justification of it. The criticism that can be leveled at this ''school'' is that it tends to interpret and use literature and art as deceptive sublimations of material motives, thus downgrading them as morally rather devious instruments of power. This is the way much of New Historicism has projected forth, but one should note that the method can yield fruit in a more positive direction, namely of disclosing the lower roots that propelled to the surface the lofty branches of cultural projects and images.

It should be interesting to explore how some aspects of early Renaissance culture come out under the light of some recent, theory-inspired research. I shall begin with a note on the relationship between the socio-cultural environment and the ideological framework reflected by some humanistic production. Historians have commonly related humanism to the social environment of the burghers' communes, stressing the humanists' frequent professional affiliations with the law, the notarial art, and chancery bureaucracy. But civic humanism also had a counterpart in what one historian has labeled as ''courtly humanism'' and another one as ''subdital humanism,'' with reference to the use of the renovated classical ethos to support, praise, and illustrate the new seigniorial rulers.[3] Indeed, humanists could be courtiers, too, and their fashionable panegyrical displays distilled a heady brew of old and new ideals that applied some of the features of the medieval knight and courtier to the uses of the modern warrior statesman. The humanistic view of literature, and especially eloquence, as the highest human endeavor is reflected in the way humanists evaluated public achievements. A most successful funeral oration by the Venetian patrician Leonardo Giustinian for the Venetian civic leader and general Carlo Zeno (1418, at least 64 manuscript copies and six printed editions are extant) typically praised him as a model captain, even more excellent than the Athenian Themistocles, for having won not by force of arms but through the humanistic virtues of authority, humanity clemency, affability, civility, and eloquence (*auctoritas, humanitas, clementia, affabilitas, comitas, eloquentia*). The Ciceronian matrix, put to a new use, had helped to transform the image of the chivalric leader and refined courtier into that of the modern condottiero in the garb of a humanistic orator: literary virtues could be higher and more effective than practical ones.[4]

The topic I would like to focus on is that the notion of literature that became the center of attention for humanistic education and conduct was a rather new concept both in theory and in practice. Historians who stress the orality of literary production and transmission, signally and typically the formalist Paul Zumthor and, in a completely independent way, Mikhail Bakhtin, appear to assign a considerable role to commoners as active public, viewing them rather as the German Romantics used to view the *Volk*.[5] More specifically, Zumthor proposes to read all of medieval literature according to a sharp opposition between a written literature (*de rigueur* the only "literature" by our definition), which began around Chrétien de Troyes no earlier than 1160, and all other literary production which until at least the end of the fifteenth century continued to be orally produced and orally transmitted. A largely "popular" public of producers and consumers of oral literature is thus sharply opposed to a distinct élite public of written literature. In the oral mode of artistic production the text enjoyed no special privilege outside the actual performance "here and now," and the texts lived through a continuous evolution of "féconde intertextualité orale."

This view of things amounts to a type of global "deconstruction" of the whole history of western literature on the premise that (differently from figurative art and even poetry) written art literature as we know it is neither a perennial human activity nor, as the humanists firmly held, the highest product of civilization and the very foundation of humanity: it would be a temporary affair, largely confined to the modern period, and perhaps already extinct. For we are now witnessing a type of paraliterature (mass literature, what the Germans call *Trivial-Literatur*) which tends to merge with "true" literature as indistinguishable from it, in a process of confusion that some German theorists decry with the heavy yet telling term of *Entdifferenzierung,* 'de-differentiation.' In this sense much of medieval "literature" looks to us more like our own mass culture than like the "classical" literature of 1500-1900.[6]

We should now turn to Francis Petrarch's role in the shaping of the modern literary tradition. As a lyrical poet Petrarch, the "Prince of Humanists," was not only the most illustrious heir of the Provençal troubadours, but also a product of the curial tradition. After all, much as he came to loath it in his mature years, the highly corrupt yet equally sophisticated curial court of Avignon was Petrarch's nurturing ground, with close personal association with some of its leading figures. But his way of working was also shaped by certain important modifications that his Italian predecessors introduced into the methods of literary production. The consequences were far-reaching, with a decisive impact on the literature of the courts, which also used these new formal manners of composition and transmission to convey some powerful new themes. Some of these themes that constitute original elements of the Italian contribution have not yet been properly dealt with. One example on which I shall not dwell in the present essay is the theme of death in Dante and Petrarch: death "improves" the beloved, making her more perfect as pure spirit, so that in the Earthly Paradise Dante made Beatrice blame him for not having loved her more after her passing away, and Petrarch presented to us a humane, compassionate Laura only after her death.

Life at court had been especially conducive to oral literature. The early bishops and the educators at imperial and episcopal chapels and cathedral schools often did not care, like new incarnations of Socrates, to put their teachings down to writing, since their efficacy rested on their live voice. One of the greatest medieval poets, Wolfram von Eschenbach, stated outright that he was not one who could write. Literary life at court had been based on live performance, verse compositions being delivered with musical accompaniment. Yet, even at a time when oral transmission in all genres (including the scientific and philosophical ones) was still the general rule, writing started to play a more decisive role in Italy. This means that recitation at court went hand in hand with the use of the manuscript, which circulated and propagated motifs and forms beyond the courts to the more literate burghers.[7] The change was soon to affect the whole of the Italian cultural scene, preparing the ground for making written literature the core of humanistic education. The most important early consequence of this shift is seen in the mode of transmission of Provençal poetry.

Typically, Dante invented the difficult form of the terzina also in order to make sure that the scribes would be restrained from their customary rewriting of texts—a natural and perfectly legitimate aspect of the transmission of a *live* culture that was normally tied to a verbal, hence constantly moving and evolving delivery. In a terzina it was not possible to introduce any substantive verbal changes without rewriting a whole canto—at least if rhyme was affected. Any accidental dropping or interpolation of lines would have been immediateiy apparent by disturbing the tight movement of the rhyme structure.

Above all others, Petrarch started a new habit of paying scrupulous attention to the precise wording of a poet's written text (a habit that was to lead to the great achievements of humanistic philology). He did so by leaving to his disciples a painstakingly accurate record of his work, page by page, word by word, variant by variant, many of them often marked by glosses and specific annotations as to the exact time and circumstances they were entered into a draft. He was making sure, for the first time in medieval Europe, that his writings would be regarded as *ne varietur* editions. His rather novel desires were heeded by the following generations, and autographs of final drafts (including the *Canzoniere*) were religiously preserved, even together with many a preliminary draft. This was unprecedented at a time when no autograph was ever destined to survive. Zumthor (1987: 165) notes that "we possess no autograph manuscript of poetry before the end of the fourteenth century: this means that, up to that date, in all our texts, without exception, what we perceive in our reading is the stage of reproduction, not of production." Zumthor ignores Petrarch's case, indeed a hard one to overlook, and when he mentions Boccaccio (1987: 166) for being the first to show "un véritable souci d'authenticité auctoriale," he thinks only of his autograph corrections to the scribal copy of the *Decameron*, and entirely forgets Boccaccio's illustrious predecessor. This degree of attention to form and style, composition and structure was formerly limited to Latin writing, and only occasionally so. Petrarch and his Italian predecessors methodically extended it to the vernacular (starting perhaps with Provençal). It is remarkable that this phenomenon occurred in a country with a relative paucity of both Latin and vernacular poetry compared with Germany, France, or England before, say, 1230. At the same time, however, in their respect for the letter of the literary text, the Italians were guided by the invigorating example of the ancients.[8]

Italian was to become the language of diplomacy, hence an international medium of communication, replacing Latin in this function. Now knights and clerics as well had been cosmopolitan classes in the Middle Ages, but only the clerics had an international language at their disposal, kept relatively invariant and universal by its being constrained within fixed grammatical structures that were dead for the man of the street. The knights, instead, had at their disposal only regional, unstable dialects both for their everyday life and for their cultural expression. Even Occitan literature, so successful internationally, had barely faced the problem of standardization, overcoming the motley situation of sharply variant dialects simply by relying on the early models from the Limousin. The Italians were the first to confront the problem squarely and to become seriously preoccupied with a "national" standard: even before Dante intervened with his *De vulgari eloquentia* and the doctrine of the *vulgare illustre*, the Sicilians had already profited from the cosmopolitan ambiance of Frederick II's court to begin a process of linguistic homogenization.

Petrarch was also responsible for the crystallization of an idea of love as the trademark of the literate gentleman and writer, and he achieved this remarkable feat by using and transforming the themes of courtly love he had inherited from the Provençal poets. It is interesting to observe how well-tested motifs that corresponded to specific aspects of feudal relationships at the twelfth-century courts were changed by Petrarch into abstract patterns for ideal love. Troubadours and Minnesingers displayed the apparent contradiction of constantly protesting total devotion while threatening a change of heart if reward was not forthcoming, and we can conclude that this was part and parcel of that "game of love" that was conventionally and artificially verbal and yet, at the same time, a very earnest strategy for survival. In a way, it can be said, Petrarch conclusively sealed that contradiction for all posterity of imitators by framing his whole *Canzoniere*—the most consistent and prolonged expression of total dedication to an evanescent and elusive, even physically absent, ideal woman—inside the recantation of his passion as "a youthful error" in poem 1 and the transcendent hymn to the Virgin in the closing poem 366. Beyond the Provençal heritage, this inner ambiguity was perfectly consonant with the whole personality of that supreme lyricist, who embedded into his lifetime work a "discovery" of the inner tensions of the self and the contradictory nature of the psyche.[9] Differently put, what had been a witty and elegant game to be played for one's survival (the knight/courtier's career) became a symbolic expression of man's ambiguous, dialectic predicament.

Despite its incompatibility with Christian love, courtly love had imposed itself on court life because of its social function. But when the amatory lyric outgrew those precise social boundaries, as was the case, for instance, with the early Bolognese and Tuscan poets who had no contact with any court of the Provençal or French type, the conflict between sacred and profane love stood out clearly enough to demand a solution. The Stil Nuovo doctrine of the *donna angelicata* came to the poets' rescue and, just as Dante had profited from that new departure for his sublime ends, so did Petrarch proceed within this new intellectual framework that had transcended the Provençal context. In other words: despite the fact that the sociological settings had become incompatible in the transition from the feudal courtly environments to the republics and signories of fourteenth-century Italy, the Stil Nuovo managed to codify the ideology of the former to the taste and understanding of the latter in a language that eventually became Petrarchan. A similar situation characterized Catholic Spain in that and the following century, where the adulterous definition of courtly love was commonly deemphasized: the lover, aristocrat or no, could look to a love within marriage—or the writer could directly attack the implications of a sinful passion, as did the author of the *Celestina* (1499).[10] The case of Castilian and Portuguese amorous poetry is interesting for the use of Petrarchism in establishing a firm context of psychological analysis of a moral predicament, in a tense polarization between a rational sublimation of love and the condemnation of an alienating passion, futile at best, destructive at worst. In that poetry a universal ethos filled the forms inherited from a court setting that could no longer be operative, since it no longer existed.

The ideology of courtly love gains in intelligibility in light of such recent researches as those of C. Stephen Jaeger, a Germanist who has focused on the rich tradition of courtly and "curial" ethical training (i.e., pertaining to the imperial and royal chapels) and those of a medieval historian like Georges Duby and a Romanist like Erich Köhler.[11] These researches can be combined to fill their respective gaps. Jaeger does not explain the survival of the curial *mentalité* after the end of the imperial bishoprics; Duby and Köhler do not ask, let alone answer, why the poor knights developed an ideology that reproduced so much of the language and ethos of the *curiales*. Taken together, the two views explain how this unique ideology (absurd, for example, when seen in isolation in Petrarch) could acquire so much vitality as to survive almost intact for several centuries, especially through the realistic and skeptical experiences of the Cinquecento. One could explain this outstanding example of the enduring character of aesthetic forms and artistic themes—namely the universal phenomenon of Petrarchism—by Geörgyi Lukács's argument that, beyond mere sociological relativism or determinism, the superstructure has a dynamic life of its own: as reflection or mirroring of a past reality it can live on in the collective memory for the pleasure of recalling the past.

In Italy, Petrarchism grew steadily in the Quattrocento, producing, before Bembo came to canonize it along classicizing criteria, potentially aberrant forms, especially in courtly environments. The outstanding example is Serafino Aquilano (d. 1500), a page at Naples in his youth and then an acclaimed court entertainer at Urbino and north Italian courts. In line with the progressive Christianization and Platonization of erotic poetry after Petrarch, the virtues of the lovers sounded more and more like the standard Christian virtues: *onestade, temperanza, vergogna, continenza,* and such, will dominate both in stanzas of European love poetry like the *Cantos de amor* of the fifteenth-century Catalan poet Ausias March or in pages of philosophical speculation on love like Mario Equicola's successful *Libro de natura de amore* (1509).

Petrarch's model of frustrated love as the noblest form of love, his latter-day interpretation of courtly love taken out of its social context, became canonical for much of the subsequent European lyric—thanks mostly to Bembo's authoritative endorsement in his 1525 *Prose della volgar lingua*.[12] But his success must not make us oblivious to the availability of other options both at his time and before. For not only could a frankly uncourtly view of love be presented (or perhaps advocated) even in such an extended treatment as the *Roman de la rose*, but a chivalric dressing could be used for transparent uncourtois allegories disguising daydreams about subduing a woman with knightly force instead of worshipping her lofty resistance. Typically, at least as early as 1214 a festival at Treviso included a victorious siege by young males of a Castle of Love held by fair maidens.[13]

Petrarch should also enter our discourse for his more technical contribution of codifying some typical chivalric and courtois clichés by turning them into a method of lyrical expression—what became the main ingredients of European Petrarchism in the lyric, including the conventionalized uses of them that can be termed "manneristic."[14] I am referring, first, to his adoption of courtois motifs in the form of stylistic antitheses and oxymora as well as the symmetries of his "correlaciones plurimembres," to use Dámaso Alonso's terms. Petrarch brought to its most consummate level the habit of composing "logically" rather than by simple successions of lyrical moods, which has been observed in the passage from the earlier Provençal, French, and German lyric to the more mature Italian lyrical modes, especially with the Stil Nuovo. An impressive example of the compositional structures that Petrarch canonized is Giacomo da Lentini's (fl. 1233–1240) "Lo basilisco a lo speco lucente." In this sonnet, the first known Sicilian poet exploited the form, which he invented, for the most architectonic compositional format it could encompass by using not only a correlative pattern (in the quatrains) but also a recapitulation of its members (in the tercets), all of it in the midst of continuous antitheses.[15]

Antithesis as well as its most concentrated form, the oxymoron, abounds in Giacomo: see, e.g., the sonnet "Chi non avesse mai veduto foco," ending with a most effective pre-Petrarchan antithetical treatment of his relationship to Love and the beloved: "Certo l'Amore fa gran vilania, / che non distingue te che vai gabando; / a me, che servo, non dà isbaldimento" ("Surely Love does wrong: / he does not subdue you, who only mock, / he has no reward for me, who truly serve"), reminiscent of the close of more than one of Petrarch's most memorable sonnets.[16] Likewise in Rinaldo d'Aquino, canzone "Amorosa donna fina": "d'uno foco che non pare / che 'n la neve fa 'llumare, / ed incende tra lo ghiaccio" ("with a fire that does not show, / that shows its light in the snow, / and flares up inside the ice"); and in Guido delle Colonne's (b. 1210) "che fa lo foco nascere di neve" ("which makes fire arise out of the snow"—sonnet "Anchor che l'aigua per lo foco lassi"). These are paradoxical antitheses in the form of adynata of a kin with Petrarch's "icy fire."[17] Such figures were also common in the earlier French, Provençal, and German poets. For one more striking, final example, I turn to the famous passage in Gottfried's Tristan (vv. 60–64) where the poet espouses the type of true love of his tragic couple, and where we find even the equivalent of Petrarch's neologism *dolceamara* 'bittersweet':

ir süeze sur, ir liebez leit,
ir herzeliep, ir senede not,
ir liebez leben, ir leiden tot,
ir lieben tot, ir leidez leben:
dem lebene si min leben ergeben.

Their sweet bitterness, their loving sorrow,
their hearts' love, their yearning misery,
their loving life, their wretched death,
their loving death, their wretched life:
let my life be devoted to that life.
(W. T. H. Jackson's trans., 1971: 54.)

And again

daz honegende gellet,
daz süezende siuret,
daz touwende viuret,
daz senftende smerzet....

love's gall, with honey fraught,
bitterness, sweet though tart,
pain, soothing though it smart,
fire, quenching though it burn....
(vv. 11,884–87 Ranke ed., 11,888–91 Zeydel 1948 trans.)

Indeed, Gottfried favored antitheses and oxymora throughout his poem, climaxing in the definitional one he adapted from Thomas: "Isot ma drue, Isot mamie, / en vus ma mort, en vus ma vie!" ("Isold my love, Isold my friend, / in you is my death, in you my life," 19,409–10, in French in his text).[18] He had described Isolt as Tristan's "living death" ("sin lebender tot"—14,468).

Petrarch, moreover, transmitted to his Quattrocento imitators and beyond the medieval conceit of the heart or soul detached from the lover. Compare sonnet 16, "Io mi rivolgo indietro a ciascun passo": while he is away from his beloved he wonders how it can be that his limbs are detached from the spirit that sustains them, "come posson queste membra/ da lo spirito lor viver lontane?" Besides Provençal and French (and German) antecedents, he had Italian ones as well. Listen to Rinaldo d'Aquino ("Amorosa donna fina"): "che vita po l'omo avere, / se lo cor non è con lui? / Lo meo cor non è co' mico, / ched eo tutto lo v'ho dato" ("How can one live / without a heart? / Mine is not with me, / since I have given it entirely to you.") Of course, the roles could also be reversed, and Guido delle Colonne, in the canzone already quoted, could say that he thought the soul happily dwelling inside his body was really his lady's own: "Lo spirito ch'i' aggio, und'eo mi sporto, / credo lo vostro sia, / che nel meo petto stia / e abiti con meco in gran diporto" ('I think that the soul that sustains me is your soul, which dwells in my breast with great delight!').[19] Traditional motifs that embody the notions of sweet enslavement and liberation through poetic singing come down from the troubadours all the way to the most recent models, like Guittone d'Arezzo (ca. 1253–1294): "come l'augel dolci canti consono, / ch'è preso in gabbia e sosten molti guai" ("I sing sweet songs like the bird who is kept in a cage and suffers much woe") (sonnet "Dolcezza alcuna," ending with the antithesis "credendomi appressare, io m'allontano" ["in the illusion of coming closer I drift further away"]). Or take the motif of the pilgrim who looks for the sacred relics as the poet looks for the likes of his beloved (cf. Petrarch's "Movesi il vecchierel"), as in Lapo Gianni's (ca. 1250–1328 or later) sonnet "Sì come i Magi a guida della stella": "Sì come i Magi a guida della stella / girono invèr le parti d'oriente / per adorar lo Segnor ch'era nato, / così mi guidò Amore a veder quella" ("Just as the Magi, guided by the star, / turned toward the East / in order to worship the newly born Lord, / so Love guided me to behold that woman").

We can now conclude by bringing our several threads together. First, language indeed holds with the world; the sign with outside reality. Seigniorial courts had been a fitting environment for oral culture and literature both in the curial setting of clerical teaching for ecclesiastical and administrative instruction and in the social relationships that fostered troubadour poetry as live singing of the lady's praises. In Italy the new political setting of the Frederician court of Palermo as well as the new social and professional setting of notarial circles that produced the Stil Nuovo brought about a decided privileging of the written text, fixed and transmitted by copying and reading rather than reciting and singing. Petrarch inherited the curial and courtly traditions in this new "grammatological" form, and radically crystallized it by making the

Petrarchan lover part of a written elitist culture with a set of canonized, universalized motifs that established a text as trademark of the new man of the world.

New York University

NOTES

1. Concerning the derivations of modern philosophical trends from Hegelianism and competing philosophical traditions see Remo Bodei, "Dialettica, contraddizione e sviluppo nel moderno," in *Forme e pensiero del moderno*, ed. Franco Rella (Milano: Feltrinelli, 1989), 140–57.
2. Cf. Heidegger, *Basic Writings from* Being and Time *(1927) to* The Task of Thinking *(1964)*, ed. David F. Krell (New York: Harper & Row, 1977), "Letter on Humanism," 225–26.
3. See Werner L. Gundersheimer, *Ferrara* (1973), 129–31, for the first label, and Benjamin Kohl "Political Attitudes of North Italian Humanists in the Late Trecento," *Studies in Medieval Culture* 4 (1974): 418–27, for the second. "Subdital" refers to the rule of princes being praised as beneficial to the subjects, *subditi*.
4. John M. McManamon, *Funeral Oratory and the Cultural Ideals of Italian Humanism* (Chapel Hill: U of North Carolina P, 1989), 88–91.
5. Paul Zumthor, *Essai de poétique médiévale* (Milano: Feltrinelli,1974); "Genèse et évolution du genre," *Grundriß der romanischen Literaturen des Mittelalters* 4.1: *Le roman jusqu'à la fin du XIIIe siècle*, ed. Jean Frappier and Reinhold R. Grimm (Heidelberg: Carl Winter, 1978), 60–73; and especially, now, *La lettre et la voix* (Paris: Éditions du Seuil, 1987).
6. Cf. Zumthor (1987) 319–22.
7. Aurelio Roncaglia has conjectured one important episode in this story by identifying the Occitan manuscript that in about 1230 Frederick II may have made available to his court poets. Cf. Roncaglia, "Per il 750° anniversario della scuola poetica siciliana," *Rendiconti dell'Accademia Nazionale dei Lincei*, Classe di Lettere, Serie 8^a:36 (Roma: Accademia dei Lincei, 1983–84), 321–33. Cf. Zumthor (1987), 164–66 on the first methodical uses of written documents for literary transmission.
8. Ronald G. Witt, "Medieval Italian Culture and the Origins of Humanism as a Stylistic Ideal," *Renaissance Humanism: Foundations, Forms, and Legacy*, 3 vol., ed. Albert Rabil (Philadelphia: U of Pennsylvania P, 1988), 1: 29–70 at 52.
9. On this aspect of Petrarch's poetic and moral psychology see my "Petrarca 1974: A Sketch for A Portrait," in *Francis Petrarch, Six Centuries Later: A Symposium*, ed. A. Scaglione (Chapel Hill: U of North Carolina P—Chicago: Newberry Library, 1975), 1–24; A. Scaglione, "Classical Heritage and Petrarchan Self-Consciousness in the Literary Emergence of the Interior 'I'," *Altro Polo 7* (1984): 23–34, rpt. in *Modern Critical Views: Petrarch*, ed. Harold Bloom (New York: Chelsea P, 1989), 125–37.

10. Cf. Lucie Brind'Amour in T. Klaniczay et al., eds. (1988), 450–53. The key texts and authors for Castille are *El cancionero de Baena* (1445), Juan de Mena, the Marquis of Santillana, Juan del Encina, Jorge Manrique, and Hernando de Ludueña (*Doctrinal de gentileza*); for Catalonia. especially Ausias March.

11. See C. Stephen Jaeger, *The Origins of Courtliness: Civilizing Trends and the Formation of Courtly Ideals 939–1210* (Philadelphia: U of Pennsylvania P, 1985); Id., "Cathedral Schools and Humanist Learning, 950–1150," *Deutsche Vierteljahrsschrift für Literaturwissenschaft und Geistesgeschichte* 61.4 (1987): 569–616; Georges Duby, esp. *Hommes et structures du Moyen Age: Recueil d'articles* (Paris-La Haye: Mouton, 1973); Erich Köhler, *Trobadorlyrik und höfischer Roman* (Berlin [Ost]: Rütten & Loening, 1962); Id., *Ideal und Wirklichkeit in der höfischen Epik. Studien zur Form der frühen Artus- und Graldichtung.* Beihefte zur Zeitschrift für romanische Philologie 97 (Tübingen: Max Niemeyer, 1956, 2nd, expanded ed. 1970); trans. of 2nd ed. by Eliane Kaufholz, *L'aventure chevaleresque. Idéal et réalité dans le roman courtois: études sur la forme des plus anciens poèmes d'Arthur et du Graal* (Paris: Gallimard, 1974); Id., *Esprit und arkadische Freiheit. Aufsätze aus der Welt der Romania* (Frankfurt/M.-Bonn: Athenäum, 1966; rpt. 1972); Id., *Sociologia della fin'amor*, trans. and introd. by Mario Mancini (Padova: Liviana, 1976); Id., "Literatursoziologische Perspektiven," *Grundriß der romanischen Literaturen des Mittelalters* 4.1, ed. J. Frappier and R.R. Grimm, 82–103; id., ed. *Grundriß der romanischen Literaturen des Mittelalters 2.1, Les genres lyriques*, (Heidelberg: Carl Winter,1979–87).

12. On the codification of Petrarchistic practice in the lyric after Bembo, especially with regard to the influential work of Girolamo Ruscelli, see Amedeo Quondam, "Livelli d'uso nel sistema linguistico del Petrarchismo," *Sociologia della letteratura*, Atti del 1° Convegno Nazionale, Gaeta 1974, ed. Fernando Ferrara et al. (Roma: Bulzoni, 1978), 212–39.

13. Roger Sherman Loomis, "The Allegorical Siege in the Art of the Middle Ages," *American Journal of Archaeology* 2.23 (1919): 225–69, and Thomas M. Greene, "Magic and Festivity at the Renaissance Court," *Renaissance Quarterly* 40.4 (1987): 636–59 at 642.

14. E.g., A. Scaglione, "Cinquecento Mannerism and the Uses of Petrarch," *Medieval and Renaissance Studies* V, ed. O.B. Hardison (Chapel Hill: U.N.C. Press, 1971), 122–155.

15. The text is worth quoting:

> Lo basilisco a lo speco lucente
> tragge a morire cum risbaldimento,
> lo cesne canta plù gioiosamente
> quand'egli è presso a lo so finimento,
> lo paon turba, istando plù gaudente,
> cum a soi pedi fa riguardamento,
> l'augel fenice s'arde veramente
> per ritornare in novo nascimento.

In tai nature eo sentom'abenuto,
che allegro vado a morte a le belleze,
e'nforzo 'l canto presso a lo finire;
estando gaio torno dismarruto,
ardendo 'n foco inovo in allegreze,
per vui, plù gente, a cui spero redire.

The basilisk before the shining mirror / comes to death with joy, / the swan sings
with greatest pleasure / when it approaches its end, / the peacock becomes perturbed
when, / at the height of its rapture, it looks at its feet, / the phoenix burns itself
to come back to a new life. / I feel I have acquired the nature of one of these
animals / when I see I go toward my death in the name of beauty, / and sing more
sharply as the end approaches; / even while I feel merry I become lost, / burning
in fire I renew myself in joy, / all this because of you, most gentle one, to whom
I seek to return.

Text from *Le rime della scuola siciliana* 1, ed. Bruno Panvini (Firenze: Olschki,
1962). Translation mine.

16. Text from *Letteratura Italiana delle Origini*, ed., Gianfranco Contini (Firenze:
Sansoni, 1970). Frede Jensen's new edition of the Sicilian School is useful for
its criteria of selection: cf. *The Poetry of the Sicilian School*, ed. and trans. Frede
Jensen (New York-London: Garland, 1986).

17. Leonard Forster, *The Icy Fire: Five Studies in European Petrarchism* (Cambridge:
Cambridge UP, 1969; 1978), is a brilliant study of Petrarch's antitheses within
the whole Petrarchist tradition.

18. The symmetric arrangement of this passage reminds the reader of the similar cadence
in Marie de France' *Lai du chèvrefeuille*. Tristan discloses to Iseut his being near
her in the forest by sending her a message in the form of a twig where he has
carved the couplet: "Bele amie, si est de nus: / ne vus senz mei, ne jeo senz vus!"
("This is the way with us, my sweet friend: neither you without me, nor I without
you!"). The Norman Marie, perhaps the natural daughter of Geoffrey IV of Anjou,
writing in France and England, is supposed to have composed her *lais* between
1175-1189, and the *Isopet* and *Espurgatoire Saint Patrice* after 1189.

As to the precedent of Thomas, cf. *Les* Tristan *en vers*, ed. Jean Charles
Payen (Paris: Garnier, 1974), 178 and 231: "La bele raïne, s'amie / en cui est
sa mort e sa vie" ("The beautiful queen, his friend, in whom lies his death and
his life"—vv. 1061-62); "cum a dame, cum a s'amie, / en qui maint sa mort e
sa vie" ("as with a mistress, his friend, / in whom resides his death and his life"—
vv. 2711-12).

19. Contini, ed., *Letteratura Italiana delle Origini* (1970), 64.

Paradiso XXIII:
To Read The Human Condition[1]

MARISTELLA DE PANIZZA LORCH

Regina caeli, laetare,
Quia quem meruisti portare
Resurrexit, sicut dixit
Ora pro nobis Deum

How are we to link the "human condition" with *Paradiso* XXIll? On one level a great significance lies in a very original fusion of classical models (Ovid, Horace, Virgil, Statius, and Lactantius) with those similes or metaphors Bosco called *comparationes domesticae*.[2] At a more profound level, I shall attempt to show that XXIII reflects a moment in Dante's pilgrimage when his relationship to Beatrice and the constantly-silent, but all-encompassing presence of Mary becomes humanly functional. Each woman in her own way aids the pilgrim to en-vision a second life, a true *vita nuova* in which the body and soul are unified through an aesthetic transcendence.

The key lies in the mystery of incarnation, an incarnation that is pivotal to the acceptance of physical death at the onset of a new life. Both Beatrice and Mary guide Dante's perception of that mystery which only Mary fully represents. For Beatrice this canto implies the drama of an Earthly Parardise and anticipates her silent presence in *Paradiso* XXXIII. In the present canto Beatrice constitutes an intermediation between Dante and the divine experience, of which Mary is a direct

236

part. Both women share in the experience of an "essential being," and each in her distinct way reveals Dante's human perception of it. For the reader this vision can only be represented in image and simile.[3]

In the canto's narrative, the "human condition" is first concretized in the image of Christ Triumphant. Here for the first time Dante is offered a vision of Christ, not in his double nature (which he will obtain only in *Paradiso* XXXIII), but in his humanity: "l'umanità di Cristo," which Buti explains as "the resurrected body of Christ which with its splendor pierces through the light that envelops it, as it will happen to all bodies after the resurrection."[4]

> vid' i' sopra migliaia di lucerne
> un sol che tutte quante l'accendea,
> come fa 'l nostro la viste superne;
> e per la viva luce trasparea
> la lucente sustanza tanto chiara
> nel viso mio, che non la sostenea.

> Over a myriad of lamps prëeminent
> I saw one Sun which kindled each and all,
> As light from our sun to the stars is lent;
> And through the living light shone forth the whole
> Irradiated Substance, so intense
> Upon my eyes, I needs must let them fall.
>   (Paradiso XXIII.28–33)

The vision of the *lucente sostanza* ("Irradiated Substance"), unbearable to Dante's eyes, represents the apex of the narrative, an occasion for the poet to touch upon the motif of *trionfo*. Beatrice acts in this connection as the direct intermediary for Dante's experience. She transforms that experience into words: "E Bëatrice disse: 'ecco le schiere / del trïunfo di Cristo e tutto 'l frutto / ricolto del girar di queste spere!'" (" 'Behold the assembled hosts,' Beatrice said; / 'Behold Christ triumphing, and all the fruit / These spheres have in their circling harvested' "—19–21).

Her words are pronounced with such ardor in her countenance that Dante can only voice an adynaton, "che passar men convien sanza costrutto: ("and I must needs be mute"—24).

If Dante is not able to respond to Beatrice's words, what kind of *trionfo* can he experience? In general Dante conceives the *trionfo* in the human terms Buti describes: "a Roman triumph when in front of the chariot is displayed the prey taken away from their enemies; thus the author imagines Christ with the prey he has torn away from the devil. . . ."[5]

Bosco observes that Dante uses the word *trionfo* in the sense of both "victory" and "joy": victory over sin and joy of beatitude.[6] This victory and/or joy can be experienced by an individual soul, by all the blessed souls or by the Church. In *Paradiso* V.115–116, the Church Triumphant constitutes a *trionfo* in the sense of an ensemble of the blessed in their seats or thrones: "O bene nato a cui veder li troni / del triunfo etternal concede grazia" ("O happy born, whom grace lets contemplate / The thrones of the eternal triumph"). The Church triumphant is concretized in the totality of blessed souls. In *Paradiso* XXIII, however, Dante sees Christ's triumph in terms of the blessed who surround him. Their joy of victory over evil takes the form of *human* joy, if not analogous, apparently at least not dissimilar to the soul's "triumph" over the devil in *Valla's* paradise.[7]

Dante's vision of this kind of triumph calls upon our intuition, not our reason, to respond as humans to the "humanity" of Christ, his death as a man and his victory over it. Christ's victory and joy is with and through the blessed souls that surround him. This vision of Christ Triumphant in the act of redemption defines Beatrice as the *frutto* of Dante's pilgrimage.

Such a *trionfo* has been the goal of Dante's own experience from the moment he, a pilgrim in preparation for his heavenly voyage, stepped across the *limen*, that wall of fire, in order to partake of the beatitude of the Earthly Paradise (*Purgatorio* XXVII). The metaphor of the fruit and its fertility is, in fact, an all pervasive image in that canto: "come al fanciul si fa ch'è vinto al pome" ("As on a child by an apple's bribe cajoled"—45), says Virgil, smiling ironically and jokingly scolding Dante: " 'Come! / volenci star di qua?' " (" 'Do we hold / Our wish to stay on this side?' "—43–44). At the same time, the *name* of Beatrice as the desired *fruit* (*pome*) is the constant subject of the dialogue between the two poets during the harsh experience of the "burning beyond measure" ("'ncendio sanza metro"—51), a conversation executed by Virgil in an intimate, familiar tone: " 'Li occhi suoi già veder parmi' " (" 'Already I seem to see her face' "—54).

Solemnly the night is described. Dante sleeps and wakes to hear Virgil's definition of his pilgrimage's aim as a *fruit* (*pome*):

"Quel dolce pome che per tanti rami
cercando va la cura de' mortali,
oggi porrà in pace le tue fami."

"That apple whose sweetness in their craving keen
Mortals go seeking on so many boughs
This day shall peace to all thy hungers mean."
(*Purgatorio* XXVII.115–117)

At this Virgil ceases functioning as Dante's guide. His words give wings to Dante's upward ascent: "al volo mi sentia crescer le penne" ("I felt wings on me growing to waft me higher"—123). After Virgil's *commiato* and before Beatrice appears, Dante remains for a moment alone—the only time in his voyage—and enjoys "l'erbette, i fiori e arbuscelli / che qui la terra sol da sé produce" ("the young grass, the flowers and coppices / Which this soil, of itself alone, makes grow"—134–135): the spontaneous product of Earthly Paradise. This moment of pause and meditation and the subsequent intervention of the beautiful Matelda prepare Dante for the apparition of Beatrice, love's first and foremost flame of youth, his *antico amor*, his *antica fiamma* (*Purgatorio* XXX.39, 48).

Yet, note that, following her appearance, Beatrice reproachfully indicates a transition in their relationship which had been provoked by her physical death:

Quando di carne a spirito era salita,
    e bellezza e virtù cresciuta m'era,
    fu'io a lui men cara e men gradita;
e volse i passi suoi per via non vera,
    imagini di ben seguendo false,
    che nulla promession rendono intera.
Né l'impetrare ispirazion mi valse,
    con le quali, e in sogno e altrimenti,
    lo rivocai: sì poco a lui ne calse!

When from the flesh to spirit I had clomb
    And beauty and virtue greater in me grew,
    Less dear to him, more strange did I become;

And with perverted steps on ways untrue
He sought false images of good, that ne'er
Perform entire the promise that was due.
Nor helped me the inspiration won by prayer
Whereby through dream or other hidden accost
I called him back; so little had he care.
(*Purgatorio* XXX.127–138)

Beatrice points here to Dante's reaction to her physical death, her transition or metamorphosis into a *new* life which Dante had not accepted as such.

The metamorphosis Dante himself will undergo in *Purgatorio* XXX through XXXIII that he might accept the *new* Beatrice is prefigured in XXVII. There Dante makes an especially sophisticated use of Ovid's narration in the *Metamorphoses* of the myth of Pyramus and Thisbe, in particular of the "fact" that the fruit of the mulberry tree changed color. This chromatic metamorphosis symbolizes a change in the *frutto* or aim of Dante's voyage, as he journeys away from the Earthly Paradise in the last cantos of the *Paradiso*. The *frutto* or *pome* for which Dante longs may be earthly happiness in the Earthly Paradise. It is, however, in XXIII the triumph of Christ and Mary, his first approach to the mystery of incarnation. The intensity of the latter increases in proportion to his increasing experience of Beatrice's beauty in her *new* life.

Beatrice is literally the sub-stantia of Dante's "'divine" experience. Yet, our understanding of her relationship to Dante here must be predicated on her first appearance to him as a woman, loved in flesh and blood. A simile leads us to relate these two images of Beatrice from the *Purgatorio* and the *Paradiso*. A simile that describes the "painting" of the sky at dawn by the rising of the sun precedes her appearance in *Purgatorio* XXX:

Io vidi già nel cominciar del giorno
la parte orïental tutta rosata,
e l'altro ciel di bel sereno addorno;
e la faccia del sol nascere ombrata,
sì che per temperanza di vapori
l'occhio la sostenea lunga fïata:
così, dentro una nuvola di fiori
che da le mani angeliche saliva
e ricadeva giù dentro e di fori,

sovra candido vel cinta d'uliva
donna m'apparve, sotto verde manto
vestita di color di fiamma viva.

I have seen ere now at the beginning dawn
  The region of the East all coloured rose,
  (The pure sky else in beauty of peace withdrawn)
When shadowed the sun's face uprising shows,
  So that the mists, attempering his powers,
  Let the eye linger upon him in repose;
So now for me amid a cloud of flowers
  That from the angels' hands up-floated light
  And fell, withinside and without, in showers,
A lady, olive-crowned o'er veil of white,
  Clothed in the colour of a living flame,
  Under a mantle green, stole my sight.
                    (*Purgatorio* XXX.22–33)

The vision of Christ in *Paradiso* XXIII is preceded by a simile,
one in which the verb "to paint" (*dipingere*) is explicitly mentioned
and the central image is one of the sky at night:

Quale ne' plenilunïi sereni
  Trivïa ride tra le ninfe etterne
  che dipingon lo ciel per tutti i seni,
vid' i' sopra migliaia di lucerne
  un sol che tutte quante l'accendea,
  come fa 'l nostro le viste superne;
e per la viva luce trasparea
  la lucente sustanza tanto chiara
  nel viso mio, che non la sostenea.

As in the full moon's tranquil brilliance
  Trivia smiles among the nymphs who paint
  Eternally Heaven's uttermost expanse,
Over a myriad lamps preëminent
  I saw one Sun which kindeled each and all,
  As light from our sun to the stars is lent;
And through the living light shone forth the whole
  Irradiated Substance, so intense
  Upon my eyes, I needs but let them fall.
                    (*Paradiso* XXIII.25–34)

These two similes have something deeper in common than the fact that both focus on the sky. Beatrice's appearance in *Purgatorio* XXX reveals visually Dante's experience "within" and "without" (see Mandelbaum's essay in this volume). In this instance the experience is of a painting (or mosaic) of a Virgin on a throne among angels. In the simile of *Paradiso* XXIII that is bound to Christ, Dante transforms images of the moon and minor stars from Horace's *Epode* XV.1-2: "Nox erat et coelo fulgebat Luna sereno / inter minora sidera" (" 'Twas night, and in the cloudless sky the moon was shining amid the lesser lights") into the sophisticated painting of a court in which a royal Moon smiles (*ride*) as the mythological Trivia and the stars, her eternal nymphs, "paint" (*dipingon*) the whole firmament. The "painted vision" evokes the inside of a church completely covered with a fresco or mosaic, not the image of stars but of blessed souls around the central image of Christ. Not only is the heavenly simile more concise than that of *Purgatorio* XXX, it is also much more ambitious. Nonetheless, both share the poet's human condition reflected in a spiritual immersion, not in natural phenomena, but in the iconography of church painting that Dante saw before him during the liturgical experience of his everyday life. In *Paradiso* XXIII, the "humanity" of Christ is projected (again see Mandelbaum) through Dante's own poetic en-visioning of a religious painting into something which lies beyond the "human": the idea of the co-presence of millions of blessed souls in Heaven who adore Christ in his "humanity."

Beatrice, both human and blessed, acts as an intermediary between Dante and his transcendent experience. Throughout his heavenly journey, Dante strives to render the transition from the old love (the *antico amor* or *antica fiamma*) to the new. Yet, in Dante's "new" life, in spite of the immersion into the waters of the Lethe and Eunoe, his "new" love never ceases to appeal humanly to the "old" in simile and metaphor.

In *Paradiso* XXIII, it is human experience that relates Dante to Beatrice, a kind that triumphs over the ephemeral through a miraculous "conquest" of physical death. Physically dead, but a participant in the "new" life, Beatrice is able to form a relationship to Dante as would the Virgin Mary. This is not the Beatrice of *Purgatorio* XXX.

Purgatorio XXX and *Paradiso* XXIII must, however, in the end be related to the closing of St. Bernard's prayer to the Virgin at the opening of *Paradiso* XXXIII. " 'vedi Beatrice con quanti beati / per li miei prieghi ti chiudon le mani!' '' ('' 'See, Beatrice with how many of the blest, / To second this my prayer, lays hand to hand' ''—38–39). Here is expressed the *summa* of Dante's vision of Beatrice, and from it we may retain a pictorially rendered vision, a tryptic.

This tryptic's central section lies in *Paradiso* XXIII and evokes (as does the opening image of the canto) Beatrice as a nesting mother bird, anxious to feed her young and anxious for Dante to face the vision of Christ and then of Mary in Triumph.

Is it by chance, Bosco asks, that "every time Dante has to describe visions which respond to some of the most difficult religious questions, he should recur to the image of the relationship of an "infant" to his "mother?" It so happens, for instance in high Paradise. When he has to sharpen his eyes in order to penetrate the nature of the Empyreon's river of light, he declares:

> Non è fantin che sì sùbito rua
> col volto verso il latte, se si svegli
> molto tardato da l'usanza sua. . .

> No child is there that flings him at such speed
> With face turned to the milk, if he awake
> For later than his wont. . . .
> (*Paradiso* XXX.82–84)

When he finally avows that he cannot articulate the supreme truth within a human language, Dante will describe his *favella* ("speech") as more limited ". . .che d'un fante / che bagni ancor la lingua a la mammella" (". . .and less than could an infant's store / Of speech, who at the pap yet sucks"—*Paradiso* XXXIII.107–108).[8]

How is this particular simile used in canto XXIII?

Through an ecstatic vision, Dante first perceives Christ's human nature in order to experience the vision of Mary in concert with the archangel Gabriel and an army of the blessed. After Mary vanishes beyond a height that Dante's eyes can follow, the blessed distend toward the Empyreon in their intense longing for her (75–129).

The human relationship that Dante nourishes for both Mary and Beatrice is exposed precisely through the mother-infant and infant-mother similes, one at the opening, the other toward the end of the canto. At the onset of XXIII, the mother bird, longing to feed her little ones that try to anticipate the first beams of the sun, is Beatrice (1–12). At the closing of the canto, the infant who, after being breastfed, stretches its arms toward the mother "per l'animo che 'nfin di fuor s'infiamma" ("the spirit flaming outward to respond"—123) expresses the ardor of the blessed souls' longing to join Mary in the Empyreon. The second simile, one is tempted to conclude, complements the first: Beatrice prefigures Mary. Yet, how so?

Mary is rendered in the most human, domestic, familiar tone:

> Il nome del bel fior ch'io sempre invoco
> e mane e sera, tutto mi restrinse
> l'animo ad avvisar lo maggior foco.

> The name of the fair flower, which day and night
> My lips continually invoke, compelled
> My mind to gaze upon the greatest lights.
> (*Paradiso* XXIII.88–90)

Then too, Beatrice's relationship to Mary is lodged in more than the recurrence of the mother-child simile. Both share the power of "the name," that *image* binding Dante as human being to both Beatrice and Mary, as one woman draws him "beyond" and "through" the other.

Dante's pilgrimage of love begins in *Purgatorio* XXVII when, in the mention of Beatrice, Virgil finally induces Dante to cross the barrier of fire:

> "Or vedi, figlio:
> tra Bëatrice e te è questo muro."
> Come al nome di Tisbe aperse il ciglio
> Priamo in su la morte, e riguardolla,
> allor che il gelso diventò vermiglio;
> così, la mia durezza fatta solla,
> mi volsi al savio duca udendo il nome
> che ne la mente sempre mi rampolla.

> "Look now, this same
> Wall is 'twixt Beatrice and thee, my son,"
> As Pyramus at the sound of Thisbe's name
> Opened his dying eyes and gazed at her
> Then, when the crimson on the mulberry came,
> So I did turn to my wise Leader,
> My hardness melted, hearing the name told
> Which like a well-spring in my mind I bear.
> (*Purgatorio* XXVII.35–42)

After having crossed the wall of fire, the *nome* of Beatrice is already giving the signs of its spiritual, inner "fertility": Dante's world has never been so rich and so peaceful. Yet it is a world dominated by physical images. From Ovid's world of the poetic image, Dante devises instruments within the process of sight (*vedere*). They instinctively evoke in him a metaphor and stimulate a movement of vision from the outer *senso* to an inner reality. He reads the Ovidian episode through the *pome*, the metamorphosis of the *arborei fetus* ("the fruit of a tree") into the permanence that in Dante's world the *nome* can bestow: "purpureo tinguit pendentia mora colore" ("[the root] tinged the hanging berries with the same purple hue"—*Metamorphoses* IV.127). He focuses instinctively on what is for him the fruitful image, which he translates from the literal into the transliteral. Pyramus dies. Only the change of the color in the fruit will remain witness of his love for Thisbe:

> ad nomen Thisbes oculos a morte gravatos
> Pyramus erexit visaque recondidit illa.

> At the name of Thisbe, Pyramus lifted his eyes,
> now heavy with death, and having looked upon her face,
> closed them them again.
> (*Metamorphoses* IV.145–146)

What must have triggered Dante's metaphorical reading of the episode of how death generates a form of life lies in Ovid's lines: "Tua te carissima Thisbe / nominat" (" 'Tis your dearest Thisbe calling you' "—143–144). For Dante it is in calling the name that the two lovers are united. In order to reach this final point he presupposes the sequence of the vivid images of the Ovidian story from the wall with the *tenuis rima* ("slender chink"); to Pyramus' fatal discovery of the torn veil and the plunging of the sword into his side with the cry, "nostri quoque sanguinis haustus!" ("Drink now my blood too"—IV.118); to the blood, leaping high, as from a broken pipe; to the fruit of the tree ("arborei fetus"—125) turning to a dark red color ("in atram / . . . faciem"— 125–126) while the soaked roots tinged the berries from the inside ("madefactaque sanguine radix / . . . tinguit"—126–127).

The metamorphosis (the change of color in the fruit) has already taken place in a natural form when Thisbe appears and, kissing the dying Pyramus, begs him to answer, to come back to life: " . . . responde! Tua te carissima Thisbe nominat. . . . " In Dante's reading of Ovid's text, the horror of the Ovidian sequence of images dissolves with *nominat*. It is the *nomen* that generates the permanence of a new life, for every summer the tree will bear *red* fruit:

> "at tu quae ramis arbor miserabile corpus
> nunc tegis unius, mox est tectura duorum,
> signa tene caedis pullosque et luctibus aptos
> semper habe fetus, gemini monimenta cruoris."

> "And do you, O tree, who now shades with your branches the
> poor body of one, and soon will shade two, keep the marks
> of our death and always bear your fruit of a dark colour,
> meet for mourning, as a memorial of our double death."
> *(Metamorphoses* IV.158–161)

Dante reads this story of death, blood, and darkness from the powerful center expressed in *nominat*. In it lies the miraculous solution, the key to the human transformation. Expectedly, although he clearly models his text on Ovid's, he reverses the images: darkness becomes light. The *nomen* or name represents an apex of experience in both texts, but what is a brief instant of resurrection for Pyramus (he closes his eyes immediately and forever after having glanced at Thisbe) becomes a fulfilment of *ogni brama* ("every desire") for Dante, who will look at Beatrice forever with increasing intensity. Thisbe follows her love in death. Dante conquers death in the magic of a name: Beatrice, and, to be sure, her naming of him (*Purgatorio* XXX.55).

I have argued elsewhere that Ovid taught Dante how to *see* metaphorically.[9] The sensual element in Thisbe's discourse becomes an activated metaphor for Dante's relationship to Beatrice, a human device used by Dante to communicate the interiorization that the *nome* will undergo as the pilgrim crosses the wall of fire.

One specific word or image in *Purgatorio* XXVII signifies the metamorphosis from *duro* to *molle* (from "harsh" to "soft") that occurs by the magical force of the *nome*: the verbe *rampollare* ("to gush forth") in the above line "del nome che ne la mente sempre mi rampolla." The source of this verb lies within the intense sensual implications of Ovid's already cited text:

> (arbor)...
> signa tene caedis pullosque et luctibus aptos
> semper habe fetus....
> *(Metamorphoses* IV.160–161)

The natural image of a plant (in this case the mulberry tree, the vehicle of the metaphor) reveals the originally "sensual" tenor of Dante's love for Beatrice, a love that after the purification through fire, the *affinamento*, still retains *i segni de l'antica fiamma*.

Analogously, the images of a garden with its flowers inspires a simile in *Paradiso* XXIII. Dante's sources are the Bible and the mystics. Yet, the simile and the miracle of a *nome* reveal here, as in *Purgatorio* XXVII, Dante's human condition.

After the vision of Christ and Dante's reaction to it, Beatrice reproaches him for looking adoringly into her face, instead of turning to the "rose of Christ's garden," He who has appeared surrounded by fragrant lilies, leading men toward the right path.

> Come a raggio di sol, che puro mei
> per fratta nube, già prato di fiori
> vider, coverti d'ombra, li occhi miei;
> vid'io così più turbe di splendori,
> folgorate di sù da raggi ardenti,
> senza veder principio di fulgóri.
> O benigna virtù che sì li 'mprenti,
> sù t'esaltasti per largirmi loco
> a li occhi lì che non t'eran possenti.

> As, with my eyes in shade, I have seen
> A meadow of flowers flashed over by the sun,
> When cloud breaks and a pure ray glides between,
> Many a clustered splendour, blazed upon
> By ardent beams, was to my eyes revealed,
> Although I saw not whence the blazing shone.
> O benign Power, who hast these spirits sealed,
> Thou didst withdraw thee on high, that to my sight,
> So feebly empowered, this room thou mightest yield.
> (*Paradiso* XXIII.79–87)

The simile betrays a visual experience of nature analogous to the one with which Dante introduces the reader to Beatrice's appearance in *Purgatorio* XXX:

> Io vidi già nel comminciar del giorno
> la parte orïental tutta rosata,
> e l'altro ciel di bel sereno addorno;

e la faccia del sol nascere ombrata,
sì che per temperanza di vapori
l'occhio la sostenea lunga fïata.

I have seen ere now at the beginning dawn
The region of the East all coloured rose,
(The pure sky else in beauty of peace withdrawn)
When shadowed the sun's face uprising shows,
So that the mists, attempering his powers,
Let the eye linger upon him in repose.
(*Purgitorio* XXX.22–27)

The simile anticipates Dante's reaction to the vision of Beatrice, her "change of beauty" in all of its powerful re-experiencing of the *antico amore*.[10] In *Paradiso* XXIII the simile and the images are even more powerful and direct as they draw the vision of Mary, implicity experienced as fully and intimately as she is on earth. Mary envelops Dante now in her essence as a *bel fior*, a mystic flower or rose, because on earth she was the subject of his daily prayers.

Il nome del bel fior ch'io sempre invoco
e mane e sera, tutto mi ristrinse
l'animo ad avvisar lo maggior foco;
E come ambo le luci mi dipinse
il quale e il quanto de la viva stella
che là sù vince come qua giù vinse...

The name of the fair flower, which day and night
My lips continually invoke, compelled
My mind to gaze upon the greatest light;
And when distinct in both mine eyes were held
The glory and grandeur of the living star
Which excels there as down here it excelled....
(*Paradiso* XXIII.88–93)

Dante invokes Mary, eventually by name, through this metaphor. Yet, it is Beatrice in the text who names her *la rosa* ("the Rose"—*Paradiso* XXIII.73), not Dante, the pilgrim, who re-names her with a periphrasis: *il nome del bel fior*. It is in this metaphorical re-naming that Dante expresses his human relationship to Her. "Mary" is held within his spirit. She/it is pronounced aloud in prayer. So too is the name of Beatrice: "il nome che nella mente sempre mi rampolla" (*Purgatorio*

XXVII.42, see above). Both names reveal Dante's experiences on earth as a human being and reflect doubly an earthly love. Paradise has its roots in the human condition and its ephemeral habits. That both Beatrice and Dante agree upon an apparently "natural" metaphor in their naming of Mary in *Paradiso* XXIII in fact points to a mystical distinction in the Christian liturgy that designates the Virgin as the *rosa mystica*: Again arises the power of Dante's prayers and their spontaneous expression of an intimate love of the Virgin Mary. The proud judge of popes, theologians and emperors reveals in his relationship to the Virgin the traits of the most humble of Christians. The Triumph of Mary in *Paradiso* XXIII originates from elementary, human devotion.

The Virgin, surrounded by an army of blessed souls whose song is indescribably sweet, the Virgin encircled three times in fire by the loving archangel Gabriel ("'Io sono amore angelico, che giro...'" ("'I am angelic love and circle round'"—*Paradiso* XXIII.103), becomes the essence of overflowing, all-embracing motherly love, the concrete expression of the mystery of the incarnation. The *name* "Mary" (*il nome di Maria*), resounds (*sonare*) as it is pronounced by the blessed (109–110), and through the whole universe, it becomes a supernatural echo of the daily invocations of suffering humanity as it strives to see with different eyes visions undreamt on earth. Thus Beatrice's beauty after physical death becomes part of the beauty of the cosmos in that single phrase, "il nome di Maria."

While Dante, still a human being, strives to follow Mary in her flight upwards, he has not a vision, but an intuition of the Empyreon:

> Lo real manto di tutti i volumi
> del mondo, che più ferve e più s'avviva
> ne l'alito di Dio e nei costumi,
> avea sopra di noi l'interna riva
> tanto distante, che la sua parvenza,
> là dov'io era, ancor non appariva:
> però non ebber li occhi miei potenza
> di seguitar la coronata fiamma
> che si levò appresso sua semenza.

> The royal mantle of all the wheeling maze
> Of the universe, whose ardour burns most hot,
> Most quickened in God's breath and in His ways,

Had the inner border of it so far remote
Above, that in my vision's narrower scope,
Where I was stationed, I discerned it not.
Therefore my eyes' endeavour might not hope
To accompany the crowned flame beyond,
As after her own seed she mounted up.
(*Paradiso* XXIII.112–120)

The narrative in a crescendo of lyric moments culminates in the echo of an earthly ritual: the song *Regina coeli*, again part of Dante's daily rite. It is in this context that the second simile of the child and mother appears. The human climax of the Virgin's Triumph as an earthly phenomenon is expressed by a simile which renders the intense love (*affetto*) that the blessed souls feel for Mary:

E come fantolin ch 'nver' la mamma
    tende le braccia poi che 'l latte prese,
    per l'animo che 'nfin di fuor s'infiamma;
ciascun di quei candori in sù si stese
    con la sua cima [fiamma],[11] sì che l'alto affetto
    ch'elli avieno a Maria mi fu palese.

And as the child who toward his mother fond
    Stretches his arms when he has milked her breast—
    The spirit flaming outward to respond—
Each of those white fires strained into a crest
    Its flame, so that the affection infinite
    They had for Mary was made manifest.
(*Paradiso* XXIII.121–126)

In both *Purgatorio* XXVII and *Paradiso* XXIII, it is through the miracle of a name, invoked constantly and humanly by Dante in his earthly life, that he overcomes the difficulties of this earth and obtains the *frutto* of his pilgrimage.

One is tempted to draw a parallel: in the world created by Dante's pilgrimage of love, Beatrice stands to Thisbe as Mary stands to Beatrice. Beatrice, like Pyramus' Thisbe, constitutes for Dante the human basis for a transcendent experience. Thisbe dies with Pyramus. Beatrice, however, lives through death that she might guide and, ultimately, submit Dante to the Virgin. Mary Herself is all-encompassing love, the most elementary constitution of human emotion. While Beatrice must look upon Dante's anxious and highly-stressed dialectic as he strives from one step to another in his ascendence to the joy of an acquired victory, Mary simply embraces the intensity of his joy as he approaches his final destination.

Beatrice's role in *Paradiso* XXIII is anticipated by the role she plays in XXII, where at the onset she is represented as a mother toward Dante, a child:

> Opresso di stupore, a la mia guida
> mi volsi, come parvol che ricorre
> sempre colà dove più si confida;
> e quella, come madre che soccorre
> sùbito al figlio palido ed anelo....

> I turned, numbed with amazement, to my Guide
> For comfort, as a little child who runs,
> As always, there where it can most confide;
> And as a mother succoureth her son's
> Pale cheeks and panting breath....
> *(Paradiso* XXII.1–6)

To this point in the narrative (we are about to leave the seventh Heaven), Dante had proceeded almost inadvertently from one heaven to another. In canto XXII, after the invective of St. Benedict against the corruption of the Benedictines and his disappearance within his "collegio" ("company"—98), Beatrice literally pushes (*pinse*) Dante "con un sol cenno" ("with a sign only") up the ladder with an unnatural speed (*Paradiso* XXII.100–101). Thus Dante enters the eighth heaven, the one of the Fixed Stars, explicitly by Beatrice's *virtù*. As the mother drawn at the onset of canto XXII, she literally projects Dante into the kingdom of the divine.

In a prayer to the *gloriose stelle* at the closing of canto XXII, Dante's soul devoutly sighs to them that it might acquire *virtù*: "A voi divotamente ora sospira / l'anima mia, per acquistar virtute..." ("To you devoutly now my spirit sighs / To acquire virtue—*Paradiso* XXII.121–122). To be sure, Dante's *virtù* lies in poetic power to articulate, as a human being, the vision he is about to undergo. Beatrice then encourages him to look downward, and Dante (his text inspired by the *Somnium Scipionis*) sees the whole universe within which the earth is embraced as a whole, metaphorically rendered as "L'aiuola che ci fa tanto feroci," "the small round floor which makes us passionate"—151. Such a view, metaphorical or not, runs counter to all plausible astronomical theories of Dante's time. Thus in this anti-rational sense his is a "divine" and transcendental experience.

The poet, however, suddenly interrupts the contemplation of the universe in order to gaze upon Beatrice's beautiful eyes. Thus canto XXII ends as it began, with Beatrice as Dante's point of reference: "poscia rivolsi li occhi a li occhi belli" ("Then to the beauteous eyes my eyes returned"—154).

In his flight upward Dante's dependence upon Beatrice becomes increasingly more intense. Through her is the entree to the joy of the divine. It is possible to see in Dante's final act of canto XXII a sign of detachment from earthly things, but canto XXII must be read as a prologue to XXIII.

The opening simile of XXIII, a parallel to the one beginning XXII in its relationship of mother to infant, could in principle lead us to an understanding of Beatrice's humanity, not as a detachment from earthly things, but rather as a removal of all purely sensual experience in order to establish the underlying, natural emotion of the human condition: the relationship of mother to child, a deeply human comprehension of the "humanity" of Christ and Mary. However, the mother-infant simile with which Beatrice is introduced at the opening of canto XXIII hints at a presence that is more-than-human. This is because of the special and unusual way in which Dante deals with the simile's recurrence. Although the simile reflects human experience, it is also a sophisticated fusion of several sources.

> Come l'augello intra l'amate fronde,
> posato al nido de' suoi dolci nati
> la notte che le cose ci nasconde,
> che, per veder li aspetti disïati
> e per trovar lo cibo onde li pasca,
> in che gravi labor li sono aggrati,
> previene il tempo in su aperta frasca,
> e con ardente affetto il sole aspetta,
> fiso guardando pur che l'alba nasca;
> così la donna mïa stava eretta
> e attenta, rivolta inver' la plaga
> sotto la quale il sol mostra men fretta.

nanzi a l'acqua che ritorna equale'' (Keeping the furrow of
before /The wake behind it smoothed out again''—*Paradiso*
or where he voices the powerful cry of victory against the
tini in *Paradiso* XXV: ''con altra voce omai, con altro vello
poeta...'' (''With different voice now, nor with fleece the
hall I return, poet''—7–8).

middle of canto XXIII, overwhelmed by Beatrice's divine
of Christ, Dante admits to his trembling (*se sottesso trema*)
nbearable weight. As a poet, he admits his frustration: the
n of this divine experience.

adiso XXXIII, Dante will relate his last vision: the mystery
ity and of Christ's double nature in the geometrician's squaring
. Two centuries after Dante, the theologian-mathematician
sanus equated theological to mathematical knowledge. Only
he certainties of mathematical discourse, he claimed, might
end the materially grounded image, engage the ''oculus
''eye of the mind'') or ''visio intellectualis'' (''seeing of
. Then could one consider the infinite in the light of the finite
ate upon the ineffable divine unity wherein the divine and
osites coincide. In his *Complementum theologicum*, Cusanus
eologicalia ista oculo mentis melius videbuntur quam verbis
eant'' (''These theological matters will be seen better by
he mind than they might be able to be expressed in words'').[14]
renounced his *verba* only when the *Commedia* comes to a
that text closes with an image, not one reflecting the human
n the ''domestic'' vein, but one in the ''geometrically
one, like those in *Paradiso* XXIII, that hands us a key to
tion of the divine as transcendentally human.

University

ng of *Paradiso* XXIII is dedicated to the memory of my husband, a
cian, who loved the *Paradiso*, and of two very close common friends
y helped us both in reading the *Commedia*: Umberto Bosco and Giorgio
 This study is a first attempt to introduce the reader to a collection of
f the *Commedia* that I am projecting for future publication.

Still as the bird, 'mid the belovèd leaves,
   Reposing on the nest of her sweet brood
   Through night, which all things from our vision thieves,
Who, to have longed-for sight of them renewed
   And once again to find them, where she may
   (Hard toil she taketh pleasure in), their food,
Fore-runs the time, high on the open spray,
   And warm with love awaits the earliest light,
   Only intent that dawn may bring the day;
So was my Lady, standing all upright
   And stretched in yearning toward the region where
   The sun shows least of hasting in his flight.
                (*Paradiso* XXIII.1–12)

This particular mother-infant simile encompasses and indeed
transcends all others of its type in the poem. It is first and foremost
a paradigmatic example of Dante's use of classical models. Its precedents
include the *De ave phoenice* attributed to Lactantius.[12] Individual lexical
choices might have arisen from Statius and Virgil.[13] Yet, allusion alone
does not create powerful lyric, and above, in the first three tercets the
humus of the lyric derives from an equally human anxiety of the mother
bird, who becomes for Dante *la donna mïa* of the first verse of the fourth
tercet. Here at last Dante accepts Beatrice's anxiety and discovers solace
for his own in the hope that satisfaction might be his due (13–15). At
this point, however, the human condition clearly flows into another that
is transcendent. Metaphor becomes reality. Dante is an extraordinary
infant or baby bird whose natural desire for food is appeased by hope
alone!

Perhaps indeed to step beyond the ''natural,'' in this case, is to enter
upon a vision of Christ's humanity. Perhaps too it is to ground his
experience in the human condition that Dante invokes the ageless, natural
simile of lightning:

Come foco di nube si diserra
   per dilatarsi sì che non vi cape,
   e fuor di sua natura in giù s'atterra,
la mente mia così tra quelle dape
   fatta più grande di sé stessa uscìo,
   e che si fesse rimembrar non sape.

> As fire is from the fettering cloud unbound,
> Expanding till it needs must overflow,
> And, against nature, rushes to the ground,
> So did my mind mid these feasts outgrow
> Itself, and was dilated, and became
> What recollection hath no skill to show.
> (*Paradiso* XXIII.40–45)

Beatrice, *before and after Dante's experience*, makes him aware of the relationship of the human to the trans-human, the natural to the trans-natural. The sustaining point of reference for the pilgrim is Beatrice's *riso* ("smile") and her words, again *before and after*. Before:

> O Bëatrice, dolce guida e cara!
>   Ella mi disse: "Quel che ti sobranza
>   è virtù da cui nulla si ripara.
> Quivi è la sapïenza e la possanza
>   ch'aprì le strade tra 'l cielo e la terra,
>   onde fu già sì lunga desïanza."

> O Beatrice, dear Guide! sweet Influence!
>   She said to me: "What masters now thy sight
>   Is power against which nothing hath defense.
> Within there is the wisdom and the might
>   Which between earth and heaven the pathways found
>   Longed-for of old with longing infinite."
>   (*Paradiso* XXIII.34–39)

After:

> "Apri li occhi e riguarda qual son io;
>   tu hai veduto cose, che possente
>   se' fatto a sostener lo riso mio."

> "Open thine eyes and look on what I am!
>   Thou hast seen things which of they weakness make
>   Strength to sustain my smile, nor fear the flame."
>   (*Paradiso* XXIII.46–48)

Central to the canto (49–75) is the articulation of one of the most powerful adynata of the *Commedia*: the impossibility of describing

Beatrice's *santo riso* ("holy smile") and shining in its purity by the *santo aspetto* ("h humanity: "E così figurando il paradiso poema, / come chi trova suo cammin recis forth Paradise / Needs must the sacred p some barrier on the pathway lies"—*Pai*

Beatrice will close her circle, addre mystic rose (XXXII.7–9). Finally, in *Para* up the image of a Beatrice fully accepted proof that Dante has taken part in the j

Dante has journeyed far from *Purgatori XXIII* in his acceptance of a *new* Beatrice longs for the articulation of his experienc being avows that, as a poet, he confror exclusive acknowledgement for his po

> Ma chi pensasse il ponderosc
>   e l'omero mortal che se ne
>   nol biasmerebbe se sott' es
> non è pareggio da picciola b
>   quel che fendendo va l'arc
>   né de nocchier ch'a sé me

> But he who thinks how hea
>   Is here for mortal, should
>   Will think no blame if so
> No passage for a little barq
>   Which my adventurous k
>   Nor for a pilot losing he
>   (*F*

The love for a beautiful Beatrice human can express through poetry. T human condition within the canto sh opposition of "ponderoso tema" ("h che se ne carca" ("the mortal shoul triumphs in XXIII humanly as a poe the famous opening of *Paradiso* II, tion of those who are prepared to fo

solco / c
my keel,
II.14–15
lupi fiore
/ ritorner
same, /
   In th
reflectio
under an
articulati
   In *P*
of the Tri
of a circ
Nicolas C
by using
one trans
mentis"
intellect"
and specu
human op
writes: "
expromi c
the eye of
   Dante
close. Yet
condition
familiar":
the articul

Columbia

NOTES

1. This rea
   mathema
   who grea
   Petrocch
   readings

2. Umberto Bosco and Giovani Reggio, ed., *La Divina Commedia* (Florence: Le Monnier, 1979), 349, generally 326–36. I have made use of the Bosco-Reggio edition for the text of the *Commedia*; for a translation: *The Divine Comedy*, tr. Laurence Binyon (New York, Viking Press, 1950). For the text and translation of Horace, Ovid, Status, and Virgil, see the Loeb editions of *Horace: The Odes and Epodes*, tr. C.E. Bennett (Cambridge, Massachusetts: Harvard University Press, 1964); *Ovid: Metamorphoses*, tr. Frank Justus Miller (London, Heinemann: 1960); *Statius: Thebaid V-XII & Achilleid*, tr. J.H. Mozley (London: William Heinemann, 1969); *Virgil: Eclogues, Georgics, Aeneid I-VI*, tr. H. Rushton Fairclough (Cambridge, Massachusetts: Harvard University Press, 1965).

3. One of the most informative essays on canto XXIII to date has been for me Aldo Scaglione's in *From Time to Eternity: Essays on Dante's Divine Comedy*, ed. Thomas Bergin (New Haven: Yale University Press, 1967), 137–172. What is for me most significant is Scaglione's sensitive search into Dante's "images." For *Paradiso* XXIII in particular, a canto generally recognized as one of the lyric cantos of the *Commedia*, he points out that the Trivia simile has a function "which is neither scientific nor descriptively, sensorially realistic; it is purely *emotional* and as such not only successful, but among the most 'convincing' of the poem. Indeed that ecstatic vision of nocturnal beatitude passes from our eyes and ears to the heart, and we feel the moon-lit heaven within us" (163). "The logical discourse is overcome by the poetry of the artifact which acts through intuitive rather than rational channels" (164). In fact Scaglione states that the simile "would not contribute to a heavenly ecstasy were it not for a lack of logic, the disproportion between terms of comparison" (164). The Moon as feminine calls for the Virgin Mary, whose triumph in the canto is prevalent over the one of Christ. This final discovery, according to Scaglione, "is achieved more through the imagery than through the literal narration, for, as befits the moving homage to the Virgin, the canto's delicate melody starts out in a minor key with that arresting simile of the bird..." (166–167). More specifically, Scaglione observes that the canto opens with the image of the mother-bird referred to Beatrice and ends with the child-mother image referred to Mary (168).

Accusing the critics of having performed an injustice to the canto by overlooking "its distinctive chiaroscuro, literal and figurative" (169) that it obtains primarily through these similes, he identifies the attraction of the canto with its lyrical "intuitive" texture, rather than with the close logical context, particularly through an image that is more a consequence of the "spirit" or state of mind of the canto than through the logic of immediate comparison" (171).

I agree *post factum* with Scaglione's conclusion: "The mode of being of Dante's imagery owes more to expressive needs than to the abstract intellectual structures of the poem, and this should make the analyst of cryptographs cautious..." (172). One must also avoid an emphasis on "essential being" at the expense of the human condition (see Brandeis as quoted by Scaglione [160]). "Essential being" in my own reading of the *Paradiso* never obliterates the human. The humanly feminine, Beatrice and Mary, is directly involved in those similes and metaphors that are concerned with Dante's transcendent, more purely ontological experience.

4. *Commento di Francesco da Buti supra la Divina Commedia di Dante Alighieri,* 3 vols. (Pisa: Nistri, 1858–62). See on *Paradiso* XIV.52–57.
5. *Ibid.,* on *Paradiso* XXIII.19–20.
6. Bosco-Reggio, *Paradiso,* 364.
7. Lorenzo Valla, *De vero bono* (New York: Abaris, 1977), III.21.
8. Bosco-Reggio, *Paradiso,* 368.
9. Maristella & Lavinia Lorch, "Metaphor and Metamorphosis: *Purgatorio* XXVII and *Metamorphosis* IV," *Dante and Ovid: Essays in Intertextuality,* ed. Madison W. Sowell (Binghamton: MERTS, 1991), 99–121.
10. What Dante is offered in *Purgatorio* XXX is a first vision of a Beatrice in her new sublimity, in her "ascension of the flesh to the spirit." This *new* Beatrice is not the young woman he had loved on earth; yet, by a hidden *virtù,* he still experiences the symptoms of the old love on earth:

> E lo spirito mio che già cotanto
> tempo era stato ch'a la sua presenza
> non era di stupor, tremando, affranto,
> sanza de li occhi aver più conoscenza,
> per occulta virtù che da lei mosse
> d'antico amor sentì la gran potenza...

> My spirit that a time too long to name
> Had passed, since, at her presence coming nigh,
> A trembling thing and broken it became,
> Now by no recognition of the eye
> But virtue indivisible that went out from her
> Felt old love seize me in all its mastery.
> (*Purgatorio* XXX.34–39)

On this occasion when *l'alta virtù* overcomes Dante, he turns to Virgil, "...quale il fantolin corre alla mamma / quando ha paura o quando elli è afflitto" ("as a child that is afraid / Or hurt, runs to his mother with his pains—*Purgatorio* XXX.44–45). (*Mamma* in this case rhymes with *fiamma*: "Conosco i segni de l'antica fiamma" ("I recognize the old flame within my veins"—*Purgatorio* XXX.48). In this particular case, however, the relationship between mother and child becomes the object of a reproach on the part of the *new* Beatrice. Dante must not act like a child. He must grow into a new understanding of love and its beauty, one that does not deny the original experience in childhood, but both incorporates and transcends it.
11. See Bosco-Reggio, *Paradiso,* 391.
12. Natalino Sapegno, ed., *La Divina Commedia* (Milan/Naples: Ricciardi, 1957), 1057.
13. "L'amate fronde" (1) from "laeti / inter se foliis strepitant" ("joyous... [they] chatter to each other amid the leaves"—Virgil, *Georgics* I.412–413), or/and "qua fronde domum suspendat inanem, / ...vix stetit in ramus et protinus arbor amatur" ("on what branch to hang her [a mother bird's] empty home...scarce has she alighted on the boughs, and straightway loves the tree"—Statius, *Achilleid*

I.213–216); "dolci nati" (2) from "interea dulces pendent circum oscula nati" ("Meanwhile his [a husbandman's] dear children hang upon his kisses"—Virgil, *Georgics* II.523), and/or "sed tota in dulcis consument ubera natos" ("but will spend all their udders' wealth on their dear offspring"—Virgil, *Georgics* III.178), and/or "nec dulcis natos exoptatumque parentem" ("or my sweet children and the father I [Sinon] long for"—Virgil, *Aeneid* II.138), and/or "nec dulcis natos Veneris nec praemia noris?" ("and know not sweet children of love's rewards?"— Virgil. *Aeneid* IV.33); "la notte che le cose ci nasconde" (3) from "et rebus nox abstulit atra colorem," ("and black Night had stolen from the world her hue"— Virgil, *Aeneid* VI.272).

14. This reference is quoted from Percy Brooks' interesting discussion in his Ph.D dissertation, Columbia University, May 1990.

Vision and Visibilia

ALLEN MANDELBAUM

I. "TRA QUESTE ROTE"

Any assembly, symposium, or *convivio* of Italianists merits an ecumenical epigraph. May I then propose as incipit:

> Diverse voci fanno dolci note;
> cosi diversi scanni in nostra vita
> rendon dolce armonia tra queste rote.

> Differing voices join to sound sweet music;
> so do the different orders in our life
> render sweet harmony these spheres.
> (Par. VI, 124–126)[1]

Yet, despite the benevolent ecumenical nature of the epigraph, there is we realize, diversity in it too: on the one hand, the audibility of *note*, on the other the visibility of *rote*. To bridge that diversity there is rhyme: the iconic incarnation of harmony that reconciles the rights of the ear and eye.

In addition to the rhyme, a somewhat obsessed scrutinist could add the harmonized nexus of the obvious alliteration between *diverse and dolci* or, more particularly, the double discord in the suffixes of *diverse* and *voci*, and *dolci* and *note*, a discord regularized by the chiasmus in the aligned suffixes of *"diverse-voci-dolci-note."* And the same scrutinist, ignoring the nouns and aligning only the adjectives, might point to another chiasmus: *diverse-dolci-diversi-dolce*.

Another scrutinist—more lakeside in spirit—still mortgaged to the Saussurian hypograms in the eight cases and 115 books of memoranda on the shores of Lake Geneva, could exclaim: ''Remember Chlebnikov with his macho mockery of vowels as 'feminine elements of language' adapted only to connect the masculine sounds.'' Or he could murmur in accents more meditative: ''Remember Mandelstam with his admonition: 'The word reproduces itself not through the vowels but through the consonants. The consonants are the seed and the confirmation of a language's posterity. The atrophied sense of the consonant is evidence of a weakened linguistic conscience.[2] So certainly take notice of the revealed hypogram, but only of the *consonants* and at a decidedly deeper level than banal alliteration. It is clear that the fundamental word here is *note*; its N and T stabilize the double vertical axis with the N always infixed in the sixth position of the hendecasyllable (fanno-scanni-armonia) and the T in the final one (note-vita-rote).''

A more pedantic agonist could now assert that the scrutinists who privilege the adjectives *diverse* and *dolci* and the nouns in rhyme, *note* and *rote*, neglect *nostra vita*. This configuration is too important not to direct our steps to the passage from Spitzer's ''possessive of human solidarity'' (*nostra*) at the incipit of *Inferno*, to the possessive *nostra* of the blessed in Heaven, and to link it, in a more comprehensive application of Mandelstam's consonantal lesson, with that *nostra* that incorporates the N, the T, and the R of *note* and *rote*. It is the *nostra* of the blessed that sums up both the *note* and the *rote*.

At this point the *convivio*, despite its tolerance, is certainly prepared to eject the scrutinists and perhaps with them the English translator, or better the beleaguered translator, who is taken with desperation in his attempt to weave an isomorphic, phonic fabric as counterpart to Dante's web or who, *in extremis*, is encouraged and rescued by the breadth of the poem itself. It is this breadth that allows the same effects as Dante's, perhaps not at the place chosen by the poet but with the means he taught us.

This sorely beleaguered translator is the one who stutters, ''I cannot mime Dante's rhymes, but I do at least have the possibility (in *Purg.* XIII, 128) of displacing the 'Pettinaio' of Piero Pettinaio to the end of the verse, and then, with the aid of the double T and the N, almost anagramming it with 'petitions' at the next line end: 'Pier *Pettinaio* / remembered me in his devout *petitions*.' '' The same translator, despairing over doubling the L and the G of the initial *luogo* with the L and the G of the final *Malebolge* in ''Luogo è in Inferno detto Malebolge,'' can, if also mindful of the admonition of Mandelstam, at least recoup the L of *luogo* in the fifth position between three single Ls and two double Ls in the English line: ''There is a place in Hell called Malebolge.''

Even if we dismiss the translator, however, we can sympathize with his plight: he is afflicted by the specter of corporeality in Dante's lexis. In the end, that corporeality is a good deal different than the attempts of the painted word—I'll go back in a bit to Giovanni Pozzi—or the infigured one, both with their sense of being tinted or painted with an emphasis on the surface. Dante's is an *incised* corporeality that endeavors to transform into inscription not only the writing at the entrance to Hell but *every* vowel and consonant.

The phono-mysticism of Grammont—I cite him as an emblem—may be insufficient and confused, and the *plaisir poétique et plaisir musculaire* of André Spire, inadequate, but their haze probably accompanies certain glimmerings that Anglo-Saxon clarity has obscured. (I think of Wimsatt, for example, for whom poetic ''music'' compared to a Beethoven quartet is banal.) In fact it is the realization of something lacking, an aridity inherent in structure's grids, that explains, I believe, the residue of phono-mysticism in Jakobson. What is fluctuating fog in Grammont is realized clarity in Dante.

It is semantic weight and the increase of that weight that motivates and permits his *technē* to arrive at a denser terrain than that reached by any other of Dante's predecessors in the romance languages—and here I include Arnaut Daniel. One is tempted to see in that prosodic apotheosis an inheritance from the *De Musica* of Augustine. But let us resist this temptation. After all, *technē* is already much more autonomous in Dante than in Augustine, unless we are able to see already in the latter a strong separation between the last book of *De Musica* and the rest of the volume.

To speak of this corporeality as word incarnate would be blasphemous; it could fall into a type of Hellenistic-Alexandrian magic. *Technē*, however, is not magic.[3] Dante's *technē*, moreover, depends on an intuition that is, at least to my knowledge, unique in the history of prosody. (We speak or, better, often spoke, in a structuralist vein or a phenomenologically Ingardenian one, about the isomorphism in poetry between various, hierarchically ordered linguistic levels. There is no prosodic form aside from Dante's, however, that *exemplifies* that isomorphism at so many levels.) By far the most frequent phonemes at the end of Italian words are vowel-consonant-vowel or VCV, that is the final phonemes of the word in rhyme are isomorphic with the ABA of the rhyme in terza rima (thus, the *piano* endings -*ita*, -*ura*, etc. are VCV). There is, too, another ABA in each and every canto. At the very beginning and very end of a canto the rhyme family has two members, but throughout the course of the canto, each rhyme family has three members. Two equals A; three equals B. And so the rhyme families give us still another ABA. (John Freccero, to be sure, saw the last-mentioned ABA, but without reference to the first kind.)[4]

To these three levels of ABA—the final phonemes in a word, words in a rhyme family, and the rhyme-in-two and rhyme-in-three in any single canto—one may add, I should say, another isomorphism. Given the frequencies of iambic verses in Dante and the unequal constituents of the hendecasyllabic verse line, it is possible to find in his text, especially if one gives a value to secondary accents, verses that rotate to the right and to the left around the sixth position with both homeopodic and antipodic symmetry. This links what I indicated above to the research of Giuseppe Sansone on the possible symmetries in the hendecasyllable.[5] And so, we can sometimes add a *fourth* ABA to the other three, that of the verse itself, centering about the sixth position.

My principal emphasis here would be the continuity between the ''natural'' humus of Italian, the ABA of the VCV, and Dante's form. It is precisely from that micro-level of phonemes that he drafts a law for rhyming that *forbids* contiguous rhyme. Together with this law a profound consciousness intervenes that elevates from that humus not only the stressed elements in the verse, but *all* the phonic elements, accentuated and *non*-accentuated. After all, in the VCV arrangement at line end, the only phoneme accentuated is the first. It is from this consciousness, I believe, that arises, almost precisely halfway through the *Commedia*, the first of three enjambments on the definite article composed by unstressed CV *after* the tonic V of the rhyme.

That this consciousness shows itself at almost the middle of the *Commedia* is like unto a ''revelation.'' It is, I should say, a sign of the temporality not only of what is narrated but also of the temporality of poetic toil and the intimate, ongoing relationship between natural and poetic languages.

(In fact, Dante's projection into the future and into the future exploitation of the poetic potential of natural language is so aggressive and prophetic that it foregrounds the great difference between the career of Auditus [What Is Heard] and the career of Visus [What Is Seen]. Northrop Frye has spoken of pictorial conventions that Andrea del Sarto could not have imagined.[6] About Dante, however, one cannot formulate an analogous reflection. In fact it would be difficult to discover any modern poetic conventions that would lie beyond his own imaginative capacities.)

Despite the caveat in the just-closed parentheses, the inscriptional corporeality of Dante's lexis is, if not a sister, a step-sister to visuality. This is implicit even in the tercet with which I began. Chimenz, who certainly does not belong to the sect of scrutinists I paraphrased above, noted in reference to "rote" or the heavens the inexactitude of expression (to be taken, therefore, in a loose sense) because, after all, all the blessed are in the Empyrean.[7]

Here, naturally, we remember the function of compromise, the concessive position of all the massive mises-en-scènes of the *Paradiso* in relationship to the needs of us on earth. Yet, despite this sense of "concession," there is in Dante a resolute separation between him and St. Thomas' view of poetry as *infima doctrina*. *Visibilia* do not embarrass Dante's vision.

Now, tracing the connection between the sacred and *visibilia*, it is worth remembering that despite the non-imagistic nature of Judaism, the saying of Rav Ishmael that "The Bible spoke the language of man" was not seen as an emblem of the philosophers' embarrassment in the face of biblical anthropomorphism until many centuries later. Maimonides (1135–1204) only gave a more precise articulation to this unease a full millennium after Ishmael. Remember, too, however, that the first wave of the iconoclasts' complaint appeared in Christianity already during the eighth century with a second wave in the ninth. We can hazard the possibility that Dante, even if he had known Greek and had at his disposal the thirty manuscripts of the *Sacra parallela*, would have chosen the *only* illustrated one, and have delighted himself with the 1658 miniatures. (He might have changed a little the proportions between the 402 scenes and the 1265 portraits, but not the categories.)

In any case, without having read Kurt Weitzman, he would have aligned himself retroactively with John Damascene against the iconoclasts. It would not be legitimate to identify generically and *tout court* the "poetic" position with one that is pro-visibilia. The history of poetry does have memorable examples of the anti-visibilia position, a position that favors Pythagorean-Platonic celebration of the powers of sound and ear in contradistinction to the eye. One indelible instance lies in the poetry of Fray Luis when he speaks of the musician of Salamanca, Salinas. (Let us not forget, however, as Macrì says, that "*Lo visible* can be a delicate allusion to the blindness of [Fray Luis'] friend").[8]

> A este bien os llamo
> gloria del apolineo sacro coro,
> amigos, a quien amo
> sobre todo tesoro;
> *que todo la visible es triste lloro.*
>
> Friends, more dear to me than any treasure,
> this is the good to which I summon you,
> the glory of the choir of Apollo:
> for all the visible is but lament.
> ("To Salinas" v. 35–38, italics mine)[9]

This is not Dante's position, nor is it, I should say, even given his doctrine of *infima doctrina*, that of Thomas. Dante's vision includes *visibilia* (but one must distinguish it from the excessive emphasis in certain strains of the New Criticism on the graphic nature of Dante's text or, if there be a trinity composed of spirit, body, and nerves, on his appeal to the nerves.) Yet if Dante is one who scrutinizes *visibilia*, he is also given to a dimension of vision like that described by Giovanni Pozzi:

> Here on earth the vision of the divine does not have as its terminus the production of images; in fact, the theory of the icon asks the sacred painter to place himself in the situation of the celestial vision, to reverse the relationship of beholder and beheld. There, then, God and the saints are not objects that the spectator sees; they are, on the contrary, subjects that watch the faithful and offer him of themselves the vision of the invisible.[10]

For "sacred painter" let us read "sacred poem" and also "sacred poet." Pozzi, in my opinion, requires only one modification. When he speaks of the *Paradiso* he argues:

> That does not mean that the blessed can point to or de-scribe or in-scribe the object that they contemplate face to face. The crosses, the eagles, the roses, the writings, even when they contemplate themselves in Dante's heaven, absolve only one task on behalf of the occasional and privileged wayfarer beside the didactic one. They are made uniquely for the homo viator; for the chosen they are totally pleonastic.[11]

The image of Dante as homo viator is widely held, but I am inclined to accept the following suggestion of Piero Di Vona in his "Dante filosofo e San Bonaventura:"

> I should note that St. Bonaventure in his *Itinerarium* and likewise in his last work, the *Collationes in Hexaëmeron* describes the condition of the *homo viator* and not that of the *homo in patria,* while Dante clearly places himself in the *Commedia* from the point of view of the man having already arrived.[12]

So despite the unappeased hopes inherent in Dante, despite the consciousness of us readers that without the disillusion in and with the *polis* (or better perhaps what Padoan called "the great illusion"), the *Commedia* very probably would not have been created; despite our knowledge that the intermediate stages in the emergence of the *Commedia* are also the death of Beatrice and Dante's quasi-death, the fear so "amara che poco è più morte" ("So bitter–death is hardly more severe"—*Inf.* 1.7)—despite all of this, there is in him something that transcends the condition of the *homo viator.*

Another formulation: Dante, if we wish, does not obscure "Lo visibile es triste lloro" Of the Old Man of Crete he affirms:

> Ciascuna parte, fuor che l'oro, è rotta
> d'una fessura che lagrime goccia,
> le quali, accolte, fóran quella grotta.

> Each part of him, except the gold, is cracked;
> and down that fissure there are tears that drip;
> when gathered, they pierce through that cavern's floor.
> (*Inf.* XIV. 112–114)

He also provides us with other visibilia that reinforce these tears. But more central to the point, I should say, is the force of certain of Dante's *visibilia* that arrive at the stage of vision, things that reverse "the relationship of the viewer and the viewed" or that hesitate at the boundary between the two. These are not so much in things that we can recognize in a lightning-flash (the "ramarro sotto la gran fersa / dei di canicular," "the lizard... / ...beneath the dog days' giant lash— *Inf.* 25.79-80), nor in the rhetoric of hyperbole and marvel of the spectacle of *Diligite* (even though that spectacle serves us as a magnifying lens, letter by letter, of that which I have called Dante's sense of inscription). No, such *visibilia* becoming vision are to be found in the structure of Hell itself, not in the ethical taxonomy, but in the "edifice" of Malebolge; in the icon of the Old Man of Crete; in the cadenza on the *paralimnion* of the Mountain of Purgatory; in the solitude of the entrance to the Earthly Paradise; in the end of the tenth canto of the *Paradiso*. (This list applies both to the diagrammatic and to that which is difficult to "illustrate.")

These *visibilia* that become visions include the visibility of Virgil himself. (Consider for a moment the differences between Dante's Virgil and the less than compelling transformation of Homer into a peacock in the verses of a poet whom Dante did not know: Ennius.) They also include what Botticelli captures in full: the *visibility* of Beatrice and Dante.

More than anything it is the *Paradiso* that watches and measures us. And perhaps we should explain a large part of Croce's evasion and escape from this text in this way:[13] On the one hand, there are the metaphorizations implicit in our apotheosis of the short lyric, which are the result of the fleeting equilibrium between concept and symbol, mediated by Kantian *Einbildungskraft* (Imagination); on the other hand, there is a poem that, though it "deploys" eternity and the trans-temporal, is itself the fruit of much time, of profound temporality, whether in its making or in its condensation of two centuries' meditations on previous centuries. Croce refuses and eludes the challenge the second mode of poesis offers to the first.

When I refer to Dante's meditation on the "co-ordinating" toil of previous centuries, I do not mean the angels or the diagrams of Ptolemy or Alfraganus. In the *Paradiso* the base of visibility is essential—the knowledge of light in its progressive augmentations, the dazzling wonderment of vision that serves as a ground for *visibilia*, and for the indistinguishable figure and ground in the rapport between the immortal and humanly mortal incarnation. (And as Di Vona reminds us, this is *not* to be found in the *Liber figurarum*.[14]) This light is also the ground for the cognitive act. Canto Two of the *Paradiso*, therefore, is not so pedantic, after all; for to seek the roots of the "turbo ed il chiaro" ("the dark and the light") is totally proper for the poet who discovered chiaroscuro.

It is in regard to images that watch and measure us—remember Pozzi—that, in long iconographic work with Barry Moser, the illustrator of the California Dante, we decided on a predominant frontality in the drawings and, in the progressive illumination of the *Commedia*, decided to adopt a progressive obscuring for the images. We did not take this as some kind of negative theology (we were not that presumptuous), but as negative burin or pen. Such a negative pen designed the completely black final pages in the *Paradiso* with a simultaneous unravelling shock of the visible page, the unyielding material paper of *visibilia*.[15]

II. "FUORI O DENTRO"

Dal centro al cerchio, e sì dal cerchio al centro
movesi l'acqua in un ritondo vaso,
secondo ch'è percosso fuori o dentro.

From rim to center, center out to rim,
so does the water move in a round vessel,
as it is struck without or struck within.
(*Par.* XIV. 1-3)

Between the "rote" of *Paradiso* 4 and "the wheel revolving uniformly" of the penultimate verse of the *Paradiso*, there is a long road (not only from plural to singular)—long and perhaps more winding than straight.

That journey intersects and absorbs, or, better, is intersected and absorbed by, another path that moves from *Purgatorio* 24.53-54 ("e a quel modo / ch'e' ditta dentro vo significando"), touches the beginning of *Paradiso* 16, and then culminates in the last verse of that canticle.

For the first two stages of that journey, if "significando" means "tell and give external form" (or as I translate the passage, "What he within dictates, / I, in that way, without, would speak and shape''), then both of the textual stages speak of ''without'' and ''within.'' The text of *Purgatorio* 24 cannot boast of being unique, for behind it is the *Epistola ad Severinum de Caritate*, which is now attributed to Fra Ivo. Yet, it can certainly boast that it is the emblem that defines and asserts Dante's achievement in the vulgar tongues, where Love flanks and, at times, supplants the Muses. This interlaces in a convincing way the idiom of the romance languages with the idiom of theology. (Moreover, in reference to ''Io son un . . .'' that precedes this announcement, the verses of *Purgatorio* 24 are linked with the *''Ieu seu Arnaut''* of *Purgatorio* 26.) This conquest and linkage will culminate in the last verse of the *Paradiso*.

The *incipit* to *Paradiso* 14, however, is able to boast another unique quality both inside the *Commedia* itself and, I suspect, also in the Romance vernacular and the classical epic. As you will remember, Beatrice is at the center; Thomas, instead, is part of the circle of the ''circumference'' of souls. She speaks from the center to the circumference; he, from the circumference to the center. However, from the moment that the canto begins, the vehicle of this tenor (in I.A. Richards' sense) becomes syntactically autonomous, like many other passages in Dante. It journeys beyond the microcontext just as Dante's deictics can point to varied contexts. For example, ''here'' can refer to Malebolge, to the complex of Hell or to the other world; or the ''here'' of the ''qui registra'' (''she [Justice] had registered''—*Inf.* 29.57) of Robert Hollander and Giovanni Serravale can be applied to ''this text.''[16]

It is of course true, as Bosco and Reggio assert (on *Par.* XIV.1-3): ''to be exact, from without one strikes the vessel, *within* you must instead strike the water.'' Such an observation is in strange, but comprehensible, oxymoronic proximity to their notation: ''It is a common physical phenomenon that Dante observes with his usual *extreme exactness''* (italics mine).[17] The oxymoron resolves itself or, better, is muted if we hear the more extended resonances of ''without'' and ''within,'' resonances that extend from the microcontext to the circumference of a circle that comprehends the mind of Dante and the visionary canticle that is the *Paradiso*. (This applies also to the Italian poetry after Dante and to the uses of Dante by other poets both in Italian and in other languages.) We are invited to welcome these resonances when we remember the emblematic passage from *Purgatorio* 24, but more than anything the incontestable uniqueness of the verses of *Paradiso* 14 that follow the first three of the *incipit*. They show us a mind that stops for the only time in the *Commedia* to detail the "occasion," the "case," of the birth of a simile in that mind.

> ne la mia mente fé sùbito caso
> questo ch'io dico, sì come si tacque
> la glorïosa vita di Tommaso,
>   per la similitudine che nacque
> del suo parlare e di quel di Beatrice
> a cui sì cominciar, dopo lui, piacque.

> What I am saying fell most suddenly
> into my mind, as soon as Thomas's
> glorious living flame fell silent, since
>   between his speech and that of Beatrice,
> a similarity was born. And she,
> when he was done, was pleased to start with this.
>   (*Par.* XIV. 4-9)

We recognize, then, the mind of Dante both as the "water" and as the "vessel": it is the "mind" of Dante that resolves the oxymoron in the comment of Bosco-Reggio.

Moreover, with this "mind" in mind we are able to stop at the "without" and at the "within" and make various suppositions:

1) We are able to presume—above all, with Edward Cranz—that antiquity, including the late antiquity of Augustine, did not have a "without" and a "within" in the sense that these terms were used in the West in the high medieval period when it became not so much the pre-Renaissance but *the* modern.[18] Secondly, we can presume that the ontological argument of Anselm could not have arisen in the climate of Augustine. (I admit that some shadow, although, I should say, not definitive, can be cast on this thesis by reading the end of Plato's *Phaedrus* and sundry crepuscular passages in the *Aeneid*.)

2) We are able to presume that the early Auerbach who discerned a close relationship between Dante's and Petrarch's realism "within," did not err completely when he arrived at a truth inferior but complementary to the thesis of *Mimesis*, a thesis that would see division between Dante and Petrarch, inserting instead Boccaccio and the principle of individuation in the line that goes from Dante to Balzac.[19] (This is a basically Hegelian thesis that will be corroborated by Contini's demolition of Petrarch's language.[20])

3) We are able to presume that the "without" of the journey involves not only an external individuation along Auerbach's pattern, but also an intellectualization, the sort of development traced by Gilson, Van Steenbergen, and a recent synopsis by Piero Di Vona in the same essay cited above:

> After the second half of the 13th century various authors came to sustain the argument that not two, but three *principatus* rule this world: the *Sacerdotium*, the *Regnum* and the *Studium*. To the tradition of the *translatio imperii*, the idea of the *translatio studi* is thus connected. Paris, that is the medieval Paris, was seen as the new Athens; the *Studium* of Paris, the Sorbonne, the third universal power of the Christian West.[21]

In relationship to Dante, this is not, at least for me, an abstract scheme contingent on the presence of Siger in the *Paradiso*. It is sufficient to think that the water with which Dante seeks to satiate himself at the end of the *Purgatorio* and in the beginning of its twenty-first canto is not comparable (although he compares it) to the water of the "Woman of Samaria"; I don't think she would have formulated her curiosity as Dante does his, when he inquires about the "quaking" of the mountain and the "perché tutto ad una / parve gridare" ("[Why the mountain] shook and shouted, all of it— / for so it seemed..."*Pur.* XXI.35–36). This, at least, is certain: the stylistic and intellectual woof of the *incipit* of *Purgatorio* XXI has little to do with *sermo umilis* and a good bit to do, instead, with the *principatus* of the *Studium*.

4) We may suppose that the "without" and the "within" are analogous to the "praise" and "vision" defined by Pozzi: "Praise is differentiated from vision in so far as vision predicates a relationship that flows as does God's Spirit, except inversely."[22] We may suppose that Dante, in his confrontation "within" and "without," strives to unite the two. After all, both are acted upon by an external and unique force, just as the "water" of our simile in *Paradiso* XIV can be assimilated to the "water" that "recepe / raggio di luce permanendo unita" ("will accept / a ray of light and yet remain intact"—*Par.* II.35-36). In following this up, one is able to return to our initial epigraph and see these diverse "wheels" as having become, in the last simile of the *Commedia*, the "wheel."

5) An emphasis on unity would accord well with reading "mio *disio* e 'l *velle*" as a hendiadys. At the same time, along with this reading, we can entertain "my desire" (remembering also "my mind") as the "within," and "will" as the "without," "la *sua* volontade" (*"His* will") with which the "within" of Dante is now in accordance. The "muovere" (movement) of the "mossa" (moved) is a cousin of the water's "movesi" (moving itself) in *Paradiso* XIV. Both are the sources of similes, but sources also of the similes' concurrence, of the "igualmente" ("uniformly").

In fact a fanatic Chlebnikovian might think it not blasphemy to see in the pairing of *disio* and *velle* the pairing of consonants and vowels.[23] This scrutinist, moreover, could take joy in thinking about an accord between "without" and "within" along the same lines as the accord between *visibilia* on the one hand and vision, voice, and notes on the other. In the end, having returned to the relationship between the viewer and the viewed (Pozzi), we can think that Dante himself is an icon that watches the spectator. Not for nothing was Yeats sensitive at a crucial point of passage in his own poetic journey, in his "Ego Dominus Tuus," to the summons of personification in the *Vita Nuova*, to the edifice of the *Commedia*, and to the visage of Dante.[24] Not all of the poets whom a culture summarizes require faces; Virgil, Chaucer, and Shakespeare, in this sense, are without them. But the "io sol uno" ("I myself alone) and the individualized and watching face of Dante is an emblem of Christian semantics, of *individual* and *individuated* redemption.

This vision is defined in the finite space of the canticles ("son tutte le carte / ordite," "all of the pages pre-disposed / for this"—*Pur.* XXXIII.139–140). But it is a vision that perhaps anticipates (despite the amphitheater with its reserved seats-thrones of the Mystic Rose), what Hans Blumenberg calls Cusanus's "explosive metaphor," a metaphor Blumenberg retrieves in Simmel's diary:

> The cosmic process seems to me to be like the turning of an enormous wheel, precisely like the premise of the eternal return. Yet, the cosmic wheel—unlike the eternal return—does not involve an identical repetition of reality. Why? Because the cosmic wheel has an infinitely extended radius. It is only after an infinite amount of time has passed that the wheel will return. The same radius, therefore, can never return again to the same place. Nevertheless, it is still a wheel that turns and that, according to its own idea, tends toward the exhaustion of qualitative multiplicity without ever truly exhausting it.[25]

But we can see this becoming in effect a directional line in a poet so sensitive to closure in canto and canticle as Dante. And this directionality is what Mandelstam meant when he said that Dante was the poet of the "future."[26] There is in Dante a projection that invites us to travel an infinite line of exegesis; and because this invitation is presented with such urgency that we readers have to accept it, Dante reads and trans-reads us.

For me this final characteristic of Dante has been renewed in our century, not by a poet but by another "sol uno" in exile, the prose-writer Joyce.

Wake Forest University

NOTES

1. This essay was originally given as the opening paper (thus, an incipit) at the University of Toronto at the 12th International Conference for the Study of the Italian Language and Literature in May 1985. Its first form was published in Italian in *Letteratura italiana e arti figurative: atti del XII Convegno dell' associazione internazionale per gli studi di lingua e letteratura italiana* (Toronto, Hamilton, Montreal), 6–10 maggio 1985, 3 vols, ed. Antonio Franceschetti (Florence: L.S. Olschki, 1988), 1:29–40. The present essay was derived through a joint translation of Janet Dickman and the editor. Because the text several times refers clearly to the author's translation of the *Commedia* (Berkeley: University of California Press, 1980, 1982, 1984), I have made use of that text for all necessary translations for this essay and refer to it, as does the author, as the "California Dante"—Ed.

2. See Allen Mandelbaum, *Chelmaxioms* (Boston: David R. Godine, 1977) 155, 161.

3. On the other hand, for the marriage between *technē* and magic, see Robert Klein, *La forme et l'intelligible* (Paris: Gallimard, 1970), 160–170.

4. John Freccero, "The Significance of the *Terza Rima*," *Dante: The Poetics of Conversion* (Cambridge, Mass.: Harvard University Press, 1986), 258–271.

5. Giuseppe Sansone, *Le Trame della poesia: per una teoria funzionale del verso* (Florence: Vallechi, 1988), 40–59, 235–42.

6. Northrop Frye, *Letteratura italiana e arti figurative*, I:13–26.

7. Siro A. Chimenz, *Commedia* (Turin: Unione tipografico-editrice torinese, 1967), 675.

8. Oreste Macrì, ed., *La poesia de Fray Luis de Leon* (Salamanca: Anaya, 1970), 315.

9. As translated by Allen Mandelbaum, *Journeyman* (New York: Schocken, 1967).

10. Giovanni Pozzi, *La parola dipinta* (Milan: Adelphi, 1981), 344.

11. *Ibid.*

12. Piero Di Vona, "Dante filosofo e San Bonaventura," *Miscellanea francescana*, vol. 84, 1984, I–II, 15.

13. Benedetto Croce, "The Last Canto of the Paradise." In *Philosophy, Poetry, History: An Anthology of Essays*, trans. Cecil Sprague (London: Oxford University Press, 1966), 825–833.

14. Piero Di Vona, *op. cit.*, 9–10.,

15. Pages 279–280 of the *Paradiso* in the California Dante.

16. Robert Hollander, "Dante's 'Book of the Dead': A note on 'Inferno' XXIX.57," *Studi danteschi*, vol. 54, 1982, 31–44.

17. Umberto Bosco and Giovanni Reggio, eds., *La Divina Commedia* (Florence: Le Monnier, 1979), *Paradiso*, 228.

18. Edward Cranz in private discussions.

19. Eric Auerbach, *Dante: Poet of the Secular World*, trans. Ralph Manheim (Chicago/London: Chicago University Press, 1961), 57, 176.

20. Gianfranco Contini, *Francesco Petraca Canzoniere* (Turin, Einaudi, 1968), vii-xxxviii.

21. Piero Di Vona, *op. cit.*, 5.

22. Giovanni Pozzi, *op. cit.*, 344.

23. See Allen Mandelbaum. *Chelmaxioms*, 151.

24. Allen Mandelbaum, " 'Al mente che non erra' (*Inferno* II, 6)," *Letture classensi*, vol. 18, 1989, 42.

25. Hans Blumenberg, *Naufragio con spettatore*, trans. Francesca Rigotti, (Bologna: Il Mulino, 1985), 125. The original German edition, *Schiffbruch mit Zuschauer* was published in 1979. The citation from the German paperback edition is on p. 84.

26. See "Conversation about Dante," *Osip Mandelstam: Selected Essays*, trans. Sidney Monas (Austin: University of Texas Press, 1977), 43.

Naming The Rose:
Petrarch's Figure In And For
The Text And Texts

RAYMOND ADOLPH PRIER

What's in a name?
Romeo and Juliet II.2.43

"That which we call a rose / By any other name would smell as sweet."
Names do not smell. At best they sound, and when the Petrarchan
Shakespeare went about composing the wistful sophistry of Juliet's
speech, he knew not only that a name could entail a great deal, he knew
also that one man's metaphor might well be another's immediate
experience. Romeo, for all of Stampa's mirrors and twists, was no Laura.
Nor was a certain Chariteo's Luna. Why? The answer, if carefully
understood, lies hidden in Petrarch's text, in the whole text. At the center
of that text speaks, "Laura." Once grasped within the *Canzoniere,* how
does the name effect the imitator; to be exact, how does "Laura", effect
the late fifteenth, early sixteenth-century Spaniard turned Neapolitan
poet: Chariteo, a major Petrarchan once famous, now long fallen from
the canon?

Laura, like Beatrice, is a *figura* in the sense of a linguistically protreptic
focus that for the poet-narrator raises into consciousness both his past
and future states. The similarity between the two *figure* is present, despite
Auerbach's arduous attempts to deny Petrarch's *donna* such a status.[1]
It is the locus the two pinpoint and the direction toward which the two

275

draw the poet and the reader-listener that dictate their figural difference. For Dante the *figura,* as Auerbach knew well, is placed "without" and impels a human being outside the isolated self and into a religious transcendence (see also Maristella de Panizza Lorch's essay in this volume). Petrarch's "Laura," however, lies "within" and impels "within." In terms of our simplistic dichotomies, "Laura" is "more subjectively placed" than "Beatrice." However, merely to establish her name more deeply "within" the poet and, consequently, more deeply "within" the text can only *begin* any literary study of Petrarch's "Laura" as a poetic figure.

Perhaps to broach the problem of "Laura" we should first consider an example of her and its unusual poetic context. No short poem reveals the idiosyncratic power of that name better than *Canzoniere* 291:

> Quand'io veggio dal ciel scender l'**Aurora**
> co la fronte di rose et co' crin' **d'oro,**
> **Amor** m'assale, ond'io mi *di*s**coloro,**
> et dico sospirando: Ivi è **Laura ora.**
>
> O felice Titon, tu sai ben l'**ora**
> da ricovrare il tuo *caro tes***oro:**
> ma io che debbo far del dolce **alloro?**
> che se 'l vo' riveder, conven ch'io **mora.**
>
> I vostri dipartir' non son sí duri,
> ch'almen di notte suol tornar colei
> che non a schifo le tue bianche chiome:
>
> le mie notti fa triste, e i giorni oscuri,
> quella che n'à portato i penser' miei,
> né di sé m'à lasciato altro che 'l *nome.*
>   *(Canzoniere* 291, emphasis mine)

> When I see Aurora quit the sky
> With rosy brow and tresses glist'ning gold,
> Then Love assaults me that my color flies,
> and sighing do I say, "There's Laura now."
>
> Glad Tithonus, you well know the hour
> When once again you'll take your treasured prize,
> But what's my course about the laurel dear?
> If once again I see it, I must die.

Between you two the cleft works little harm,
At least at night she's wont to slip on home,
Who dislikes not the white locks of your crown.

My nights are sad, my days beset with gloom,
The woman who did steal my thoughts is gone
And left me nothing but a name: a noun.[2]

The last line tells us that for the poet-narrator "Laura" is a name or noun. That name, however, is not in a grammatical sense a "proper noun," for it is never self-enclosed, but entrapped in sound, an assonance and rhyme, the roots of which are much deeper than some play on words: *l'Aurora, d'oro, Amor, discoloro, aura, ora, l'ora, caro tesoro, alloro, mora.* Between the poles of love and death she and it suggest Dawn, gold, the poet's paleness, the name, "there now," the mythological time and treasure of Tithonus, that dear laurel which the poet-narrator will never see again. The poem's plot rests solidly upon the ancient Orpheus myth with its irreversible event of death. Petrarch sings but *his* Eurydice is lost. Not so is Tithonus' Dawn. A hero, such as Tithonus, whose actions or condition is directly opposed to that of a suffering narrator, has a long history. (One thinks immediately of Propertius' narrator's morose reference to the successful Milanion in the incipit of the *Monobiblos.*) Petrarch's sonnet is simple in its narrative construction, its oppositions, so that it might better accent the ringing reiterations of "Laura's sounds." The affect is paratactic, but what or who signifies these sounds in a multiplicity of lexical choices? Laura or "Laura?" A name, the citation of which becomes lost within a nexus of its very sounds, or an elusive "self" heard beyond the surface of the text but faintly. Or both?

The questions that beg for the asking are: "What kind of name or noun is 'Laura'?" "What does 'she' accomplish in and for Petrarch's text?" "What does 'she' provide the poet and the listener-reader, whether he or she be a later Petrarchan or us?"

The answers lie in other texts, but even from a glance at 291 we are forced to suggest that the common denominator solving the puzzle is the *underlying cohesiveness of sound.*

Petrarch qualifies his obsession with sound in the incipit to the *Canzoniere.* That we could escape it says a great deal about our education of the eye over the ear that alienates us from the sense of a poem and its book.[3] Holding much too close to the blinding postmodernist "grammatology of sight," we fail to hear the resonating parameters of a poesis "within"—within the text and within what, for the lack of a more appropriate word in English, must be dubbed "the self" of the narrating poet. From the very first line of the incipit to the *Canzoniere*, Petrarch elevates the prelexical power of sound, not the read lexical remains of written words, as he attempts to illustrate the narrating self and a private, but central poesis.

It is best to argue from the text. Lexical choices relevant to the argument are in boldface:

> *Voi* ch'ascoltate in rime sparse il **suono**
> di quei sospiri ond'**io** nudriva 'l **core**
> in sul **mio** primo giovenile *er***rore**
> quand'era in parte altr'uom da quel ch'**i' sono,**
>
> **del** *vario* stile in ch'**io** *piango* et *ragiono*
> fra le vane speranze e 'l van *dolore,*
> ove sia chi per prova intenda **amore,**
> spero trovar pietà, non che *per***dono.**
>
> Ma ben *veggio* or sí come al popol *tutto*
> favola fui gran tempo, onde sovente
> di **me medesmo meco mi** ve*rgogno;*
>
> et del **mio** vaneggiar *vergogna* è 'l *frutto,*
> e 'l pentersi, e 'l conoscer chiaramente
> che quanto piace al *mondo* è breve **sogno.**
> (*Canzoniere* 1, emphasis mine)

> You who hear as scattered rhymes this sound
> Of sighs whence I have fed and reared my heart
> Engulfed atop a young man's first-made error,
> A time I was in part another man,
>
> From varied modes in which I reasoning weep
> Between these empty hopes and empty griefs,
> Where I find those who know by trial of love,
> I hope for mercy, and that they forgive.
>
> But well I see now how to all without
> I was so long a laughing stock, whence oft'
> I feel ashamed for me myself within;

And of my wand'ring thought shame is the end,
And too deep-felt regret, to know full plain
That what delights the world is but a dream.

This sonnet addresses two major areas of human experience: the sound of the human voice in song and the distinction between the resonance of that voice "within" and its audience "without." Petrarch does not refer here to the sociological difference between "private" and "public," but that distinction between "me" and "you," between the "self" (whatever it might "be") and "the rest," in other words between "the one" and "the many." The poem is "self-centered." How well, however, does the poet define this center, especially in the context that he has chosen to employ? In what form must the "self" necessarily emerge?[4] In what form for the poet? In what form for the audience?

"You," the audience, hear the *rime sparse*. "I," Petrarch, emit the *suono*. "Voi ch'ascoltate in rime sparse il suono" ("You who hear as scattered rhymes this *suono*"). The audience as it hears and reads does indeed perceive "scattered rhymes" as it confronts Petrarch's text, but "rhymes" (*rime*) is the key word in this phrase. Does Petrarch speak of the diachronically read phenomena of "scattered verse" (*versi sparsi*)[5] or of the separate, concrete, lexical choices (*parole sparse*)? No. Hence from the first line of the incipit we are thrust into a view of language and poesis little suited for a deconstructionist's reduction.

While the audience "without" hears sound as scattered rhymes, the poet-narrator experiences sighs (*sospiri*) whence he has fed his *heart*, in the West the locus of feeling and of at least some experience "within" since Homer. Yet Petrarch's "heart," his *core*, because of the very rhyme to which Petrarch draws our attention in line one, immediately attracts our *sense* into the "heart" or interiority of the poem itself: his error (*errore*), his grief (*dolore*), his love (*amore*). The poet-narrator's self does not resonate beatitude, to be sure, but there can be no doubt that the sonnet as language is that self's representation, however *sparse* or varied in mode (the *vario style* that opens the second quatrain).

Yet, whither leads Petrarch's "sound," his *suono*? To *uom, sono, piango, ragiono, perdono, vergogno, frutto, sogno* ("man," "I am," "I weep," "I reason," "they [human beings without] forgive," "I feel ashamed," "the end," "a dream"). *Suono* attaches itself also to the "vario" of his *vario style* and his realization or "sight" of those without (*veggio*). On a pronomial level (*io, mio, me*), Petrarch leads us to the paratactic, ultimately Socratic definition of a first-person *autos kath' auton* ("a self in itself"): *di me medesmo meco mi* ("of me myself within," literally "of me, the very same, with me myself [I am ashamed]"). The poet-narrator projects the self as target of his rhyme within.

Suono, however, must be linked to *mondo*, the world "without," and it is in the sonnet's last verse that this assonance forces the poet's and our recognition that only sound links the "within" and the "without," the "one and the "other" or "many." In the eyes and ears of these, Petrarch proposes to suggest a resonating center, as he draws their attention to their and his moral view of that "first-made error" (*mi primo giovenile errore*). They are to know that his "error" was "another's," at least in part another man's" (*in parte altr' uom*) than that man he is now (*sono*). The sonnet closes with two tercets weighed between the audience's perception of a self from without and the hope, grief, and shame within. Our perception of the poet-narrator's error perhaps indeed has made him a laughing stock. It is our mistake if we read this poem as a non-ironic palinode of a passive poet-narrator.[6] Petrarch treats his audience rather roughly (one may not exclude the critic) whose ethical, even aesthetic pretensions isolate and trivialize the poet. What delights the world without is at best a short dream. What pains the poet is "me myself within," especially in so far as his audience and he, the reflecting poet-narrator, seem to be unable to grasp his own centrality.

The poet-narrator, however, possesses means that will exteriorize the "I myself" in such a way that the audience will hear and sense this center as they are drawn beneath the surface of his text.

The key to his plan is "Laura," the *nome* ("name," or "noun"), but first he must direct his audience's attention and interest to that *name as language*:

Quando **io** movo **i** *sospiri* a chiamar **vo**i,
e 'l *nome* che nel *c*or mi scrisse **Amore**,
LAUdando s'incomincia udir di *fo*re
il suo*n* de'primi *dolci accenti* **su**oi.

Vostro stato REal, che 'ncontro *po*i,
RAddoppia a l'alta impressa il mio *val*ore;
ma: TAci, grida il fin, ché farle *hon*ore
è d'altri homeri soma che da' *tu*oi.

Cosí LAUdare et REverire *insegna*
la voce stessa, pur ch'altri vi *chiami*,
o d'ogni reverenza et d'onor **degna**;

se non che forse Apollo si *dis***degna**
ch'a parlar de'suoi sempre *verdi RA***mi**
lingua mortal *presumptuosa* **vegna**.
(*Canzoniere* 5, emphasis mine)

When I do bend these sighs to cry to you,
And bend Love's name inscribed upon my heart,
In LAUra's praise, at once you hear without
Its sound of accents first intoned and sweet.

Your true and REgal rank, do I then meet,
Twice great thus strengthens me for lofty deeds;
But no! "Be TAcit," shrieks the end, "her praise
Weighs hard another's shoulder's down, not yours.

Therefore to LAUd, adoRE does educate
This voice, what yet another calls your name,
fore'er *re*vered and honored in *re*spect:

Unless suppose, perhaps, Apollo scorns
To set his limbs forever green in speech
Of morTAl tongue that preens its arrogance.

Petrarch forges an immediate link between his first and fifth sonnets when he reiterates those underlying sonantly non-morphemic sighs he "bends" to cry the name of his beloved. His sounds are not passive, that is as if simply moved by the wind, but painfully intentional. His sighs become a bent experience, created into poetry by him. Once again a sonnet turns on the central distinction between "within" and "without." The poet-narrator's "voi" to whom he addresses these sighs signifies "the other," but also commands that the "other" regard that which is implanted within. "Voi" must adduce "a name." Yet note that "Laura" has never yet been spoken in the *Canzoniere*; the name has only been "inscribed upon my heart." [7]

It is here in the second verse that Petrarch toys with the central issue of his sonnet: the sometime compatibility between sound and writing. One might well imagine why this distinction cannot be fully explored by postmodernist readings. [8]

A "name inscribed upon the heart," that is within, should never be confused with some act of non-metaphorical writing or Gutenberg's now critically problematic printing upon the object that for some has become the text. Petrarch never intended that "Laura" be directly read on the surface of *his* text (see note seven). The first time the sound of the name veers toward the surface of the text in *LAU-RE-TA* (*LAUdano-REal-TAci*) there appears "intermixed" a *LAU-RA: LAUdando-RAdoppia*. The second time, the reader-listener is inundated with a proliferation of the "second syllable": *LAUdaRE-REveriRE-REverREnza*, another *LAU-RA: LAUdare-RAmi*, and a "TA" that lies inside the lexical choice: *morTA*, but was not stressed visually in the line until relatively recent editions of the *Canzoniere*. By the sonnet's end, "Laura" has long since sunk below the surface. Her name was to the poet experience within, that is below the surface, and her reflection, her reception by his audience could only be transmuted in the intoned sounds and stresses of his verse, the sound of a name's "accents."[9] In semiotic terms, "Laura" as a signified is always indistinct and possesses the tendency to return to her and its hidden signifier.

In the second quatrain, Petrarch muses further on the true and real condition that "Laura" suggests within. He knows intimately this name's force (*valore*) that elicits the inadequacy of the lexical choices he proposes on the surface of his text. Yet, he collides here with a very ancient problem in modern guise: if he were to allow "Laura" an inscription or direct, unqualified citation on the surface of his text would his poesis not be somehow stripped of its power and, hence, dead? Would not his text scream "TAci" and obliterate the sonant nuances that regulate the dialogue between the "within" and "without?" (Perhaps this intuition explains the one probable citation of "Laura" in 332.50 that makes of her and it a dead, black image even the poet's own sorrowful style cannot displace.)

No, "Laura" must sustain her and its "condition within." This is her and its *valore*, and it rests on the impossibility of the name "ending without," that is received as cited in the text. What appears on the surface of the text, as was indicated by the sonant multiplication of assonance and rhyme in sonnet one, is the language, the *honore* of another. Of God? Of Petrarch as humanist critic? Of the commentators? Of his imitators? Of us? The common denominator underlying all of these categories is a "locus without."

In sonnet five the poet-narrator has entered into a dialogue with his doubts in terms of the important distinction between sound and the "objectification of citation," the vitality of "Laura" resonating within and the difficulty of exteriorizing the name, the center, the self without. Petrarch's is truly a chivalric quest (see Aldo Scaglione's essay in this volume), but its painful ambiguities and resolutions do create a text for a vast audience commanded to interiorize its meaning.

The first tercet, to my view, concerns the resonance of "Laura" as name and sound. "La voce stessa" ("this voiced sound," literally "the same voiced sound") is named by others, that is the poet-narrator as audience and the greater audience of other human beings. Again here lies the entrée for Petrarchan imitation that in rhyme (*chiami-rami*) forces an imitator to address the idiosyncratic use of language Petrarch advocates (see note nine). "Laura" educates the poet-narrator through the multiplicity of her and its possible lexis, which, one must never forget, is ultimately under the tight control of Petrarch. As, however, the poet-narrator and we gaze within upon the figural centrality of "Laura," "Laura" her and itself assumes a substantive state or condition. It is primarily in this mutual infiguration from without and within that we suddenly realize that what we are viewing can be nothing other than the poet-narrator as subject-object, that is as self.

Thus both externally on the surface of the text and within it, at its center, Petrarch has achieved figurally both a stasis and a fluidity which Dante construed quite differently. Little wonder if Apollo in the final tercet might find fault with this new poesis that does not exteriorize the god's verses for a god without, but directs an audience within by a "self-directed" sound of alliteration, assonance, and rhyme.[10] Petrarch is well aware of his arrogance here. His poesis literally appropriates (*arrogo*) his audience for him-self in an attempt to turn it inside out as he only *partially* exteriorizes a "Laura" in her and its sonant multiplicity on the surface of his text. His poet-narrator has embarked with us all upon a Socratic task: to know the self.

This command is tantamount to God's will in the verses of Chariteo. It is difficult to imitate a text that demands much more than it defines. The imitator's problems, however, can become the critic's almost insurmountable obstacle.[11] To reduce a reception of the *Canzoniere* and, subsequently, its imitation to a play of classical or medieval rhetorical tropes, postmodern semiotics, or, for that matter, Christian or classical myth is unsatisfactory, primarily because each of these reductions necessitates a clear exteriorization of its own rhetoric at the expense of a philological ambiguity of the text. As "Laura" is cited almost clearly but once on the surface of the *Canzoniere*, as "Laura" finds its and her way into Chariteo's *Endimione* but once (see below), so the critic must do his or her best not to deny the imitator that resonating multiplicity of language that Petrarch's "Laura" creates and must forever imply.

To avoid such a misstep, some pragmatic questions need asking: if we acknowledge the philological, semiotic ambiguity of "Laura," what were Chariteo's subsequent options? What did he wish to retrieve from Petrarch's text for his own? How did he "reflect" upon his then circumscribed world? Was this reflection superficial or profound?

One needs to understand that the roots of Chariteo's *poesis* weave deeply into classical as well as Italian sources, both philological and cultural,[12] and that the poet is conscious of this historical fact. In canzone 20, the poet, clearly in his own voice, acknowledges Homer, Virgil, Pindar, Horace, Callimachus, and Propertius, the last classical poet mentioned in the catalogue and, hence, especially stressed (canzone 20.12–19).[13] He alludes to Dante, Petrarch, and, probably, Polizano, Luigi Pulci, and Lorenzo de' Medici of the fifteenth-century Florentines (23–25), and to his own Neapolitan school (Panormita, Pontano, Sannazaro) (26–44). Expectedly he claims that his principal poetic source is Christian (55–76).[14] It is only in an historical retrospective of poets that Chariteo may disassociate himself as poet entirely from his poet-narrator and tie his *poesis* with the *figure* of the past.

Canzone 20 ends with the direct praise of the state but before the poet praises the efficacy of his sources and himself *as an imitator*, a Hercules: "Nè vuo' tacer del tuo ramo fraterno / Il bel frutto, di tue vertute excelse / Imitator, che, come Hercule scelse..." ("Nor does the fair fruit of your fraternal bough desire silence, from your sublime power the imitator, who, as Hercules, chose..." [canzone 20.88–90]). Self-praise is scattered throughout the *Endimione*. Yet, what insight ordered and made possible such claims? Chariteo's remarkable citations of "Laura" and "Beatrice" are the key:

> Se i duo soli, di cui l'Arno si gloria,
> Onde Beatrice & Laura hor son divine,
> Offuscan l'altre stelle Fiorentine,
> Non torran a Sebetho la sua gloria.
> Vivon le Muse....
>
> (canzone 20.23–27)

> If two suns the Arno glorify,
> Where now both Beatrice and Laura reign,
> And dim the other stellar Florentines,
> Not Naples' glory do they here deprive.
> The Muses are alive. . . .

The five lines are deceptively concise, but, in their short historical statement, they contain the only instance of the citation of either ''Beatrice'' or ''Laura'' in the *Endimione*. Is it merely because of a rhetorical trope that they are cited as suns among other stars? Some kind of ''celestial apparatus'' is indeed at work here, but it is one addressed directly to Chariteo's creation of his text. Stars and heavenly bodies partake of an exteriorized universe of signs that draw Dante's poet-narrator and those of subsequent poets perforce ''out and up'' from the human condition. Such power over the exteriorization of the self is figural. As suns ''Laura'' and ''Beatrice'' are *figure*.

Yet why ''perforce?'' One because of an imposed poetic necessity. Two because of a philological one.

Petrarch's interdiction on citing ''Laura'' effected a radical shift in any subsequent imitator's point of view: a citation of a ''beloved's'' name had to assume a reflection of ''Laura'' without either citing her and its name or overstressing the sonant nexus Petrarch had created about his *donna*. To ''hear'' her and it would be tantamount to citation in another's text in any case and block the later poet from exploring his or her own avenues of poesis, that is from including in the humanly self-revealing assonance, alliteration, and rhyme that was the poetic gift poetry Petrarch freely offered.

How was Chariteo tacitly to *reflect* ''Laura'' and at the same time *deflect* Petrarch's binding command? Like Dante in a different context, Chariteo chose the medium of the heavens where Dante had already set the *figura* of ''Beatrice.'' Because both ''Laura'' and ''Beatrice'' are linguistically protreptic *figure*, Chariteo could regard them both as suns, celestial figures to whom he could add yet another, although traditionally lesser luminary, his ''Luna,'' the moon. In this way, Chariteo's *figura* takes her place ''without'' and finds an unexpected, but neatly predicated citation on the surface of his text. Petrarch's philological multiplicity is saved without any direct allusion to ''Laura'' in any form, except, to be sure, in Chariteo's last poem where he wishes to advise his audience that he has established her and its place in a celestial poesis for reasons that are historical, personal, and ultimately for the "poetic good." Whether or not, in any case, the constellation of two suns and a moon is traceable to Dante's genius or Petrarch's or Chariteo's, it is to Chariteo that it bears sweet fruit. And it bears it in a doubly subjective *and* objective sense.

First Chariteo's idiosyncratic arrogation of Petrarch's world allows him a use of classical sources in a way Petrarch preferred to ignore, at least in the Italian of the *Canzoniere*. Although Chariteo, like Petrarch, utilized classical myth (he named his book the *Endimione* after the young man loved in myth by the moon), the textual citation of a mistress' name devolved from Greek and Latin elegy. In this particular case, "Luna" has her and its roots in Propertius' Augustan text: "Cynthia," that poet's mistress, was one name of the goddess of the moon, and Chariteo's fondness and deep understanding of the Propertian text is easily proven. Thus a classical citation provides an extratextual validation of "Luna" that does not lie in the *Canzoniere*. Chariteo's claim to "Luna," like Scève's to "Délie," frees the poet and his narrator from the surface of Petrarch's text and grants an extended parameter of language, literally a "freedom of speech." For a modern critic to destroy the possibility of such a freedom in the name of false "canonicity," no matter what the political agenda, is nothing less than totalitarian. (See Brenda Schildgen's essay in this volume.)

Second the *figura* of "Luna" is double-edged. So, to be sure, is "Laura." Yet in Chariteo's text is the *figura* merely rhetorical?

"Luna" is a "Beatrice" because of her and its place in the poet's celestial poesis and because of the protrepsis of her and its *virtù*. She and it are a spiritually animating *figura* (an "alma figura") to be admired and contemplated, one whose eyes "di mente mi privaro" ("stripped me of my mind") (sonnet 139.9–10). The poet-narrator's position and responsibility toward his *donna* are simple, clear, and already in a well-established tradition since at least the poets of the *dolce stile nuovo*:

> Ponmi sotto 'l più vivo ardor del sole,
> Seguerò sempre amando quella Luna,
> Che dolcemente parla & dolce ride.
>   (sonnet 93.12–14)

> Place me 'neath the ardor of the sun,
> My steps will always love and trail that moon,
> Who so sweetly speaks and sweetness smiles.

Chariteo here links "Luna" unequivocally to the earlier style, not by the conventionality of some Petrarchan trope but by a shared concern for the human condition. Hence arises the poet-narrator's obsession with what might be called, conveniently, the "dark side" of "Luna." It is in experience the "dark" anxiety of the poet-narrator. A common psychological source lies in the anxiety with which Petrarch's and Propertius' texts are imbued. In a sonnet addressed to his "donna" the poet-narrator exclaims:

> Splende da terra al ciel vostra figura,
> Nè d'human seme nata esser dimostra,
> Ma d'immortale angelica natura.
>   Hor che vuol dire: è forse mia ventura,
> O costume d'Amore, o culpa vostra,
> Che'n tanto lume io viva in vita oscura?
>   (sonnet 29.9–14)

> Your figure radiates from earth to heav'n,
> Not proven to be born from human seed,
> But from the angels' nature, far from man's.
>   What is my gist: perhaps it is my due,
> In this Love's dress, oh this my sinful need,
> That in such light I only night accrue?

What is the poet-narrator's fate? In the third canzone, the poet-narrator addresses those who in empty and fraudulent gloom reign unknown and dark by means of magic ("...che'n l'ombre vane & fraudulente, / Per arte tenebrosa, / Haveti imperio incognito & occolto..."). He begs these witches to convert his *donna*'s intransigent intellect ("Convertite la dura, immobil mente...") and to make use of their powers "to turn one by one the stars with the moon" ("...voltare ad una ad una / Le stelle con la luna") (canzone 3.56–64). I shall speak of "una ad una" subsequently. What strikes the reader-listener in the present context is the attempt to exchange a potentially inconstant *figura* for an unambiguous Dantean one, Petrarch's dilemma from the beginning and one that necessarily informs Chariteo's poet-narrator.

Hence Charitean poesis, although overwhelmingly Petrarchan, cannot be merely superficial. "Luna" as a "joyful figura" ("lieta sua figura") encounters a poet-narrator, "miserable and unlucky" as he gazes upon her and it ("misero & infelice chi la mira"). This narrator provides a psychological, not rhetorical, insight when he understands that "because of such a light a dark and gloomy life awaits" ("Che di tal luce aspetta vita oscura") (sonnet 38.9–11). Love, moreover, not witches, is the key to Chariteo's profound implication in his own celestial poesis:

> **Amor**, tu vuoi ch'**io creda**,
> Che'l ciel *fa* movimento
> Per **memoria** del *pianto* & **morte** *mia*.
> Io 'l **credo**, & par che 'l *veda*:
> Che 'n *quella hora* & *momento*,
> Che **parte** il sol, la **Luna** si **partia**.
> *Sorte maligna* & *ria*,
> *Che due volte* in *occaso*
> Hai *voluto eclipsare*
> Le due luci più *chiare*;
> Ond'**io** de **l'una** son *cieco rimaso*:
> *Cosa inaudita* & *nova*,
> Che per *dolore humano* il ciel si **mova**!
>   (canzone 15.40–52, emphasis mine)

> Love, you will that I believe
> The heavens far above me heaved
> In memory because I cried and died.
> I do believe and seem to see:
> In time's fleet momentality,
> When parts the sun, the moon itself does hide.
> Oh fate, most cruel, for ill conceived,
> At one sun's set does twice retrieve
> in willed eclipse, oh infamy,
> The two in light the most refined,
> Whence of the two from moon I still am blind;
> It is a thing unheard and new
> That for a human's sorrow heaven moves!

In this thirteen-versed stanza, Chariteo, in rhyme and assonance, confronts an experience lodged in the doubly Perarchan and Propertian obsession with Love, death, and grief (*Amor, morte,* and *dolore*—40, 42, 52). The poet's act is human, another significant call for a poetic latitude to free an "embattled hemmed-in self"[15] "Love you will that

I believe'': *io creda* (*io: movimento, pianto, credo, momento, occaso, voluto, io, cieco rimaso; creda: fa, memoria, mia, veda, quella, hora, Luna, partia, maligna, ria, l'una, cosa inaudita & nova, mova*). The two verses, ''che due volte in occaso / Hai voluto eclipsare'' (''At one sun's set does twice retrieve / in willed eclipse, oh infamy'') draw their rhyme in assonance with *che parte* and *sorte* of the previous two lines. Note that this assonance itself is introduced through ''initial *par-*'' (*parte-partia*). This type of sonant metamorphosis is characteristic of Petrarch's verse. Chariteo has received well one of his master's most enduring gifts. Here it introduces and then isolates those verses (48 and 49) that thematically stand furthest apart from the context of the rest of the stanza, the heavenly bodies of which are made into objects by Chariteo's celestial poesis.

There is, moreover, a disturbing significance about Chariteo's play with his ''heaven'' in this stanza, especially in terms of his imitated and present *figure*. He speaks of an instant (*momento*) when both sun and moon disappear, in other words when neither of his historical *figure* radiate the poet-narrator's gloom. His ''Moon'' the ''One and one'' (*Luna* and *l'una*), slips entirely into the ''celestial apparatus'' and in reflex to the apparatus itself, emphasizes a human, over a celestial power: '' 'Tis a thing unheard and all quite new / That for a human's sorrow heaven moves.'' Chariteo's celestial poetics become here distinctly unlike Dante's. The latter's ''Beatrice'' directs the poet-narrator toward Mary and beyond to the light of God. Chariteo's poesis points within by figural reflex and reflection. It is a product of a Petrarchan's intensified projection of Petrarch's text.

The extraordinary place of Petrarch's model, in one instance even at the expense of a Dantean lexis, is established in the incipit to the *Endimione*, a book of poetry:

> Se 'l foco del mio casto, alto desio
> Non havesse aspirato a vero, *hon**ore**,*
> Sarebbe stato insano & folle *err**ore**,*
> Havere aperto al mondo il voler mio.
>   Poi che vertù lo mosse, ardir pres'io
> Di far chiaro ad ciascun, senza *tim**ore**,*
> Il tanto honesto & si pudico *ard**ore**,*
> Che contra il *Re del ciel* mai non fallio.

Per la mia diva io vidi *exempio in ter*ra
Degli angeli, & in opre & in *figura*,
Che contra il vil pensier fe' sempre *gu*erra.
    Io l'adorai come *sustanti*a *pu*ra,
Da presso & da lontan: ché l'huom non **erra**,
Il fattor a*dorando in su*a *factu*ra.

(sonnet 1, emphasis mine)

If my desire, enfired and most fair
Had not aspired to this honored view,
It would have been insane, the wildest error,
To open wide my will 'fore all of you.
    Since a power moved it, then I burned,
Remote from fear, to clarify my tale,
A pure, thus chastened fire in me turned,
Which strove 'gainst heaven's Lord and did not fail.
    Thus through my lady-god I viewed on earth
The angels, thus infigured in their works,
Whose will vile thought in constant war rebukes.
    The both I thus adored as substance pure,
From near and far: Because no man does err,
A maker loving in his facture's lure.

A certain hyperbolic moralism, aligned strongly to self-praise, rings through the *Endimione*, and it can be somewhat difficult for the modern reader to tolerate. The above incipit, however, might border in a reader's mind on blasphemy, were he or she not aware that this particular poem deals almost exclusively with the effects of Petrarch's *poesis* and Chariteo's reception of the master's text.

The poet-narrator's burning desire to express his condition, itself already of the highest order of expression—he is, after all, a reflection of a learned man—would have assumed an incomprehensible and insane error or wandering ("insano & folle errore"—3),[16] had it not been for a power or virtue ("virtù"—5) that bent his own will and permitted its expression. In the language or, if one wishes to be less exact, style that emerges, the poet-narrator fearlessly makes manifest to every reader, that is every "other without," a very intimate part of him-self. This indeed sounds very familiar, and Chariteo makes it plain that his textual model for the exteriorization of self is Petrarch's. In a verse anticipating his celestial poetics, he claims that his imitation has successfully incorporated his model. His exteriorized self is one "che contra il Re del ciel mai non fallio" ("which strove 'gainst heaven's Lord and did not fail"—8). Again this is both a subjective *and* objective claim.

Petrarch as "heaven's Lord?" Textually for Chariteo one of the sources for this particular phrase was probably "Re del cielo invisible immortale" ("King of Heaven, invisible, immortal"—*Canzoniere* 365.6).[17] Chariteo's choice of language is less potentially blasphemous if the reader is aware that his celestial poetics is predicated upon such a particular text by Petrarch. For the later poet any part of the *Canzoniere* represents a direct entrée to the self. In the later celestial apparatus, Petrarch by necessity becomes its "King."

The last two tercets of the incipit, however, expose the central, human *virtù* of *Chariteo's text*. It is the poet-narrator's goddess, whom he claims as an "exempio in terra" (literally "an example on earth") of angels, both in perceivable works and in the protreptic power of the *figura* ("& in opre & in figura"—10). Chariteo selects a non-Petrarchan word to describe her presence. His *diva* is a pure "Dantean and Thomistic substance" ("sustantia pura"—12). Reinforcing the endline-*errore* of verse three, the poet declares, in what at first hearing rings a platitude, that "...l'huom non erra, / Il fattor adorando in sua factura" ("...no man does err, / a maker loving in his facture's lure"—13–14).

Yet, the last verse is far from platitudinous. The *fattor* or "maker" there indeed adduces God (see as lexical models Petrarch's *Canzoniere* 3.2, 327.11, 352.9), but what binds together this last verse and, for that matter, the whole sonnet is the creative relationship between the maker and his making, even more as the maker participates in his making ("Il fattor...in sua factura"—14). Pèrcopo is correct in citing Dante's "...che 'l suo fattore / non disdegnò di farsi sua fattura" ("...that its [human nature's] maker did not disdain to make himself his [own] fabrication"—*Paradiso* 33.5–6).[18] Therein lies the Dantean and Christian model, but in the "Petrarchan heaven" creation and the poet-narrator's involvement in its *operation, in its fabrication*, must rest purely on the relationship between the self and its partially subjective and objective exteriorization on the surface of a text.

The incipit to the *Endimione* is a homage to the effective power of Petrarch's poetics and to Chariteo, who has received the same poetic vision. It is, however, a *figural vision as language* that we are to understand here. In assonance and rhyme, half-Petrarch's and half-Propertius', Chariteo multiplies his "Amor" in *honore, errore, timore, ardore*.[19]

In Petrarch's tradition of more purely sonant multiplicity, the Petrarchan spins a web of *terra, figura, guerra, pura, erra, factura* and thus identifies him-self with Petrarch's entire poetic range. His own powerful, single *figura* is "Luna," one that he identifies with Petrarch's multiplicity, not fragmentation. Within a universe thus regulated by a master, a King of Heaven, and "Luna," even "Beatrice," he too will make a poetic attempt to exteriorize the self in a very intimate expanse of language. A "fatture" ("fattore") is, after all, a kind of confession. Language is its necessary medium.

Perhaps no single poem in the *Endiminone* links in practice this kind of reflecting poesis more closely to Petrarch's than sonnet 42:

> Cresc*ete*, o versi miei, & **cresca amore**,
> **Cresca** la gloria & fama a l'alta **Luna**,
> Replicate, cantando, **ad una ad una**
> Le parti del celeste *suo val*ore.
>
> **Crescan** le fiamme in **uno** immenso **ardore**
> Per questa che nel mondo è sola & **una**,
> Che la beltà con *casti*tade **aduna**,
> Et viva è degna de divino **honore**.
>
> Oda la terra e 'l ciel, mortali & dei,
> Le sue preclare lode & la mia *fede*,
> E 'l *suo*n **de** li lamenti & sospir miei.
>
> Vedran com' io, senza sperar *merc*ede,
> La servo **am**ando, & premio non vorrei:
> Nova *belt*ade un novo **amor** *rechi*ede!
>   (sonnet 42, emphasis mine)

> Oh burgeon forth, my verse, oh burgeon love,
> Oh burgeon glory, fame to highest Moon,
> Oh replicate in song thus one by one
> Her multi-prismed valor from above.
>
> Oh burgeon flames in passion, great and one,
> Through her who in the world is lone and one,
> For chastity and beauty make a one,
> And living does she heaven's praise behoove.
>
> Let hear the sky, the earth, the gods and men,
> This shining praise of her, my faith bestows,
> My rhyming sounds resounding sighs, laments.
>
> They'll see how I, devoid of mercy's hope,
> Do loving serve her, scorning recompense:
> A beauty new and fresh, new love invokes.

This sonnet is devoted to Petrarch's one and the many: the "One" of the poet-narrator's *figura* and the many of the multiple lexis with which the poet expresses his desire. Rhyme, alliteration, and a paratactic lexical repetition force the point home. On the one hand *Amor(e)* (if I were to dictate the poem's calligraphy, I should capitalize "Amor" along with "Luna") assumes a place in both the first and last verses of the sonnet and links the narrating lover (*amando*—13) and his ardor to some established, hence abstract, moral and ethical norms: "love," "valor," "ardor," "chastity," "honor," "faith," "mercy," "loving," "beauty," "love" (*amore, valore, ardore, castitade, honore, fede, mercede, amando, beltade, amor*). The poet-narrator is struggling here to define his desire. On the other hand, the *figura* involved in his conundrum deceptively demands a multiple stasis "without" and "within": "highest Moon," "one by one," "passion [ardor], great and one," "lone and one," "make a one" ("l'alta **Luna**," "ad **una** ad **una**," "sola & **una**," "ad**una**"). The "Moon as one or One" becomes almost a litany in the first two quatrains of the sonnet and suggests a figural multiplicity "without" and at the same moment a making of such a "One within," the "passion great and one" that is the poet-narrator's expression of the self. Petrarch's transcendental poesis unites Chariteo's now transformed subjective and objective states.

Perhaps, however, Chariteo allows his sense of figural multiplicity a bit more latitude than does Petrarch. The former's "ad una ad una" is part of a paratactic listing that is intimately attached to the unity of *Luna* and *l'una*, his predication in canzone 15; Petrarch's "ad una ad una" of *Canzoniere* 223 is attributed to the narration of the poet-narrator's troubles: "...narro / tutte le mie fatiche, ad una ad una" ("I narrate all my troubles one by one"—5–6). Yet, to be sure, the poet-narrator's "troubles" in the *Canzoniere* are directly identified with his sighs and laments, just as they are in the *Endimione*.

Such is the common denominator underlying both texts, and Chariteo was well aware that his text was generated from the sonant core of Petrarch's own: " 'l suon de li lamenti & sospir miei" ("My rhyming sounds resounding sighs, laments"). Chariteo had received Petrarch's text with a great deal of subtlety and understanding. He also made convincing use of the major option that text proffered: a sonant lexis of assonance, alliteration, and rhyme directed toward a discovery of the self within the parameters of a book of poetry.

Petrarch's and Chariteo's figural poesis, its replicated and, hence, continually positive formulation of a ''self,'' by its very definition explains much that draws the human being centripetally toward notions of ''God'' and ''the One.'' It defines in a single term, as Auerbach knew well, a positive phenomenology of experience that finds its place in Dante's poesis. It also is central to Petrarch's and Chariteo's. In these two poets, the exteriorization of ''the self'' necessitates an interiorization of the *figura*. Hence arises the Socratic, hidden irony inherent to that ''self.'' Thus too ''Laura'' as a ''*figura* within'' must remain uncited and obscured as she and it draws an audience below the surface of the text. There is no simple semiotics of the signifier and the signified, no deconstructionist reduction that may be applied. *This is the reason for the profound and lasting ambiguity of Petrarch's and his imitators' ever-new poesis and ever-new text and texts.*

Yet, Chariteo establishes the self in a way Petrarch does not. His collection of *rime* is not named merely ''Canzoniere,'' but ''Endimione.'' This act affirms a central property of Petrarch's book that one suspects but can only partially prove in any formal manner from the master's text alone: Petrarch's figural poesis expresses the center and unity of the poet-narrator and thus delineates more clearly the parameters of the poetic self. As a reflection of its model, the *Endimione* is able to state the hidden ''One'' in an analogical reversal. Petrarch's uncited ''Laura'' becomes a cited ''Luna'' or ''l'una,'' the one who, for all her and its potential inconstancy, her and its ''lesser light,'' reigns over the poet and poet-narrator, her and its Endimion in a purely sonant poesis.

I make no argument here whether Chariteo's poetry is ''as good as'' or ''better'' or ''worse'' than Petrarch's. However, if the reader appreciates Chariteo's ''celestial poetics,'' his clear understanding of *figura* as *donna*, and the potential lodged in his citation of ''Luna,'' he or she will recognize the idiosyncratic poesis that Petrarch left to his posterity and which Chariteo shared with his master, his *Re del ciel*. What Chariteo, therefore, reflects in his poesis is a profound understanding of Petrarch's own. His becomes a commentary on a received text, a commentary that establishes both Petrarch's and his own Socratic search for a poet-narrator's transcending self.

What I have been addressing in the past pages is the ontology of Petrarch's text, its sustaining value, its language, the poet's method made real, and his authority made open to later effected texts. At his text's core or heart lies a figure or *figura* named by voice "Laura," whose multiplicity, both concrete and abstract, burgeons throughout the parameters of that text and those Petrarchan. Although Auerbach, part and parcel of an idiosyncratic twentieth-century ontological vision, denied Petrarch a confrontation with *figure* and hence figural poesis, we have seen that Chariteo took this poesis for granted, even to the point of identifying methodologically the *figure* of both Petrarch and Dante. (After all he had no other choice.) Chariteo was not the pawn of the nineteenth and twentieth centuries' ontological periodization. It was Petrarch's right to a figural poetics, as I have shown, that created his text and dictated its reception and imitation.

Petrarch centered his poet-narrator's self in Laura's name, more precisely *in her and its naming.* Shakespeare had experienced this act too. He indirectly adduces it when Juliet naively suggests a rose's name as a subject for rhetorical speculation, the purpose of which is an all-too-reminiscently-postmodern attempt to annihilate the name altogether: *"Romeo,* doff thy *name* / And for that *name,* which is no part of *thee,* / Take all *myself."* The game, no matter how "psychologically castrating," interests Romeo, and he plays along: "I take *thee at thy word.* / Call me but *love,* and I'll be new baptize'd, / Henceforth *I* never *will be Romeo"* (emphasis mine).

How could Romeo's response be more Petrarchan? Forced more receptively than rhetorically into a position similar to Chariteo's, he speaks of words and love, in short of the figural power he well knows lies in "the rose." Romeo is, in fact, extremely sensitive to both Petrarch's and the Petrarchan dilemma. Upon Juliet's startled demand to *identify himself* ("What-man art thou...? "), he replies: "By a *name* / I know not how to tell *thee* who *I am....* / Had I *written,* I would *tear* the *word"* (emphasis mine). How near this is to Petrarch's painful predicament in *Canzoniere* 5. How far from any kind of deconstructionist reduction. Shakespeare knew well that a name meant more than the play of written signifieds made signifiers on the surface of the text.

Yet, it is Juliet, in experience and not in rhetoric who reaffirms the power of Petrarch's sounding self in Shakespeare's *figura,* by name "Romeo":

> My *ears* have not yet drunk a hundred *words*
> Of that *tongue's uttering,* yet *I know the sound:*
> Art thou not *Romeo,* and a Montague?
> (*Romeo and Juliet* II.2.47-62, emphasized by me myself)

What's in a name? A resonating figure that makes us think on love and weep. Also very subtle views of language and its meaning that are lost in the dust of postmodern reductions.

Durham, North Carolina

NOTES

1. In his important essay, "Figura," *Scenes From the Drama of European Literature* (Minneapolis: University of Minnesota Press, 1984), 11-76 (or. in German, 1944), Auerbach makes no mention of Petrarch whatsoever, relying no doubt on certain judgements made in an early work, *Dante: Poet of the Secular World* (Chicago/London: Chicago University Press, 1961) (or. in German, 1929): "Beneath the arrogance [of Guido Cavalcanti] is hidden...a kind of impotence [?] inherited from the *trobar clus,* which in Petrarch's hands was to become the basis of a radically subjective literary tradition" (57); "He [Petrarch] is distinguished from Dante above all by his new attitude toward his own person; it was no longer in looking upward...that Petrarch expected to find self-fulfillment, but in the conscious cultivation of his own nature" (176). Auerbach has had as much to do with our idea of a "second-rate" Petrarch as have had Aristotle's ontologically primary and secondary categories.

2. In citing Petrarch's text and its diacritical markings I have made use of Francesco Petrarcha, *Canzoniere,* ed. Gianfranco Contini (Turin: Einaudi, 1968); for Chariteo, *Le Rime di Benedetto Gareti detto il Chariteo,* commentator Erasmo Pèrcopo, 2 vols. (Naples: Biblioteca napoletana di storia e letterature, 1892); for Dante, *The Divine Comedy,* ed. Charles S. Singleton, 6 vols. (Princeton: Princeton University Press, 1970-1975). All translations are my own, created with the knowledge that the difficulties in transferring the sonant nexus of phonemes *and* morphemes, let alone the rhyme scheme, from one language to another makes the task at best approximate. What in the end appears can be little more than *nugae,* sometimes *in nuce,* for the translator and his audience.

3. Even contemporary critics who acknowledge an underlying presence of sound have not opted for continuity or cohesiveness. See Marguerite R. Waller, *Petrarch's Poetics and Literary History* (Amherst: The University of Massachusetts Press, 1980), who privileges difference as Derridean *différance:* "But Petrarch's *vario style* could include the notion that style (and/or his *stilus* or pen [?]) operates independently of, at variance from, experience." She cites Sarah Sturm to the effect that "what the audience of Petrarch's poetry is to hear 'is not the direct utteranc of the *sosperi,* Petrarch's sighs, but rather their sound, their *suono.* The *suono* is in turn that of verses.' " (But surely the idiosyncratic sense of a poet's lexical choice must be addressed here someplace.) She also cites Sturm's potentially non-deconstructive statement that the poem represents " 'a deliberate ambiguity in the syntax of expression' " (38-39), but does not, however, acknowledge Sturm's

deconstruing, ultimately anti-protreptic, figural stance toward the important lexical choice of *sparse:* "The adjective *sparse* suggests, then, a different sense: the individual poems are collected into a volume, but the love-poetry itself has failed to assume a coherent [?] form [?]. " She quotes the sonnet's second stanza. (Sara Sturm, "The Poet-Persona in the *Canzoniere,"* *Francis Petrarch, Six Centuries Later: A Syposium,* North Carolina Studies in the Romance Languages and Literatures: Symposia, 3, edited by Aldo Scaglione (Chapel Hill/Chicago: The University of North Carolina and the Newberry Library, 1975), 193.

4. By far the most sophisted study of Petrarch's "self" lies in Giuseppe Mazzotta, "The *Canzoniere* and the Language of the Self," *Studies in Philology* 75 (1978), 271–96. He acknowledges the previous positions, especially that of Gianfranco Contini, who "refers to the *Canzoniere* as precisely the attempt to unify experience" (271–73). (See the introduction to Dante Alighieri, *Rime,* Testo critico, introduzione e note a cura di Gianfranco Contini, (Turin: Einaudi, 1965, vii.) Mazzotta does not contradict previous views but attempts to redefine "terms such as the self, its unity and presence, in what might be called Petrarch's *poetics of fragmentation* (274, italics mine). In classical terms, the key becomes the one and the many, but not as mutually exclusive. The difference between Mazzotta's position and my own is the locus of our exegesis. Interested in "the authenticity and *exemplary* character of his [Petrarch's] moral experience" (272, italics mine), Mazzotta evaluates the text from without, as does Petrarch's audience (the *voi* of Canzoniere I.1) or as does that learned audience who must also be Petrarch reflecting on his own verse. Because the "center within" is always hidden from the exegete "without," I have endeavored to step a bit closer "within," to opt for sound (*suono*) sometimes at the expense of discrete sense. Sound must be granted its intuitive heuristic that binds together other discrete lexical choices. It, pace Mazzotta, does become the "irreducible residue of his [Petrarch's] presence," although I should prefer the slightly less Heideggerian "self." It is other than ". . . postmodernly hollow, an empty sign which points to its own insubstantiality" (295–96). If one goes in search of Petrarch's "self," one requires views both "within" and "without." I ask the reader to take Mazzotta's exegis and my own as complementary, both necessary in order to delve beneath the "paradoxical" nature of Petrarch's poesis. (*Canzoniere* 366, the canzone to the Virgin, for instance, cannot be understood without such a double vision.)

5. Sturm privileges "verse" in the mistaken assumption that verses form an easily argued relationship to sound (*op. cit.,* 193). Petrarch's sound, however, cannot be related to verses without an excursus into the complexities of meter. See Giuseppe E. Sansone, "Assagio di simmetrie petrarchesche" in *Le trame della poesia: per una teoria funzionale del verso* (Florence: Vellecchi, 1988), 97–122. (Note a similar importance to what, in this volume, Allen Mandelbaum attributes to the verses of Dante.)

6. The best argument for sonnet one as an ironic palinode is again Mazzotta's, *op. cit.,* 272.

7. "Laura" assumes an approximate citation on the surface of the *Canzoniere*'s text five times; only once does it ring clear. Four times "l'aura" is too near the surface

of the text to allow a discrete citation of the name (112.4, 278.4, 239.8, 23); once "Laura" is obscured by a foregoing nexus of rhyme and alliteration (291.1–4, see above). Only once in the *in morte* is the name cited directly in context of the ominous, assonantal identity between "Morte" and "Amor" (332.50). So to drive an unhappy metaphor to its limit, "Laura" might well be written with indelible ink on the heart of the poet-narrator, but the ink leaks out onto the surface of the text in a nexus of rhyme, alliteration, and assonance only once in direct citation.

8. One such attempted reading, although I suspect that the author was unaware of its full postmodernist possibilities, lies in Robert M. Durling's cacographics in the printing of this very sonnet, a maneuver that privileges as a poetic intent the broken fragments of a *written* or *printed* word: LAU-dando, RE-al, TA-ci, LAU-dare, RE-verire, mor-TA-l (*Petrarch's Lyric Poems: The Rime Sparse and Other Lyrics* [Cambridge, Mass./London: Harvard University Press, 1976], 41). Not only does this "rewriting" interrupt the flow of language to such an extent that the poem becomes almost unreadable, the editor's caps and hyphens reduce its signification only to the play of signified as signifier on the surface of the text. Durling, is, to be sure, not alone in his caps, but one should be aware that no such phenomena existed either in the Vatican codex 3195 or, say, the Castelvetro edition of 1582. One finds capitalization alone in nineteenth and twentieth century editions, but almost invariably the "ta" of "mortal" is in miniscule, e.g. the Contini edition which I employ in the present essay. Durling's cacography makes a deceptively destructive, only partially Petrarchan point: caps and hyphens attribute to language a false sense of concrete and material presence.

9. An *accento* is a "stress of sound," hence the hopefully more subtle way I have endeavored to translate Contini's text into English if one compares my calligraphy to Durling's.

10. Petrarch must have been well aware of Dante's invocation to Apollo near the beginning of *Paradiso I* where the older poet requests the Greek god to grant him the "loved laurel" (*l'amato alloro*) (*Par* I. 13–15). Interestingly enough these verses precede by just six a passage Auerbach quotes as an example of Dante's poetics. There Auerbach stresses *ombra*, a potent *figura* inscribed in Dante's head that he desires to manifest ("segnata nel mio capo io manifesti") (*Par.* I. 22–24) (Auerbach, "Figura," 63). When Petrarch alludes to Apollo in sonnet five, he knowingly addresses a god of a radically different character than Dante's, at least "different" from Petrarch's point of view. Dante's invocation is traditional: his infiguring act is directed without, indeed toward and for the divine, and he calls upon Apollo to crown him with the appropriate poetic power, that is the language, verse, or matter that will enable him to realize his intention ("e coronarmi de le fogile / che la materia e tu mi farai degno," 26–27). Petrarch, on the other hand, claims language as his own. His *figura* resonates within and is never totally exteriorized without. His audience, therefore, is itself turned within.

11. E.g. the disturbingly flat rhetorical reduction of Leonard Wilson Forster, *The Icy Fire: Five Studies in European Petrarchism,* (Cambridge: Cambridge University Press, 1969). He would have us believe that Petrarch's and Petrarchan poetry is a tour de force varying in the quality of antitheses, rhetorical questions, oxymora,

conceits, metaphorical description, effects, hyperbole, commonplaces, puns, etc. (1–60). In this reduction Chariteo becomes nothing but an inconsequential court poet, a transmitter of conceits and hyperbole, in short a representative of "the first ('frivolous') stage of petrarchism" (26, 37, 118, 119–120).

12. This fact does not, however, make of Chariteo "a fleeting poet" ("un poeta sfuggente"). It is true that Chariteo's position as a courtier and a humanist did not dictate the Petrarchan nature of his verse, but Petrarchan limits are less limiting than some may think (albeit Marco Santagata, *La Lirica aragonese: studi sulla poesia napoletana del secondo quattrocento* (Padova: Antenore, 1979), 299.

13. To my view Propertius exerted the major classical influence upon the text of the *Endimione*. See my "Neapolitan *Imitationes Propertianae:* Ancient Sound in the Verses of Pontano and Chariteo," to appear in *The Proceedings of the 21st Annual Conference of the Center for Medieval and Early Renaissance Studies* (Binghamton: MERTS, 1992).

14. Still by far the best introduction to the poetic sources of the *Endimione* rests in Erasmo Pèrcopo's introduction and commentary to Chariteo's works. See *op. cit.,* I.lvii-cxviii and II *passim.*

15. Allen Mandelbaum, " 'La Mente che non erra' (*Inferno* II,6)," *Letture, classensi* 18 (1989), 46.

16. Compare Milanion's "amens errabat" ("insane he was wont to wander in error") of Propertius' incipit to the *Monobiblos* (I.1.11).

17. Pèrcopo, *op. cit.,* I.7

18. *Ibid.* Pèrcopo also points us to *Purgatorio* 17.102.

19. See Prier, *loc. cit.*

ABOUT THE CONTRIBUTORS

Mark W. Andrews, Associate Professor of French, Vassar College: "Formalist Dogmatisms, Derridean Questioning, and the Return of Affect: Towards a Distributed Reading of *Triptyque,*" *L'Esprit Créateur* (1987); "The Return to Exile: Celebrating the Space of the Other in Rainer Maria Rilke and Saint-John Perse" (*Proceedings of the 12th Congress of the ICLA*) (1988)

Lilian R. Furst, Marcel Bataillon Professor of Comparative Literature, University of North Carolina at Chapel Hill: *Romanticism in Perspective* (1969); *The Contours of European Romanticism* (1979); *Fictions of Romantic Irony* (1984); *Through the Lens of the Reader* (1992)

Gerald Gillespie, Professor of German Studies and Comparative Literature, Stanford University: *Garden and Labyrinth of Time* (1988); "Here Comes Everybody/Nobody: Self as Overly Edited Palimpsest," *New Comparison* (1990); "Afterthoughts of Hamlet: Goethe's Wilhelm, Joyce's Stephen," *Comparative Literary History* (1990)

W. Wolfgang Holdheim, Frederic J. Whiton Professor of Liberal Studies, Emeritus, Cornell University: *Theory and Practice of the Novel: A Study on André Gide* (1968); *Die Suche nach dem Epos: Der Geschichtsroman bei Hugo, Tolstoi und Flaubert* (1978); *The Hermeneutic Mode: Essay on Time in Literature and Literal Theory* (1984)

Eugene F. Kaelin, Professor of Philosophy, Florida State University: *An Existentialist Aesthetic: The Theories of Sartre and Merleau-Ponty* (1962); *The Unhappy Consciousness: The Poetic Plight of Samuel Beckett* (1981); *Heidegger's Being and Time: A Reading for Readers* (1988)

William J. Kennedy, Professor of Comparative Literature, Cornell University: *Rhetorical Names in Renaissance Literature* (1978); *Jacopo Sannazaro and the Uses of Pastoral* (1983); co-editor *Writing in the Disciplines* (1990)

Dennis Looney, Assistant Professor of Italian, University of Pittsburgh: Inferno VII, *Lectura Dantis* (Spring 1990); "Recent Trends in Ariosto Criticism: Intricati rami e aer fosco," *Modern Philology (November 1990); "The Purgation and Emendation of a Simile: Purgatorio* VI & VII," *Lectura Dantis* (Fall 1990)

Maristella de Panizza Lorch, Professor of Italian, Columbia University: Ed. Lorenzo Valla, *De Vero False Bono* (1970); *A Defense of Life: Lorenzo Valla's Theory of Pleasure* (1985); With Ernesto Grassi, *Folly and Insanity in Renaissance Literature* (1986)

Allen Mandelbaum, Kenan Professor of Humanities, Wake Forest University: *The Divine Comedy: A Verse Translation* (1980-1984); *The Savantasse of Montparnasse* (1987); *The Odyssey of Homer: A New Verse Translation* (1990)

Elsa Nettels, J.B. and Mildred Hickman Professor of Humanities, College of William and Mary: *James and Conrad* (1977); *Language, Race, and Social Class in Howells's America* (1988); "Varieties of Love: Henry James's Treatment of the 'Great Relation,' " *American Declarations of Love* (1990)

Raymond Adolph Prier, Independent Scholar: *Archaic Logic: Symbol and Structure in Heraclitus, Parmenides, and Empedocles* (1976); *Thauma Idesthai: The Phenomenology of Sight and Appearance in Archaic Greek* (1989); "Laocoön IV: An Essay Upon the Pragmatics of Art and the Limits of Criticism," *The Hospitable Canon: Essays on Literary Play, Scholarly Choice, and Popular Pressures* (1991)

Peter Salm, Professor of Comparative Literature and German, Emeritus, Case Western Reserve University: *Pinpoint of Eternity: European Literature in Search of the All-Encompassing Moment* (1986); "Truthtelling and Lying in Goethe's *Iphigenie*" *German Life and Letters* (1981); *Goethe's Faust One: An English Translation* (1962, 1967, 1985)

Aido Scaglione, Professor of Italian Studies, New York University: *Nature and Love in the Late Middle Ages* (1963); *The Classical Theory of Composition* (1972); *The Liberal Arts and the Jesuit College System* (1986); *Knights at Court: Courtliness, Chivalry, and Courtesy from Ottonian Germany to the Italian Renaissance* (1991)

Brenda Deen Schildgen, Lecturer at the University of California at Davis: "Current Theories of Understanding: Juan Ruiz and the Conflict Between Art and Morality," *Chronica* (1987), "Dante's Neologisms in the *Paradiso* and the Latin Rhetorical Tradition," *Dante Studies* (1989), "Augustine's Answer to Jacques Derrida in the *De Doctrina Christiana*," *The De Doctrina Christiana: A Classic of Western Civilization* (1992)

Mary Ann Frese Witt, Professor of French and Italian, North Carolina State University: *Existential Prisons: Confinement in Mid-Twentieth Century French Literature* (1985); "*Six Characters in Search of an Author* and the Battle of the Lexis," *Modern Drama* (September 1987); "Towards a Theater of Immobility: *Henry IV, The Condemned of Altona,* and *The Balcony,*" *Comparative Drama* (Summer 1990)